ARAB CIVILIZATION

Constantine K. Zurayk

ARAB CIVILIZATION

Challenges and Responses

Studies in Honor of Constantine K. Zurayk

EDITED BY

George N. Atiyeh and Ibrahim M. Oweiss

State University of New York Press

Published by
State University of New York Press, Albany

Printed in the United States of America

For information, address State University of New York Press, State University Plaza, Albany, N.Y., 12246

Library of Congress Cataloging-in-Publication Data

Arab civilization: challenges and responses: studies in honor of Constantine K. Zurayk/edited by George N. Atiyeh and Ibrahim M. Oweiss.

p. cm.

"Some of the studies were originally written in Arabic and French but have been translated into English. Only one text offered as a critical edition was left in the original Arabic"—Editors' notes.

Includes index.

ISBN 0-88706-698-4. ISBN 0-88706-699-2 (pbk.)

1. Middle East. 2. Arab countries—History—1798- 3. Zurayq, Qusṭanṭīn, 1909- . I. Zurayq, Qusṭanṭīn, 1909- . II. Atiyeh, George Nicholas, 1923- . III. Oweiss, Ibrahim M.

DS42.4.A74 1988

909'.0974924—dc 19 87-18452

CIP

10 9 8 7 6 5 4 3 2 1

Contents

Part Three—The Modern Age: Challenges and Responses

Editors' Note

Few thinkers of the Arab world provoke as much interest as Dr. Constantine K. Zurayk. As a leader of Arab thought on questions of civilization, nationalism, and the relationship between the two, his works have not only provided directions to many intellectuals and statesmen but have also stimulated and elevated the dialogue on the meaning and destiny of Arabism and the Arabs in general. This humble endeavor to honor him on the occasion of his seventy-fifth birthday is an opportunity to bear witness to his contributions in the fields of history, political and cultural thought, and education. In the course of his career as an educator, historian, diplomat, and thinker, he has manifested a sense of responsibility, objectivity, depth, tolerance, and dedication to country and people which is a model and inspiration to all. The originality of his work resides in his unusually striking balance between reason and feeling, frankness and courtesy, and seriousness and sympathy.

The following studies and essays focus on Arab civilization in its past and present achievements as well as the problems that have faced it and are still facing it. Scholars from Europe, the Arab world, and the United States who have appreciated Dr. Zurayk as a person and as a scholar have contributed kindly and generously to bring about this volume. We thank them all.

On the editorial side, we have sought uniformity but not conformity. All foreign words found in *Webster's Third New International Dictionary* are not italicized. Their spelling follows this dictionary. Some proper names are written as they have been commonly used by the press or as they have been established by their owners. Abbreviations have been avoided as much as possible in the body of the texts. As far as transliteration is concerned, we have followed the Library of Congress system. Deviation from this system, however, was allowed where the authors requested to maintain certain minor variations or where it was thought that deviation would serve the needs of certain studies. Some of the studies were originally written in Arabic and French but have been translated into English. Only one text offered as a critical edition was left in the original Arabic.

The editors wish to take this opportunity to express their gratitude for the financial help offered by Messrs. Samī 'Alamī, Husnī Ṣawwāf 'Abd al-Majīd Shūmān, and Muḥammad Shuqayr. Their generous contributions made the publication of this volume possible.

George N. Atiyeh
Library of Congress

Ibrahim M. Oweiss
Georgetown University

Preface

It is both a privilege and a pleasure for me, as secretary general of the International Association of Universities, to be able to pay tribute to one who has so decisively and lastingly left his mark on its history: Dr. Constantine Zurayk.

Since by nature he would be reluctant to do so himself, it is perhaps especially important to recall at the outset the role which Dr. Zurayk played in the early years of the United Nations and in the formative phase of the specialized agency in the United Nations most closely related to his concerns as a scholar: UNESCO. At a time when the most catastrophic conflict in the history of the world was drawing to a close, he was one of those who strove to look beyond the horrors of human suffering and devastation in an effort to lay the foundations for a new era, an era based on mutual understanding between peoples and nations. This was no mere episode; it set the course for a long and distinguished career of service to the international community.

Devotion to the particular claims of his own field of scholarship never dimmed Dr. Zurayk's vision of the intrinsic nature of the university. He has unflinchingly pursued the same ultimate but sadly elusive goal of peace—peace defined not merely as the absence of armed conflict but as a continuing and constructive process based on mutual knowledge and assistance, on the interplay of values, and on the self-fulfillment and enrichment of cultures through their dialogue with one another. All this is what, in large measure, universities are about, and Dr. Zurayk is known to friends and colleagues in many parts of the world for his deep conviction that, individually and collectively, universities have a unique role to play in giving expression to the ideals embodied in his own person. For, although deeply committed to the history of the Arab world, he also holds the keys to many other histories which find their place in the vast realm of human thought and culture.

Thus inspired and equipped, Dr. Zurayk has been intimately connected with the life of the International Association of Universities (IAU). As the first rector of the University of Damascus, he took part in IAU's founding conference in Nice in 1950. Then, representing the American University of Beirut as its acting president at the next general conference in Istanbul in 1955, he was elected to membership of the administrative board of the association and again reelected by the general conference in Mexico in 1960. As chairman of the Board Development Committee, he played a leading role in formulating policy for the future of the rapidly growing association. His election as president by the general conference in Tokyo in 1965 came as no surprise to those who had come to know him for his devotion to the cause of interuniversity cooperation. Under his leadership, membership grew to exceed five hundred university institutions in more than one hundred countries.

As president of IAU, Dr. Zurayk gave unstintingly of his time and energy to the affairs of the association. His experience and wisdom commanded the respect of the members of its administrative board no less than that of the members of the secretariat. Those who had the privilege of working closely with him during those years came to appreciate and enjoy his warm human thoughtfulness and his remarkable ability to follow the day-to-day affairs of the association while at the same time addressing himself to the future, boldly and confidently yet always with measured prudence.

Others will pay tribute to the qualities of Dr. Zurayk as a scholar and teacher in his chosen academic field, but these same qualities also marked the exercise of his presidency. There were many lessons to be learned from one who possessed the gift of summarizing complex and seemingly inconclusive discussions and who was able to endow them with a meaningful pattern while in no way distorting the views expressed by his colleagues. An excellent interpreter of the immediate past, he was also a lucid interpreter of the thoughts of others.

A good historian must be motivated by ethical as well as intellectual qualities. Moral integrity, the ability to accept unpleasant facts, and respect for all informed opinions are no less essential for success in the leadership of a worldwide international organization. Dr. Zurayk possesses them to an eminent degree, and it has been reassuring to know that as honorary president of IAU, a title conferred on him in 1970 by the general conference in Montreal at the end of his term of office, the association can still look to him for wise advice in time of need.

Dr. Zurayk has many friends in the university community on all continents who have come to know him through the International Association of Universities, and they, too, join me in wishing him well.

Douglas J. Aitken
Secretary General
International Association of Universities

Part One

The Man and His Work

Constantine K. Zurayk: Advocate of Rationalism in Modern Arab Thought*

HANI A. FARIS

Among contemporary Arab thinkers, Constantine K. Zurayk occupies, for many reasons, a special position. His intellectual contributions over a period of almost half a century have afforded him the opportunity to establish a clear intellectual posture and have allowed many educated Arabs to become familiar with his works. Zurayk also belongs to a group of thinkers who have developed social and political doctrines that have enjoyed wide dissemination and have been influential in delineating the modern intellectual features of the Arab world. Finally, Zurayk's special position is due to the impact of his works on political movements and personalities and to his intellectual influence over successive generations of university students attained through a long career in teaching. For these reasons, the study of Zurayk's intellectual works gives us the opportunity to become acquainted with the ideas of a prominent contemporary Arab thinker and allows us to sense and perceive some of the features of modern Arab thought.

Zurayk's Career: Highlights

Zurayk was born in the city of Damascus on April 18, 1909, into a Greek Orthodox family engaged in commercial activities.[1] The family

*The author wishes to express his appreciation to the University of Kuwait for granting him a sabbatical that allowed him to carry out this study. He is also grateful to the Center for Middle Eastern Studies (Harvard University) and the Institute of Islamic Studies (McGill University) for the use of their research facilities and the intellectual challenge that the faculty and students provided during the period the author was affiliated with these two institutions (1980-82). A special note of appeciation is due to Susan Ziadeh for her insightful comments and editorial suggestions.

lived in the Qaymarīyah quarter, one of the more prestigious quarters of old Damascus and also one of the important residential areas for Damascene businessmen. His father, Kaisar, emigrated to Colombia, South America, and then returned to Damascus before the outbreak of World War I. He married and had four children, the oldest being Constantine. In 1923, Kaisar again went to Colombia, where he died one year later.

Zurayk spent his childhood in Damascus. His family moved to a new house close to the schools and cathedral of the Greek Orthodox church adjacent to the Muslim quarters. The atmosphere of tolerance and cooperation that prevailed there between the followers of both religions left an indelible mark on Zurayk's personality and mind-set. Perhaps this early experience was responsible, to a great extent, for his thinking on the two questions of Islam and nationalism which permeate most of his writings.

Zurayk completed his elementary and secondary education in the schools of the Orthodox church. These schools, their confessional connection notwithstanding, enrolled a good number of Muslim students. They were known for their openness, distance from fanaticism, and high standards, especially in the Arabic sciences. In this regard, it is important to note that the Greek Orthodox religious authorities at that time, foremost among them the patriarch Gregorius Haddad, sympathized with Syrian patriots and the Arab nationalist movement and were close to its leaders. It is said that, when the Great Syrian Revolt of 1925 broke out and some feared that the Christian quarters might be attacked, the leaders of the revolt went around the Christian quarters reassuring the people and insuring the safety of their quarters.

Zurayk enrolled at the American University of Beirut and began his university education in mathematics. Encouraged by some of his professors, he changed soon after to the study of history. At that time a chair in the history department became vacant, and Zurayk was nominated to complete his history specialization in the United States in order to prepare him to fill the chair. Upon receiving his bachelor of arts degree with distinction from the American University in 1928, he traveled to the United States. In 1929 he received a master of arts degree from the University of Chicago, and in 1930 a doctor of philosophy degree from Princeton University. The Oriental studies programs of both universities were highly respected and of particularly outstanding repute.

The positions held by Zurayk during his active career varied from university teaching to academic administration to diplomatic posts. Immediately upon graduation, he was appointed assistant professor of history at the American University of Beirut and was promoted to associate professor in 1942. For three years after World War II (1945-47), he served in the Syrian diplomatic corps as a first counsellor and then as minister plenipotentiary at the Syrian Legation in Washington, D.C. During the same period, he also served as Syria's delegate to the General Assembly and alternate delegate to the Security Council of the United Nations.

After this short experience in the diplomatic field, Zurayk rejoined the American University of Beirut. He was appointed professor of history and vice-president of the university. In 1949 he became rector of the Syrian University (Damascus) and remained in that position until 1952. In that same year he was reappointed vice-president of the American University of Beirut and dean of faculties. Between 1954 and 1957 he was the acting president. In 1956 he was made a distinguished professor of history and in 1976 distinguished professor emeritus. He was also a visiting professor at Columbia University in 1965, and at both Georgetown University and the University of Utah in 1977.

In addition to his many official positions, Zurayk was and continues to be active in many regional and international cultural organizations, occupying high positions in several of them. He is a corresponding member of the Arab Academy in Damascus, an associate member of the Iraqi Academy, and an honory member of the American Historical Association. He was also a member of the executive board of UNESCO (1950-54), a member of the administrative board of the International Association of Universities (1955-65), and president of that association (1965-70). Since 1970 he has been an honorary president. He was elected president of the Friends of the Book in Lebanon (1960-65) and chairman of the board of trustees of the Institute for Palestine Studies from its inception in 1963 to 1984, when he became an honorary chairman. He has been a member of the board of trustees of the University of Qatar since 1979.

Zurayk's distinguished achievements include his membership in the International Commission for a Scientific and Cultural History of Mankind sponsored by UNESCO (1950-69), his chairmanship of the International Committee of Experts for the Study of University Admissions (1960-62), and his participation in the Advisory Committee of Experts to the Kuwait Government on the Establishment of a University in Kuwait (1960). In recognition of his activities, he was awarded the Order of Merit, Distinguished Class, by the Syrian government, and the Education Medal, First Class, and the National Order of the Cedar, Commandeur Class, by the Lebanese government. In 1967, the University of Michigan granted him a Litt. D. honoris causa.

Zurayk's Writings: An Overview

Zurayk mastered the Arabic and English languages and writes in both. He knows French well and is familiar with German. Most of his writings, however, are in Arabic, the language he seems to prefer. Although his university education and most of his career have been associated with foreign educational institutions, he has chosen to address himself continuously to the Arabic reader and to concern himself with the contemporary Arab world and its future.

Reading Zurayk's writings is indeed a literary delight. Rarely does one find among contemporary Arab writers an author who matches the fluency, eloquence, and clarity of Zurayk's literary style. His language presents no obstacles for the reader. Although the texts can be read without undue exertion, they do not seem below the reader's level. Zurayk has been able to maintain this singularity of style at no expense to the clarity. His articles resemble a solid structure: the parts blend logically, forcefully, and clearly. He always begins by introducing the subject and conveying its importance. He then establishes the basic thesis with which he wishes to deal and explains the various elements involved in the subject. After analyzing each element, he enumerates the conclusions he has drawn and ends by presenting a summary. The format of this approach is repeated in almost all of his works. One does observe in his style a tendency to resort frequently to repetition. The same argument is explained several times and the same concept interpreted with a variety of expressions. Yet, in spite of the risks involved in this stylistic approach, the beauty of the language and the constant use of new vocabularies and forms in the process of repetition keep the reader's attention, without tedium, focused on the text.

Zurayk's research methodology is, with very few exceptions, the deductive Descartian methodology. His analysis starts with general principles, from which he infers the elements of the subject, the rules, and the conclusions. On the whole, therefore, the approach is on a high level of abstraction. Events and facts are given as evidence to support the author's argument and not as premises from which rules can be inferred. Most likely, Zurayk resorts to this methodology because of the classical nature of his training in history in particular, and in the humanities and the social sciences in general. Before World War II, the behavioral revolution and quantitative research methods had not yet had any effect on these fields. It is not surprising, therefore, that the reader of Zurayk's works can be impressed with the knowledge and comprehensive understanding of the author and feel, at the same time, the need for further information. Zurayk defends this research methodology invoking the principle that details and derivations may be easily explained once the fundamentals are made clear. The same is true with regard to ways and means when the goals are defined. It is obvious that such a principle is anchored in a philosophical outlook which considers principles, fundamentals, and goals as permanent truths that are knowable by reason.

Zurayk's books fall into three groups.[2] The first group mirrors his professional interests and consists of editions of heritage books and translations. Most of these works appeared early in his academic career. They include a translation from German of Theodore Noëldeke's *Die Ghassanische Fuersten aus dem Hause Gafna's*,[3] followed by a critical edition of a manuscript by Isma'il Beg Chol, *al-Yazīdīyah qadīman wa ḥadīthan* (The Yazidis, Past and Present).[4] Between 1936 and 1942, Zurayk completed a critical edition of volumes 7, 8, and 9 of *Tārīkh Ibn al-Furāt* (History of Ibn al-Furāt).[5] Later he edited, in association with Professor Asad Rustum, *Readings in the History of the Arabs and Their Culture.* He also edited the Arabic translation of George Sarton's *History of Science* (vol. 1).[6] Finally, he edited and published *Tahdhīb al-akhlāq* (The Refinement of Character) by Aḥmad Ibn Muḥammad Ibn Miskawayh and translated it into English.[7]

The second group consists of five books which bring together selected articles and lectures by the author previously published in various places. The first of these books is *al-Wa'ī al-qawmī: Naẓarāt fī al-ḥayāt al-qawmīyah al-mutafatiḥah fī al-Sharq al-'Arabī* (National Consciousness: Reflections on the National Life Burgeoning in the Arab East). The book, according to Zurayk, marks the launching of an attempt to clarify the concept of nationalism and the endeavor to disseminate it so that it might become the basis for collective action.[8] At the time it was published, the book enjoyed a wide circulation and established the author's reputation in the field of Arab nationalist thought, a reputation that has accompanied him to the present day. The second book in this group is *Ayyu ghad? Dirāsāt li-ba'ḍ bawā'ith nahḍatina al-marjūwah* (Whither Tomorrow? Studies of Some Motivations to Our Hoped-for Renaissance).[9] The six chapters contained in this book deal with social and cultural topics related to the prevalent situation and future prospects of Arab society. The third collection of articles and lectures appeared in a book entitled *Hadha al-'aṣr al-mutafajjir: Naẓarāt fī wāqi'inā wa wāqi' al-insānīyah* (This Explosive Age: Reflections on Our Situation and that of Humanity).[10] The book deals with the potentialities and dangers of the present age from Arab and human perspectives. The fourth book of collected articles, *More than Conquerors*, contains selected addresses delivered on various occasions at the American

University of Beirut from 1953 to 1966.[11] The fifth and latest book is *Maṭālib al-mustaqbal al-'Arabī: humūm wa tasā'ūlāt* (The Demands of the Arab Future: Concerns and Questions). Although some of these articles and lectures repeat the hypotheses found in the other books, there is a new freshness in them and a unifying thread in the outlook towards the future.

The third and last group of Zurayk's books is composed of in-depth studies of various lengths, each dealing with one topic in a unified manner. Zurayk's intellectual powers and his contributions are best exemplified in these studies because of their comprehensiveness, depth, and analytic cohesiveness. Although some of his other writings enjoyed a more enthusiastic reception when they were first published, the impact of the third group of books proved to be deeper and more permanent. It is indeed unfortunate that for an extended period of time after the start of his academic career Zurayk did not give much attention to this type of study. He focused instead on short essays of topical value, although he himself considered "the organically unified book, without argument, more valuable than a collection of essays" and saw in the scarcity of these publications a "shortcoming of the intellectuals and their society."[13] Perhaps the reason for this shortcoming is Zurayk's long involvement in teaching, administration, consultancy, and similar activities, which did not afford him the time needed to undertake such studies.

The first of Zurayk's unified books is *Ma'na al-nakbah* (The Meaning of Disaster). It analyzes the disaster of the Arabs in Palestine in 1948, attributing the causes to the internal situation of Arab societies and then offering solutions. The book aroused great interest because it presented bold intellectual theses characterized by a distance from the emotionalism prevalent in the literature of the time, which rationalized the disaster. An English translation of this book appeared in 1956.[14]

The second unified book is *Naḥnu wa-al-tārīkh: Maṭālib wa tasā'ūlāt fī ṣinā'at al-tārīkh wa sun' al-tārīkh* (Facing History: Quests and Questions on the Art of History Writing and on Making History).[15] It is the study of the basic concepts of historical writing and methodology, as well as a consideration of some problems raised by the attitude of the Arabs toward their past. The third book in this group is *Fī ma'rakat al-ḥaḍārah: Dirāsah fī māhiyat al-ḥaḍārah wa aḥwāliha wa fī al-wāqi' al-ḥaḍāri* (In the Battle for Civilization: A Study in the Nature of Civilization and its Conditions, and in the Current Situation). It deals with the various aspects and meanings of the concept of "civilization" and the theories that stem from it. Zurayk considers this work the first attempt of its kind in the Arabic language.[16] The fourth book is *Ma'na al-nakbah mujadadan* (The Meaning of Disaster Again), which appeared two months after the Arab defeat in 1967.[17] Despite the similarity in title and basic thesis with his book on the 1948 war, the two books constitute two independent studies, each exhibiting its own structure and particular material. The last of the books in the collection is *Naḥnu wa-al-mustaqbal* (Facing the Future), in which Zurayk surveys the different types of pioneering and draws a blueprint for the future directions Arab society needs to take.[18]

The Principal Pivot of Zurayk's Thought

The central issue that has engaged modern Arab thought since the beginning of the *Nahḍah* (Revival) until the present time is the "Grand Question" or the "Question of All Questions." In the form in which it is usually presented, the Grand Question consists of two parts. In the first part there is questioning of the causes that led to the weakness and backwardness of the East (the former Islamic world and the present Arab world) and to the strength and advancement of the West (the former Christian world or Europe and the present Industrialized States). A self-critical process of varying severity and depth is undertaken, in the course of which some end up defending the national personality above all errors or shortcomings while others conclude by denying the very existence of a national personality. The second part of the questioning displays a more positive side inasmuch as it contains a search for the modalities and means that would insure, once adopted and implemented, the establishment of the desired Arab society.[19]

Zurayk's thought revolves in the same sphere in which modern Arab thought revolved and is captivated by the same issue. One may safely state that Zurayk is one of those who, during the past fifty years, have dedicated themselves mostly to writing on this issue and the subjects that stem from it. He expresses himself on this issue in the following manner:

> The essential question therefore is: how can we radically and expeditiously transform Arab society from an affective, delusive, mythological and poetic society into a practical, realistic, rational and scientific one? How can we effect this revolution which assures its safety, capabilities and dignity in the modern world?[20]

It is clear from this paragraph that Zurayk's position on this issue is one of deep dissatisfaction with the present state of Arab society and that he aspires for a society that is better qualified to achieve a number of defined goals. Therefore the best way to become acquainted with his thought is to survey and analyze his ideas on Arab society, the ideal society, and the manner by which the desired transformation may be achieved.

Contemporary Arab Society and the Crisis of Arab Civilization

Arab society, in Zurayk's opinion, is in a state of revival after a period of stagnation that lasted more than five centuries. After reaching its pinnacle of achievement and becoming a symbol for human progress, Arab civilization began to weaken and lose its capacity to organize and innovate because of internal causes. A course of decline and deterioration set in. One of the most important causes for this reversal was the stalemate and rigidity that crippled the Arab mind as a consequence of society's move toward self-enclosure, the rejection of new trends, and the resistance to rationalist movements. This reversal followed an alliance between the men of the sword and the men of letters at the expense of the common people. Both wanted to maintain the status quo and to stave off the forces of change.[21] To Zurayk, these changes in attitude regarding criticism, or the shifts from an inquisitive rational outlook to a reliance on tradition, differentiated the periods of growth from the periods of decline in Arab history.[22]

The weakness that afflicted Arab civilization is best represented by the change in the Arab personality. It turned toward egoistic and material goals, its set of values declined, its productivity was reduced, and its sense of responsibility was lost. "It became passive after being active."[23] Zurayk adds elsewhere that the turning away, in the realm of collective values, from the ideas of unity, loyalty, and the universal outlook led to the replacement of the spiritual motivations with material ones. This was a major cause of the fall of Arab civilization.[24]

Contrary to the process of decline which came as a result of internal causes, Zurayk attributes the causes of the modern Arab renaissance and the accompanying process of change and transformation to external factors. Arab society, which was until recently living within a peculiar world of its own inherited from the Middle Ages, collided with the West and its modern civilization. The West now surrounds it on all sides, influences all aspects of its life, and is attempting to exercise control over its future directions. And because the West with its modern civilization will continue to impose itself on Arab society and to prevail over it whether that society wants it or not, it is imperative that the Arabs come to a correct understanding of the West and to work toward comprehending its reality in order to become able to confront it.[25] Furthermore, modern Arab life is in a transitional stage from the old to the new and is being shaped by the interaction of the "internal personality of the nation" and the West.[26] In view of the above, Zurayk dedicated many of his works to discussing his own understanding of the West on the one hand, and the essence of the Arab personality on the other, and to survey the conditions of Arab society, judging it by the standards of modern civilization.

The Essence of the West and Modern Civilization

Zurayk defines the West as that group of people which have produced or adopted modern civilization, especally its two outstanding aspects: science and technology. What distinguishes these people is their reliance on modern science and its applications on a large scale to organize the different aspects of society and to define their outlook on nature and man.[27] In one of his early works, Zurayk considers that there are three basic elements which constitute the "reality" of the West. First, the West has an economic system produced by the Industrial Revolution that is oriented toward the organization and increase of productivity through the use of the forces of nature, man, and the machine. Second, science, the basis of the Western economic system, is anchored in a methodology that promotes a constant search for the truth and relies on reason for making judgements. Third, the West has a special philosophy that distinguishes and unifies it, providing it with a weltanschauung and common scientific standards.[28] In his in-depth study of the subject of civilization, Zurayk considers the distinguishing marks of Western civilization to be a comprehensiveness of interest encompassing nature as well as society and a belief that the use of the forces of nature and the reformation of social conditions will lead to progress. Other civilizations, including the Indian, the Christian, and the Islamic, made the reformation of the individual their main objective.[29]

Zurayk did not differentiate in his writings between Western and modern civilizations. He used the two concepts interchangeably until recently, when he expressed a preference for the term *modern civilization.* This preference is justifiable, according to him, because of the expansion, increased complexity, and multiplication of the sources of origin of this civilization, which has become global in scope. Furthermore, the terms *East* and *West* have become mixed up, making it difficult to differentiate the one from the other. Nonetheless, Zurayk continues to insist on the need to differentiate between this modern civilization and the others. He considers modern civilization to have an essence of its own based on the following principles: first, the world of nature is the only real world; second, man is "the aim of existence and the object of history"; and third, reason is the distinctive mark of man and the avenue through which he arrives at the truth.[30]

The Arabs' National Personality and Civilization

In the early stages of his intellectual life, Zurayk advocated the idea of a special individuality for the Arab nation that is manifested in its particular personality, mission, and civilization. He was among the first Arab intellectuals to articulate such an idea, and it is not unlikely that his opinions influenced the doctrines of the nationalist parties that were established at the time.

In his book *al-Wa'ī al-qawmī*, Zurayk affirms that the Arab nation is endowed with a particular personality which sets it apart from other nations and which is the product of certain historical elements, the most important of which are language, culture, and a common history.[31] Furthermore, the special historical course followed by this nation and its geographical location have supplied it, in the past as well as in the future, with a mission or a special mandate. This mission consists of assimilating other civilizations, harmonizing and enriching them and then presenting them to the world in a harmoniously coordinated unity in order to become a framework for the future.[32] In addition to a personality and a mission, Zurayk concluded that the Arab nation has a civilization based on certain fundamentals, or permanent and distinguishing truths, which it offers to humanity as examples and lessons. There are four most important fundamentals: first, a nation lives and grows by spiritual visions, without which it would die and decay; second, creativity is linked to a universal outlook; third, the belief in the oneness of the truth eliminates intellectual and moral breakdowns; and fourth, assuming a cooperative spirit and openness toward other cultures enriches and beautifies life.[33]

In defining the nature of Arab civilization, Zurayk touches upon the place of Islam. The analysis he offers was adopted by numerous Arab thinkers as a model to be followed in the treatment of this issue. The starting point in Zurayk's approach is a thesis contending that religion is one of the most important components of a civilization. Understanding the spirit, doctrines, and rules of a religion allows one to comprehend the distinguishing marks of that civilization.[34] Zurayk defines religion in this context as what the society believes in and considers as the final truth.[35] Religious doctrines act as incentives for cultural creativity among individuals and groups when they subscribe to the freedom of the individual and consider the individual capable of making responsible choices. The same doctrines become a deterrent for creativity whenever they weaken the belief in the freedom of the individual and are dominated by the notion of predestination.[36]

In his writings, Zurayk focuses on the special relationship between Arab civilization and Islam. Islam has provided this civilization with its particular character "wherever it was established and spread."[37] In fact, the rise of Arab civilization is due to the spiritual awakening that Islam has brought about. This connection explains why "the Arab system of government, Arab behavior, Arab sciences, and the Arab ethos" are firmly bound to the Islamic religion.[38] Similarly, the fortunes of Arab civilization are bound to conditions of the Islamic religion. Whenever Islam was flourishing, Arab civilization abounded with vitality, creativity, and innovation. And whenever Islam reduced itself to beliefs transmitted blindly and religious laws and statutes unwisely imposed, Arab civilization waned.[39]

Like all others who touched upon the subjects of the Arab personality and civilization, Zurayk needed to deal with the relationship between Islam and Arab nationalism. Arab thinkers are divided on this issue: Islamists define the nation in terms of the religious community, and nationalists insist upon the existence of an Arab nation prior to the rise of Islam. Zurayk took a position different from both in that he saw no contradiction between true nationalism and authentic religion. To him, they are independent phenomena united by the fact that both are in essence spiritual movements that seek the same goals. The contradiction that seems to exist between the two arises when priority is given to the sectarian bond over the national, or when there is a belief that nationalist society cannot exist except over the ruins of religion. Zurayk suggests that the need to link the two movements can be achieved by having the Arab nationalists approbate Islam as the source of their doctrines and values.[40] At the same time, a national state should be established based on secularism rather than on theocracy.[41] Many of the Arab nationalist thinkers adopted Zurayk's position during the period following World War II. The focus was then set on the cultural, educational, and spiritual framework of Islam and on the approbation of the principle of nationalism as the foundation for organizing the nation and for directing its efforts toward rebuilding society.

The Arab Condition and the Crisis of Civilization

Arab society is dominated by negative values that emanate from its heritage or are inherited from an earlier period of decline, or that are transmitted from modern culture.[42] These negative values have weakened both the scientific outlook in contemporary Arab life and its ethical virtues. The absence of the scientific outlook has led to the rise of a "traditional, mythological and ignorant" society, and, equally so, the failure and lack of ethical values have led to a society which is "dissolute, sick and corrupt."[43]

Consideration of reason and ethics as the sources of individual and collective power is one of the main intellectual traits dominating most, if not all, of Zurayk's works on contemporary Arab society. The weaknesses, dissolution, and feelings of loss that prevail in this society are constantly attributed either to a rational or an ethical crisis, or to both. Because the two standards of reason and ethics rest on an absolutist concept of values such as virtue, truth, justice, beauty, and good,[44] Zurayk's evaluation of the present condition of the Arabs is unequivocal and courageous yet suffers from a tendency toward overgeneralization. This trait has led some of his critics to label his thought as utopian, divorced from objective reality.[45] Zurayk responds indirectly to this kind of criticism in his recent book *Naḥnu wa-al-mustaqbal* when he complains that thought dealing with virtuous society and virtue is presently considered dissonant, reactionary, and misguided.[46]

Zurayk speaks of an internal spiritual crisis that affects the moral and psychological aspects of Arab society and that is the origin of its weakness and the source of its ills. He considers the crisis to be more dangerous and far-reaching than any economic, social, intellectual, or political crisis.[47] This manner of thinking has led Zurayk to believe in the existence of basic ills in the Arab individual which are responsible for the problems of society and whose effects appear in the form of Arab backwardness in a variety of fields, especially those dealing with culture and civilization.[48] He ridicules those who keep uttering the popular dictum that the East enjoys a so-called spiritual superiority over the West. He asserts that there are no traces of spirituality remaining in Eastern societies. He calls upon his compatriots to be humble when it comes to spirituality and to work toward renewing the spiritual attributes for which their ancestors were renowned.[49]

Regarding rational and scientific aspects, Zurayk speaks of a crisis in the Arab mind caused by the past failure of the nation to develop the mind, which resulted in the arrest of intellectual productivity and to a rigidity lasting for hundreds of years. The end result of this failure has been the arrest of progress in Arab civilization.[50] Currently, the Arab mind is overwhelmed by fantasy and is incapable of competing with external enemies or of confronting the challenges and threats that face it internally.[51] In other words, to Zurayk, the Arab nation itself is responsible for its periods of decline because of its persecution of lively minds. He concludes by stating that civilizations "commit suicide, they are not assassinated,"[52] indicating that internal forces are responsible for the rise and fall of civilizations and that "the nation which ridicules and neglects reason deserves itself to be ridiculed, neglected and lost."[53]

The ineffectuality of rational thinking in modern Arab life is accompanied, according to Zurayk, by an absence of a scientific spirit and a predominance of literary concerns in intellectual life.[54] That trait explains why no genuine thought has yet appeared in the Arab nation.[55] It is worth noting that Zurayk's definition of science (*'ilm*) transcends mere technical knowledge and its applications. It encompasses all the capacities, rational and ethical, which have the power to discover, innovate, and apply.[56] For this reason, science, as far as he is concerned, is a basic condition for freedom, human dignity, progress, cultural innovation, and the acquisition of power.[57] In addition, the way of science is the way of the future.[58] Using this notion to gauge the capacity of present Arab society to survive and whether it deserves to survive, Zurayk pronounces a harsh judgement. He questions the capacity of Arab society to survive and, if it remains the way it is at present, whether it deserves to survive.[59]

Zurayk's stance on the issue of science and rationalism has placed him in a unique position in the development of modern Arab thought. It is a stance characterized by courageous criticism of the Arab situation for its lack of scientific and rationalist life, continuous exhortations against the dangers that might befall society because of its lack of rationalist and scientific spirit and the link between Arab developments and this situation, and finally the explanation, interpretation, and dissemination of the modern concepts of science and reason. It is not surprising, therefore, given Zurayk's reliance on these postulates in his analysis, that many were led to consider *The Meaning of Disaster*, for example, as the only objective book on the Palestine tragedy to appear at that time.[60] If we view Zurayk's long record in perspective, it should be appropriate to declare him, among all contemporary Arab thinkers, the advocate of science and rationalism.

Arab reality, according to Zurayk with all its negative aspects, tragedies, and problems, was not the cause of the crisis in Arab civilization. It would have been possible to maintain the same existence if the Arab civilization had not encountered a Western civilization that was superior in its various aspects of life. The crisis is in the Arab entity as a whole. It faces, as individuals and as a nation, tremendous challenges that require decisive responses.[61] The source of the crisis lies in the fact that the Arabs are still at the threshold of modern civilization in a state of cultural backwardness.[62] Whether this cultural condition will continue depends on how the Arabs interact with modern civilization.[63] The battle of civilization, as far as Zurayk is concerned, is the decisive battle.[64]

The crisis in civilization is reflected in the form of a struggle between the old and the new which dominates modern Arab life, divides the society into factions, and throws it into the throes of intellectual chaos with permanent and far-reaching consequences for all aspects of life.[65] Zurayk takes a clear-cut position regarding this struggle. The progress and predominance of the West is due to the progress of reason there and its neglect by the Arabs. For the Arabs to win the battle of survival and to meet the challenges head-on, they must resort to the same means discovered by the Western mind. This effort alone will position them in the modern world.[66] The situation poses what Zurayk calls the "basic question" facing the Arab world today: "Is it possible to have an Arab civilization in our modern world?"[67] The definition, explanation, and investigation of this question constitute the major part of Zurayk's concerns and efforts, as this study has shown. The rest of his endeavors were geared toward the response to this question.

Desired Changes in Arab Society

Zurayk strongly criticizes the complacence which prevails in the thinking and behavior of the Arab citizenry when it deals with issues of vital importance. He considers this condition to be the cause and effect of the present situation.[68] In his writings on the Arab future, Zurayk advocates radical change in all aspects of Arab life and calls for a comprehensive modification of the methods of thinking and acting.[69] Although Zurayk's works do not contain an integrated theory explaining the nature and characteristics of the desired society, there are certain attempts to draw some of the features of this society. Zurayk's ideas on this subject stem from four fundamental convictions which constitute the foundation of his intellectual system. The first conviction is his deep-rooted belief that peoples are responsible, to a great extent, for their own destiny.[70] In this idea, he contradicts the majority of contemporary writers, who attribute the Arabs' retrogressive situation to external factors, especially to the greed and intrigues of the colonial powers. The second conviction is that progress is determined by human will and not by material resources[71] or by natural and environmental factors.[72] By adopting such a position, Zurayk takes a different stance from those who assign to material circumstances a greater role in the interpretation of social events. Good and evil, according to him, are in man rather than in any system.[73] The third conviction derives from a philosophical standpoint which considers human will to be the outcome of man's freedom of endeavor[74] and the view that man is capable of discovering and comprehending the truth and achieving his happiness during his lifetime.[75] Here, also, Zurayk stands apart from many of his contemporaries, who adhere to religious and deterministic doctrines and interpretations which reduce human freedom and will and attribute events to metaphysical forces. Finally, the fourth conviction is his assertion that cultural creativity is a particularity of the individual and that the good and well-being of society derive from good individuals.[76] This view explains why Zurayk emphasizes in his works the high qualifications and ideals of citizenship, considering them necessary requirements for the modernization of Arab society. Moreover, he defines the liberation of the Arab individual as the goal of Arab revival.[77] In view of these intellectual convictions, it should not be surprising that Zurayk's writings are among the prominent works of liberal literature in modern Arab thought.[78]

Zurayk's prescription for a desired society is in keeping with his analysis of the negative aspects of the Arab condition and reflects the above-mentioned four convictions. The national revival of the Arabs must rest on the basis of reason and ethics now lacking in the existing society. Thus, Zurayk calls for the establishment of a society that is "modern, rational, and scientific," on one hand, and "cohesive, sound, and ethical," on the other.[79] Furthermore, Zurayk defines the attributes of the desired society as nationalism, unity, and progressiveness.[80] In another place, he announces them to be systemization, progressiveness, and cultural consciousness.[81] Yet, in spite of his use of different terminology, Zurayk consistently maintains that the future must be built on rational powers on one side, and ethical ones on the other. Rationalism is what insures the integrity and the future of the nation; without it the fate of the nation is delusion and loss.[82] The success of the Arab revival movement is bound to its ability to undo the shackles that fetter the mind.[83] The establishment of a rational society, then, is the primary challenge that faces Arab civilization because rationalism is the prerequisite that encompasses all other prerequisites. To demonstrate the importance he assigns to this matter, Zurayk concludes his study *Fī ma'na al-ḥaḍārah* with the following statement:

> If we were to reduce these requirements . . . to one requirement, we would say it is "rationalism." There is no alternative for these peoples [Arab peoples], if they wish to survive and triumph in this battle, which is the source and axis of all other battles, there is no alternative but to become rationalists. Through rationalism

they will understand that their first problem is cultural backwardness, through rationalism they will proceed to examine their conditions, yearn for a higher civilization, believe in truth and reason, look towards the future, open up to what is good no matter where it comes from, generate a capacity for production, realize their human potentials and control their political, economic and social revolutionary tendencies.[84]

Moral capacities are the capacities with which it is possible to establish the virtuous Arab society defined by Zurayk as a scientific society guaranteeing for the individual his dignity and freedom. In Zurayk's opinion, this society ascribes to a system of values, the most important of which are loyalty to truth, to duty, to generosity, to others, to the future, and to a feeling of responsibility.[85] Values are what render the homeland valuable; without them it becomes an empty entity.[86] That is what moves Zurayk to specify the moral and spiritual regeneration of the Arab classes as a condition for the generation of a virtuous Arab society.[87] Obviously, the Arab society to which Zurayk aspires is a society of science and virtue.

In his analysis of the events of 1948 in Palestine, Zurayk concludes that contemporary Arab society has reached a tragic stage of material and spiritual bankruptcy.[88] He considers the levels of civilization and culture in Arab society responsible for Arab defeat.[89] The superiority of Zionist society in the battlefield is nothing else but a reflection of the difference between the Zionist system and the system of Arab societies. The Zionist system rests on the basis of modern civilization, while Arab societies are still living in a medieval situation, deluded by dreams of past glory and disclaiming at the same time modern life.[90] The dissimilarity in power between the two societies is in reality determined by a difference in civilization.[91] If the Arabs are to achieve victory, they should battle to build the content of their civilization at the same time that they strive for self-preservation.[92] Nevertheless, the fight against backwardness remains the most important and most dangerous of battles.[93] The transition of Arab society from its current backwardness to the desired situation can be achieved only when a new attitude is adopted which considers the world of yesterday incapable of meeting the needs of today. The Arab future depends not upon outside factors but upon the resolution and sacrifice made by putting responsibility above rights, by preventing the pilfering of wealth, and, finally, by adopting the scientific mentality in the building of society.[94]

Zurayk's deep conviction that the future belongs to those who deserve it[95] and that the responsibility for Arab salvation rests with the Arabs themselves[96] has led him, given the repeated Arab military defeats, to ponder the question of whether the Arab citizen is more interested in maintaining the regimes than in the security of the country.[97] The aspired-for Arab society cannot be established if the prevailing social conditions remain as they are. The Arab must join the modern world. This revolution cannot be achieved without the following changes: use of the machine on a wide scale, separation of state and religion, organization of the national life in accordance with the latest achievements of the human mind, encouragement of the scientific spirit, maintenance of some distance from romanticism, and openness toward the rational and spiritual values of other human civilizations.[98] Zurayk suggests four standards by which to gauge the level of progress in society: first, the capacity to control the forces of nature and exploit its resources; second, the prevalence of scientific knowledge and applications; third, the degree of respect for the human personality; and fourth, the availability of free and organized personalities.[99]

It is obvious that Zurayk, in dealing with the specifications of the desired society, refrains from using the customary method, followed by many of the Arab thinkers, of resorting to the past with its real and imagined glories. One also notices that the equation upon which he anchors his analysis is free of any postulates of alleged or definite superiority of the Arab personality or civilization. On the contrary, Zurayk consistently calls for the abandonment of the historicist mentality, replacing it with a futuristic one which believes in the human mind and acts according to its rules.[100] Zurayk goes even further when he declares that rationalism is by nature progressive, futuristic, and distant from any reactionary outlook.[101] Driven by this vision, Zurayk offers in his works, as we shall see later, an ingenious analysis of an issue that preoccupied Arab thought for a long time, namely, the present and future role of heritage in Arab civilization. Regarding the directions of the future, Zurayk, in spite of his pessimistic outlook, opposes theories based on historical determinism which assert that the future of the Arabs will be determined by the quality of their response to the challenges that presently face them.[102]

It should be clear from this survey of Zurayk's ideas that his works do not contain a clear and definite conceptualization of what constitutes a model scientific and virtuous society. Rather, Zurayk's conceptualizations exhibit vagueness and were modified as time went on. This vagueness is indicated, for example, in the way he uses the concepts of "Western civilization" and "modern civilization" and how he describes the Arabs' attitude toward these concepts.

In his early works, Zurayk tends to equate the two concepts. He also makes the emulation of the West a prerequisite for the progress of the

Arab nation. He interprets the Arabs' reluctance to adopt Western civilization as the result of their failure to understand the West correctly,[103] their fear of Western colonialism and expansionism,[104] and the belief that the West looks at and treats the Arabs and other Eastern peoples as a means of attaining its own ends.[105] It is likely that Zurayk's reservations about the process of interaction with the West are not fundamental and derive from political considerations. For that reason, Zurayk prefers to borrow from the West only as long as borrowing would meet the genuine needs of the Arab world and would provide the latest achievements of the West.[106]

Zurayk's attitude toward the issue of emulating the West was determined at the time by his concept of modern civilization. Western civilization was perceived not only as reason and science but also as a philosophy which provided a nation with the capacity to build up its own powers and to acquire strength and immunity. Power was an adjunct of modern civilization. Western civilization combined in itself material power and an advanced civilization.[107] Following the path of Western civilization, according to Zurayk, was really following the call of contemporaneity and modernization.

In his latest works, Zurayk adopts a more critical outlook on Western civilization and advocates distinguishing between it and modernity. He further calls for cooperation with the liberalized elements in Western societies to fight against and defeat the motives of greed and evil that exist at the very core of these societies.[108] And in order to establish a fruitful dialogue and mutual appreciation of values between the peoples of the East and the West, he calls upon the West to abandon its exploitation of the East and upon the East to rediscover and protect the positive values in its own traditions.[109] He warns against the continuing spread of Western civilization and the Westernization of the whole world, because this spread would constitute a great loss for humanity, which is enriched by the multiplicity and variety of civilizations.[110] Zurayk talks about a crisis in Western civilization resulting from the extremism of following a concept of naturalistic truth and of stressing the value of sensory evidence. Western civilization needs to supplement these concepts with a concept of faith.[111] Further on, Zurayk abandons some of his previous concepts, denying that modernity is spiritually and morally superior.[112] He confines the superiority of Western societies and states to the areas of science and industry, and his concept of progress to advances in these two fields.[113]

Thus Zurayk finally comes closer to the position of the Arab thinkers who deny the superiority of modern civilization except in the realm of the material, after having distanced himself from them for most of his life. Zurayk's transformation is clearly manifested in his recent assertions that the moral dimension is the only dimension left to the developing nations in their competition with the advanced nations. He describes foreign influences in the moral field as being mostly negative and as furthering the weakness of developing societies. Thus, in the most recent of Zurayk's prescriptions, the desired Arab society would derive its scientific capabilities from the West and would look internally to develop its own moral ones.[114]

Mediums for Transforming Arab Society

Although Zurayk generally avoids any discussion of the applicational aspects of the subjects with which he deals, his works refer to a process for transforming Arab society from its current to its desired state which entails the use of four principal mediums. A discussion of these mediums follows.

The Nationalist Creed

After World War I, the nationalist idea began to enjoy greater acceptance among Arab thinkers, both religious and secular. Reformist-minded thinkers from both groups took part in promoting the Arab identity and in asserting the ethnic particularities of the Arabs. In so doing, they aimed to create spiritual ties which would unify a fractured society and would give direction to the national effort against the Western colonial presence. The two groups, however, differed on the final goal of the nationalist idea. The religious reformers, such as Rashīd Riḍa and his disciples, adopted a utilitarian position. They considered the establishment of a nationalist society a temporary development that would precede the resurrection of a strong and unified Islamic society. The secularists, such as Najīb 'Āzūrī, considered the Arab nation an ultimate entity and held that nationalist bonds are stronger and more important than religious bonds. With the arrival of the third decade of the current century, the secularists among the Arab nationalists grew in importance, and their concepts and programs became noticeably clearer. Zurayk distinguished himself among this group of thinkers and since then has been considered a prominent representative of secular nationalist thought.

In his first essay on nationalism, Zurayk starts with the premise that all national revivals must be preceded or accompanied by an intellectual awakening that performs two functions. First, it must provide society with a theoretical framework or a nationalist philosophy that sets the goals, aims, and direction of the movement for change and defines its means, contours, and perimeter. Second, it must offer individuals a nationalist doctrine which motivates them to achieve the goals of the collectivity. The Arab world, now undergoing a widespread revival, lacks a unified and purposeful intellectual revival which could put an end to the conditions of divisiveness and loss from which it suffers. The blame for this state falls primarily on Arab thinkers who have shied away from assuming their responsibility and have failed to explain to the public the fundamentals of nationalism.[115] Zurayk calls on Arab intellectuals to construct a national philosophy and to derive from it a national doctrine. Although Zurayk himself does not participate in developing the national philosophy, his writings nonetheless contribute to the clarification of many of the postulates of nationalist thought and direct attention to some of the significant issues in the national life of the Arabs.

It is worth noticing that Zurayk's treatment of the subject of nationalism was free, to a great extent, of the familiar attempts common to nationalist literature: namely, defending nationalism and trying to prove its superiority over other doctrines by appealing to history or to some absolutist values. This approach allowed Zurayk to call for the adoption of nationalism as a basis for the reorganization of Arab society without becoming involved in the intellectual battles which raged between the partisans of the traditional and reformist schools, and even between the reformists themselves. These battles revolved around such issues as the role of reason and revelation, the status of positive law and the *Shari'a* (sacred law), and the advantages of democracy and consultation (*shūra*). Having stayed out of the maze of controversy and argumentation, Zurayk's analysis proceeded from the hypothesis that Arab nationalism is a fact and its existence need not be proven because it is the framework chosen by Arab society to direct the process of transformation through which it is currently going.[116] Consequently, according to Zurayk, it is the duty of the Arab intellectual to explain, interpret, and popularize the nationalist doctrine to enable society to benefit in a positive way from the force of nationalist feelings among the masses.[117]

Zurayk's method of dealing with the concept of nationalism is characterized by two prominent and distinctive features. First, he considers nationalism, as a doctrine and as an identity, as a means, not an end, and he disagrees with other Arab nationalist thinkers over the definition of these ends. Zurayk's notion of nationalism as a means can best be illustrated by his explanation and defense of that notion on relativistic, transitory, and utilitarian bases. The Arab identity, for example, suits contemporary Arab needs but is not in itself a final truth. Should circumstances require it, it could change. Likewise, the attachment of citizens to the nationalist doctrine is not inevitable and depends on what progress and freedoms nationalism produces. Should it fail in this respect, its raison d'être vanishes and people are likely to abandon it for other doctrines.[118] Nationalist feelings are not the result of a natural condition: they are a means which one adopts to realize certain positive social functions, such as healing the horizontal and vertical cleavages which result from confessionalism, tribalism, feudalism, and provincialism, all ills from which Arab society suffers.[119] On the basis of this perception, Zurayk assigns to nationalism a goal that goes beyond political independence, namely, the liberation of the individual.[120] Instead of focusing on the primacy of the nation, as did Saṭi' al-Ḥuṣri, for example, Zurayk focuses on the individual and considers the realization of the interest of the individual to be the main and immediate aim of nationalism. The national struggle of the Arabs, for example, is the by-product of a personal struggle embarked upon by individuals for the purpose of building up a new Arab personality characterized first by discipline in thought and action, second, by freedom from ignorance, fanaticism, and desire for material goods, and third, by a sense of responsibility in thought, speech, and action.[121] The strong emphasis on the role of the individual is perhaps Zurayk's most important contribution to Arab nationalist thought.[122]

The second peculiarity of Zurayk's approach is his secularist and progressive notion of nationalism. He considers secularism to be an essential attribute of nationalist states and movements and warns that the Arab nationalist movement will not be able to firmly establish itself unless it adopts the principle of state secularism.[123] Nationalism and secularism are bound together in that the existence and strength of each depends on the existence and strength of the other. Zurayk states that one of the most basic challenges facing Arab nationalism is the guaranteeing of legal and real equality for all citizens.[124] As for progressiveness, Zurayk's conception envisions a nationalism that directs the thinking process toward the future when examining national issues and leads to the relinquishing of the historicist mentality which confines Arab thought.[125] It is also progressive in that it advocates a revolution against exploitation and reactionism. Zurayk states in this regard that "the greatest danger to our nationalism is reactionism in all its manifestations."[126] Consequently, in dealing with the issue of religious minorities in the Arab world, Zurayk rejects the claim that there is a conflict between Islam and Christianity and between Muslims and

Christians. According to him, any problems that exist in this context are due to the struggle between reactionaries and liberals, a struggle on whose outcome depends the future of all Arabs.[127]

Yet the secular and progressive nationalism of Zurayk does not alienate him from the Arab Islamic heritage as explained above and as further explained in the following section on the national heritage. Suffice it to point out the special place Zurayk assigns to the Prophet Muḥammad in his article entitled "Arab Nationalism and Religion" written on the occasion of the birthday of the Prophet, in which he calls upon Arab nationalists to emulate the Prophet's way of life. The Prophet is viewed as being intimately related to Arab nationalism because he is the prophet of Islam and Islam is the religion which constitutes by way of its texts, rules, and systems the bases of modern Arab culture. The intimate and special relationship between Islam and Arab nationalism derives also from the fact that the Prophet is the unifier of the Arabs and the model of a man of principle and faith.[128] This position explains why Zurayk often refers to the Messenger of God with phrases such as "the Arab Prophet," "the Arab Leader," or "the Arab Commander." It is worth mentioning in this context that Zurayk's statement on this subject precedes by several years the famous statement of Michel Aflaq, founder of the Ba'th party, on the Messenger of God in a speech delivered at the Syrian University in 1943.[129] It is not surprising, therefore, that a great many people do consider Zurayk as an authority for an entire generation of nationalists.[130]

One can conclude from the above that in Zurayk's opinion Arab nationalism is the doctrine the Arabs need to direct their efforts toward the rebuilding of their society. The content of that doctrine is determined by the national heritage and education.

The National Heritage

A student and teacher of history, Zurayk was not about to ignore the influence of the past on the present or its role in building the future. His appreciation of the distinctive and particular place the past occupies in Arab culture increased his interest in this matter. Because of this interest, Zurayk paid special attention in his works to the national heritage, considering it a major resource for transforming Arab society.

Zurayk's approach to the issue of heritage centers on responses to three questions: What position does heritage occupy in Arab culture and what is the nature of the need for it? Where do the different groups of society stand on the issue of heritage and what distinguishes each stance? What position should be taken regarding the heritage?

Zurayk views the national heritage as the distinguishing mark of the Arab nation and its common ground with other nations. Heritage endows the nation with particularity that separates it from the others yet at the same time constitutes the nation's contribution to world civilization.[131] The importance of heritage reaches the present inasmuch as it is the basis upon which the existing culture rests.[132] It touches also the future inasmuch as it is a field for learning and experimentation which may be used to meet the needs of the future.[133] And because heritage, in terms of time, enjoys this special position, Zurayk concludes that "he who has no past, likewise has no present or future."[134]

Zurayk submits a number of suggestions on how to benefit from the heritage in meeting the needs of society and achieving national purposes. Among the suggestions is the development of a national culture, inspired by heritage, which would bring out the unique characteristics of the Arab nation and generate among the citizens a mental and spiritual unity to sustain their political and social unity.[135] Zurayk also suggests that heritage serve as the inspiration for a program of historical education which would build up the nation's feeling of authenticity and would inspire self-confidence and strength in facing events.[136] Furthermore, Zurayk suggests that a return to the heritage would lead to the acquisition of a better understanding of the national and individual self. By knowing one's self, the discovery of the important and essential issues and problems that confront the nation and its citizen becomes possible.[137] Finally, because the existing standards for evaluation are chaotic and extremely unreliable because of the rapidity of change that usually accompanies a revival, Zurayk suggests the use of heritage to extract standards for judging national decisions and for stimulating creative actions.[138]

Zurayk sets a number of general rules to explain the multiplicity of attitudes in society toward heritage and the differences among them. One of these rules states that the attitude towards heritage and history reflects an attitude towards life in general.[139] Every people has its own outlook and interpretation of the past regardless of whether it is aware of this.[140] Different generations have different outlooks on historical events and different interpretations. Attitudes toward history vary because resorting to history takes place within the framework of present concerns and future hopes.[141] Zurayk invokes another rule which posits a direct correlation between the degree of openness to heritage and the scope of openness to or isolation from other civilizations, particularly the superior or prevailing ones.[142] Using this latter interpretation, Zurayk notes three kinds of attitudes. The first rejects the culture of others and therefore is driven to accept only the Arab heritage. Its adherents are characterized by fanaticism and fundamentalism. The second accepts without qualifications whatever comes from the outside and totally rejects its own heritage in the belief that this approach is the best and shortest way to modernization and development. The failure of this attitude is almost unavoidable, and heritage quickly reasserts itself in different styles and forms. Zurayk indicates that once heritage has reasserted its being, this second group rationalizes its position on the ground that its final purpose is to preserve and protect the heritage, thus confusing the distinction between the modernist and the traditionalist and between the progressive and the reactionary. The third and final category includes holders of a great variety of positions which differ only in the degree of outside influence they will accept or reject, but all agree on the principle of borrowing and the necessity of interaction between the new and old. What differentiates these positions is their final goals and approaches to those goals. Regarding goals, this third category may be divided into two groups. One accepts the assimilation of some elements of the more advanced civilizations but rejects its values. The aim of this group is to acquire the sources of power and, at the same time, to defend its own heritage and personality. The second group seeks to acquire the principles upon which advanced civilizations are built in addition to those elements that are of practical value. There are also two approaches, or styles. One group would like the borrowing to take place gradually to insure its effectiveness and durability. The second group would resort to revolution to expedite change out of a desire to eliminate backwardness as quickly as possible.[143]

Zurayk uses the following rationale to define the position that should be taken regarding heritage. The tragedies that befell the Arab nation were an incentive for it to reflect on its past. The knowledge it gained in this process of reflection contributed to its revival.[144] However, these reflections on the history of the nation have brought forth a great number of trends which differ in their vision of the past they seek to revive and the goal which the process of revival seeks to achieve.[145] Of these trends, two should be strongly rejected. The first is characterized by a vigorous attachment of its followers to the past which leads them to pay no attention to the present and to confine their interest to a segment of the nation's history. By glorifying history and placing a halo above it, they become less and less compelled to go beyond it.[146] The followers of this trend do not seem to be aware that defeat is the fate of all who attempt to fight the present with the past.[147] The second trend that needs to be rejected is one that calls for the invalidation of the heritage. This approach would lead to the destruction of the heritage in all its aspects, good and bad. Furthermore, to extract oneself and become separated from the past is neither desirable nor, practically speaking, possible.[148]

Zurayk designates these two trends as "retrograde reactionism" and "recalcitrant futurism," and he considers both as dangerous to heritage.[149]

In addition to his explanation of existing trends in society, Zurayk discusses a correlation between society's cultural level and its general attitude towards heritage. In periods of decadence, society normally adopts the forms and traditions of its heritage but not the content. History thus becomes a mental illness further weakening society because its use is limited to boasting and haughtiness.[150] And when society finds itself confronted with a more developed civilization, it wakes up to its heritage. The effect of heritage on society will depend on how much rationalism is developed in its midst and its psychological disposition. Whenever rationalism is weak and is accompanied by insecurity, society is led to the illusory belief that heritage will shelter it; but if rationalism is strong and is accompanied with a feeling of security, society will differentiate between the various elements of its heritage and select whatever is more appropriate.[151]

Zurayk's own position on heritage is based on a principle that affirms the need of any live populace to continuously reevaluate its history and extract from it the positive elements of its heritage. By "positive elements," Zurayk means an assortment of historical actions characterized by innovation and progressivism which have contributed to an atmosphere of freedom and dignity for the citizen and for humans in general. Accordingly, Zurayk considers history as both a burden and an incentive. He maintains that a nation needs to pass judgement on its history to better understand it and to use it wisely in meeting the needs and demands of the future.[152] One judges one's history to discover those values of the heritage that are suitable for regeneration with the aid of a liberated and organized mind, which the Arabs need to borrow from modern civilization.[153] Zurayk concludes by stating that society enhances its authenticity and strengthens its futurist mentality when the creative actions of its ancestors are extracted and emulated.[154]

National Education

Zurayk's works dealing with the systems of education, teaching, and culture (*thaqāfah*) in the Arab world are oriented toward explaining the major features and philosophical bases of the above three fields, and toward a clarification of their expected role in the rebuilding of Arab society.

Zurayk defines national education as that acquired refinement which cultivates in the majority of the people the feeling of belonging to the nation. Such feelings lead citizens, in turn, to fulfill their duties toward the nation. National education performs for the nation the same functions that scholastic education performs for the individual. It preserves the integrity of the nation by reducing the level of conflict within society. It also counterbalances conflicting behavioral and intellectual trends by providing society with a definite and cohesive identity and definite goals. Finally, national education prepares society to contribute to human civilization by unleashing its powers and directing them toward the realization of higher ideals. For an education to acquire a national character, Zurayk states that it should be inspired by a national philosophy and be based on real-life experiences. If these two conditions are met, education gains stability and steadiness and becomes appropriate to the environment and its circumstances. In his works, Zurayk deals with the means used in the dissemination of national education, which include, among others, educational organizations, the media, political parties, and the family. He pays special attention to the importance of newspapers and ideological political parties.[155]

Zurayk compares religion and education as vehicles for reforming the individual and introducing needed social changes. He concludes that the role of education has been more significant, especially since the spread of schools in the modern age has ended the monopoly on education exercised by a small conservative and fundamentalist minority allied to governmental authorities.[156] In addition, Zurayk maintains that education provides the best means to reform Arab society and to lead it toward modernization.[157] Through education, heritage is handed down from generation to generation and the leadership class needed to direct society is created.[158] Zurayk expresses here the same conviction held by most modern Arab reformists and best represented by Muḥammad ʻAbduh's school of thought.

Zurayk alludes to two crises facing Arab education. One is particular to the educated Arabs and the other to the educational system in the Arab world. The crisis of the educated is caused by a lack of understanding of what really constitutes science and culture and by a preoccupation with deceptive appearances and sophomoric knowledge.[159] The essence of the crisis of the educational system resides in its inability to meet the present and future needs of Arab society.[160] Zurayk announces the complete failure of the educational system to explain national issues and national risks to the youth, to reconcile inherited and modern values, and to graduate new ranks of leadership. He attributes these failures to current policies, such as the state's control of the teaching apparatus, excessive centralization, constant changes in educational policies, discouragement of innovation, reliance on indoctrination, lack of concern to develop the moral side of the personality, and finally, ignorance of the two most important elements in the educational process: the student and the teacher.[161]

Zurayk warns that the continuation of the present system of Arab education will not only compound Arab problems, but will act as a deterrent to progress. To remedy the crisis, he recommends two sets of measures, one to produce radical changes and the other to remedy the present situation for the short run. The first set covers two areas: one, educational concepts; and two, organizational systems and teaching methods. On the level of concepts, Zurayk calls for emphasizing the cultivation of the personality rather than indoctrination and for adopting the principle of comprehensive rather than limited and fragmented education. He also calls for programs which promote the values of production and development in lieu of programs that endorse the values of consumption and profiteering. On the level of organization and method, he calls for introducing new technologies into the educational process, revolutionizing educational administration, creating and developing educational institutions such as communal councils and centers for research and planning, and coordinating Arab efforts on a national basis. The second set of measures consists of fighting the politicization of education and the use of education for commercial purposes, reducing laxity and squandering in the educational system, improving conditions for teachers, linking educational programs to the development process, and equipping the educational apparatus with what is needed to meet the goals of development and growth.[162]

In addition to dealing with education and teaching, Zurayk's works deal with the concept of culture (*thaqāfah*) on the personal and national levels. Zurayk defines personal culture as acquired knowledge of the basic concepts upon which rest the different human sciences, supplemented with specialization in one aspect of knowledge. True personal culture is supported by certain attitudes, such as a constant desire to learn the truth, doubting of appearances, effort and agony in searching, humility, and seeking of education for its own sake and not for material purposes.[163] On the national level, Zurayk concludes that it is impossible to define Arab culture at this stage because of the absence of consensus among the Arabs on what is meant by Arab culture. He calls upon the nation, however, to struggle to maintain its own cultural character. Using a number of principles to guide the struggle, he mentions among others the need to link it to the national political struggle for the liberation of the country; the recovery of full authority over cultural institutions; and the definition of the essence and content of Arab culture by way of reviving the heritage, getting acquainted with the effective forces in its actual culture, and disseminating Arab culture among the people by all possible means.[164]

Although Zurayk refrains from stating his understanding of what the current Arab culture is, he nevertheless makes his thoughts clear regarding the qualifications required in setting up the desired culture of Arab society. The future culture is characterized in Zurayk's opinion by a wide popular basis, response to the needs of society, belief in reason and its rules, authenticity, and openness to, and participation in, human civilization.[165] Zurayk singles out the universities as the institutions with the most basic and most important role to play. In many of his works, he explains what this role should be.[166]

To conclude, Zurayk's approach to the questions of education, teaching, and culture is distinct in three aspects. First, he emphasizes the decisive role of education in national life. His writings in this field should be placed at the same level as those of Sāṭi‘ al-Ḥuṣri. Second, he introduces and disseminates the modern concepts of education. The third and last aspect is his dedication since the 1930s to the evaluation, criticism, and reform of the educational systems that were introduced in the contemporary period to the Arab world. His contributions in this field were more marked than those of his contemporaries among the Arab reformers, whose efforts were aimed mostly at proving that traditional religious education is inadequate given the needs of the modern age. There should be no doubt that the modern education Zurayk received and his advocacy of secularism and nationalism had the greatest effect on defining and directing his concerns.

The National Elite

It is obvious that the three mediums of nationalism, heritage, and education are not capable by themselves of transforming society to its desired state because all three are static and require an effective outside agent to activate, direct, and exploit the potentialities inherent in them. Without the introduction of such agents, the intellectual structure proposed by Zurayk would by necessity lose every practicality or realism. It would remain merely an impractical utopian exercise in theorization. The fourth medium that endows his theorization with a dynamic dimension is the idea of the elite, which he strongly and consistently calls for in almost all his works.

Zurayk equates the concept of the elite with concepts such as leadership, the vanguard, leaven, messengers of God, and companions (of the Prophet).[167] To him, all those concepts indicate a distinguished minority capable, through its creative powers, of producing civilizations. He even goes further in asserting the importance of the elite by stating that, on the one hand, the value of civilizations and the state of societies depend a great deal on the quality and qualifications of their elite, and, on the other hand, that society is correlated to the conditions of the elite.[168] The elite embody the highest degree of consciousness in society and are the element qualified to create because they do not refrain from transcending the status quo and venturing into the unknown. They are the energy that supplies society with vitality and the power of renovation. Finally, the elite are the source of progress and advancement.[169]

In Arab society, the ideal state will be established only in proportion to the cultural achievements of the Arab elite.[170] What is more critical is that the starting point in the social transformation process lies with the existence of an elite. Without it society will be devoid of the only element capable of producing change and reform. Meanwhile, the elite will succeed in its mission to the extent that it integrates the nation's goals, enrolls in ideological parties, and supplies the nation with the needed leadership from within its ranks.[171] The availability of an elite leadership is therefore "the primary requirement for nation-building and 'civilizational' creativity."[172]

The elitist concept adopted by Zurayk is a natural consequence of the hypothesis underlying his interpretation of progress and civilization. By attributing these phenomena to the creativity of certain individuals, he logically concluded that the existence of a distinguished human element inevitably leads to the establishment of an advanced and civilized society. That is why Zurayk engaged himself in the task of exhorting the role of the elite instead of focusing his attention on objective social conditions. Zurayk's belief in elitism might also be attributable to his perceptions of the Arab situation during the interwar period. Zurayk belongs to that early generation in the Arab East who received their modern education in academic institutions outside the Arab or Islamic worlds. It was only natural for Zurayk and his peers to look at themselves as members of a tiny circle differing from the rest of Arab thinkers dominated by traditionalism and conservatism, and also as different from the general public, which suffered from a high degree of illiteracy and ignorance. This position is clearly reflected in the conclusions Zurayk makes in his first book, *The National Consciousness.* There he says that the Arab world lacks authentic thought and is living in intellectual chaos; that Arab thinkers are not shouldering their responsibilities the way they should and generally misunderstand the nature of modern civilization and science; and that they are distracted by secondary issues and partial research and therefore in all these things should be stopped. Finally, it should be pointed out that Zurayk's use of the concept of an "elite" suffers from a major drawback. Except for his suggestion that academic institutions play an important role in the creation of the elite, Zurayk fails to explain how, without any prior or simultaneous basic changes in the actual conditions of society, traditional institutions in a backward society can identify the required elite to set in motion the development process. The failure of Zurayk and his colleagues to posit or to explain this issue gave the Arab nationalist school of thought, in its early stages, its idealist character.

Conclusions: Review and Evaluation

I have tried in this study to survey Constantine K. Zurayk's thought and his contributions to modern Arab thought in the hope of delineating the general precepts contained in his works. To accomplish this task, I have sought to bring out the underlying themes or the fabric in which they are woven. For this reason, I have foregone the traditional approach of presenting the accomplishments of a thinker within the framework of the time sequence or the chronological succession of dates of publication.

It is clear from the above that in the totality of his works Zurayk has developed a number of basic concepts which form an intellectual scheme uniquely his own. Of these concepts three stand out as the most important: civilization, rationalism, and nationalism. Zurayk chose the first of the three as a springboard for dealing with all the issues of Arab society, considering civilization "the domain from which all national and human issues arise and within which they find their place." The concept of civilization imbues Zurayk's thought with a universal dimension. It also gives him the opportunity to consider the different aspects of society as an organic and interactive unity. Furthermore, the concept of civilization allows Zurayk to develop his ideas within a universal and human framework, thus escaping the pitfalls of self-containment which characterized the majority of trends in modern Arab thought. As Zurayk explains, the concept of civilization is a gauge for comparing societies, a measurement of the scope of their progress and advancement, a means of judging things, and an indication of the unity of the human race and of its destiny in the past as well as in the future.

As for rationalism, this concept constitutes the means through which Zurayk wants to achieve the Arab passage to modern civilization. In this respect, he adopted a definition of rationalism composed of two basic elements: science and morality. Finally, the concept of nationalism received the greatest attention. Zurayk considered the question of nationalism to be the "question of Arab life." He worked hard to crystallize a nationalist consciousness and to promote a nationalist system of education. And although he did not develop in his works an integrated national philosophy and did not approach national issues in "a specialized, detailed and conclusive way," he nevertheless succeeded in drawing the attention of other Arab thinkers to them. One of his most important contributions in this respect is the way he dealt with the Palestinian Question, which he considered to be the litmus test for Arab revival. Through his many works on the Palestinian Question, Zurayk was able to enrich Arab thought by motivating it to adopt new points of departure in the consideration of national issues.

Perhaps the best summary of Zurayk's intellectual work is found in a section of a letter he sent me, dated October 18, 1981, in which he explains the major issues that preoccupied him.

> The primary motivation for concerning myself with the issues I dealt with in my works . . . is the deep awareness of the all-encompassing crisis through which Arab society is passing and of the responsibility of the intellectual—no matter what is his or her scientific or professional specialization—to face the issues raised by the crisis. This twofold and interactive awareness permeates all my works . . . Perhaps I considered what first should be done, once the issues are raised, is to proceed to clarify the basic concepts contained in them which are shrouded by a great deal of confusion and perplexity in our theoretical and practical environments. What is a nation, what are its components? Is there an Arab nation, and what is its nature in the past, at present and in the future? What is nationalism? Is it simply a movement for liberation from colonialism or should it have a more positive content, and what is this content? Is it possible to separate the nation and nationalism from its civilizational context? Therefore, what is civilization and what distinguishes civilizations from one another? What are the distinguishing marks of the earlier Arab-Islamic civilization and the civilization for which we aspire at present and in the future? This raises the question of our relationship with history, with the past, on the one hand, and the future, on the other. Which side should be given priority and control over the other? In this context, what is the meaning of progress and progressive society, and what is reactionism and a backward society? Since our backwardness forces us to strive for an expeditious revival, to leap forward and be radical and revolutionary in thought and action, what then is the desired revolution? And can we separate our situation, past, present, and future, from the situation of other peoples and humanity as a whole, especially at this juncture in time when the bonds among peoples have become stronger and the destiny of humanity has almost become one? I believe that (1) raising the major issues facing contemporary Arab society, and (2) the explanation of the basic concepts contained therein, and (3) the investigation of the links that connect these issues to each other and ranking them according to priority and importance, are among the most important responsibilities the Arab thinkers of today must assume. I hope I have contributed—even a little—to the fulfilment of this responsibility.

The process of evaluating Zurayk's thought underscores notable contributions to modern Arab thought in different areas, the most important of which are the crystallization of a secular conception of Arab nationalism which accentuates the human and individual side of nationalism, and an innovative way of dealing with the issue of heritage and the relationship between Arabism and Islam. Probably his most outstanding contribution is that he acted as a catalyst to some Arab intellectuals to involve themselves in the investigation of the issues he raised and to deal with them in a more detailed and conclusive way. Perhaps this is what Constantine K. Zurayk aspired to and what he really wanted.

Notes

1. The information dealing with Zurayk's family background and education is based on the author's interviews and correspondence with Zurayk.
2. This section surveys only Zurayk's books. Articles are listed at the end of this chapter.
3. Translated jointly with Bandali Jawzi (Pendali Jousé) and printed by the Catholic Press in Beirut in 1933.
4. Printed in Beirut by the American Press in 1934.
5. Najla Abu-Izzeddine participated in editing volume 8 and the second part of volume 9 (Beirut: American University Press, 1936-42).
6. *Readings* was used as a textbook at the American University of Beirut. The translation of Sarton's *History* was done with others and published in three parts in Cairo at intervals between 1957 and 1961.
7. Both the Arabic and English editions were published on the occasion of the centennial anniversary of the American University of Beirut in 1966.
8. Published in Beirut by Dār al-Makshūf in 1939. The second edition came out in 1940. References in this study are to the second edition. See p. 7 of that edition.
9. Published in Beirut by Dār al-'Ilm lil-Malāyin in 1957.
10. Published in Beirut by Dār al-'Ilm lil-Malāyin in 1963.
11. Published by the American University of Beirut in 1968.
12. Published in Beirut by Dār al-'Ilm lil-Malāyin in 1983. Three of the articles were originally in English.
13. *Hadha al-'aṣr al-mutafajjir*, pp. 7-8.
14. Published in Beirut by Dār al-'Ilm lil-Malāyin in August 1948. A second edition appeared in October of the same year. References here are to this second edition. Translation by R. Bayly Winder, as a part of the Near Eastern program of the American Council of Learned Societies, was published by Khayat's, Beirut.
15. Published in Beirut by Dār al-'Ilm lil-Malāyin in 1959. References here are to the fourth edition, which appeared in 1979. See pages 7-8 for the author's objectives from this study.

16. Published in Beirut by Dār al-'Ilm lil-Malāyin in 1964. See p. 8.
17. Published in Beirut by Dār al-'Ilm lil-Malāyin in 1967.
18. Published in Beirut by Dār al-'Ilm lil-Malāyin in 1977. References are to the second edition, which appeared in 1980.
19. For further readings on modern Arab political thought, see Adīb Naṣṣūr, "Muqaddimah li-dirāsat al-fikr al-siyāsi al-'Arabī fī mi'at 'ām," in *al-Fikr al-'Arabī fī mi'at 'ām*, eds. Fuad Ṣarrūf and Nabih Amin Faris (Beirut: American University of Beirut, 1967), pp. 82-149.
20. *Ma'na al-nakbah mujadadan*, p. 17.
21. *Naḥnu wa-al-mustaqbal*, pp. 319-320.
22. *Naḥnu wa-al-tārīkh*, p. 93.
23. *Ayyu ghad?* pp. 92-93.
24. "al-Ḥaḍārah al-'Arabīyah," *al-Abḥāth* (Beirut), Vol. 2, No. 1 (March 1949), p. 9.
25. *al-Wa'ī al-qawmī*, p. 45.
26. Ibid., pp. 41, 51.
27. *Hadha al-'aṣr al-mutafajjir*, p. 89.
28. *al-Wa'ī al-qawmī*, pp. 45-51.
29. *Fī ma'rakat al-ḥaḍārah*, p. 349.
30. Ibid., pp. 354-357. For further details on Zurayk's approach to the different meanings of civilization (*ḥaḍārah*) see "Fī mafāhīm al-ḥaḍārah," *Majallat al-Majma' al-'Ilmī al-'Arabī* (Damascus), Vol. 39, No. 1 (January 1964), pp. 99-112.
31. *al-Wa'ī al-qawmī*, p. 40.
32. Ibid., pp. 54-55.
33. "al-Ḥaḍārah al-'Arabīyah," pp. 5-19.
34. *Fī ma'rakat al-ḥaḍārah*, pp. 95, 138.
35. Ibid., p. 96.
36. Ibid., pp. 185-186. Zurayk adds that the tension between reason and revelation during the early history of Islam was one of the greatest motivations of creativity in Arab civilization. See *Tensions in Islamic Civilization* (Washington, D.C.: Georgetown University, Center for Contemporary Arab Studies, 1978).
37. *Naḥnu wa-al-mustaqbal*, p. 25.
38. "al-Ḥaḍārah al-'Arabīyah," p. 6.
39. Ibid., pp. 6-7.
40. *al-Wa'ī al-qawmī*, pp. 125-128. Zurayk's position has prompted some Western writers to classify him as a Christian Arab extremist in order to distort and invalidate his thesis on the relationship between Arabism and Islam. See, for example, Sylvia Haim, *Arab Nationalism: An Anthology* (Berkeley: University of California Press, 1962), pp. 61-62.
41. *Naḥnu wa-al-tārīkh*, p. 203.
42. *Naḥnu wa-al-mustaqbal*, pp. 306-308.
43. Ibid., pp. 237-238.
44. As an example, he wrote the following in one of his articles: "Since truth is one, right must be one. The fragmentation we are witnessing now in the

world is caused by our attempt to know the right by way of subjectivism, which is wrong, and to divide the right which is indivisible." "al-Ḥaḍārah al-'Arabīyah," p. 12.

45. See, for example, Bassam Tibi's accusation that Zurayk's thought is reactionary, traditional, compromising, metaphysical, bourgeois, and superficial in his article, "al-Fikr wa-al-hazīmah, arā' Constantine Zurayk fi hazīmat ḥuzayrān," *Mawāqif*, Vol. 2, No. 8 (March 1970), pp. 160-165.
46. *Naḥnu wa-al-mustaqbal*, p. 310.
47. *al-Wa'ī al-qawmī*, pp. 71, 215-216.
48. *Naḥnu wa-al-mustaqbal*, p. 277. See also *Ayyu ghad?* p. 130.
49. *Ayyu ghad?* p. 88; see also *al-Wa'ī al-qawmī*, p. 233.
50. *Ayyu ghad?* p. 25.
51. Ibid., p. 147.
52. *Hadha al-'aṣr al-mutafajjir*, p. 71.
53. Ibid., p. 182.
54. *al-Wa'ī al-qawmī*, pp. 49, 159.
55. *Ayyu ghad?* p. 34.
56. *Naḥnu wa-al-mustaqbal*, p. 245.
57. *Hadha al-'aṣr al-mutafajjir*, p. 150.
58. *Naḥnu wa-al-tārīkh*, p. 216.
59. *Ayyu ghad?* p. 166. This pessimistic evaluation is also reflected in his article, "al-Waṭan al-'Arabi fī al-thamānīnāt," *al-Mustaqbal al-'Arabi*, Vol.2, No. 13 (March 1980), p. 146, where Zurayk foresees the Arabs' power to face the challenges of the eighties as being less than what is was in the seventies.
60. See, for example, Nadīm al-Biṭār, *al-Fa'ālīyah al-thawrīyah fī al-nakbah* (Beirut: Dār al-Ittiḥād, 1965), p. 147.
61. *Ayyu ghad?* p. 71.
62. Ibid., p. 148. See also *Hadha al-'aṣr al-mutafajjir*, p. 11.
63. *Ayyu ghad?* p. 130.
64. *Fī ma'rakat al-ḥaḍārah*, p. 411.
65. *al-Wa'ī al-qawmī*, pp. 172-173. See also *Ayyu ghad?* p. 104.
66. *Ayyu ghad?* pp. 25-26.
67. "aḷ-Ḥaḍārah al-'Arabīyah," p. 20. For a second approach to this question, see Constantine Zurayk, "Naẓrah fi tārīkh al-'Arab wa-al-'ālam," *Tārīkh al-'Arab wa-al-'ālam*, Vol. 1, No. 1 (November 1978), pp. 5-10.
68. *Ayyu ghad?* p. 156.
69. *Ma'na al-nakbah*, p. 42.
70. *Ayyu ghad?* p. 29.
71. *Hadha al-'aṣr al-mutafajjir*, p. 14.
72. *Fī ma'rakat al-ḥaḍārah*, p. 202.
73. *Naḥnu wa-al-mustaqbal*, p. 310.
74. *Fī ma'rakat al-ḥaḍārah*, p. 201.
75. *Ayyu ghad?* p. 132.
76. Ibid., p. 182.
77. *al-Wa'ī al-qawmī*, p. 115.
78. Zurayk's postulates and approach have been frequently condemned by

leftist writers. An Egyptian author wrote: "He propagates in a style that gives the impression of neutrality and objectivity for the values of bourgeois democracy and chauvinistic nationalist ideas." See Ghāli Shukrī, "Istrātijiyat al-isti'mār al-jadīd fī ma'rakat al-thaqāfah al-'Arabīyah," *al-Ṭalī'ah* (Cairo), Vol. 3, No. 7 (July 1967), p. 16.

79. *Naḥnu wa-al-mustaqbal*, pp. 237-238.
80. *Ma'na al-nakbah*, p. 46.
81. *Ayyu ghad?* p. 7.
82. *Hadha al-'aṣr al-mutafajjir*, pp. 10, 145-147.
83. Ibid., p. 145.
84. *Fī ma'rakat al-ḥaḍārah*, pp. 410-411.
85. *Naḥnu wa-al-mustaqbal*, pp. 291-306.
86. *Hadha al-'aṣr al-mutafajjir*, p. 188.
87. "al-Ḥaḍārah al-'Arabīyah," pp. 21-22.
88. *Ma'na al-nakbah*, p. 49.
89. *Ayyu ghad?* p. 130.
90. *Ma'na al-nakbah*, p. 42.
91. *Ma'na al-nakbah mujadadan*, p. 14.
92. *Hadha al-'aṣr al-mutafajjir*, p. 79.
93. *Naḥnu wa-al-mustaqbal*, pp. 266, 405. For a second treatment of the problem of backwardness, see Constantine Zurayk "al-Ṭālib wa-mas'ūlīyatuhu al-waṭanīyah," in *al-Ṭālib al-jami'i fī Lubnān: Mustaqbaluhu wa mushkilātuhu* (Beirut: Rābiṭat al-Asātidhah al-Jāmi'iyīn fī Lubnān, 1969), pp. 30-31.
94. *Hadha al-'aṣr al-mutafajjir*, pp. 148-150.
95. *Naḥnu wa-al-mustaqbal*, p. 239.
96. *Ma'na al-nakbah mujadadan*, p. 82.
97. Ibid., p. 67.
98. *Ma'na al-nakbah*, pp. 46-49.
99. *Ayyu ghad?* pp. 48-65.
100. *Naḥnu wa-al-mustaqbal*, p. 198.
101. Ibid., p. 204.
102. *Naḥnu wa-al-tārīkh*, p. 242.
103. *al-Wa'ī al-qawmī*, p. 45.
104. "al-Ḥaḍārah al-'Arabīyah," p. 21.
105. *Hadha al-'aṣr al-mutafajjir*, p. 93.
106. *Ayyu ghad?* p. 107. Although Zurayk considers both the capitalist and communist systems products of one civilization, the Western, he nevertheless uses the term *Western world* as equivalent to the Western Alliance. In his works that appeared immediately after World War II, he calls on the Arabs to emulate and ally themselves with Western policies. He is thus reflecting the general position of the nationalist movements and thought at the time. He writes in one of his articles, "As I do this I find myself standing on the side of the Western system, and deciding that the future of the Arab countries would be safer and better off if they stand on the same side" (Constantine Zurayk, "al-Qaḍīyah al-'Arabīyah, 1953," *Muḥaḍarāt al-Nadwah al-Lubnāniyah*, Vol. 7, Bulletin 9-10 [May 1953], p. 242).

Zurayk adopted a less partisan position in his later works.

107. *Fī ma'rakat al-ḥaḍārah*, p. 226.
108. *Ayyu ghad?* p. 28.
109. *Hadha al-'aṣr al-mutafajjir*, pp. 91-100.
110. *Fī ma'rakat al-ḥaḍārah*, p. 336.
111. Ibid., p. 141.
112. *Ma'na al-nakbah mujadadan*, p. 13.
113. *Naḥnu wa-al-mustaqbal*, p. 292.
114. Ibid., p. 298. Zurayk expresses himself on this issue in another work, where he says, "Genuine knowledge is not merely a mental acquisition, but also a moral struggle, . . . and here is the opportunity to benefit from heritage" (Constantine Zurayk, "al-Mustaqbalīyah al-mu'āṣirah wa bawa'ithuha," in *Muḥādarāt al-mawsim al-thaqāfī li'ām 1974/1975* [Abu Dhabi: Wizārat al-I'lām wa-al-Thaqāfah], p. 279).
115. *al-Wa'ī al-qawmī*, pp. 12-22; see also *Ayyu ghad?* pp. 19-20.
116. *Naḥnu wa-al-tārīkh*, p. 204.
117. *al-Wa'ī al-qawmī*, pp. 7-19. It is worth noting that Zurayk did not propose a definite political framework for Arab nationalism until recently. One can gather, however, from some passages in his earlier works, that he would have liked to have seen a merger of the different political units into one entity. In one of his latest works, he focuses on the importance of common loyalties and the coordination of public policies as a prelude to the establishment of a federal Arab system. See *Naḥnu wa-al-mustaqbal*, pp. 224, 394.
118. *Naḥnu wa-al-mustaqbal*, pp. 220-226.
119. *Ayyu ghad?* p. 103. Zurayk's concept becomes clear as he defines nationalism as a process of nation building which requires the transformation of capabilities into a practical and effective unit. See Constantine Zurayk, "Arab-American Relations: Dangers and Opportunities," *Arab Studies Quarterly*, Vol. 2, No. 2 (Spring 1980), p. 121.
120. *al-Wa'ī al-qawmī*, p. 115.
121. Ibid., pp. 238-258.
122. I am indebted to Mr. Ramiz To'meh, who called my attention to this point in his unpublished paper, "The Arab Nationalist Thought of Professor C. K. Zurayk."
123. *Naḥnu wa-al-tārīkh*, p. 203.
124. *Naḥnu wa-al-mustaqbal*, p. 223.
125. *al-Wa'ī al-qawmī*, p. 108.
126. *Ma'na al-nakbah*, p. 45.
127. Constantine Zurayk, "al-Masīḥīyūn al-'Arab wa-al-mustaqbal," in *al-Mustaqbal al-'Arabi*, Vol. 4, No. 27 (May 1981), pp. 30-33.
128. *al-Wa'ī al-qawmī*, pp. 125-132.
129. For the text of the speech, see "Dhikra al-Rasūl al-'Arabī," in Michel 'Aflaq, *Fī sabīl al-Ba'th* (Beirut: Dār al-Ṭali'ah, 1963), pp. 50-61.
130. See Albert Hourani, *Arabic Thought in the Liberal Age, 1798-1939* (London: Cambridge University Press, 1983), p. 309.
131. *Hadha al-'aṣr al-mutafajjir*, p. 62.

132. *al-Wa'ī al-qawmī*, p. 128.
133. *Naḥnu wa-al-mustaqbal*, p. 203.
134. *al-Wa'ī al-qawmī*, p. 155.
135. Ibid., pp. 135-136.
136. *Naḥnu wa-al-tārīkh*, p. 169.
137. Ibid., pp. 165-167.
138. Ibid., pp. 227-231.
139. Ibid., p. 28.
140. Ibid., p. 136.
141. Ibid., pp. 160-161.
142. *Fī ma'rakat al-ḥaḍārah*, p. 237.
143. *Fī ma'rakat al-ḥaḍārah*, pp. 238-245.
144. *Naḥnu wa-al-tārīkh*, pp. 17-20. In another place, pp. 28-45, Zurayk classifies the attitude toward the heritage as traditional, nationalist, Marxist, and scientific.
145. *Naḥnu wa-al-tārīkh*, p. 45.
146. Ibid., p. 212.
147. *Ma'na al-nakbah*, p. 38.
148. *Naḥnu wa-al-tārīkh*, p. 18.
149. *Naḥnu wa-al-mustaqbal*, p. 215.
150. *Fī ma'rakat al-ḥaḍārah*, p. 397.
151. Ibid., pp. 235-237.
152. *Naḥnu wa-al-mustaqbal*, p. 212.
153. *Ma'na al-nakbah*, p. 49.
154. *Naḥnu wa-al-mustaqbal*, pp. 212-214.
155. *al-Wa'ī al-qawmī*, pp. 75-93.
156. *Naḥnu wa-al-mustaqbal*, pp. 315-321.
157. Ibid., p. 395.
158. *Fī ma'rakat al-ḥaḍārah*, p. 324.
159. *al-Wa'ī al-qawmī*, pp. 194-195.
160. *Naḥnu wa-al-mustaqbal*, p. 373.
161. *Ayyu ghad?* pp. 102-120.
162. *Naḥnu wa-al-mustaqbal*, pp. 372-400.
163. *al-Wa'ī al-qawmī*, pp. 185-194.
164. Ibid., pp. 199-212.
165. *Ayyu ghad?* pp. 166-177.
166. The role of the university is discussed in the following articles: "Risālat al-jāmi'ah fi 'ālam 'Arabī mutajaddid," in *Falsafah tarbawīyah mutajaddidah li-'ālam 'Arabī mutajaddid* (Beirut: American University of Beirut, 1956); "Dawr al-jāmi'ah fi al-ḥayāt al-waṭanīyah," *al-Ma'rifah*, Vol. 1, No. 3 (May 1962); and "al-Jami'āt amām mas'ūlīyātiha," *al-Abḥāth*, Vol. 18, No. 1 (March 1965).
167. *Fī ma'rakat al-ḥaḍārah*, p. 203.
168. Ibid., pp. 323, 346.
169. Ibid., pp. 203-204.
170. *Ayyu ghad?* pp. 176-177.

171. *Ma'na al-nakbah,* pp. 51-53.
172. *Ayyu ghad?* p. 106.

References (in order of publication)

"al-Ḥayāt al-'Arabīyah fī al-shām 'alā 'ahd Ṣalāḥ al-Dīn" (Arab Life in Syria during the Period of Saladin), *al-Mawrid al-Ṣāfī,* Vol. 18, No. 2 (March 1934), pp. 193-208.

"al-Tijārah al-Islāmīyah wa athāruhā fī al-ḥaḍārah" (Islamic Trade and its Influence on Civilization), *al-Muqtaṭaf,* Vol. 87, No. 5 (December 1935), pp. 541-548.

"al-Tarbīyah al-qawmīyah" (Education for National Life), *al-Ḥadīth,* Vol. 11, Sp. No. (January 1937), pp. 15-25. Reprinted in *al-Wa'ī al-qawmī,* 2nd ed. (1940), pp. 73-93.

"Kayf afham al-tārīkh" (How I Understand History), in *al-Funūn al-adabīyah* (Beirut, 1937), pp. 65-86.

"Jundī min jaysh Salāḥ al-Dīn" (A Soldier in the Army of Saladin), *al-Makshūf,* Vol. 3, No. 88 (March 1937), pp. 2, 14-16.

"al-Wa'i al-qawmī" (National Consciousness), *al-Ḥadīth,* Vol. 13, No. 8 (August 1939), pp. 641-645. Reprinted in *al-Wa'ī al-qawmī,* 2nd ed. (1940), pp. 33-59.

"Wājibāt al-mufakkir al-'Arabī fī al-waqt al-ḥāḍir" (The Duties of the Arab Intellectual at Present), *al-Abḥāth,* Vol. 1, No. 1 (March 1948), pp. 3-17. Reprinted in *Ayyu ghad?* pp. 9-39.

"Naḥū thaqāfah 'Arabīyah jadīdah: Khidhlān al-muthaqqafīn" (Towards a New Arab Culture: The Failure of the Intelligentsia), *al-Abḥāth,* Vol. 23, No. 3 (March 1948), pp. 3-22.

"The Essence of Arab Civilization," *Middle East Journal,* Vol. 2, No. 2 (April 1949), pp. 125-139. Arabic translation in *al-Abḥāth,* Vol. 2, No. 1 (March 1949), pp. 3-22.

"Ahamīyat al-in'āsh al-ijtimā'ī fī al-mujtama' wa-al-dawlah" (The Importance of Social Welfare in Society and the State), in *Jāmi'at al-Dūwal al-'Arabīyah, Idārat al-Shu'ūn al-Ijtimā'īyah wa-al-Siḥḥīyah* (League of Arab States, Department of Social and Health Affairs), *Ḥalqat al-dirāsat al-ijtimā'īyah,* (First Session) (Cairo, 1950), pp. 7-15.

"The National and International Relations of the Arab States," in T. Cuyler Young, ed., *Near Eastern Culture and Society* (Princeton: Princeton University Press, 1951), pp. 205-224.

"al-Qaḍīyah al-'Arabīyah, 1953" (The Arab Question, 1953), *Muḥaḍarāt al-Nadwah al-Lubnānīyah,* Vol. 7, Nos. 9-10 (May 1953), pp. 225-248.

"al-Tarbīyah al-'Arabīyah" (Arab Education), in *al-Mujtama' al-'Arabi* (Beirut: Arab Studies Program of the American University of Beirut, 1953), pp. 58-79. Reprinted in *Ayyu ghad?* pp. 95-125.

"Mabādi' al-takāful al-ijtimā'ī" (The Principles of Social Solidarity), in *Jāmi'at al-Dūwal al-'Arabīyah, Idārat al-Shu'ūn al-Ijtima'īyah wa-al-Ṣiḥḥīyah* (League of Arab States, Department of Social and Health Affairs), *Ḥalqat al-dirāsat*

al-ijtimā'īyah (Third Session) (Cairo, 1955), pp. 582-587.
"al-'Arab wa-al-thaqāfah al-hadīthah" (The Arabs and Modern Culture), in Ma'ārif al-Kūwayt, ed., *Muḥaḍarāt al-mawsim al-thaqāfī al-thānī* (Cairo, 1956), pp. 293-315.
"Durūs min al-tārikh" (Lessons from History), in ibid., pp. 317-335.
"Risālat al-jāmi'ah fī 'ālam 'Arabī yatajaddad" (The Message of the University in a Reviving Arab World), in *Falsafah tarbawīyah mutajjaddidah li-'ālam 'Arabī yatajaddad* (Beirut: Department of Education of the American University of Beirut, 1956), pp. 151-163.
"Min ma'ānī al-azmah al-Lubnānīyah" (Some of the Meanings of the Lebanese Crisis), *al-'Ulūm*, Vol. 3, No. 8 (August 1958), pp. 5-8, 63, and No. 9 (September 1958), pp. 7-11, 51.
"Fatrat al-ḥurūb al-ṣalibīyah" (Period of the Crusades), in *Ma sāhama bihi al-'Arab fī al-mi'at sanah al-akhīrah fī dirāsat al-tārīkh al-'Arabi wa-ghayrih* (Beirut: Arab Studies Program of the American University of Beirut, 1959), pp. 94-121, 196-206.
"The Effects of New Social Changes," in *University Education and Public Service* (Paris: International Association of Universities, Paper 4, 1959), pp. 135-148.
"Conditions for the Mutual Appreciation of Eastern-Western Cultural Values," in *Cultural Values: Eastern-Western* (Washington, D.C.: Committee of International Relations of the National Education Association of the U.S.A., 1959), pp. 23-43. Arabic translation in *al-Abḥāth*, Vol. 12, No. 4 (December 1959), pp. 485-499, and in *Hadha al-'aṣr al-mutafajjir*, pp. 86-109.
"al-Tawjīh al-qawmī fī al-ḥaql al-tarbawi" (National Orientation in Education), *al-Thaqāfah al-'Arabīyah*, Vol. 3, No. 2 (April-June 1959), pp. 3-6.
"al-Turāth al-ḥaḍārī" (Cultural Heritage), in Wizārat al-Thaqāfah wa-al-Irshād al-Qawmi, *Muḥaḍarāt al-mawsim al-thaqāfī 1959-60* (Pt. 2) (Damascus, n.d.), pp. 145-170, and *al-Abḥāth*, Vol. 13, No. 1 (March 1960), pp. 3-24. Reprinted in *Hadha al-'aṣr al-mutafajjir*, pp. 51-85.
"Min mushkilāt al-tarbīyah al-ḥadīthah" (A Modern Educational Problem), *al-'Arabī*, No. 17 (April 1960), pp. 84-88.
"Djami'a" (University), *Encyclopedia of Islam*, 2nd ed.
"Nahji li-muwājahat al-'aṣr al-mutafajjir" (How to Face the Explosive Age), in Wizārat al-Thaqāfah wa-al-Irshād al-Qawmī, ed., *Muḥaḍarāt al-mawsim al-thaqāfī, 1961-62* (Pt. 6) (Damascus, 1963), pp. 301-323, and *al-Abḥāth*, Vol. 15, No. 1 (March 1962), pp. 3-24. Reprinted in *Hadha al-'aṣr al-mutafajjir*, pp. 19-50.
"Dawr al-jāmi'ah fī al-ḥayāt al-waṭanīyah" (The Role of the University in National Life), *Muḥadarat al-Nadwah al-Lubnāniyah*, Vol. 18, Nos. 5-6 (1963), pp. 36-68, and *al-Ma'rifah*, Vol. 1, No. 3 (May 1962), pp. 6-23.
Forward to Frank Bowles, *Access to Higher Education*, Vol. 1 (Paris: UNESCO and the International Association of Universities, 1963), pp. 9-19 (French edition, Paris, 1964, pp. 9-21).
"Fī mafāhīm al-ḥaḍārah" (On the Concepts of Culture), *Majallat Majma' al-Lughah al-'Arabīyah bi-Dimashq*, Vol. 39, No. 1 (January 1964), pp. 99-112.
"al-Jāmi'āt amām mas'ūlīyātiha" (The Universities in the Face of Their Respon-

sibilities), *al-Abḥāth*, Vol. 18, No. 1 (March 1965), pp. 3-20, and *al-Thaqāfah al-'Arabīyah*, Vol. 8, No. 3 (March 1965), pp. 2-16.

"'Ilm al-nakbah" (The Study of the Disaster), *al-Ma'rifah*, No. 49 (March 1966), pp. 68-74.

"al-Jāmi'ah wa-mustaqbal al-fikr al-'Arabī" (The University and the Future of Arab Thought), in *al-Fikr al-'Arabi fī mi'at sanah* (Beirut: American University of Beirut Centennial Publications, 1967), pp. 631-656, and in *al-Jāmi'ah wa-insān al-ghad* (Beirut: American University of Beirut Centennial Publications, 1968), pp. 159-182.

"Universities and the Making of Tomorrow's World," in Algo Henderson, ed., *Higher Education in Tomorrow's World* (Ann Arbor: University of Michigan, 1968), pp. 18-30.

"Ghiyāb dawlat al-'aql," (The Absence of the Realm of Reason), *al-Adāb*, Vol. 18, No. 1 (January 1969), pp. 2-3.

"al-Ṭālib wa-mas'ūlīyātuh al-waṭanīyah" (The University Student and His National Responsibilities), in *al-Ṭālib al-jami'i fī Lubnān: mustaqbaluh wa-mushkilātuh* (Beirut: League of University Professors in Lebanon, 1969), pp. 27-51.

Preface to *International University Cooperation* (Paris: International Association of Universities, Paper 9, 1969), pp. VII-X.

"Gandhi wa-taḥarrur al-shu'ūb" (Gandhi and the Liberation of Peoples) in *Gandhi, taḥīyah min Lubnān* (Beirut: Dār al-Nahār, 1970), pp. 88-106.

Preface to *The University and the Needs of Contemporary Society* (Paris: International Association of Universities, Paper 10, 1970), pp. XI-XV.

"The Palestine Problem: An Introductory Survey," *Middle East Forum*, Vol. 46, No. 1 (1970), pp. 27-36.

"The University and the Creation of the Future," Presidential Address at the Inaugural Session of the Fifth General Conference of the International Association of Universities, Montreal, Canada, in *Report of the Fifth General Conference of the International Association of Universities* (Paris, 1971), pp. 65-73 (French edition, Paris, 1971, pp. 69-78), and *al-Kulliyah* (Autumn 1970), pp. 2-7. Arabic translation in *Maṭālib al-mustaqbal al-'Arabi*, pp. 86-96.

"'Abd al-Nāṣir al-Mubdi'" ('Abd al-Nāṣir's Creative Achievement), *al-Adāb*, Vol. XIX, No. 1, January 1971, pp. 3-5.

"The Relevance of Traditional Cultures in an Age of Accelerating Change," in John Burchard, ed., *Thoughts from the Lake of Time* (New York: Josiah Macy, Jr. Foundation, 1971), pp. 169-177.

"al-Takhalluf al-fikrī wa-ab'āduhu al-ḥaḍārīyah" (Intellectual Underdevelopment and its Cultural Dimensions), *al-Adāb*, Vol. 12, No. 5 (May 1974), pp. 38-40, and *al-Ma'rifah*, No. 148 (June 1974), pp. 83-92.

"'Ibrah min 'aṣr Abi al-Fidā'" (Lessons from the Age of Abī al-Fidā'), *al-Ma'rifah*, No. 154 (December 1974), pp. 24-41.

"al-Jāmi'ah al-yawm wa-ghadan" (The University Today and Tomorrow), in Jāmi'at Qaṭar, ed., *Min thimār al-fikr, al-mawsim al-thaqāfī al-rābi'*, (al-Dawḥah, 1978), pp. 185-197.

Tensions in Islamic Civilization (Washington, D.C.: Center for Contemporary

Arab Studies, Georgetown University, Seminar Paper No. 3, 1978; reprinted 1984). Arabic translation in *Maṭālib al-mustaqbal al-'Arabī*, pp. 228-253.

"al-Tā'rikh min ayn wa-ila ayn?" (History, Whence and Whither?), *al-Fikr al-'Arabi*, Vol. 1, No. 2 (July-August 1978), pp. 4-17. Reprinted in *Maṭālib al-mustaqbal al-'Arabi*, pp. 97-119.

"Naẓrah fī tārīkh al-'Arab wa-al-'ālam" (A View of Arab and World History), *Tārīkh al-'Arab wa-al-'ālam*, Vol. 1, No. 1 (November 1978), pp. 5-10. Reprinted in *Maṭālib al-mustaqbal al-'Arabi*, pp. 254-268.

"al-Ḥaḍārah al-insānīyah ila ayn?" (Wither Human Civilization?), *al-Fikr al-'Arabi*, Vol. 1, No. 10 (March-April 1979), pp. 48-62. Reprinted in *Maṭālib al-mustaqbal al-'Arabi*, pp. 19-45.

"Cultural Change and Transformation of Arab Society," in *The Arab Future: Critical Issues* (CCAS Studies in Arab Development-2) (Washington, D.C.: Center for Contemporary Arab Studies, Georgetown University, 1979), pp. 9-17.

"Arab-American Relations: Dangers and Opportunities," *Arab Studies Quarterly*, Vol. 2, No. 2 (Spring 1980), pp. 113-126.

"Naḥū ḥulūl 'amalīyah lil-taghallub 'ala al-'aqabāt fī sabīl al-waḥdah al-'Arabīyah" (Towards Practical Solutions of the Problems Facing Arab Unity), *Qaḍaya 'Arabīyah*, Vol. 7, No. 7 (July 1980), pp. 5-16. Reprinted in *Maṭālib al-mustaqbal al-'Arabi*, pp. 204-227.

"al-Masiḥīyūn al-'Arab wa-al-mustaqbal" (Arab Christians and the Future), *al-Mustaqbal al-'Arabī*, Vol. 4, No. 27 (May 1981), pp. 24-33, and in Ilyas Khūri, ed., *al-Masiḥīyūn al-'Arab: Dirāsat wa-munaqashāt* (Beirut, 1981), pp. 109-127. Reprinted in *Maṭālib al-mustaqbal al-'Arabi*, pp. 67-85.

"Maṭālib al-mustaqbal al-'Arabī" (Demands of the Arab Future), *Shū'ūn 'Arabīyah*, No. 11 (January 1982), pp. 8-18. Reprinted in *Maṭālib al-mustaqbal al-'Arabi*, pp. 46-66.

"al-Nahj al-'aṣrī: Muḥtawāh wa-hūwīyatuh, ijābiyātuh wa-salbiyātuh" (The Contemporary Way of Life: Its Content and Identity, Its Positive and Negative Elements), *al-Mustaqbal al-'Arabī*, Vol. 7, No. 69 (November 1984), pp. 106-121.

Humanism and Secularism in the Modern Arab Heritage: The Ideas of al-Kawākibī and Zurayk

GEORGE N. ATIYEH

The forces of history which are unremittingly at work produce different but simultaneous movements. In a complex culture, several trends can become integrated into one. This integration produces a richness of human experience and adds color and life to the national heritage.

One of the main characteristics of classical Arabic culture is its ability to accommodate both a religious and a humanist tradition. The *Nahḍah* (Renaissance) in the nineteenth century was, in a sense, a return to the enriching experience of that culture. As in the golden age of Arabic and Islamic culture, the ideals and values of reason, human dignity, justice, and freedom acquired prominence and visibility, but always within the confines of a religious environment.

The social and political circumstances under which the Arab world witnessed the burst of humanism and secularism upon the modern historical scene were such that the resurgence of these ideals seemed inevitable. Long centuries of subjection to foreign rule, disregard for human rights, and technological backwardness motivated many intellectuals to seek new avenues for achieving progress. With the spread of the idea that international law is one and indivisible, the colonized peoples of the Middle East began acting to redress the lack of freedom, justice, and equality. It became evident to political leaders, intellectuals, and social scientists—even to poets—that only an order based on the principles of freedom, equality, and justice for all could meet the challenges of the modern and future ages and be congruent with the natural rights of man. I plan, therefore, to examine the ideas expressed by two Arab writers, one a Muslim, ʻAbd al-Raḥmān al-Kawākibī (1854-1902), and the other a Christian, Constantine K. Zurayk (1909-), both of whom, I believe, epitomize the modern Arab humanism and secularism, and whose social thinking could serve as an inspiration to "rehumanize" the present Arab society.

However, before I examine the thoughts of these two eminent intellectuals, it behooves me to elucidate briefly the meaning and scope of the two terms *humanism* and *secularism*. Historically, humanism is a product of the Western culture. To the Greeks, it meant the consideration of man as the center of thought. Even the Greek gods were conceived anthropomorphically. Greek art concentrated on depicting the human form in sculpture and painting. Their philosophy culminated, one might say, in the aphorism "man is the measure of all things." In fact, the Greek state cannot be understood well unless viewed as the "force which shaped man and man's life."[1]

Humanism during the Renaissance period meant, in more than one way, a return to the Greek culture. However, the Renaissance humanists were also rebels. They rebelled against a medieval way of life centered around the supernatural, against a methodology of knowledge based on authority, against artistic values predicated on the complexities and fatuousness of the Gothic style, and against the concept of the supremacy of the Church in state affairs. The ideals of the supreme authority of the people, social justice, and the inalienable right of man to enjoy freedom culminated in the affirmation of the independence of the human spirit, the human mind, and the inherent value of man and his dignity.

In our time, humanism does not address itself solely to the revival of the Greek and Roman antiquity. Although man remains the center of its preoccupation, it has assumed a variety of postures regarding his place in the universe and consequently his very nature. It has branched out into many schools: secular humanism, socialist humanism, liberal neohumanism, existential humanism, and Christian humanism. A few voices talk shyly, here and there, of a Muslim humanism. The sum total of this proliferation in modern times has been an obfuscation of the meaning and scope of the concept of man and his nature. Secular and existential humanisms understand true being to be man himself, independent and self-sufficient. It is a humanism without God. Humanism without God cannot exist in any of the three monotheistic religions—it would be a contradiction in terms. The three monotheistic religions have a common concept of man as the creature of God, but they differ somewhat on the ways and means that man's dignity is acquired and on the substance of his freedom. The tendency in the humanistic philosophy is to consider the end of man's earthly existence to be the development of his human capacity and of the creative powers inherent in him, especially the powers of the mind. This end is, by no means, opposed by any of the three religions. Nor is the other goal of humanism opposed, namely, the goal of harnessing the focus of physical nature into instruments of man's liberty. It is only when man declares his self-sufficiency, and his complete independence from the supernatural, that an unbridgeable gap arises.

It is not my intention here to discuss the possible and real differences between Muslim and Christian humanism that derive from the differences in their concept of man and from the redemptive theology of Christianity. I will only look into the common ground wherein humanism is seen as an affirmation of the exceptional value of man as man, the belief in the strong powers of the mind, and the belief in continuous progress through education. My attention will focus on the questions of rationalism and freedom. Rationalism manifests itself in many aspects of religion and society. In religion, it manifests itself particularly in the reduction of the role of religion in the legal, social, and economic aspects of life. In society, rationalism manifests itself in the affirmation of the universality of freedom. Secularism is a derivative of freedom. This statement might sound controversial to some, but in the Middle East secularism carries the strong connotation that all citizens are equal and should enjoy the same rights regardless of creed. It is not necessarily anticlericalism. Secularism assumes that equality, unless based on freedom, is a false equality. Predicated on that principle, secularism looks toward the achievement of the separation of state and religion, but not toward atheism. In my opinion, secularism, although it may seem anticlerical, does not deny or affirm the basic principles of religion; it is simply concerned with the affirmation of the principles of freedom and human rights.

Conscious of the difficulty of achieving a comprehensive view of the role of humanism and secularism in the modern Arab heritage, I will limit myself to a consideration of the two representatives mentioned above, who perhaps epitomize in their thoughts and deeds the different dimensions of this trend. I will further limit myself to those aspects which highlight the tendencies of humanism and secularism in their thought. I would like to mention in passing that both, although highly appreciated, have not been given their due in Western scholarly circles.

ʻAbd al-Raḥmān al-Kawākibī was born in 1854[2] and flourished during the period of the Arab *Nahḍah* (Renaissance) at a time when the ruling Ottoman Empire was experiencing a decline as a cohesive force in Islam. The *Nahḍah*, as commonly understood, was a period of awakening and a manifestation of a new social process brought about by increasing contact with the West and characterized by reformist aspirations for more freedom, self-assertion, and technological advances. The enlightened persons who spearheaded the *Nahḍah* were no doubt influenced by the ideas of the French Revolution—equality, fraternity, and liberty—which had reached the Arab East through different channels, but in particular through education.

As a result, the idea of nationalism took root and blossomed. The educated classes called for constitutional government and demanded greater participation in decision making. The growth of nationalism, or the consciousness of a separate socio-political identity, indicated a greater interest in self-identity, human rights, and respect for individual freedom. A new spirit of laicism and belief in science spread and found fertile ground among the younger generation.

Naturally, the response to the new ideas was varied. Three broad opinions appeared on the scene. Some enlightened persons aspired to modernize society without breaking away from religion; they hoped to adapt the life of the faithful Muslim to the new social, intellectual, and economic conditions of the time. Others called for a strict adherence to traditional Islam, rejecting any innovations. A third group, more rationalistic, called for secularization or emphasized the love of country above religion. Conscious of the backward, I should say "weak," condition of the Arab countries, they all sought to find the causes of "backwardness" and to conjure up remedies accordingly. In their search for remedies, not only did they seek to set up new social and political programs, but they also went further to search out new formulations of the concept of man, his freedom, his place in society, and the components of his progress.

al-Kawākibī and His Concept of Man

al-Kawākibī, a Muslim from Aleppo, Syria, was descended from a distinguished family. He was educated in the traditional manner of his day but kept himself well informed on the intellectual and social stirrings going on at the time. He led an active literary and political life editing the official Aleppo paper *al-Furāt* from 1875 to 1880. In collaboration with Hāshim al-'Aṭṭār, he brought out, in 1878, a weekly, *al-Shahbā'*, which lasted only for fifteen weeks. This, as well as a second paper, *al-I'tidāl*, were closed by order of the Turkish governor in 1879. Proud, honest, and opposed to injustice, he struggled to defend the weak and poor until, under the pressure of the Turkish authorities, he lost his effectiveness and had to emigrate to Cairo, where he joined the company of eminent reformists such as Muḥammad 'Abduh and Rashīd Riḍa. Shortly after touring some Muslim countries on behalf of the Egyptian Khedive, he died in 1902.

al-Kawākibī published two books in Cairo, both drafted in Syria: *Umm al-qura* (The Mother of Cities) (Mecca) and *Ṭabā'i' al-istibdād wa maṣāri' al-isti'bād* (The Characteristics of Tyranny and the Death of Despotism).[3] Two other books, in manuscript form, which are attributed to al-Kawākibī were confiscated with his other papers by the agents of Sulṭān 'Abd al-Ḥamīd II after his departure to Egypt.

Umm al-qura, written as if it were a verbatim record of the proceedings of a congress of Muslim leaders, addresses itself to the problem of "backwardness." In it the Muslim leaders belonging to different nationalities gather in Mecca to discuss the causes of the decline of Islam and to offer remedies. The question of the caliphate is discussed, and it is argued that the problem of Islam would be solved if the caliphate were returned to its rightful holders, the Arabs.

In the second book, al-Kawākibī formulates a pointed criticism of tyranny, alluding to the despotism of Sulṭān 'Abd al-Ḥamīd II. He states that despotism is destructive to man and is caused by ignorance. Only through education and enlightenment can ignorance be eradicated.

To reconstruct al-Kawākibī's concept of man, one has to glean it from his statments on this subject inserted in a variety of unsuspected places. One also has to infer it from the general framework of his philosophical outlook on life. The shortcomings of this method are obvious, however, because one has to remember that he was a political and religious thinker, not a philosopher.

In his relationship to God, man is a "witness to God the Sovereign" (Koran 28:88). As His creature, man bears witness to the existence of God, and he serves Him by obeying His laws in order to achieve his own true liberty and dignity within the community, and in order to achieve eternal life in the hereafter. Man's liberty does not consist in blind acceptance of fate or authority. True liberty is obedience to God achieved through the use of reason. God has created man free and guided by reason; ungrateful to his Creator, man prefers to remain a slave guided by ignorance. God has provided man with a father and a mother to sustain him until he reaches maturity, and He has made for him the earth a mother and work a father, but man has turned his own mother into a slave and his own father into a ruler.[4] Approaching the concept of fall, al-Kawākibī determines that man's rationalism is equivalent to his original innocence. True Islam confirms this position because it is based on reason. This might not be the Islam of the majority of Muslims, but it is the Islam of the Koran.[5]

The thrust of al-Kawākibī's thought is directed toward going back to the first principles, the *uṣūl*. This is nowhere more obvious than in his opening statement to the fictitious meeting he describes in *Umm al-qura*. There he calls for a return to the *uṣūl*, that is, the Koran and the ascertained Sunnah (the Prophet's sayings and actions). The revival of Islam cannot be achieved except by removing the dross of superstitions and considering as marginal the heresies that accrued during centuries of immobility and reliance on authority. Any true revival has to resort to *ijtihād*, that is, personal opinion, or personal reasoning, and has to consider it among the first principles.[6]

Like 'Abduh and al-Afghānī, al-Kawākibī's starting point, the return to first principles, was not meant to make Islam freeze itself back into the first decades of its history, but to move forward on what is considered its true pillars: reason, freedom, and justice. It is only by considering Islam at its authentic best and not in terms of its periods of decadence that a fair assessment of these three aspects of Islam can be made. A religion replete with false beliefs cannot exist in one and the same head with an enlightened mind.[7]

A return to pure Islam, therefore, is not a return to a rigid fundamentalism; it is simply making reason and wisdom a companion to the Sacred Law. The value of reason is not in challenging the revealed and uncontested doctrines of Islam but in helping the establishment of a free and just society. In summary, what might appear as al-Kawākibī's conservatism (*salafīyah*) is in reality a call to an open-minded, commonsensical, and true revival of Islam. Its implications are an affirmation of the need for reform, for the renewal and updating of Islam. In fact, his "conservatism" addressed itself to propelling Islam into new channels of modernity and progress.

Reform Inspired by Rationalism

Because of the closeness between the spiritual and the political in Islam, it is obvious that political, social, and moral reform for a Muslim believer like al-Kawākibī should derive from the doctrines of Islam. How did al-Kawākibī conceive of the needed reform? Freedom was al-Kawākibī's main preoccupation, not only in individual but also in national terms. In fact, the Arab nationalist possibilities were first expressed by him. He was opposed to the Ottoman rule over the Arabs as much as he was opposed to the despotism of 'Abd al-Ḥamīd II over the citizens. His book *Ṭabā'i' al-istibdād* is nothing but an outpouring of his great desire and appreciation for freedom. Unlike any other Arab writer before him, he deals with the problem of despotism comprehensively and systematically. He examines the relationship of despotism to religion, knowledge, glory, wealth, morality, education, and progress. He also offers some of the most enlightened solutions for doing away with it. The rationalistic approach to reform comes out clearly and strongly in al-Kawākibī's criticism of those oppressed among the Muslims who, instead of fighting despotism, console themselves with the hope of a better life in the next world, and who consider this world as "the prison of the faithful." Some rulers, he believes, have encouraged this otherworldly resignation in order to strengthen their hold over the citizens.

Islamism, according to al-Kawākibī, is based on freedom and the inherent dignity of man. All those who attempt to abridge man's dignity are encroaching on the divine prerogatives. The Islamic doctrine of the Oneness of God implies that God alone is great. Therefore, no human being is greater than another before God.[8] God created man to think for himself. He endowed him with the right to live free and to improve his life on this earth socially and morally through education. The espousal of *ijtihād* is an assertion of this freedom. Are not all the teachings of the great scholars and founders of the schools of jurisprudence merely personal interpretations? Consequently, a Muslim does not have to follow the opinions of any particular school, because, except for the Prophet, none speaks with the authority of a Messenger of God. The differences of opinion should not be a cause of friction but an opportunity to relate the Sacred Law to the constantly changing conditions of the world. Even *talfīq* (selections and combinations), as a method, may be considered when reason dictates it could or should be used.

In *Umm al-qura*, the value of this personal interpretation, or personal reasoning and the repudiation of authority, is clearly expressed in the pronouncement of the Russian Orientalist (in his dialogue with the Mufti of Qazān), who is a fervent partisan of the use of reason and personal interpretation in all questions related to the social order:

> Even if the matter were of a positivist nature, it would be unwise for the people of our time to be under the obligation to follow the opinions of those who have preceded them ten centuries, or for the people of the West to be under the obligation to follow the laws of the people of the East. It seems to me that this act of restriction has led to what you view as the decline of respect for the Sacred Law.[9]

Freedom is Democracy

Ijtihād, therefore, represents the capacity and obligation to use one's own reason: it also represents the God-given right to enjoy freedom. In politics, al-Kawākibī's conception of freedom is close to the liberal definition, which opposes any abridgment of it by government. He makes this definition very clear in both his extant works:

> Free nations have guaranteed freedom of expression, authoring, and publishing, placing limitations only on defamation of others. They [free nations] opted to tolerate the impairments that might result from chaos rather than impose restrictions [on freedom] because there is no guarantee against a ruler's turning

a hair of restriction into an iron chain with which to strangle the eternal enemy: freedom.[10]

To me the affliction is our loss of freedom . . . the other dimensions of which are the equality of rights, the accountability of rulers inasmuch as they are the custodians, the temerity to demand [one's rights] and to offer advice. The freedom to speak out and to publish, freedom to carry out scientific research are its other dimensions. Also total justice so that no man dreads a tyrant, nor a usurper nor a treacherous assassin. Other dimensions are security for religion and life, security for honour and dignity, and security for knowledge and its exploitation.[11]

If man is then born rational and free, how can this freedom be translated into political action? The principles of freedom in Islam, according to al-Kawākibī, are based on the elimination of all kinds of tyrannical domination and arbitrariness: Islam commands justice, equality, fairness, and brotherhood, and encourages charity and love of one another. True government rests on the principle of democratic consultation of the community representatives (*Ahl al-ḥall wa-al-'aqd*), those who "untie and tie." These are the people who use their minds and not their swords. Islam sets up

the principle of the nation's administration on democratic legislation, that is socialist, as we shall see later . . . It is well known that in Islamism there is no religious authority absolutely except in questions related to religious rites [*Sha'ā'ir*], also the general legislative principles which do not exceed one hundred principles and rules. All are among the best and noblest discovered by legislators ever.[12]

One of the striking aspects of al-Kawākibī's thought is his distinction between freedom and the democratic form of government. The first is one and indivisible, whereas the second may be adapted to different circumstances. However, whatever the form of government is, its basic role is service to people. It is only under such governments that man can develop his mental potentialities, his personal, religious, and intellectual freedoms. A constitutional government can also be a despotic government unless a balance of power is set up between the executive, legislature, and judiciary, and all branches are made accountable. The purposes of governments should be defined clearly in accordance with the wishes of the total population, or the opinion of a majority comprising three-fourths of their number.[13]

Another striking aspect of al-Kawākibī's thought is his belief that the Islamic system is a socialist one. Moved by the injustices against the poor, he thought that socialism, like Islam, aimed at establishing equality of standards of living among mankind, people's ownership of the land, immovable property, and large industrial factories. Socialism, according to him, is at the origin of Christianity and Islam, but the socialist life in Christianity has remained in the realm of the potential, whereas in Islam, the Rāshidūn (Orthodox) caliphs were able to found a government that equalized even their own persons with the poor of the nation in happiness as well as in misfortune. They produced among Muslims feelings of brotherhood and links of a socialist society the likes of which did not exist even among brothers who are provided for by one father and cared for by one mother.[14]

The socialist tendencies which distinguish al-Kawākibī from the reformist school of 'Abduh and al-Afghānī need to be further considered, and I hope this task will be undertaken on another occasion. However, al-Kawākibī stands clearly apart from this school in his promotion of the liberal doctrine of the separation of church and state.

In the chapter on despotism and religion in *Ṭabā'i al-istibdād*, al-Kawākibī surveys the historical stages in which religion and politics interlocked. In all stages, he notices the appropriation of divine attributes by human beings, which is contrary to the doctrine of the oneness of God. Islam has refined the doctrines of both Judaism and Christianity by putting an end to all association (*shirk*, worshipping others besides God) permanently. It has set up a system of political freedom which combines the best in democracy and aristocracy.[15] Unfortunately, this system was practiced only for a short period, up to the time of the third caliph. Since then Islam has been trying in vain to recapture and reinstate the system. Muslims will keep crying to the Day of Judgment unless they substitute their present system with the consultative political system, which constitutes the true miracle of the Koran, "the system discovered by certain Western nations who, so to say, benefited from Islam more than the Muslims themselves."[16] This consultative rule is similar to the assembly of chiefs of clans in the Bedouin tribe that advise the shaykh and consent to his decisions. Consultative rule is ingrained in the true Arab tradition.

This concept of democratic rule and political equality as represented by consultative government is extended by a liberal outlook on individual religion:

> Religion is what the individual believes in, not what the crowd believe in. Religion is certainly an action, not mere knowledge and memorization by heart. Is not the collective duty [*Farḍ kifāyah*] one of the bases of your religion, which means that a Muslim fulfills his own obligation without much heeding whether the others fulfil theirs or not?[17]

al-Kawākibī's secularism is made even clearer in his call for a nationalistic approach to government, following in the footsteps of those nations that have separated state from church:

> Oh, people, I mean you who are speakers of Arabic among the non-Muslims. I call upon you to think no more of past wrongs and grudges and to overlook whatever offenses have been perpetrated by our fathers and grandfathers. Enough has been done at the hands of trouble-makers. I don't consider it beyond you, you who have been forerunners in enlightenment, to discover the means for unity. Look at the nations of Austria and the United States, which have discovered through science several means and solid principles to achieve patriotic rather than administrative association. Why shouldn't we consider following one of these or similar means, thereby enabling our wise people to say to the instigators of hatred, whether foreigners, or non-Arabs, please, dear sirs, leave us alone to manage our own affairs; to communicate between us in our own Arabic; to have, through brotherhood, compassion for each other; to console each other in adversity, and to share equally in prosperity? Leave us alone to manage our worldly affairs and to make religion rule only in the next world. Let us unite under one slogan: Long live the nation, long live the homeland, long live freedom and self-respect.[18]

Whether al-Kawākibī's secularism was complete or not is a debatable question in more than one way. His introduction of the idea of spiritual caliphate led him necessarily to consider politics as an autonomous discipline, a position which placed him almost alone among the modern reformers of Islam. This impression becomes stronger when we look at his ideas in the perspective of the times. He certainly was more outspoken in his secularist tendencies than any other Muslim intellectual of his age. Even his friend Rashīd Riḍa was very much aware of this position when he pointed out his disapproval of al-Kawākibī's concept of the separation of state and religion.[19] Furthermore, when Riḍa serialized *Umm al-qura* in his *al-Manār*, he attempted to delete al-Kawākibī's attack on the Ottoman Empire, the seat of the Muslim caliphate.[20]

In an article entitled "Pan-Islamism," published in *al-Muqattam*,[21] and signed by a "Muslim Free Thinker," al-Kawākibī criticizes those Muslims who believe that the dangerous situation in which Islam finds itself will not disappear until the Christians are humiliated. He affirms that such an attitude is what drives the Christians to seek the protection of Europe. The solution to this problem, he asserts unhesitatingly, is the separation of state and religion. Those who think that the state does not stand by itself without support from religion are mistaken. The purpose of the state's existence in our time is a worldly purpose, that is, the protection of people, the legislation of just laws, and the application of those laws. Religion, on the other hand, has one purpose in all times and places, that is, providing the opportunity for man to lead a sane life in this world in order to gain paradise in the next. Religion is a relationship between God and the individual, and each individual has his or her own religion—"If God had willed it, He would have made all the peoples into one nation." If this is not secularism, what else could it be?

To sum up, although a contemporary and in some ways a disciple of 'Abduh and al-Afghānī, al-Kawākibī differs from them in that he clearly differentiates between the Arab movement and Pan-Islamism; he explores the concept of Arab nationalism and the return of the caliphate to the Arabs. He holds socialistic views in his consideration of the distribution of wealth, and he especially espouses the doctrine of separation of state and religion and the protection of the state from religious hegemony.

Constantine K. Zurayk

Constantine (Costi) K. Zurayk, the second of the two intellectual leaders under discussion, was born in Damascus, Syria, seven years after the death of al-Kawākibī. Although he is officially retired, his career, fortunately, has not come to an end. He is still intellectually and politically active, and his wisdom and expertise are sought after by governments as well as by institutions, individuals, and scholars.

Historian, author, and editor of many classical works, Zurayk is no doubt one of the most respected intellectuals in the Arab world. His works are many and varied. He wrote mostly in Arabic, but his contributions in English are substantial. Perhaps the most important of his books are *al-Wa'ī al-qawmī* (National Consciousness), *Ma'na al-nakbah* (The Meaning of the Disaster), and *Naḥnu wa-al-mustaqbal* (Facing the Future).[22]

Zurayk's vision spans the past, present, and future. History, for him, is not merely a record of events in time. It is not passive and should not be passive, for knowledge of things past could not be an end in itself. Unless knowledge contributes to our understanding of the present and our preparation for a better future, it is incomplete and useless. The true historian, therefore, is not one who is satisfied with amassing information or editing old manuscripts but one who realizes that intellectual and patriotic responsibilities transcend his professional expertise.

Zurayk's view as a historian has greatly permeated his style and his methodological approach. His style is lucid and his presentation is extremely well organized and organically brought together. He is cautious not to see things as simply black and white, to look with perspective at all aspects of a question, to weigh the evidence pro and con, and to consider the implications carefully. He provides the depth, insight, and rationality that characterize the writings of great philosophers. Like a philosopher, he does not let his patriotism obscure truth, which is the ultimate goal of the historian. History, like truth itself, is a value. Falsified history is not history at all.

Humanism and Rationalism

The intellectual milieu in which Zurayk built his career was that of the American University of Beirut, which during the twenties and thirties was a stimulating house of learning and a forum for such ideas as nationalism, democracy, and science, all characteristics of Western rationalism. Faced with the problem of cultural transformation, from a metaphysically or otherworldly oriented society to a modern one with a scientific and technical mentality, many Arabs began, more and more, to appreciate the categories of Western thought and culture and to adopt them. Nationalism, which was a vague feeling of patriotism during the time of al-Kawākibī, manifested itself at the time of Zurayk in the form of ideologies and convictions that were bound to affect the whole national outlook. Associated with the question of identity, nationalistic thought was soon confronted with the problem of defining an Arab. What makes an Arab an Arab? Is it religion, language, historical traditions, or is it geography and the human will to create a nation? All these questions were the subjects of a great debate among the intellectuals, and Zurayk was certainly one of their leaders.

In Lebanon and Syria ideological parties appeared and took a major role in the debate, giving rise to a new activism and structured organizations anchored mostly in rationalistic principles. The parties involved themselves in the endeavors to transform not only governments, but the Arab mentality into one that was more sophisticated, scientific, and technically oriented. They aimed also at transforming a tribal society into one organized along modern principles of full suffrage and participation. The question of the primacy of the individual or of the group acquired great importance when the urgency of transformation was used as justification for giving priority to collectivity. However, the hope of changing the social order along democratic lines and of setting up governments by and for the people as well as establishing new legality based on equality for all citizens gained favor among a great number of the educated. Modernization in the form of Westernization, the fashioning of the new Arab society in the image of the superior and more advanced West without relinquishing the Arab heritage, became the greatest aspiration. Science and technology, the mainstays and symbols of the West, were considered the best tools with which to achieve modernity.

Zurayk's basic approach rested on these principles, especially on the principle that people are responsible for their own actions and destiny.[23] The only measure of a true civilization is the rational, moral, and spiritual values it supports: This is the critical test that makes a judgment for or against its view of man. Zurayk also thought that social progress is determined by human factors and not by any material ecological or physical circumstances.[24] Man's freedom derives from his own will to determine his own destiny. Man is capable of discovering the truth and of achieving his own happiness in this world.[25] Progress and innovation proceed from the individual; therefore any reform should start by reforming the individual. To reform the individual is to reform society. Education is the best tool for reform inasmuch as it starts with the individual. In other words, Zurayk advocated the theory of the centrality of man and the individual in opposition to the collectivists, who wanted to steamroll or bypass him.

Both al-Kawākibī and Zurayk were greatly concerned with the problem of reform, the problem of how to move the Arabs from their "backward" situation into the modern world. Both, nationalists at heart, wanted to see the Arabs catch up with the West and adopt the best that is there. Both appreciated the Arab heritage driving force, but they never thought that change could be accomplished by resting on one's oars or by mere rhetoric. Zurayk's program for modernization was based on his vision of the free individual and the latent potentialities in him. The disaster that befell the Arabs in 1948 spurred him to analyze its remote causes and to set up guidelines for its remedy. The defeat of seven Arab armies by the army of Israel was seen as a defeat for the actual Arab civilization and as a challenge, if responded to positively and rationally, that would lead to a true resurgence of Arab culture and civilization: "The source from which all other aspects of life branch out, and our problems in Arab society are, in the final analysis, problems of culture and civilization."[26]

The modern civilization Zurayk has in mind is the civilization of the Renaissance, which has brought a new vision of man, a new respect for his rights, a vision that has led to a greater interest in this world of ours and away from the other world. It drove man to discover the mysteries of the visible universe and to strengthen his faith in his own capacity to control nature through discovery, and to thus produce wealth, happiness, and continuous progress.

The achievements of modern civilization may be attested to by the great material production, great advances in the protective sciences against the hazards of nature and disease, and the shrinking of distances and widening of the areas reached by man. It is also achieved by a more orderly and more complex society, continuous efforts to bridge the gap between classes and between rich and poor, better understanding of human rights and human dignity, and patient and deeper research into nature as well as into the universal problems with which the human mind has wrestled since the dawn of history. These questions include the nature of man, the limits of his mind, and man's destiny. Although numerous, praiseworthy, and highly impressive, man's modern achievements have not been able to solve his basic problems. The gains in human rights, for example, are counterbalanced by the acquisition of the most lethal capacity for destruction.[27]

Although al-Kawākibī has a modernistic social outlook, his starting point is metaphysical. Zurayk's starting point is more rationalistic. Both nonetheless arrive at a similar appreciation of the centrality of man and of his dignity. In the case of al-Kawākibī, human dignity and human rights are a derivation of one's servitude to God. This is a basic Islamic doctrine. Man's dignity, in the case of Zurayk, is a derivation of man's natural right to freedom. Zurayk does not deny or affirm the ontological link between religion and freedom. His main concern is man. The essential truth in *this universe* is man; therefore all endeavors should be directed toward the liberation of man, toward freeing him from external bondage as well as from his internal shortcomings. Zurayk the educator never parts company with Zurayk the historian and thinker. Man derives from religion inspiration and spiritual guidance, but his freedom is his birthright as a human being. All men are brothers, and consequently no peace or justice can be established in the world unless the principles of human brotherhood are put into practice. The future of humanity depends in great measure on the removal of the barriers that block the road to brotherhood, be they barriers of nationalism, race, or class. Unless man overcomes his egotistic dispositions and assumes the noble virtues of altruism, cooperation, and generosity, the safety and dignity of man may remain threatened, more so as our world keeps shrinking as a result of advanced technology. The justification of Arab nationalism is measured by its contribution to the liberation of the Arab man, and to his individual and collective progress.

Zurayk's formula for the Arabs to catch up with the modern age is directly derived from his vision of man and the present situation of Western civilization. The Arabs, according to Zurayk, are far outdistanced in the modern parade of achievements. Arab society, as a whole, is still medieval and feudal in character. If Arab society is to survive, greater attention must be paid to social and economic reforms. The prescription for a remedy should include the following: (1) the acquisition and use of the machine more extensively in developing the natural resources of the Arab world; (2) complete separation of Arab states from the religious organization, since in a truly advanced community there is no place for sectarianism or theoretical principles, and national unity cannot be achieved in a theocratic state; and (3) greater attention to education in the applied sciences, since scientific training, along with a scientific approach, is the mainstay of modern civilization. There is nothing like an organized mind for uprooting falsehood and for erecting the life of the nation on secure foundations.[28]

All the above is to be accompanied by a constant seeking of cultural values and of intellectual and artistic creation. Freedom of expression and belief must be permanently secured. For any significant cultural activity, freedom is like air. Without freedom, culture suffocates and withers away.

Nationalism and Secularism

One major aspect of Zurayk's thought deals with Arab nationalism. The first book authored and published by him had to do precisely with the question of Arab nationalism. Entitled *al-Wa'ī al-qawmī* (National Consciousness), it came out in 1939, two years after the publication by Anṭūn Sa'ādeh of his book *Nushū' al-umam* (The Development of Nations), which elicited a great deal of discussion at the time for its approach to the question of determining what factors go into the making of a nation. In formulating his general theory of nationalism, Sa'ādeh placed more emphasis on the geographic factor and its interaction with the human will. People and territory are the key components of a nation. He considered language to be merely a medium of expression and not a determining factor. Neither is religion a determining factor. On these bases Sa'ādeh concluded that there is a Syrian but no Arab nation. Sa'ādeh's theories were seen as a challenge to Arabism. At the time there existed no systematic and rationalistic formulation of the doctrine of Arab nationalism. Zurayk faced this task with his usual serenity and thought-provoking ideas. He believed in one Arab nation and in Arab nationalism. Language and history were determining factors in the making of nations. However, like Sa'ādeh, he considered secularism an essential characteristic of nationalism. Language and history, yes, were determining factors, but not religion. He warned that Arab nationalism would not be able to sustain itself unless it adopted a secularist approach to state building.[29]

Nationalism and secularism go hand in hand and rely on each other's moral support. One of the major challenges to Arab nationalism, he declared, is the insurance of equality for all citizens.[30] The raison d'être of nationalism is the liberation of the individual, that is, the actual adoption of laws and attitudes that provide the individual with a sense of freedom, combined with responsibility and attachment to one's country.

Facing the question of the place of Islam in Arab nationalism, Zurayk offers a distinction between "religious spirit," which is supportive of freedom, equality, and high morality, and "sectarian solidarity," which is exclusivist. True nationalism in no case can be incompatible with true religion, because in its essence nationalism is nothing but a spiritual movement which aims at the regeneration of the inner forces of a nation and the realization of its mental and spiritual potentialities. The moral principles of religion are those same principles which are required to build a stable and prosperous society. The symbols in which these principles are expressed differ from one religion to another, but the difference is cultural rather than intellectual. It is in this sense that there is no essential connection between Arabism and Islam. However, Zurayk's secular nationalism does not stop him from emphasizing the cultural connection between the two. Muḥammad was the creator of Arab culture as well as the founder of Islam. He was the unifier of the Arab people, the man of conviction from whom they can draw their inspirations,[31] but there is no suggestion that they should draw more than that from him, such as sole guidance by Islamic law or the reinstitution of the caliphate. If the Arabs' goal is to become a modern people, they must adopt those institutions that guarantee for the individual his freedom and must educate Arab minds to become organized, systematic, and forward looking. Islam as a civilization is the Arab past, not the future.

Conclusion

al-Kawākibī and Zurayk, both little studied in the West, represent the underlying aspirations of the modern Arab heritage for a humanistic approach to life. al-Kawākibī's starting point was the unadulterated Islamic religion, but man and his freedom were indeed the focal point of his deliberations. He was as much concerned with man's happiness and self-fulfillment in this world as in the other. The essence of the Islamic creed of the Oneness of God was not so much theological as it was moral. In his consideration of this doctrine, al-Kawākibī made clear that he has in mind the moral implications and the social and political consequences resulting from it. Both al-Kawākibī and Zurayk saw in Islam a spiritual force and moral values that should strengthen Arabism and Arab nationalism and not necessarily stand in opposition to it. al-Kawākibī's first loyalty, however, was perhaps to Islam, although this is a question that requires further investigation. Zurayk's primary loyalty has been to Arab nationalism, which, to a great extent, has replaced religion as the driving and spiritual force that unifies the Arabs. Zurayk, a Christian, realized that the religious and ethical values of Islam were so ingrained in Arab society that they could not be ignored as a basic ingredient for Arab nationalism. However, the finality of man's freedom and individuality were uppermost in his mind. He attempted sincerely to find out the subtle intellectual and moral connections between man's freedom, Arab nationalism, and Islam that could keep the three together. Maintaining such a connection was the only way to bring the Arabs into the modern world and into their rightful place under the sun.

Notes

1. Werner Jaeger, *Paideia: The Ideals of Greek Culture*, tr. from the second German edition by Gilbert Highet (New York: Oxford University Press, 1939), p. xxiii.
2. The birth of al-Kawākibī could have occurred in 1849. See *The Encyclopedia of Islam*, 2nd ed., s.v. "al-Kawākibī," 4:775.
3. 'Abd al-Raḥmān al-Kawākibī, *al-A'māl al-Kāmilah*, ed. Muhammad 'Imārah (Cairo: al-Hay'ah al-Miṣrīyah al-'Ammah lil-Kitāb, 1970). Includes *Umm al-qura* and *Ṭabā'i' al-istibdād.*
4. *Ṭabā'i'*, p. 23.
5. Ibid., p. 130.
6. *Ijtihād*, or the right to form an opinion from first principles, was abandoned in favor of *taqlīd* (authority) around A.D. 900. A consensus gradually established itself around that period to "close the door" of *ijtihād.*
7. *Umm al-Qura*, p. 173.
8. One of the works of al-Kawākibī confiscated by the agents of Sulṭān 'Abd al-Ḥamīd II was entitled *al-'Aẓamah lillah* (Greatness is God's Only). See Muḥammad Kurd 'Ali, *al-Mudhakkirāt* (Damascus: al-Taraqqi Press, 1948), p. 611.
9. *Umm al-Qura*, p. 237. All quotations in this study are my translations.
10. *Ṭabā'i'*, p. 102.
11. *Umm al-Qura*, p. 154.
12. *Ṭabā'i'*, p. 102.

13. Ibid., p. 101.
14. Ibid., p. 34.
15. Ibid., p. 33.
16. Ibid., p. 34.
17. Ibid., p. 148.
18. Ibid., pp. 148-49.
19. *al-Manār*, 5, no. 6 (1902): 279.
20. Ibid., no. 23 (1903): 910.
21. *al-Muqattam*, no. 3148 (August 5, 1899): 3; and no. 3149 (August 7, 1899): 1.
22. For a complete list of Zurayk's works, see the study by Dr. Hani A. Faris in this volume.
23. Constantine K. Zurayk, *Ayyu ghad? Dirāsāt liba'ḍ bawā'ith nahḍatina al-marjūwah* (Beirut: Dār al-'Ilm lil-Malāyin, 1957), p. 29.
24. Constantine K. Zurayk, *Fī ma'rakat al-ḥaḍārah* (Beirut: Dār al-'Ilm lil-Malāyin, 1964), p. 202.
25. *Ayyu ghad?* pp. 132-33.
26. Ibid., p. 130.
27. Constantine K. Zurayk, *Naḥnu wa-al-mustaqbal* (Beirut: Dār al-'Ilm lil-Malāyin, 1977), p. 143.
28. Zurayk's prescription for reform appears all over his creative writings. The above three points are explicitly stated in *Ma'na al-nakbah* (Beirut: Dār al-'Ilm lil-Malāyin, 1948), pp. 50-51.
29. Constantine K. Zurayk, *Naḥnu wa-al-tārīkh* (Beirut: Dār al-'Ilm lil-Malāyin, 1956), p. 122.
30. Ibid., p. 122.
31. *Naḥnu wa-al-mustaqbal*, p. 223.

Part Two

The Classical Heritage

On the Use of Islamic History: An Essay

MUHSIN MAHDI

I

What can one learn from Islamic history that may prove relevant to the place of politics in Islam as spiritual message and quest for justice? As I interpret this question, *spiritual message* is meant to refer to the formation of a Muslim's character as a pious man, which is largely an affair of the heart and the mind. The *quest for justice*, on the other hand, is both private and public: private to the extent that it refers to the proper ordering of the elements of the soul, but largely public in that it is the quest for the proper ordering of society. Piety in its various forms—ascetic, mystical, intellectual, and philosophic—is not always in harmony with the quest for legal and political justice, the equal or proportional distribution of rewards or punishments. Political justice cannot take into account the particular needs of the different forms of piety, for these require things that go beyond the limited demands imposed on all members of the community. This problem has led to certain tensions in Islamic history, especially in times and places where pious men tried to reform or transform the public order, either in cooperation with or in open rebellion against the ruling authority. But I have the impression that readers of this volume are not as concerned with this particular issue as they are with the lessons of Islamic history for the present and future conduct of public life in the Islamic world. I must therefore speak as a concerned citizen who has observed the work of professional and amateur historians of Islam and has wondered about the use made of Islamic history in dealing with the problems of contemporary life in the Islamic world.

There is a long tradition of critical historical scholarship, beginning with the earliest Muslim scholars who compiled the documents on which this history rests and extending to modern Muslim and non-Muslim scholars. This tradition has offered different and even conflicting views of some of the major events of Islamic history. Even more important for our immediate purpose is the fact that, regardless of their scholarly pretension, almost all the interpretive histories of the rise and development of Islam and Islamic civilization are based on a mixture of conjecture and preference. It is perhaps not an exaggeration to say that among modern Muslims, in particular, almost every movement of thought, whether religious, political, or social, has tried to anchor itself to real or imagined facts of Islamic history, carefully selected and interpreted to justify or attack a current practice or a future course of action. The fact that these movements of thought have been so numerous, often radically different, and sometimes even opposed to one another has meant that the resulting views of Islamic history might appear to the disinterested observer as ideological weapons rather than accounts of the past. Yet such is the nature of Islam (and other so-called historical religions) that there has always been and always will be a relationship between what Muslims believe to be true and right and what they believe to have taken place in early Islamic history. Their quest for justice seems to be closely related to their quest for the practice of the early Muslim community.

This relationship between the Muslims' view of their past, their judgment on their present condition, and their hope for the future makes it difficult to disentangle the elements that enter into how they deal with the pressing problems of the day, or to judge the relative weight of their attachment to the past and to precedent, their dissatisfaction with the present state of affairs, and their desire for change. It is sometimes even difficult to say whether the common tendency to turn back to early Islamic history has done more good than harm. I have in mind the common use of early Islamic history to reactivate sectarian, regional, racial, and national conflicts within the Muslim community, to silence rational discourse on proposed courses of action, and to justify regimes and laws that would have been considered evil and barbarous were they judged on their own merit by a decent and enlightened citizenry. This does not mean, of course, that Islamic history is something that can or should be bracketed or removed from the mind and life of contemporary Muslims, but it does mean that recourse to Islamic history is an activity that demands critical attention. Muslim thinkers need to persuade themselves and their coreligionists that not every aspect of the past, good or bad, should be allowed to impinge on their lives today, and not every current of belief and fancy and desire and interest should be permitted to claim its truth and roots in the past. Otherwise, the past will lose its meaning and cease to be an inspiration for noble deeds. Muslim thinkers must face and resolve a paradox: on the one hand, the Muslim community is unalterably tied to its history, especially to early

Islamic history, and to break with that history is tantamount to no longer being a Muslim community; on the other hand, the Muslim community needs a certain distance from its history and (as it faces its present and thinks of its future) needs to make use of God's gifts of reason and freedom and sense of responsibility to judge what is right and wrong, desirable and undesirable, useful and harmful.

Perhaps the main lesson of Islamic history is the success of Islam in forming a religious community (the *ummah*) out of a multitude of ethnic, linguistic, and cultural communities, not by forcing them to deny or suppress their traditions, but by providing them with a common faith, common ethical standards, a common language, and eventually a common cultural heritage that was superimposed on and integrated with their particular traditions. In addition, one can point to significant achievements in the position of women, abolition of racial barriers, and treatment of other religious communities. But today's Muslims cannot and should not go back to Islamic history with the intention merely to reinstate the past. Certainly, they can and should look at this past to find out where they may have lost sight of past achievements, which should inspire them to move forward. But as they do this, they must also ask themselves whether these past achievements were not limited in their scope because of the exigencies of time and place, whether they represent the full realization of the demands of the divine revelation, and whether their present conditions and their hopes for the future do not require them to go back to the divine revelation for a new understanding that is more commensurate with their needs today: to develop as fully as possible the principles of human freedom, equality, and brotherhood among Muslims and between Muslims and members of other religious communities, and to embody these principles in clearly defined social and political institutions. The study of the achievements of the past does not absolve Muslims from the careful and intelligent assessment of their present condition and the wider context in which they find themselves and in which they must function.

The breakup of the Muslim community into relatively well-defined national entities, each of which experienced its own linguistic and cultural revival, is a fact of modern Islamic history that cannot be ignored. Yet all of these national entities face internal pressures that need to be dealt with creatively before they endanger the very existence of these entities. There is hardly a group of Muslims or non-Muslims today within these national entities that can continue to preserve their ethnic, linguistic, religious, or cultural isolation and continue to practice their customs and beliefs with only marginal attention to the customs and beliefs of their neighbors. This situation leads them to fear the loss of their identity and to strive to preserve it in some fashion. Most of them do not consider this desire as necessarily incompatible with their desire for full participation in national life, but there are some who do. This is surely one of the most immediate and urgent questions deserving the attention of thinking Muslims today. It is a difficult question because the borderlines between an arrangement that can disrupt national unity and a nation's ability to develop and to defend itself against outside interference and an arrangement that can satisfy the genuine needs of the different segments of the population without leading to the disruption of national unity are not always clearly demarcated or easy to agree on. Yet there are a number of models outside and inside the Islamic world that show the way to a solution. A good recent example is the legal arrangement for Kurdish autonomy and local rule in the Republic of Iraq; given time and good faith, such an arrangement cannot but strengthen the country and provide a model for other Islamic countries that face similar pressures from ethnic and linguistic groups. The pressures from religious groups, whether Muslim or non-Muslim, for full equality as citizens and the abolition of all kinds of discrimination must be faced with equal ingenuity and good faith. The same is true of the pressures for equality for women. All these are questions that can no longer be ignored or swept under the rug if the present national entities are to achieve more than superficial internal unity and realize their full potential as communities of free and equal men and women who need to work together for a common purpose out of inner conviction that they do indeed have a common destiny.

Equally important are the external pressures felt by the national entities in the Islamic world. They continue to face political, economic, and ideological pressures from both the so-called capitalist and socialist blocks, leading to the transformation of their social and political fabric and intensifying the desire for economic and technological development and the quest for social justice. They continue to import a multitude of foreign forms and ideas that seem to be indispensable for the realization of that desire and that quest. But the more a nation advances in these directions, and the more people adopt foreign forms and foreign ideas as their own, the more it appears that these forms and ideas are not always harmonious among themselves or in harmony with their inner convictions. The result is the kind of chaos that one observes in the Islamic world today: there are states that wish to be Islamic but do not seem to know how to go about it, others that wish to be Western but find they cannot make it, and still others that muddle through the best they can in the hope that things will somehow arrange themselves. Thinkers, ideologues, poets, journalists, and semieducated intellectuals pander to this or that view and accuse each other of ignorance, lack of faith, or worse. Nationalists, reformists, fundamentalists, and neo-fundamentalists present themselves as the true interpreters of Islamic history and of Islam itself and think they alone have the key to the salvation of the Islamic world. In the meantime the rapid transformation of society; the destruction of traditional agriculture, crafts, and trades; the exploitation of natural resources for foreign use; and the importation of foreign technology continue at a relentless pace. The resulting cultural and social confusion that is disturbing the life and thought of Muslims today is a situation that is hard for the human soul to tolerate; it has threatened their inner peace, and they see it as a mortal danger to their very existence.

Thus has come into being reaction and the desire to stop this process, return to a premodern state of affairs, stand against external pressures, reject foreign ideas and forms, and go back to the forms and ideas of former times, when the Islamic world was presumably united, at peace with itself, and in control of its own destiny—ideas that prove attractive both to the confused, tired, dislocated, and dispossessed men and women, who thirst for peace and repose and love to work for and possess what they can call their own, and to the revolutionaries, who thirst for change but are unable to mobilize the masses by means of the ideas in which they really believe.

A return to a golden age is surely one of the most fundamental and potent ideas in Islam, and the desire of the Muslim community to return to a golden age is not something that can be ridiculed or stifled. But what does it mean to return to a golden age? It cannot mean to reestablish the time of the Prophet without a prophet, for it is a fundamental principle of Islam that Muḥammad was the last prophet. Nor can it mean to recreate the conditions of early Islamic history, with all the political, social, cultural, and doctrinal divisions and conflicts of the first and second centuries of the Islamic era. Nor, again, can it mean to recreate the particular synthesis of the cultures of the ancient world that was realized in the third and fourth centuries of the Islamic era and to return to the thought of its illustrious philosophers, scientists, and men of letters of whose achievements both Muslims and non-Muslims have been justly proud. There is no return to any of that; and those who think that such a return is possible are deluding themselves and adding to the current chaos.

The only return that is possible and necessary for Muslims today is the task at hand: to learning to understand what makes for the chaos and confusion in which Muslims live, to knowing themselves—for "he who knows himself knows his Lord"—and to looking to the future, to a life worthy of their past and their faith. Islamic history is many things and can be all things to all men. What is relevant to the current predicament is that a religious community, after a long period of conflict and confusion, was able to create out of its inner resources a degree of harmony between its faith and the cultures of the ancient world and in that context create for itself and for the rest of humanity a civilization that was the wonder of the age. But that age is now a thing of the past. We need to study it, recover it, be proud of it, be inspired by it, but also be critical of it and try to understand and transcend its limitations. Ours is a new age. We may have been thrust into it without wishing to be, it may have been forced on us from the outside, we may not have been ready for it, or we may wish it had not come to us. But this is neither here nor there; we have gone too far into it to turn back now, and there is no place to return to even if we wanted to return.

Whatever one may say about the initial period in which the new age was forced on the Islamic world from the outside, Muslims have subsequently embraced it and gone out of their way to learn about it and identify themselves with it—and in this they have done much more than their ancestors did when they received the cultures of the ancient world. Muslims have taken advantage of the greater accessibility of foreign languages, literatures, history, arts, and inventions. They have traveled to and lived in different regions and nations in greater numbers, learned their languages, studied under great masters, and returned home to teach what they have learned to their students and spread it among their coreligionists. They have even learned to look at themselves and their past through foreign eyes. The range of what Muslims have learned and continue to learn is immensely more vast than what their ancestors learned or could have learned about ancient cultures. They are learning it from nations that are still full of life, creativity, and inventiveness rather than from nations that have reached senility or are in decay. The period needed to digest what is being learned and to keep up with new inventions may last longer. The range of what can be seen as original is narrower; nothing invented or developed by any nation, past or present, in the West or the East, can be assumed not to be there or not to be learnable from its source. The danger of self-deception, of presuming that one has come up with something new when one has not, is far greater. And so is the temptation to conclude that there is nothing that has not been said or done apart from the new and impressive achievements of modern science and technology. This makes the current predicament seem oppressive because impossible to master; the time never seems to come when one feels ready to make use of what one has learned, to move from learning into creating and acting and enjoying the fruits of what one has learned. All this may be true. But to think that this process is reversible, that the Islamic world can abandon its venture into the modern world that has lasted for almost two centuries and retreat into a distant past, may be comforting to some, but it is an invitation to a fool's paradise in the land of nowhere.

Turning to early Islamic history can be useful only if it is done as part of a wider and deeper effort at self-examination and as an examination of the present predicament of the Islamic world with a view to a creative response. For just as the return to early Islamic history cannot provide the full answer to what Muslims must do here and now, the long experience of constant imitation and borrowing, importation of foreign forms and ideas, and dependence on foreign products cannot be accepted as a normal state of affairs, at least not for a community that cherishes the hope of standing on its own feet and making its own contribution to our age. Yet the present situation of almost total dependence cannot be terminated by wishful thinking. It requires a special effort on the part of the intellectual elite of the Islamic world (who must be open to the currents of thought inside and outside the Islamic world) to look for the common element that can form the cement of a new community. This need not be yet another ideology. Rather, it must be an organic fusion of or balance between the main ideas that have always existed in or have more recently found their way into the Islamic world (indigenous notions of law, morality, and communal life; nationalism, socialism, and so forth). That common element must be such as to command willing loyalty on the part of the common man and sustain the elite so that they can take their bearing from it and function within its horizon. Unless a horizon is established within which the community and the elite can develop a wide measure of consensus as to the basis of legitimate thought and action, the current state of chaos may extend indefinitely and indeed get worse. Universal education, urbanization, and foreign contacts are likely to add to the existing confusion of forms and ideas, and the elite are likely to continue to challenge openly and forcefully the very roots of traditional Islamic societies, which leads to reactions on the part of conservatives, with the result that social conflicts will sap whatever strength is left in these societies. Whether or not the present chaotic condition will result in the total transformation of the Islamic world into a backyard of the industrialized world, from which they draw their raw material and into which they dump their finished product, will thus depend on the ability of the new elite to understand this predicament and create a new order out of the chaos.

II

Let me therefore state what I consider the most important task. It is not, I submit, any one of the many useful things that engage the attention of most thinking Muslims today, such as tinkering with Islamic law, protecting Muslims from exposure to the so-called materialistic philosophies of the modern world, or the race to catch up with the West in the economic, scientific, and technical fields. Important and useful as some of these efforts may be, they are bound to fail so long as they lack a comprehensive framework, and that framework can be no other than a political framework. To put it differently, the most important task is not the quest for economic, social, or legal justice in isolation; these are partial and subordinate forms of justice. It is, rather, the quest for political justice, the just political order within which these other forms of justice have to find their place.

The quest for the just political order today in the Islamic world seems to take two negative forms: revolutionary resistance to change on the one hand, and revolutionary change on the other. Those who espouse these revolutions must realize that no political order can survive if subjected to permanent revolution, that preservation and reform must go hand in hand, that change must be gradual. This is perhaps the fundamental principle of a healthy order: a way of life in which tradition and collective memory form the foundation, and change is carefully grafted into the existing tradition. The political order, like language, has a life of its own. It is not a machine that can be discarded and replaced by a new, shinier, or more efficient model whenever one fancies that it has become old and obsolete. It does admit of improvement or reform. But this must be done in a way that avoids throwing away the baby with the bath water.

Ever since the failure of the attempts to establish liberal democracies in a few Islamic countries—attempts that were halfhearted, ill-prepared, and without firm foundations that could stand the weight of internal social changes and the new external global order generated by World War II and its aftermath—what political thinking emerged in the Islamic world has taken the form of restating the case for or against nationalism and socialism. But nationalism and socialism are not types of political regimes. They can exist in tyrannies and in free societies; in monarchies, aristocracies, and oligarchies; in regimes that respect the rule of law and regimes that do not respect the rule of law. Whatever else one may say about the military regimes that seem to rise and fall in most Islamic countries, they are symptoms, not causes, of the absence of an adequate level of political thinking, education, and commitment on the part of leaders of thought and the public at large. The attempt to reestablish certain aspects of Islamic law will not resolve this problem, for it is not a legal but a political problem. The kind and scope of the legal system one must have is an important aspect of the political order, but without the right political order laws can be used and misused, instituted or abolished, applied or not applied. The political order has to do with who has the monopoly of power, how power is shared among various organs of the state, and the ground of legitimacy. The quest for just laws does not absolve Muslims from the quest for a just political order.

And it is here, in the quest for political justice and for the just or good political order, the best political order that is possible given the conditions of modern life, that we lack clear guidance when we look back at the course of Islamic history and much of Islamic thought. Let me pose a simple question. Was the quest for political justice, which should have resulted in the just political order, realized in Islamic history after the expansion of Islam and the establishment of empires by the Ummayads and the Abbasids? The difficulty in answering this question is not caused by the fact that most leading Muslim thinkers of those times either answered it negatively or were satisfied to live under less than ideal conditions. It is, rather, that they left us a host of ideas and positions from which we can learn to oppose unjust regimes or submit to them, but not how to think about political life and conduct ourselves politically, that is, how to preserve and yet reform the political order. They left us a variety of political maxims and a vast literature on the qualities of imams and caliphs, most of which are of little use to us today when there are no ruling imams or caliphs. We need to go beyond political maxims, understand the structure of our political life, and decide what is worthy of being preserved and what needs to be reformed.

The only group of theologians who made justice one of their primary quests was the Mu'tazilites. They understood that this quest required a comprehensive rational inquiry into the totality of human life rather than a limited effort to ascertain the literal meaning of the revelation, to imitate, or to engage in legal reasoning. Even they, however, did not develop the political implications of their quest for justice into a coherent and detailed reflection on how it can be embodied in a just political order. Some Muslim philosophers were more successful in this respect, but their political teachings are now almost forgotten; the discipline itself is either absent or else banned in a number of Islamic countries, while in others it has been transformed into theology or mysticism, or one or another version of recent or contemporary Western schools of thought. Political philosophy, the disciplined and coherent reflection on political life, has been replaced by ready-made political ideologies and political propaganda, as if all the answers have been found and all that remains is to convert the unbelievers and inform the ignorant.

What the Islamic world needs today is neither ready-made ideologies nor political propaganda, but political thinking. Such political thinking cannot begin so long as the elite of the Islamic world are forced to adopt ready-made ideologies, function as part of the state propaganda machine, or else remain silent. They need to study the great political philosophers of the past: Greek, Muslim, as well as Western. And they need to supplement this effort with direct reflection on the current state of affairs in their own countries; the tradition and character of their own people; and, above all, the source of the strength of the West, its impact on their countries, and the nature of the crisis in which the Western culture seems to find itself.

This reflection must distinguish between theoretical and practical opinions. Theoretical opinion, or belief about religious or philosophic questions, varies among individuals or groups within the community. They may hold different and even conflicting positions, and they must be allowed to argue in a civilized manner by engaging in earnest dialogue. We can learn a great deal from the periods of tolerance in Islamic history, when Muslims were free to hold a variety of opinions regarding all sorts of issues and when jurists refused to judge as unbelievers any Muslim who professed the *shahādah* (The Muslim Creed). We need to develop a similar degree of broad-minded tolerance toward our fellow citizens, respect their opinions, and allow them to argue for their views without fear of being branded as infidels or traitors just because we disagree with them. We cannot expect that all individuals or groups within a vast community will always agree in their opinions about the deepest questions and highest principles of human life and the nature of the world, especially in these times of intellectual ferment and ever-widening cultural horizons. Differences of opinion regarding these matters need not disturb the social fabric and can even be a source of strength if the members of the community are educated to respect and make an effort to appreciate differing or opposing opinions. A political community is not a military camp. In practical matters, however, it is necessary to achieve consensus on those issues in which the community must act together or about which it must be in implicit or explicit agreement.

Next, we must pursue our reflections on the relation between the Islamic world and the Western world with greater acumen and realism. In the face of the massive trend toward universalizing Western culture and Western ways of life, and when traditional cultures appear to engage in rearguard action or are condemned to become museum pieces, we cannot afford to think and act as if modern science, technology, education, bureaucracy, urbanism, and so forth are somehow detachable from everything else in Western culture that we do not happen to like. How much of modern science and technology, for instance, is detachable from the rest of Western culture? The use of a few gadgets? The factories that produce them? The engineers who build these factories? The scientists who discover the properties of the materials used by the engineers? The scientists who investigate the theoretical foundations of the applied sciences? The philosophers who investigate the grounds of scientific inquiry? Can we continue to argue that Islam is a whole—a religion, society, economy, and so forth—and that one cannot detach from it any one of these aspects, and yet think that modern science and technology can be separated from Western culture and can be grafted on Islamic societies without harmful results? On the other hand, if this kind of limited borrowing is not possible and if the Muslim community has already gone a good distance in opening itself to a whole range of Western ideas, does it not make better sense to urge Muslim thinkers to penetrate as far as they can into the very foundations of Western culture, engage in a dialogue with it on a less superficial level than they are accustomed to, and go beyond the elementary, questionable, ignorant, and prejudiced ways in which they usually speak about it? Those who believe that Islam is still a living force cannot be afraid of such an open encounter with modern Western culture.

Finally, we must decide what kind of society we want to live in and what kind of human being we want to be. If this decision is to be based on knowledge or reasoned inquiry, we must learn to inquire what is the just or good order of society, and what is noble or base for man in the here and now. This we cannot learn from contemporary Western scientific social thought. Western scientific social thought tells us that these are value judgments relative to historical epochs, cultures, interest groups, and individuals. The crisis of political thought in the Islamic world is largely the result of the widespread adoption of this type of thought.

The Expression of Historicity in the Koran*

JACQUES BERQUE

The Koran is no more a history than it is a code, an encyclopedia, or a lyrical meditation. It embraces all of these genres and many others in a powerful spiritual synthesis. Thus one can rightly say that, not only in the eyes of the believers, the revelation constitutes a decisive event in the course of humanity and nature. It is equally legitimate to study the text (the Koran) from a historical angle. However, since Western thought has encumbered the concept of history with so many connotations, the latest of which—Romanticism, Marxism, and most recently Heidegger—hold sway over some of us, we must avoid falling into the trap of anachronism and abusive assimilation as well as, in a contrary sense, of exaggeration of specific Islamic and Arabic features.

The most advisable way to proceed is to move from the simpler to the more complex, from the more obvious to the more hypothetical. First we will consider how the language of the Koran expresses temporal succession. Next we will examine particular references chosen from the Book, and then we will conclude by an examination of what may profanely be called the "vision of duration" or the "philosophy of history."

The Articulation of Time

The expression of time in a text of this kind is not self-explanatory. On the one hand, as we all know, the temporality in the Latin verbal structure is represented in classical Arabic as well as in ancient Greek by a whole range of verbal aspects. In the Koran, on the other hand, this characteristic is accentuated by the fact that the divine speaker, letting his gaze sweep over a simple temporal sequence, uses the perfect (*al-māḍī*) to convey that which, in the eyes of man, is still resting in the future, such as the coming of the Last Hour and everything that concerns life in the Hereafter. God encompasses in a concurrent vision what we humans discern as past, present, and future. In the apocalyptic and eschatological passages, the use of the perfect and, less frequently, the imperfect (*al-muḍāri'*) responds to extratemporal finalities, to which one should devote a prior study. This does not mean to say that there is no expression of human time. The particle *qad*, used with the perfect, specifies the past; *sawfa* with the imperfect specifies the future. A second combination of the two tenses corresponds to the French *imparfait* tense. We should, however, take care to note that the universal implication of the message is not taken as a mere "announcement" (*nabā'*) coming from the Beyond. It is in metahistory that human time is anchored and thus, if I may say so, twice made relative: once with respect to the Absolute and once again with respect to the moment in which the Absolute reveals Himself.

We should take note, on the other hand, that the announcement, enlarged to that eschatological and cosmic dimension, does not apply to man alone. The earth also has its own history (Surah XCIX, 4 and 5). In this case the term used is no longer *nabā'*, but *khabar*—that is, "predicate."

Man's past, then, together with that of the world, is plunged into a metaphysical vicissitude whose recurrences bring in the countless uses of the root (*DH-K-R*). The "recall" of past messages that come again and again encourages *tadhakkur* in the present (in the fifth form[1])—that is, "remembrance," and also "reflection." The Koran itself refers to it as *dhikr*. We will return to this essential character later.

Let me mention a few specific issues.

1) For example, the curious use of the plural *aṭwār* in Surah LXXI, 14: "He created you by 'phases' or 'stages.'" The full usage of both the term and the concept reappears in Ibn Khaldun, with the anticipatory power that we know of.

2) The old grammar called "corroborative" or "intensive," a verbal form ending in a simple or double *n* of the Arabic conjugation. The Koran uses it often to indicate commitment, imprecation, and solemn affirmation. This is how it is used in Surah XVII, 4-8. This extract from the Book of Destiny refers to the Israelites and mentions a double destruction of the temple. Has the second destruction already taken place or is it going to take place in the future? This is a passage whose exegesis requires some pause. It seems to us that, in this passage, modal violence—if one may call it that—prevails over temporality.

3) The binomial *bayna yadayhi* is used as an adverb, even when it occurs in a second-person proposition. The meaning seems to us to arise from the context, which joins it together with a derivative of the root *S-D-Q* thirteen times and opposes it to *khalfa*, "after," "behind," five times. In the first case, we hear that the new revelation has come to confirm what was already "in hand," "previous," or "current." In the second case we hear that the actual is in contrast with what "comes later," that is, "afterward."

There is a certain ambiguity here that is brought out in the commentary of polytheism and animism.

What we call "prehistory" is not far from such perspectives. Otherwise, who are these People of the Rock, People of the Bush, and so forth? We on Surah XXXVI, 45, by Shaykh Ibn 'Āshūr:

Sometimes we perceive a representation of what is added when we go toward a place: what we have "in hand" then is that which is reached, and what we have "behind" is that which comes later in the journey. At other times we perceive a representation of what the agent adds: If it is in "his hands," he has already gone past it in his journey; and if it is "behind" him, it is what befalls him later, hence what comes "afterwards."

If our interpretation is correct, *bayna yadayhi* aims essentially at the immediate, at what is in use or is imminent, and *khalfa* indicates the more or less distant future. If we were to try to visualize this figure of speech, we would repeat with Paul Valery that "man enters into the future walking backward."

Here is what further reinforces the motive force of the concept of *dhikr*. The future slumbers in memory. Its activation depends more on a revival of memory than on an activation of what has not been experienced. The future takes part, with all that has preceded it, in a homogenous range of recurrences. Yet, not everything new is merely a renovation. The message transmitted by Muḥammad is not limited to restoring the contribution of Moses. His revelation is the last one, being at one and the same time recapitulative, actualizing, and innovative. The route traversed by man from Adam to the revelation of the Koran and from thence on to the present does not only propagate—if one may say so—a wave originating from the sources, but it also records a number of events and vicissitudes in which man's destiny as well as his responsibility are brought into awareness as they are put to the test.

Factual Soundings

In effect, the Book of Islam contains many references to staggered events from prehistoric antiquity up to the recent past or present. That is why it sometimes takes the form of a chronicle. In this respect the Abyssinian invasion and the struggle between the Greek and Sassanian Empires furnish the framework for the larger history where the internal movements occuring within the Arabian Peninsula are inscribed (expansion of Tamīm, the movement of Banū 'Āmir, the establishment of Mecca as a communal center, and so forth). At its highest reaches one enters into a zone in which the flow of legends plunges into an atmosphere of polytheism and animism.

What we call "prehistory" is not far from such perspectives. Otherwise, who are these People of the Rock, People of the Bush, and so forth? We are undoubtedly dealing with pre-Arabs such as 'Ād, Thamūd, and Madyan. Sabā', however, brings us into history. The bursting of the dyke of Ma'rib is a proven fact, one that has left traces on the landscape. Finally, it is to be noted that one of the cities through which the caravan between Ḥijāz and Syria passes—Hijr (literally, "the Forbidden")—carries a name that puns on Ptolemy, "Hegra." All this has an imprint of authenticity that is confirmed by external and archaeological sources.

In the case of Egypt, a large number of allusions are made to an agricultural civilization and centralized state. They are of a striking precision and color. It should also be noted that the only time in the Koran that the Egyptian dynast is not called "Pharoah" is in the Surah of Joseph. Could this be because, in the epoch this prophet was presumed to have come upon the scene, along with the installation of the Hebrews, the continuity of the Egyptians sovereignty was interrupted by the reign of the Hyksos?

Dr. Maurice Bucaille, with the eyes of a scientist, reading the *kawnīyah* verses of the Koran—namely, the verses dealing with astronomy, biology, etc.—has underlined their objective accuracy. He does the same with the interpretation of Surah X, 92: "So today we shall deliver thee in thy body . . . " which he takes literally. In fact, it would appear that the mummy of the pharaoh of the Exodus has recently been found. But al-Amir 'Abd al-Qādir, in No. 265 of his *Mawāqif*, gives the verse a completely moral interpretation based on the final redemption that this guilty person would have received for a tardy repentance (Surah X, 90). Here we have given preference to the mystical over the scientist. Let us say, however, that to us it is not historical objectivity that counts in the Koran or should matter when reading it, but the moral teachings or the symbolism that can be attached to it. Moreover, it is not the succession of time as such which is important, but the qualitative variations that come forth from that succession.

Consider, for example, Surah XXXIII, 9ff, which concerns the Battle of the Trench. The narrative mixes exhortations on permanent values and forecasts for the future. This is even truer of Surah LXXXV (the Holocaust of Najran). The Koranic discourse does not seek to record the facts as they are. It encloses them in a network of meanings which it does not penetrate except in an elaborate or elliptic way.

Ṭabari has noted with great satisfaction, with reference to Surah CV (*al-Fīl* [the Elephant]), the decisive step which achieved the defeat of the Abyssinian invader, a defeat to which the firm attitude of the grandfather of Muḥammad contributed. Muḥammad himself was born that same year. Who knows whether the enigmatic term *sijill* (stones of baked clay) is not an omen of sorts connected with this event. On the other hand, the commentators say the question of the term *abābil* (flock of birds in flight) still goes on. But isn't there a striking echo of the (biblical) Babel?

Another notation. Surah of the *Rūm* (The Byazantines) (XXX) (let us dare to translate it as "Rome") opens with the famous prediction of a victory by Heraclius (627-628), following the ravaging of Syria and Palestine by Chosroes (611-614): Gibbon points out that this anticipation of events confused the medieval Christian apologists. Let us remember, for our part, that it is notable (but not uniquely) with reference to the Romans that the Koran glorifies the superiority of ancient civilizations (Surah XXX, 9). And this glorification is linked up with a whole system of thought. The sense of the unlearned lesson, of the past gone without recall, laid the ground for a meditation that would be melancholic were it not for the hopes attached to a New Promise. At this moment, a "revival of the message" intervenes (*Muḥdath*, XXI, 2: XXVI, 5).

Because of its very repercussions, does not this message look like it has created a zone of silence at its own upper reaches? "And how many a generation We destroyed before them! Dost thou perceive so much as one of them a whisper?" (Surah XIX, 98). Thus all the past previous to the Koran is animated with recurrences. But in this immense fabric of facts, ideas, and words, there is a sorting and selection which could lead to a total obsolescence.

The messages of unitarianism (Oneness of God) are vivid and glorified. The vicissitudes of the ancient peoples, with the exception of the lessons which are drawn with respect to their own goals, are thrown into justified oblivion. Their works are obliterated, grandiose though they may have been, and the prophecies open a new era.

The Idea of Duration in the Koran

From a text of this kind, then, we cannot expect an idea of uniform and cumulative time—other concepts of the industrial age—nor of an ascending duration, or "progress," an optimistic elaboration of our eighteenth and nineteenth centuries. The rejection, however, of these two ways of looking at things as anachronistic must not lead us to attribute to the Koran a position of being outside of time or of cyclic involution.

In support of this last thesis, Louis Massignon has cited Surah XVIII, "The Cave." According to him and to many others, Islam—as "momentalist" in its concept of time as it is "atomist" in its conception of space—would show signs here of an attitude opposed to that of the West, at least such as has produced the industrial centuries. But the Surah (in question) is faced with two types of being in time, the metahistorical and the historical; it does not sacrifice the second at all, for to lead a life outside of time, the Seven Sleepers (of the Cave) must in fact withdraw from the evolving context of the world around them. The Surah, on the other hand, develops a chronological reckoning. Archaeology itself enters into the game. It is explicitly said that a memorial will be built upon the cave. The Seven Sleepers are designated as *The People of al-Raqīm*—that is, we think, the people of the "epitaph." It is indeed a City of the Late (Roman) Empire that is invoked. It is a city rich in monuments, legends, and precarious longevity, all of which are overwhelmed by any comparison with the eternity of the afterlife.

Let us go further. God, according to the Koran, acts not only in eternity, but also in time, and He endows and renews it with laws. He intervenes in the chain of cause and effect. He moves from what is outside of time to the metahistorical and on to the historical, not without different procedures, to carry out the flux and reflux among the three series.

Prophecy is one of the procedures. Let us recall that according to some Islamic tradition, there are some three hundred thousand prophets as opposed to only three hundred messengers. Even though reminded in the most urgent manner of the universe of mystery or of *ghayb*, man does not any the less function as God's custodian over what is here below, though still obligated to fulfill his responsibilities. If, in moving from the cosmic to the eschatological, man can have at his disposition only a temporary delay (*ila ḥīn*), he nevertheless exercises at his own level mastery over his own affairs. In this way he can "promote" by what his hands "gain for him" his retribution in the other world.

It is not less true that the general meaning of life is progress toward God, a theophoric "becoming" (this term *becoming*, the literal translation of *maṣīr*, is used twenty-eight times). Nature itself rejoins this movement and somehow takes part in this finality. The world is by no means a vale of tears. Its joys and sorrows are fully measured by a system that takes into account the "here-below"—*dunyā*—as well as the "here-after"—*ākhirah.*

In all these instances, and more, communities, races, and sects are taken into account as much as individuals. Thus they enter into this great game in which anthropology appears as an active and responsible waystation between the cosmic and the eschatological.

Forecasts

The interpretation I have risked could be charged with engaging in rationalizing and historicizing. It will not be contradicted, I think, by any Koranic text; on the contrary, it will be confirmed by many of them. Nevertheless, I willingly concede that other interpretations are possible, such as the mystical, whose essence is far removed from the present remarks. Still, have I not leaned on the side of the mystical exegesis in the case of Surah X, 92?

What seems more difficult to admit is the retrospective interpretation, which, as mentioned earlier, does not seek to infer what I have invoked as a future of remembrance or, in another term, the historicity of *dhikr*, but to drag this future backward toward an alleged golden age. To this interpretation are linked the deterministic perceptions that limit the role of research and induction, and, to the contrary, as far as the true text is concerned, expand the role of reactionary applications of it and narrow inferences from it (*taqlīd*). Conversely, it goes without saying that not only our preferences but also the suggestions which a prolonged reading of the Book inspires in us are on the side of a progressive Islam.

At the level of events, the Koran has indeed been acting as a historical catalyst for the people to whom it was revealed. One can justly apply to the Arabs of the first century of the Hijrah the famous Koranic verse "God changes not what is in a people, until they change what is in themselves" (Surah XIII, 11). Thus we are obviously led to a plane of which the *jihād* (Holy struggle) and *ijtihād* (personal judgment) are nothing more than special forms. This exegesis is confirmed by the circumstances surrounding early Islam. Burning with a faith that was not escapist but was directed instead at personal and collective realization, the Arabs, who had been for a long time marginal in relation to the Byzantine and Persian Empires, entered into the realm of that larger history that had until then relegated them to its outer reaches, or treated them as vassals of the Byzantines or the Romans.

Of course, many things had occurred earlier in the peninsula: warrior raids, caravan journeys, merchant traffic, and trade with the empires of the time, or refusal of such. Poetry was no less than the highest expression of this people and really the only thing which was truly original. It was in it that the Arabs expressed their thought of themselves. This poetry touched on legends, even myth. Note, for example, the end of Ṭarafah and of ʻAbīd ibn al-Abraṣ: one finds an analogy in Greek mythology.

But since the Hijrah, the Arabs laid the foundations of their own historicity: an admirable mixture of religious ethics, esthetic creativity, and economic realism. In the first century in which they held sway from the Pyrenees to the Indus, they found themselves trapped between two eras—one that fades away, that of the myth, and another that gains strength, that of history. Allowing for many differences, this situation, in some respects, is reminiscent of the one in which the first Ionian thinkers found themselves. The same unveiling of existence denoted the same sort of development in both cases. For Islam it is a religious text upon which it is anchored and by which it is explained. The believers are left free to think that the Koran reaches deeper into the truth of existence than does Heraclitus or Parmenides.

But here another kind of question arises. Fifteen centuries after the revelation of the Koran, will technology—in which Arabs and Muslims in general are more and more involved—and their growing involvement in the affairs of the world—a world which, in turn, has involved them more and more profoundly—will all this change the shape of their history? Or, rather, is the change already under way? Yes, certainly, but not without their often rediscovering as an ideal, excuse, or even as a longing for the past the connection between the historical and the sacred.

It is true that in the West already the historical is no longer what it was, and what it seems to yield on many points to the new synchronic and formal powers. Where are Arabs and Muslims in general with respect to this new debate that affected them even before they had overcome the previous one? These are formidable questions that we cannot avoid.

Notes

* Translated and revised by Professors Khalil Semaan and Charles Butterworth.

1. From every "root," theoretically, the verb in Arabic generates forms, ten or more: from the root *DH-K-R*, *tadhakkara* is form 5, *tadhakkur* is the verbal noun-gerund of form 5 (translator's note).

Equity and Islamic Law

MAJID KHADDURI

In the development of some of the major Western legal systems—Roman law and common law, to mention but two—some form of equity seems to have come into existence when the judicial process was in need of reform. At these times it adopted a higher level of legal justice apart from the established legal system. However, since the general principles of Islamic law (*Shari'a*), derived from the Revelation and Divine Wisdom (not to mention human reasoning), were considered the embodiment of divine justice (*jus divinum*), it would indeed be strange to speak of equity as a higher level of justice, since the justice embodied in the *Shari'a* is the expression of God's essence and perfection. But although equity and the *jus divinum* may mean the same thing in theory, they may not necessarily mean the same thing in practice, when the need for equity arises in the administration of justice. What are these situations?

First, the general principles and rules of law are characterized by uniformity and universality, since they are laid down to govern not specific instances but general categories and events and situations. "All law is universal," said Aristotle, "but . . . it is not possible to make a universal statement which shall [always] be correct."[1] In other words, no rule of law can possibly be always just without exception. For these exceptions, the need for equity arises to correct the error of injustice. This is true in Islamic law as well as in other revealed laws—for example, Jewish and Christian—because the principles and rules of law are too broad and cannot possibly be applied to all events and incidents.

Second, unless exceptional cases are specifically dealt with in the law, hardship and injustice contrary to the very spirit of the law, which aims at justice, may result. Even if the case is indirectly covered, the effect of the strict application of the law is injustice. *Summa jus summa injuria.* In such a situation a different ruling is called for.[2] In the absence of new legislation, lawyers have often resorted to legal fiction as a solution.[3]

In earlier ages, the problem of the inadequacy of legal rules to achieve justice was dealt with in accordance with different judicial procedures.

Special courts presided over by men were entrusted with cases arising from extraordinary situations. In Rome the praetor dealt with such situations, and in England chancery courts were established for the same purpose. The praetor was given extensive power over the entire judicial process to give relief against the rigidity of the legal system.[4] In England the chancellor, appointed by the king, decided cases outside the common law in accordance with what seemed to him to be the merit of the case. In time, the cases decided in the chancery courts provided ample precedents for establishing a set of rules to achieve justice through equity apart from the rules of the common law. In practice, the chancellor tended to pursue his conscience, guided by precedents. Equity was thus a form of discretionary justice intended to correct the injustice resulting from the application of the common law. However, the history of the chancery courts showed that not all cases were decided on their merits. Some cases, presumably decided in accordance with equity, betrayed corruption and unworthy motives. Originally designed to achieve corrective justice, the chancery courts were an expression of the king's conscience. But in time, precedents and rules evolved to insure equity as a corrective to legal justice.[5]

In Islamic experiences, as in the experiences of other nations, the need for equity was just as keenly felt. Nonetheless, Muslim jurists maintained that the divine justice enshrined in the law was ideal and perfect, that there was presumably no need for equity, although in practice it was compromised by the judicial processes. The situation was compounded not only by judicial procedure, but also by subsequent development of the legal system. Apart from substantive justice, the law lacked uniformity for the simple reason that it developed outside the state as a jurist law. As a result, several schools of law emerged—not to mention heterodox schools—but only four were recognized. Differences on credal and legal grounds necessarily led to differences in the scale of procedural justice from one school to another and from one province to another. For this reason, the judicial structure did not develop as a hierarchy, and judges were not bound by such rules as *stare decisive*, which requires judges to make their decisions consistent with those of a higher court as well as consistent with one another.

The establishment of the Abbasid dynasty (A.H. 132/A.D. 750) brought in its train changes in the political regime which reconciled religious scholars and tempted jurists to serve in the state. The need for the establishment of some form of harmony in the legal system was keenly felt, and it seems to have been discussed in high political circles. Ibn al-Muqaffa' (d. A.H. 139/A.D. 756), an official in the provincial administration of Baṣra, prepared a memorandum for the Caliph al-Manṣūr in which he proposed, among other things, certain specific reforms in the legal system. He called the attention of the caliph to glaring discrepancies in judicial decisions from court to court and from province to province in dealing with similar cases. Some judges, said Ibn al-Muqaffaʿ, claimed that they made their decisions on the basis of the Prophet's Traditions (sunna), but in practice they often followed their own opinions. Others, claiming to make decisions on the basis of analogy (*qīyās*), inflicted injustice on one party or the other, although the purpose of analogy was to seek equity in favor of the injured party in accordance with a general principle or the judge's own discretion. To repair this situation, Ibn al-Muqaffaʿ proposed that a unified code of law should be promulgated by the caliph and applied to all the lands.[6] The caliph himself, perhaps persuaded by other counselors, seems to have realized the need for reform. It is reported that he asked Malik (d. A.H. 179/A.D. 795), head of the school of law bearing his name, to compose a digest of law for possible adoption as the standard *corpus juris*. Malik, however, seems to have been dubious about the need for codification (perhaps he was expressing the prevailing opinion of jurists) and did not think that his digest should be the only text to be followed in the lands. Indeed, the jurists were opposed to the idea that the authorities should impose a unified code and tended to stress diversity (which would enrich the development of the law) rather than uniformity in the legal system at the expense of justice.

In the absence of equity courts, the lawyers resorted to legal fiction (*al-Ḥīyal al-sharʿīyah*)—which seems, not unlike the experiences of other nations, to have existed before Islam—by virtue of which an act may seemingly be lawful in accordance with the literal meaning of the *Shariʿa* but could hardly be in conformity with its spirit. The purpose of the *ḥiyal*, according to the Ḥanafi jurists (Abū Ḥanīfah, founder of the Ḥanafi School, was the principle exponent of this concept), was to assist men in difficult situations where the law could be very harsh and unjust. There is an element of equity in the *ḥiyal*, but not all jurists sought to achieve equity. A case in point is the oath made by one party to the other in a business transaction concerning which he was not anticipating an adverse legal effect, such as "If I do such and such a thing (or if such and such a thing is not carried out), my wife is divorced."[7] In accordance with procedural justice, such an oath is binding, especially to judges who assert the literal meaning of the declaration. In such circumstances, in which the person's oath leads to an unjust situation, the Ḥanafi jurists claimed to provide corrective justice by arguing that the oath is not binding. As a device to help victims of injustice, the *ḥiyal* might be justified in cases of extreme hardship, such as obligations undertaken under pressure or the inevitable choice between two wrongs. In this sense the *ḥiyal* served the cause of equity, but it was a negative step, for, in a positive sense, the *ḥiyal* undermined the very idea of justice enshrined in the *Sharī'a* as a whole.

Perhaps an even more important positive attempt at correcting injustice was the establishment of the Maẓālim and other special courts noted earlier, It is, however, not my purpose to provide a detailed account of the composition and functions of these courts. Suffice it to say that they came into existence in the third A.H./ninth A.D. century, although some form of procedural justice was achieved by occasional councils presided over by the imam or his representatives. Like regular courts, they were to deal with private litigations resulting in a wrong or injustice done to an individual, but they were not to pursue an appellate procedure. They were, however, separate courts and applied essentially a set of political (almost secular) rules and not necessarily the *Sharī'a.* The litigations that were considered outside the jurisdiction of regular courts, where the law was applied, were taken almost always to the Maẓālim councils. The Maẓālim, deriving their power of jurisdiction from the imam and entrusted to men in high authority—*wazīrs* (ministers), *wālis* (governors) and other high offices—proved more efficient, and their decisions were carried out more promptly than in regular courts. In this respect, the Maẓālim councils may be said to have fulfilled the functions of equity courts.[8]

However, the Maẓālim councils differed from their prototype of Western equity courts in two important respects. First, no rules or precedents were established to guide the Maẓālim magistrates, their procedure often proved arbitrary, and litigation varied considerably from case to case. Some litigations were conducted by the imam himself, others by his representatives. But in most cases, the litigation fell into the hands of lesser officials, who paid little or no attention to the merit of the case. Second, the Maẓālim councils did not develop into a strictly separate judicial system as equity courts, since no regular magistrates were entrusted to attend to equity functions and the lesser officials appointed to function as magistrates made their decisions under the vagary of shifting circumstances. Therefore no set of equity rules could develop. Accordingly, the Maẓālim councils could hardly be regarded as true equity courts; they could neither correct procedural justice nor improve on the judicial process. For this reason, most jurists did not recognize them as courts at all, for they paid little or no attention to the law.[9]

Closely connected with the judicial process relevant to equity is the institution of *futya* (*iftā'*)—equivalent to the Roman institution of the *jus respondendi*—in which the principle of consultation (*shūra*) is given practical expression. The jurist who exercises *iftā'* is called the *mufti*, whose function consists mainly in answering questions relating to law. Since the law evolved as a jurist law, the need for interpretation was essential for its development. Moreover, the *mufti*'s opinion (*fatwa*) provided flexibility for the law, since reason for the *fatwa* was not required. So equity might be the basis for the *mufti*'s legal opinion, provided it was consistent with the general legal and moral principles of the law.[10] But *fatwas* could lay no claim to altering specific rules, since they were *respons* to practical situations. In its early development, the *iftā'* was exercised by private jurists, but it gradually passed under state control and served as an instrument to effect a change in the scale of justice from the perspective of the individual, guided by conscience and public morality, to that of the state, whose functionaries were not always sensitive to public opinion. Compilations of *fatwas* proved useful for the development of the law and provided guidance for other *muftis* were they to seek equity.

The judicial system, needless to say, proved inadequate for the requirements of procedural justice, let alone for equity. True, in structure there existed separate courts—the Maẓālim and others—which might have developed into equity courts; but courts whose function was to correct decisions made on the basis of the law were not acceptable in principle. Moreover, the absence of the principle of separation of powers rendered the courts subservient to political pressures, which made it impossible to achieve procedural justice. Only in the modern age, when Muslim states became fully sovereign, did the judicial system begin to assert its independence and seek the paths of justice and equity. In most Muslim states, the rulers have accepted the principles of separation of powers, although the courts have not yet become immune to political pressures. Though not yet fully independent, the courts have made their position clear on the matter: unless the judicial process acts freely, legal justice and equity cannot be achieved.

Notes

1. Aristotle *Nichomachean Ethics* 1137b10. 13-14. Translation by W.D. Ross.
2. According to Aristotle, "When the law speaks universally . . . and a case arises on it which is not covered by the universal statement, then it is right, where the legislator fails us and has erred by over-simplicity, to correct the omission—to say what the legislator himself would have said had he been present, and would have put into his law if he had known" (*Nichomachean Ethics* [1137b10. 19-24]).

3. See C.K. Allen, *Law in the Making* (Oxford: Clarendon Press, 1958), pp. 368-69.
4. For the nature and functions of the praetorship, see Barry Nicholas, *An Introduction to Roman Law* (Oxford: Clarendon Press, 1962), pp. 19-28.
5. See J.W. Ehrlich, ed., *Blackstone's Commentaries* (San Carlos, Calif.: Nourse, 1959), pt. 2, pp. 23-37, 269-78; and Allen, pp. 382-96.
6. See Abdallah Ibn al-Muqaffa', "Risāla fī al-Ṣaḥāba," *Rasā'il al-Bulaghā'*, 3d ed., ed. M. Kurd 'Ali (Cairo: Lajanat al-Ta'līf wa-al-Tarjamah, 1946), pp. 117-34.
7. For other cases of *ḥīyal*, see Ibn Qayyīm al-Jawzīyah, *I'lām al-Mūwaqqi'īn 'an rabb al-'ālamīn*, 4 vols. (Cairo: al-Maktabah al-Tijārīyah, 1955) 3: 264ff.
8. For the composition and functions of the Maẓālim councils, see 'Ali Ibn Muḥammad al-Māwardī, *Kitāb al-aḥkām al-sulṭānīyah*, ed. M. Enger (Bonn, 1853), pp. 128-64.
9. Ibid., pp. 140-41. Apart from the Maẓālim councils, there were other special courts, such as the army and *shurṭah*, established to deal with limited jurisdiction. But these courts, though separate from the regular courts, observed the same law enforced by the courts and could hardly be considered to function as equity courts. Nor could other courts presided over by the *ḥājib* (chamberlain), who derived his power of jurisdiction from the imam or the *wazīr* to deal with specific civil litigations, be considered equity courts, since they too functioned as special courts and applied the same law as regular courts.
10. The *muftī*'s opinion might also be based on *ijtihād* (personal reasoning), which expresses his own personal discretion for equity. For the use of reason as a source of equity, see John Maqdisi, "Legal Logic and Equity in Islamic Law," *American Journal of Comparative Law* 33 (1985): 63-92.

The Devolution of the Perfect State: Plato, Ibn Rushd, and Ibn Khaldun

MĀJID FAKHRY

I

The concept of a perfect state is not an empirical one arrived at through observation or induction. The stark realities of political life and the failure of ruler and ruled alike, throughout human history, to live up to the most modest expectations have militated against the possibility of approaching, however tentatively, the ideal of moral and political perfection. However, there is in human nature an undeniable urge to seek perfection, and, accordingly, it may be useful to inquire how the concept of a perfect state actually arises. To describe it as an aspiration of human nature clearly begs the question, since the question might still be asked: How does this aspiration itself arise? The aspirant, in any case, must have a vision or mental conception of what a perfect state would really look like. I will call this vision "utopian" and contend that the father of all utopianism is really Plato of Athens (432-348 B.C.). No other philosopher has been so obsessed with the concept of perfection, not only as a mode of being which belonged to the soul prior to its terrestrial existence, but to what the whole system of archetypes or ideas, which, for him, formed the very stuff of reality.

Prior to Plato, the Greek poets, especially Homer and Hesiod, had depicted the gods as partaking of a mode of being which by Plato's standards was far from being morally perfect; hence his vehement strictures in the *Republic* against the poets for ascribing shameful and immoral actions to the gods, or their ability, like magicians, to appear in various forms. For, as he observes:

> The divine nature must be perfect in every way, and would therefore be the last thing to suffer transformation.[1]

In the biblical tradition, which was perpetuated in the Koran, the concept of God's transcendence insured His unqualified perfection. (That He is occasionally guilty of some of the lapses of the Homeric gods, exhibiting jealousy, venom, or partisanship, need not detain us here.) The perfection of this transcendent God sets the stage for the perfection of his favorite creation, Adam, made in His image and likeness, at least up to the time of his expulsion from Eden.

We might call the origin of the Platonic concept of perfection philosophical, and that of the biblical concept theological. These two concepts are by no means the only possible ones, but they are the most significant for the purposes of the present study. For Ibn Rushd (d. A.D. 1198), the origin of the perfect state, as we shall see, is partly philosophical or Platonic, partly theological or Islamic, whereas for Ibn Khaldun (d. A.D. 1406), it is thoroughly theological or Islamic.

II

However, it is not with the concept of the perfect state as such that I will be concerned in this paper, but rather with its devolution, or the process of its progressive deterioration and the principal forces which contribute to this process. Plato, it will be recalled, had described in Book VIII of the *Republic* how the ideal or aristocratic state will, under the pressure of inexorable forces, degenerate first into the timocratic, then the oligarchic, the democratic, and finally the despotic types.[2] The forces which cause this degeneration, according to him, are partly cosmic, stemming from a universal law of change or mutability, and partly genetic, stemming from the fallibility of the guardians responsible for the breeding of the citizens in determining the right seasons of procreation.[3]

At the root of the transition from the ideal to the inferior constitutional forms, argues Plato, is the breakdown of political unity and the rise of civil strife, accompanied by an insatiable lust for gain at the top. In timocracy, military virtues are cultivated or admired, whereas in oligarchy it is the passion for money that is the ruling principle. This passion ultimately leads to the splitting of the state into two: the city of the rich and that of the poor, with the two constantly plotting against each other. As the rich grow richer through usury and other devious means, and are weakened by "luxurious indolence of body and mind," the poor suddenly wake up to their own importance and strength by reason of their numbers and their ruggedness. "Lean and sunburnt," they conclude that their enemies are rich because they themselves are cowards, and eventually rise against their enemies, seize power, and distribute property and office equally among all the citizens by lot. In addition, they declare their commitment to the ideal of liberty for all, and thus the third degenerate form of government, democracy, comes into being, according to

Plato.[4] Finally the general lawlessness which democracy inevitably breeds will lead to despotism, or the monopoly of power by a demagogue who, originally acclaimed by the masses as their liberator, soon becomes their oppressor.[5]

III

My main purpose in this paper is to show that both Ibn Rushd, in his commentary on Plato's *Republic*, extant in Hebrew and Latin (and now in two English translations),[6] and Ibn Khaldun, in the political parts of his *Prolegomena*,[7] are dependent on the *Republic* in their account of the devolution of the perfect state, identified by Ibn Rushd with aristocratic kingship or the state based on the Law, on the one hand, and by Ibn Khaldun with the Islamic caliphate on the other.

Before I proceed, however, a word is needed to explain why the great Aristotelian commentator, Averroes, has chosen to write a commentary on (or rather a paraphrase of) the *Republic* of Plato instead of the *Politics* of Aristotle. The reason is one of the strange accidents of literary history; the *Politics* is the only major work of Aristotle to have gone untranslated into Arabic during the classical period. (In fact, it was first translated from Greek by Augustine Barbara in 1957.) Averroes, who does not appear to be aware of this fact, simply states in his preface that he undertook to comment on Plato's *Politics* (*siyāsah*) "since Aristotle's book on governance has not yet fallen into our hands."[8]

I will not dwell on the paraphrase as a whole, but only on Ibn Rushd's comments on the transformation of the perfect state into the four corrupt forms and the way in which Ibn Khaldun was undoubtedly influenced by them in his account of the stages through which the state passes. In his comments Ibn Rushd tends, in general, to follow Plato rather closely, but departs from him on occasion to apply his conclusions to the political situation in Arab Spain during the eleventh and twelfth centuries.

Like Plato, Ibn Rushd recognizes, as already mentioned, that the transformation of the ideal state is the result of cosmic and genetic factors which are almost unavoidable and which lead to the rise of timocracy, a state in which wisdom is superceded by honor as the goal of the state or its rulers.[9] The deterioration of the state at this point is not complete, since honor is the closest thing to wisdom and a shadow thereof. However, timocracy bears within it the seeds of further deterioration: first into oligarchy, in which the love for money predominates; secondly to democracy, in which love for liberty holds sway; and finally to despotism, in which lust for power is the ruling principle.

In all these transformations, it is wealth which, according to Ibn Rushd, plays the most nefarious role. At first the timocratic ruler is not excessively moved by love of money, but as his nature is flawed as he grows older, his love for money grows by the day.[10] As this love intensifies, the ruler and his cohorts "accord *dirhams* and *dinārs* a shameful honor," and the government of the strong gives way to the government of the rich. Oligarchy next changes into democracy, because the rich proceed to encourage the young to spend their money as freely as they please, in accordance with the twin precepts of liberty and equality, which are the hallmarks of democracy. Sensing their numerical strength, the poor turn like drones upon the rich and, with the assistance of strangers, plunder and despoil them of their wealth and take the reins of government.[11]

Although, according to both Plato and Ibn Rushd, democracy is capable of breeding any form of government because of its variegated fabric, its natural offspring is despotism. In their cult of excessive freedom, the people, especially the propertied class, turn to a popular hero who becomes their champion. However, instead of serving their interests, he serves his own; he concentrates power in his own hands, subjugates the masses, and despoils them of their wealth. Here, too, the despot finds it necessary to rely on "wicked foreigners" as his bodyguards or retainers, to the exclusion of his fellow citizens, whom he no longer trusts. In what I take to be a reference to the bond of solidarity or kinship (*'aṣabīyah*) which Ibn Khaldun later placed at the center of his political theory, Ibn Rushd argues that the despot, once in power, will begin to conspire against the "association" which originally appointed him as its ruler. The "association," feeling betrayed, rises up in rebellion against him, and when they fail to remove him by force, his hold over them is simply consolidated.[12] This kind of transformation of democracy into tyranny, according to Ibn Rushd, actually took place in Cordova after A.D. 1106. The Almoravid dynasty, founded by the Berber chief Yusuf Ibn Tashfin (A.D. 1061-1106), was originally benevolent, but soon turned into tyranny under his successors. At first, under its founder, the reign of this dynasty was based on the Holy Law; but under his son Ali (A.D. 1106-43) it became a timocracy, then a "hedonistic" democracy under his grandson Tashfin (A.D. 1143-46) and finally disintegrated into tyranny.[13] Ibn Rushd gives as the date of this unfortunate development the year A.H. 540 (A.D. 1145), corresponding, roughly, to the reign of Almohades, who succeeded the Almoravids in A.D. 1147 and under whose rule Ibn Rushd himself flourished.[14]

IV

Ibn Khaldun was most probably acquainted with Ibn Rushd's paraphrase of the *Republic.* A tradition ascribes to him the writing of epitomes of Ibn Rushd's works.[15] I hope to show in this section that Ibn Khaldun's concept of the transformation of the state and its eventual dissolution is influenced directly by Ibn Rushd's analysis and, indirectly, by Plato's. More specifically, the five stages through which the state passes and the factors determining this dissolution are analogous to, if not identical with, Ibn Rushd's.

To begin, Ibn Khaldun distinguishes two types of government, the one "rational," resting on laws promulgated by "the learned, the dignitaries of the state and the sagacious elements in it", and the other "religious," resting on laws laid down by "God through the Lawgiver [the Prophet], who determines and promulgates them."[16] Insofar as "religious" government, identified by Ibn Khaldun with the caliphate, ministers to the welfare of mankind both in this life and in the life to come, it is clearly superior to the "rational" identified with "natural kingship." The ideal caliphal regime, which started following the Prophet's death in A.D. 632, endured, according to Ibn Khaldun, throughout the reigns of Mu'āwīyah (A.D. 661-80) and his immediate successors and the first group of Abbasid caliphs until the reign of Hārūn al-Rashīd (A.D. 786-809) and his immediate successors, whereupon "the essential attributes of the Caliphate vanished and only its name remained, the whole matter becoming pure kingship."[17] In spelling out the causes of this transformation, Ibn Khaldun explicitly mentions two: (a) the way in which power was used as a means of domination or subjection and (b) the pursuit of luxury and indulgence in the pleasures of the body.

In contrast, Ibn Rushd draws the line of demarcation between the "virtuous rule" of the Orthodox caliphs (A.D. 632-61) and timocracy, the first form of degenerate rule, more specifically at the beginning of the Umayyad period (A.D. 661-750). During the early period, he says, the Arabs "imitated the virtuous government" (Plato's aristocratic kingship). "Then they were transformed into timocrats in the days of Mu'āwīyah,"[18] founder of the Umayyad dynasty. Ibn Khaldun, who appears to accept Ibn Rushd's premises, is at pains to whitewash Mu'āwīyah and his immediate successors up to 'Abd al-Malik's reign (A.D. 685-705). For Mu'āwīyah did not oppose 'Alī, the fourth Orthodox caliph, out of malice; he argues, "he sought the right, but erred."[19]

V

A more graphic instance of Ibn Khaldun's dependence on Ibn Rushd's theory of the transformation of the state is his well-known theory of the five stages through which the state passes before its final dissolution.[20] He begins, like Ibn Rushd, with a cohesive stage in which the ruler is bent on consolidating his authority and which he describes as "the stage of achieving the set goal and subjugating the opponents and recalcitrants." During this stage, the ruler shares the privileges and advantages of office equitably with his subjects, drawn originally from his own kinsmen, as stipulated by the principle of tribal solidarity (*'aṣabīyah*). This principle is soon shattered as the ruler lords it over these subjects and bars them from sharing with him in the fruits of political and military victory. To secure his throne, he can no longer rely on the support of kinsmen, but must rely on foreign clients (sing. *mawla*) and mercenaries, on whom he lavishes honor, privilege, and wealth.[21] Thus from a "timocratic" regime, the state soon passes into an oligarchy and then into tyranny. The final collapse of the state comes when, following a period of relative stability and prosperity, the ruler begins to squander the public treasure on the gratification of his pleasures or those of his retainers, who are soon corrupted by soft living and luxury and can no longer render him the services they were intended to render. Ibn Khaldun describes this final stage of deterioration as a form of aging attended by "incurable sickness" from which the state cannot possibly recover.[22]

VI

It should be noted at this point that Ibn Khaldun appears to depart from the Platonic-Averroist model in a number of ways. According to him, theocracy, the ideal or divinely ordained state, is succeeded by timocracy, designated by him as "natural kingship." Timocracy next passes into oligarchy and then into downright tyranny, without passing through democracy, which Plato regarded in *Republic* VIII, 562D., as its necessary predecessor. However, it is noteworthy that Plato quite inadvertently had explicitly stated earlier that "a democracy is so free that it contains a sample of every kind," so that a state founder "ought first to visit this emporium of constitutions and choose the model he likes best."[23] In other words, democracy could be regarded as the fertile ground for the growth of any kind of constitution and not exclusively tyranny. Conscious perhaps of this inconsistency, Ibn Rushd is less dogmatic; "the democratic cities," he writes, "*mostly* change into tyranny and tyrannical cities."[24] Even the ideal (or virtuous) city, and, indeed, any kind of constitution, could arise from democracy, because they all exist potentially in it, as he says.[25] As to the predecessor of democracy, which Plato had identified as oligarchy, here, too, Ibn Rushd is in apparent disagreement with Plato, since for him democracy grows out of the "necessary city," a state which in the Arabic political tradition initiated by al-Fārābī (d. A.D. 950) is the primordial form of political organization. This "necessary city" is the first type to grow up by nature, and from it democracy as well as the remaining types eventually develop.[26] Plato, who was more interested in determining the right moral and political relations, especially justice, binding the various parts of the state together, did not altogther ignore the "necessary state." At the very outset of his account of the genesis of the state in the *Republic*, he identifies the essential economic and social needs which lead to political association.[27] However, his remarks on these needs are very brief, and accordingly he does not list a necessary state among the five generic types which form the core of his constitutional theory, a gap which is filled in the Arabic tradition by al-Fārābī, whom Ibn Rushd follows in this regard. For this tenth-century philosopher, the "necessary city" is characterized by "collaboration in the acquisition of all that is necessary for the upkeep of the body" through such means as husbandry, tending of flocks, and even highway robbery.[28]

VIII

We might call this transition from the necessary city to the democratic and subsequently the other constitutional forms, as described by al-Fārābī and Ibn Rushd, the "evolution," or upward movement, of the state. This paper, however, was intended to deal with the devolution of the state, or its downward movement, and the parallels between Ibn Rushd's and Ibn Khaldun's accounts of this devolution. These can now be summed up as follows:

For both writers, the devolution of the state begins at the top, as a consequence of political divisions which the despotic policies of the ruler are bound to generate. From a cohesive political system the state now passes into one racked by dissension. The unity which originally held the state together under a single ruler enjoying the full support and loyalty of his kinsmen-subjects is now broken, and the state is launched on its career of gradual deterioration. For Plato, too, "revolution always starts from the outbreak of internal dissension in the ruling class. The constitution cannot be upset for long because that class is of one mind, however small it may be."[29]

A specific cause of the state's devolution is the love of money. Interpreting Plato, Ibn Rushd writes:

> Now this lordship [timocracy] is the first lordship that Plato asserts the virtuous city is transformed into, because preference for honor, violence and love of lording it over prevail over the souls of the virtuous.[30]

But this is only the first step. At first the timocratic ruler, moved exclusively by honor, despises money, but as he grows older there grows in him the love for money and thus the stage is set for the rise of the next corrupt form, oligarchy, which is essentially the rule of the rich. This state, too, is rent by dissension and is, in fact, not a single city but two, a city of the rich and a city of the poor.[31] Hence to the evil of disunity is now added that of avarice. Ibn Khaldun elaborates on this point at great length and describes how, from the third stage through to the last, the ruler is moved to follow the "natural human bent" of accumulating wealth and spending it either on ambitious public projects or on his pleasures and those of his retainers on a grand scale.[32] Plato, too, saw in "the flow of gold" the secret of timocracy's downfall, and argued that oligarchy, which is its successor, is essentially a mixed state which has lost its unity and in which the measure of moral and social standing is no longer honor or virtue, but simply wealth.[33]

An ancillary cause of the devolution of the state is the eventual dependence of the ruler on foreign aides. Plato had observed in connection with the rise of democracy that, when strife between rich and poor becomes rampant, one or the other of the conflicting parties will call in allies from outside.[34] Dependence on foreigners, however, reaches its pitch when democracy eventually degenerates into tyranny, and the tyrant, fearing for his own life, demands a bodyguard, which is recruited either from emancipated slaves or foreign mercenaries, whom he supports from the public treasury.[35]

Both Ibn Rushd and Ibn Khaldun stress the need of the ruler to turn to "evil foreigners," as Ibn Rushd calls them, since he can no longer trust his own subjects. Ibn Khaldun links this development to the weakening of the bond of tribal solidarity, which was the hallmark of the state's cohesion, as was already mentioned. Like other Arab historians, he imputes the downfall of the Islamic caliphate in large measure to its dependence, starting with the reign of al-Mu'taṣim (A.D. 833-42), on foreign "clients and mercenaries" (*Ahl al-wilāyah wa-al-iṣṭinā'*). This Abbasid caliph was actually the first ruler to enlist the support of Turkish, Daylami, and Persian elements.[36]

Other parallels between Ibn Rushd and Ibn Khaldun, stemming ultimately from Plato, may be briefly outlined. Plato refers at the beginning of his account of the devolution of the ideal state, as we have seen, to inexorable genetic and cosmic forces which bring about its eventual downfall. It is not idle to draw a parallel between this theory of genetic and cosmic determinism and Ibn Khaldun's own theory of historical determinism. After all, the transition from a nomadic to a sedentary phase is subject to ecological as well as genetic factors, without which the social and political permutations to which the state is exposed cannot be understood. (Ibn Rushd, I might mention, simply expounds Plato's own view of genetic and cosmic determinism with tacit approval.)

There is, finally, a key feature which all three theories of the state and its devolution have in common: the obsession with psychology as a clue to understanding political and social change. It is well known how Plato, in the *Republic*, had developed a nearly complete parallel between the state and the individual, between the types of constitutions and the corresponding types of individual souls. Ibn Rushd explicitly and Ibn Khaldun implicitly corroborate this psychological-political model, ascribing decisive importance to the goals, attitudes, and idiosyncracies of the ruler at every stage of political and social development. This idea can best be understood as a legacy of Plato's "psychological politics" or "political psychology."

Notes

1. Plato *Republic* II. 380. (London: Oxford University Press, 1966). For Plato's strictures against the poets, see 376f, passim.
2. See ibid., 544f.
3. Ibid., 546.
4. Ibid., 555f.
5. Ibid., 563f.
6. See E. I. J. Rosenthal, *Averroes' Commentary on Plato's "Republic"* (Cambridge: Cambridge University Press, 1956, 1966, and 1969); and Ralph Lerner, *Averroes on Plato's "Republic"* (Ithaca and London: Cornell University Press, 1974).
7. See Ibn Khaldun, *al-Muqaddimah* (Beirut, n.d.), pp. 154-225. Cf. *The Muqaddimah*, trans. F. Rosenthal, abridged and edited by N. J. Dawood (Princeton: Princeton University Press, 1967), pp. 123-66. Hereafter F. Rosenthal.
8. Lerner, *Averroes*, p. 4.
9. Ibid., pp. 117f. Cf. *Republic*, 548.
10. Lerner, *Averroes*, p. 119.
11. Ibid., pp. 126f. Cf. *Republic* 556.

12. Lerner, *Averroes*, p. 135.
13. Ibid., pp. 125, 133.
14. Cf. ibid., p. 133.
15. For references, see M. Fakhry, *A History of Islamic Philosophy* (London: Longman, 1983), p. 324 and notes.
16. Ibn Khaldun, *al-Muqaddimah*, p. 190. Cf. F. Rosenthal, pp. 154, 256f.
17. *al-Muqaddimah*, p. 208. Cf. F. Rosenthal, pp. 165f.
18. Lerner, *Averroes*, p. 121.
19. Ibn Khaldun, *al-Muqaddimah*, p. 205. Cf. F. Rosenthal, p. 164.
20. *al-Muqaddimah*, pp. 175f. Cf. F. Rosenthal, pp. 141f. The five stages through which the state passes are given by Ibn Khaldun as follows: *first*, achieving the set goal and subjugating opponents and recalcitrants; *second*, lording it over kinsmen and monopolizing power; *third*, leisure and tranquility in the reaping of the fruits of authority; *fourth*, contentment and pacification; *fifth*, extravagance and lavish expenditure in the gratification of one's desires and those of one's retainers.
21. Ibid., p. 183. Cf. pp. 175f. and F. Rosenthal, pp. 141, 135.
22. Ibn Khaldun, *al-Muqaddimah*, p. 176. Cf. F. Rosenthal, p. 142.
23. *Republic* 557C.
24. Lerner, *Averroes*, p. 130.
25. Ibid., p. 128.
26. Ibid.
27. *Republic* 369-71.
28. See al-Fārābī, *al-Siyāsah al-Madanīyah* (Beirut: The Catholic Press, 1971), p. 88. Cf. *al-Madīnah al-fāḍilah* (Beirut: The Catholic Press, 1959), p. 110.
29. *Republic* 545C. Cf. 465B.
30. Lerner, *Averroes*, p. 118.
31. Ibid., p. 122. Cf. *Republic* 550.
32. Ibn Khaldun, *al-Muqaddimah*, pp. 176, 206f. Cf. F. Rosenthal, pp. 142, 245.
33. See *Republic* 550.
34. *Republic* 556.
35. Ibid., 567f.
36. Ibn Khaldun, *al-Muqaddimah*, pp. 206, 155. Cf. F. Rosenthal, pp. 166, 124. For historical details, see Philip K. Hitti, *History of the Arabs* (London: Macmillan, 1953), pp. 466f.

al-Khwārizmī's Concept of Algebra

ROSHDI RASHED

I

Muḥammad Ibn Mūsa al-Khwārizmī[1] wrote his renowned *Kitāb al-Jabr wa-al-muqābalah*[2] in Baghdad between A.D. 813 and 833, during the reign of al-Mamūn. It was the first time in history that the term *algebra* appeared in a title to designate it as a discipline.[3] Its recognition was not only insured by the title, but was confirmed by the formulation of a new technical vocabulary intended to specify objects and procedures.

The event was crucial and was recognized as such, as much by ancient as by modern historians; its importance, furthermore, was not lost on the mathematical community of the time. Even in al-Khwārizmī's lifetime, or at least shortly afterwards, mathematicians were quick to comment on his book. Of his immediate successors alone, Ibn Turk, Thābit Ibn Qurrah, al-Ṣidnāni, Sinān Ibn al-Fatḥ, Abū Kāmil, and Abū al-Wafa al-Buzjānī should be cited. Some of these commentaries clearly constituted a fundamental contribution to the formulation of algebra. In writing the history of their discipline, these mathematicians, like their successors, agreed unanimously to assign precedence to al-Khwārizmī.[4] There was one dissenting voice: that of Ibn Barza, who gave that honor to his grandfather, a claim rejected out of hand by Abū Kāmil.[5]

Although generally accepted, these few facts are difficult to interpret. In fact, as long as he remains unacquainted with the work of mathematicians preceding al-Khwārizmī, the historian is likely to find himself in a position which at first sight seems enigmatic. But this is a situation that, at least for the time being, remains irremediable.[6] The question is still open how this newly conceived discipline was developed, and how it is that this particular contribution, several aspects of which suggest the culmination of past activity, emerges as a radical departure. Unable to find a satisfactory answer, historians have for some time engaged in an endless debate around two complementary themes: the origins of algebra and the sources used by al-Khwārizmī, referring in turn to the Hellenistic mathematician (Euclid or Diophantus, depending upon the case) and to Indian or, more recently, Babylonian mathematics. The very fact that so many contradictory opinions exist indicates that no single one can prevail and that no historian has been able to establish effectively a link of any kind between al-Khwārizmī and any of the supposed sources. The difficulty is the same whether it is a question of the work as a whole or of chapters of more restricted scope, such as those concerned with the measurement of surface and volume, *al-Misāḥah.* One has only to remember the contradictory theories on the relationship between al-Khwārizmī's book and the Mishnat ha-middot.[7]

It is not uncommon under these conditions for historians to have recourse to theories which raise more problems than they resolve, such as the well-known hypothesis of the "geometric algebra" of the Greeks. In addition to the problem of establishing the genesis of al-Khwārizmī's contribution to the history of algebra is the further problem of a different order. Even if one accepts the breakdown of al-Khwārizmī's book to identify the traces of ancient mathematics, it must be allowed that these are merely vestiges which do not in the least clarify the theoretical form of the new knowledge. This paper will be confined to an examination of this form in an attempt to grasp the concept of algebra as formulated by al-Khwārizmī. Then it will perhaps be possible to make a more rigorous enquiry into the genesis of al-Khwārizmī's algebra.

II

In the introduction to his book al-Khwārizmī announces his plan: to provide a manual which people could use for arithmetical problems, for commercial transactions, in cases of inheritance, and for the measurement of their lands.[8] Sections of his book develop these themes.

The first section, a theoretical one, is concerned with this method —*ḥisāb*—of algebra and *al-muqābalah,* its early terminology and concepts. In the second, al-Khwārizmī determines the bases of the normal procedures which allow practical calculations to be reduced to fundamental algebraic types. The last sections, of purely practical intent, are concerned with the application of this method to commercial transactions, to land surveys, to geometric measurements, and, lastly, to testaments. From reading al-Khwārizmī's book it is clear that algebra appears from the outset as a theoretical discipline, extended to be applicable in both the field of numbers and of metric geometry.

Therefore, if algebra is an arithmetic—*ḥisāb*, as al-Khwārizmī writes—

it is so for at least two reasons. On the one hand, the laws of calculation can be applied to different objects (arithmetic or geometric) once formulated in the primitive terms of algebra—number, unknown, and unknown squared (al-Khwārizmī had studied these laws from a book now preserved in its Latin translation).[9] On the other hand, algebra is found to have been envisaged from the outset with all the possibilities of application, and as such answers to the practical needs of mathematics. It may be apodictic knowledge, but algebra is also an applied science. Its object is not specific since it is concerned with numbers as well as with geometric size.

It is impossible to overstress the originality of the conception and style of al-Khwārizmī's algebra, which did not rise from any "arithmetic" tradition, not even that of Diophantus. Analysis of al-Khwārizmī's book reveals two kinds of primitive terms: those purely algebraic and those common to algebra and arithmetic. The algebraic terms, as already mentioned, are the unknown, designated without distinction —root, thing, and its square, *māl*. To these may be added rational positive numbers, the laws of arithmetic $\pm$, $\times/\div$, $\sqrt{}$, and the equals sign. All of these operations are designated by words of unequal occurrence. For example, speaking of multiplication, al-Khwārizmī uses *ḍarb*—to multiply—but uses *ḍ'f* just as often; and more rarely (two appearances each) he uses *tny* and *tlt*. The relation *fī* functions equally as an operator of multiplication according to the model "n *fī* (in, by) n."

As regards algebraic terms proper, it would be astonishing if al-Khwārizmī knew only the two cited previously. In his book, it should be noted, he deals with a problem whose context suggests that he knows the third power, although this term is not named by al-Khwārizmī. He writes in effect: "If one speaks of a square—*māl*—multiplied by its root, it comes to three times the first square." By *māl* al-Khwārizmī almost invariably intends the square of the unknown. He does express the same term *the thing*, at times. However, juxtaposed to the root, the term *māl* only expresses the first sense, thus: $x^2 . x = 3x^2$. This being established, even independently of the example, al-Khwārizmī must have known the cubic power, at least. It is known that the cubic root was extracted at that time, as in the *Opuscule* in the measurement of the plane and spherical by Banū Mūsa,[10] and that the solid number can be found in the al-Hajjāj translation of Euclid's *Elements*. Banū Mūsa and al-Hajjāj were contemporaries and, so to speak, the colleagues of al-Khwārizmī, at the "House of Wisdom." The extension of the notion of algebraic power was effected, furthermore, after a single reading of al-Khwārizmī's book by at least two mathematicians independently from each other, Abū Kāmil Shujā' and Sinān Ibn al-Fatḥ.[11] The latter explicitly formulated the general concept of integer positive power. It seems, then, that if al-Khwārizmī limited the usage of algebraic terms to two, it was not the result of a misunderstanding of the superior powers of the unknown, but reflects a whole concept of algebra, its domain, and its scope. It is equally necessary to return to the constituent concepts of algebraic theory in order to understand al-Khwārizmī's intention and at the same time to grasp the sense and the import of this deliberate limitation to primitive terms.

The principal concepts used by al-Khwārizmī are the first- and second-degree equation, the related binomial and trinomials, normal form, the algorithmic solution, and the demonstrability of the solution formulae. However, if one wishes to understand how these concepts are realized and coordinated in the original algebraic theory, the best method is a rapid perusal of al-Khwārizmī's explanation. Having introduced the terms of his theory, he writes: "Of these three types, some can be equal to others, as when you say: squares are equal to roots, squares are equal to a number."[12] He continues: "I have found that these three types—*al-ḍurūb, modus*—which are the roots, the squares and the numbers combine, and that there are therefore three composite kinds—*ajnās muqtarinah, genera composita*— which are squares, plus roots equal a number; roots plus a number equal squares."[13] It can then be seen that al-Khwārizmī retains three binomial equations and three trinomial equations:

$$ax^2 = bx \qquad ax^2 + bx = c$$
$$ax^2 = c \qquad ax^2 + c = bx$$
$$bx = c \qquad ax^2 = bx + c$$

Even at this stage, al-Khwārizmī's text can be seen to be distinct not only from the Babylonian tablets, but also from Diophantus' *Arithmetica.* It is no longer a question of a series of problems to resolve, but of an exposition which departs from primitive terms in which the combinations must give all possible prototypes for equations, which henceforward explicitly constitute the true object of study. On the other hand, the idea of an equation for its own sake appears from the beginning and, one could say, in a generic manner, insofar as it does not simply emerge in the course of solving a problem, but is specifically called on to define an infinite class of problems. To gauge the extent of the breakthrough, it is sufficient to recall a survival of the ancient tradition in al-Khwārizmī's book. Having found the value of the unknown, he concludes by giving that of the square. This appears to derive from a tradition which was not concerned with the study of equations but with the solution of problems—with finding, for example, a square, such as its product by a given number is equal to its root by another given number.

In this situation it might be anticipated that al-Khwārizmī's exposition would evolve in an ever more general manner. Indeed, a second stage of generality is attained when the notion of normal form is introduced. al-Khwārizmī requires the systematic reduction—*yarudd, reducere*—of each equation to the corresponding regular form. For the fourth equation, for example, he writes: "In the same way, if one postulates two squares, or three, or more or less, reduce that to one square, and reduce the roots and numbers found at the same time to that to which you have reduced the squares."[14] This is true, in particular, for trinomial equations:

$$x^2 + px = q, \quad x^2 = px + q, \quad x^2 + q = px$$

Everything is therefore positioned to allow the establishment of algorithmic formulae to solutions. al-Khwārizmī then deals with each of the three cases. The fact that the coefficients are given in no way diminishes the generality of the reasoning. Take the best-known case, the first of the three equations cited, with $p = 10$, $q = 39$. al-Khwārizmī writes: "The rule in this—*fabābahu, cujus regula*—is that you divide the roots into halves. In this problem five is the result, which you multiply by itself, you have twenty-five, you add it to thirty-nine, you have sixty-four; you take its root which is eight, you deduct from it half of the roots, which is five, and three is left, which is the root of the square you are looking for, and the square is nine.[15] In other words, he obtains the following expression:

$$x = [(P/2)^2 + q]^{1/2} - P/2.$$

For the other two cases, he obtains the following expressions:

$$x = P/2 + [(P/2)^2 + q]^{1/2}$$
$$x = P/2 \pm [(P/2)^2 - q]^{1/2}, \text{ if } (P/2)^2 > q.$$

In this last case, he condenses it: if $(P/2)^2 = q$, "then the root of the square is equal to half of the roots, exactly, without surplus or diminution"; if $(P/2)^2 < q$, "then the problem is impossible—*Fa-al-mas'ālah mustaḥīlah-tunc quaestio est impossibilis.*"[16] To conclude this chapter, al-Khwārizmī writes:

These are the six types which I mentioned at the beginning of my book. I have finished the explanation and I have stated that there are three types, the roots of which are not divided into halves. I have shown the rules for these—*qiyāsaha, regulas*—and their necessity—*iḍṭirāraha, necessitas*. Concerning those of the three remaining kinds, the roots of which must be divided into two, I have explained them with correct reasons (*bi-'abwāb ṣaḥīḥah*), and I have invented for each a figure by which the reason for the division can be recognized.[17]

al-Khwārizmī demonstrates the different formulae not only algebraically but with the aid, he writes, of figures—*ṣūrah, forma*—that is, by means of the notion of the equality of surfaces. Each of these demonstrations is presented by al-Khwārizmī as the "cause"—*'illah*—of the solution. This treatment was very probably inspired by a recent knowledge of the *Elements*. In addition, al-Khwārizmī not only requires each case to be demonstrated, but occasionally proposes two demonstrations for a single type of equation. Such requirement adequately illustrates the extent of progress and certainly distinguishes al-Khwārizmī from the Babylonians, but also, in his systematic approach, from Diophantus. It is thus, in a brief resumé, that al-Khwārizmī's exposition evolves, and that he handles preceding concepts. All problems dealt with by means of algebra must be reduced to an equation, to a single unknown, and to rational positive coefficients of almost the second degree. Such is the only equation admissible in al-Khwārizmī's book. Algebraic procedures, transposition and reduction, are then applied so that the equation may be written in regular form. The procedures then make possible the idea of the solution as a simple question of decision: an algorithm for each class of problem. The formula for the solution is then justified mathematically with the help of a protogeometric demonstration. al-Khwārizmī then finds himself in a position to write that everything stemming from algebra "must lead you to one of the six types which I have described in my book."[18]

al-Khwārizmī's exposition is followed by four brief chapters dedicated to the study of certain aspects of the application of elementary laws of arithmetic to the most simple expressions of algebra. He studies, in order, multiplication, addition and subtraction, and the division and extraction of the square root. For example, this is what he proposes to show in his short chapter on multiplication: "how to multiply objects [the unknown] which are roots, by each other, if they are single, or if they are added to a number, or if a number is subtracted from them,"[19] that is to say, products of the following type:

$$(a \pm bx)\ (c \pm dx)\quad a, b, c, d, \in Q+$$

These chapters are far more important for the intention behind them than for the results that they enclose. If one considers al-Khwārizmī's declarations, the position that he gives these chapters (immediately after the theoretical study of the quadratic equation), and finally the autonomy conferred on each, it appears that the author wished to undertake the study of algebraic calculation for its own sake, that is, the properties of binomials and trinomials considered in the preceding section of the book. However rudimentary it may seem, this study nevertheless represents the first attempt at algebraic calculation per se, since the elements of this arithmetic do not simply emerge in the course of solving different problems, but provide the subject of relatively autonomous chapters.

al-Khwārizmī's concept of algebra can now be grasped with greater precision: it concerns the theory of linear and quadratic equations with a single unknown, and the elementary arithmetic of related binomials and trinomials. If al-Khwārizmī was confined to the second degree at best, it was simply through following the notion of solution and proof in the new discipline. The solution had to be general and calculable at the same time and in a mathematical fashion, that is, geometrically founded. In fact, only a solution by means of the root answered to al-Khwārizmī's requirements. The restriction of degree, as well as that of the number of unsophisticated terms, is instantly explained.

From its true emergence, algebra can be seen as a theory of equations soluble by means of roots, and of algebraic calculations on related expressions, before the notion of the general polynomial had been formulated. This idea of algebra lasted long after al-Khwārizmī's death. His immediate successors were concerned strictly with the study of superior-degree equations, which could nevertheless be reduced to second-degree equations. Others were to be tempted by the solution of cubic equations through the radicals. al-Khayyām's refusal to accept the solution of a cubic equation by the intersection of curves as algebraic (which definition he reserves for the solution by radicals) provides further evidence of al-Khwārizmī's influence.

After his theoretical chapters al-Khwārizmī returns to the different applications of the theory, arithmetic or geometric, the great majority of which can be seen to be established on the generality of the theory. He endeavors in each case to transpose the problem into algebraic terms in order to bring it under the demonstrated types of equation. It is not until the second section of his book that he meets certain problems of Diophantine analysis.[20]

It would be useless to look for a similar theory before al-Khwārizmī. Certainly it is possible to find one or another of his concepts in certain texts of antiquity, or late antiquity, but they are never found together and are never bound into a structure such as his. It is precisely this illustrated theoretical structure that explains the apparent poverty of technique in al-Khwārizmī's algebra and the mathematician's intentional innovative terminology. Compared to the *Arithmetica* of Diophantus, for example, al-Khwārizmī's book appears to describe no more than an elementary algebraic technique; but this simplicity corresponds exactly to the limitations imposed by the constitution of the theory. Similarly, the terminology was designed to create a language capable of translating, without distinction, geometric and arithmetic terms. Thus, in expressing a requirement of the theory, the terms reflect the desire to distinguish the new knowledge.

No description of al-Khwārizmī's algebra is complete without indicating where its fertility lies. A science is defined not only by the procedures it develops, but also by its cumulative power; the obstacles generated and confronted—in short by all the channels of research that it is able to open. It is precisely in this area that al-Khwārizmī distinguishes himself from all possible predecessors: he alone determined the scope of a whole vein of algebraic research which has not yet been exhausted. This historical dimension of al-Khwārizmī's algebra must therefore be examined.

III

The different elements of classical algebra can be traced already in al-Khwārizmī's book. But to develop the traces effectively and to give body to al-Khwārizmī's concept of algebra, his successors had to diverge from his tracks. New inroads had to be made not only to surmount theoretical and technical problems which limited the execution of his program (the resolution of the cubic equation by radicals, for example), but also to aim the project in a more arithmetical direction for the development of abstract algebraic calculation. One can therefore isolate two new departures for algebra and two areas of research undertaken following al-Khwārizmī's lead but in a direction opposite to his. The first was arithmetic, the second geometric; both modified the nature of the discipline profoundly. (Of course, I can only briefly outline the results of the arithmetic tradition of algebra.)

Shortly after al-Khwārizmī's death, perhaps even during his lifetime, attempts were made to follow his lead. While Ibn Turk adopted the theory of equations to give demonstrations,[21] still protogeometric but firmer, al-Mahāni translated certain biquadratic problems from Book X of the *Elements* and cubic problems from Archimedes[22] into algebraic terms. Equally prompt was the extension of the notion of algebraic power. There are two testimonies confirming that this effort had been suggested by a reading of al-Khwārizmī's book: that of Abū Kāmil, whose work is known and has been analyzed,[23] and that of Sinān Ibn al-Fatḥ.[24] The latter studied trinomial equations which, if divided by a power taken from the unknown, are brought into the realm of al-Khwārizmī's equations, in other words, equations which consist of the following terms:

$$ax^{2n+p},\ bx^{n+p},\ cx^{p}$$

All these findings, especially Abū Kāmil's improved study of rational positive numbers, as well as other results obtained by algebraic mathematics in the study of algebraic irrationals, and finally the translation of Diophantus's *Arithmetica*, coincide with the development of the project of the "arithmetization of algebra" (as it has been called) by al-Karaji. It is concerned first, according to the words of a successor of al-Karaji, al-Samaw'al, "with operating on unknowns with every arithmetic tool, in the same way as the arithmetician operates on the known," and with opting more and more for algebraic demonstrations at the expense of geometric demonstrations. Thus the movement is towards a systematic application of elementary arithmetic procedures to algebraic expressions. This application was made possible by the first elaboration in general terms of the idea of the polynomial. It is this application, evident in al-Karaji's work, which has permitted the extension of abstract algebra and the organization of the algebraic exposition around different arithmetic operations successively applied to algebraic expressions. Furthermore, it is in this way that the best treatises on classical algebra have been presented since then. It has been shown elsewhere in detail how such a project was constituted and what the principal results were.[25]

It would be too lengthy to enumerate the consequences of this arithmetization of algebra here; but it should be remembered that algebra itself is affected—the theory of numbers, numerical analysis, and the resolution of numerical equations, as well as rational Diophantine analysis and even the logic and philosophy of mathematics. I would like to conclude here on the theory of the equation itself in order to show, with the help of unpublished and unknown documents, that, contrary to the accepted idea, the successors of al-Karaji had in fact attempted an algebraic solution to the cubic equation.

First, with regard to the theory of equations, in *al-Fahri* as well as what has already been seen in Sinān Ibn al-Fatḥ's work, the following equations can be found:

$$ax^{2n} + bx^n = c \qquad ax^{2n} + c = bx^n \qquad bx^n + c = ax^{2n}$$

But al-Karaji himself says nothing about the cubic equation.[26] It is one of his successors, al-Sulamyi, who suggests that the question preoccupied algebraist mathematicians in the tradition of al-Karaji. He himself envisages two possible kinds:

$$x^3 + ax^2 + bx = c \quad \text{and} \quad x^3 + bx = ax^2 + c.$$

However, he imposes the condition $b = (a^2/3)$. He therefore gives a true positive root for each equation:

$$x = (a^3/27 + c)^{1/3} - a/3 \quad \text{and} \quad x = (c - a^3/27)^{1/3} + a/3.$$

We may, it seems, piece together the mathematician's progress in the following manner: by a related transformation, he restores the equation to its normal form. But instead of finding the discriminant, he annuls the coefficient of the first power of the unknown in order to bring the problem to that of the extraction of the cubic root. Thus, for example, for the first equation $x \rightarrow y - a/3$ is taken for a related transformation; the equation can be rewritten as follows:

$$y^3 + py - q = o$$

Here $p = b - a^2/3$ and $q = c + a^3/27 + (b\,a/3 - a^3/9)$ postulate $b = a^2/3$; it comes to $y^3 = c + a^3/27$, whence the value of x. It should be remembered that the role of the discriminant was identified by Sharaf al-Dīn al-Ṭūsi in the particular case $x^3 - bx + c = o$.[27]

As we have seen in the preceding pages, it was therefore al-Khwārizmī who established the unity of algebra, not merely because of the generality of mathematical entities which the discipline deals with, but above all because of the generality of his procedures. It is a question of successive operations designed to turn a numerical or geometrical problem into one of equations expressed in normal form, and of equations which lead to the canonical formulae of solutions, which, moreover, must be demonstrable and calculable.

The algebra worked out by al-Khwārizmī is a science of equations and algebraic calculations on related binomials and trinomials, an autonomous discipline which commanded already its proper historical perspective and carried with it the potential of a first reform, the arithmetization of algebra.

al-Khwārizmī's contribution is clearly irreducible, reflecting the essence of mathematical rationality. If attempts to discover the origins of his algebra continue to fail, this failure may be the result of insufficient insight in analysis as much as of a lack of historical information, and of an uncontained regression in linguistic and ideological terms. Rather than ask what al-Khwārizmī may have read, it would be preferable to enquire how he conceived of what none of his predecessors had been able to conceive.

Notes

1. This is the name of the author according to the testimonies of historians, bibliographers, and mathematicians. al-Ṭabari, in his *Tārīkh al-rusul wa-al-muluk*, ed. M. Abū al-Faḍl Ibrahim (Cairo: al-Ma'ārif Press, 1966), gives his name as such in relating the events of A.H. 210: "Muḥammad Ibn Mūsa al-Khwārizmī is reported to have said . . ." (vol. 8, p. 609). However, speaking of the events of A.H. 232, he gives a list of the names of astronomers present at the death of the caliph al-Wāthiq. "Amongst those present were al-Ḥasan Ibn Sahl, the brother of al-Faḍl Ibn Sahl, al-Faḍl Ibn Isḥāq, al-Hashimi Isam'il Ibn Nubakht and Muḥammad Ibn Mūsa al-Khwārizmī al-Majūsi al-Qutrub-bulli, Sanad, the companion of Muḥammad Ibn al-Haytham and all of those interested in the stars" (ibid., vol. 9, p. 151). In view of both of al-Ṭabarī's testimonies, and taking into account the consensus of other authors, there is no need to be an expert on the period nor a philologist to see that al-Ṭabarī's second citation should read "Muḥammad Ibn Mūsa al-Khwārizmī *and* al-Majūsī al-Qutrubbullī," and that there are two people (al-Khwārizmī and al-Majūsī al-Qutrubbullī) between whom the letter *wa* has been omitted in an early copy.

   This would not be worth mentioning if a series of errors concerning the personality of al-Khwārizmī, occasionally even the origins of his knowledge, had not been made. Recently G. J. Toomer, in an article "al-Khwārizmi" in the *Dictionary of Scientific Biography* (New York: Scribners, 1973), vol. 7, p. 358, with naive confidence constructed a whole fantasy on the error, which cannot be denied the merit of amusing the reader. (All translations are by author.)
2. I refer to the edition of A. Mustafa Musharrafah and M. M. Aḥmad (Cairo: al-Jāmi'ah al-Miṣrīyah, 1939).
3. Ibn al-Nadim, *al-Fihrist*, ed. Reda Tajaddud (Tehran: n.p., 1971), pp. 334-338; see also entries under Abū Kāmil and Sinān, pp. 339-340.
4. Abū Kāmil described al-Khwārizmī as "the one who first succeeded in a book of algebra and *al-muqābalah;* who pioneered and invented all the principles in it." Cf. Abū Kāmil, mss. Kara Muṣṭafa, 369f. 2+. Cf. Sinān Ibn al-Fatḥ, who in the introduction to a small work (mss. 260 Riyāḍiyāt, National Library, Cairo, f. 95V) mentions al-Khwārizmī alone, and asserts that the science is his: "Muḥammad Ibn Mūsa al-Khwārizmī wrote a book which he called

al-Jabr wa-al-muqābalah." Still later, al-Hassan Ibn Yūsuf (in *al-Jabr wa-al-muqābalah*, mss. 200 Riyāḍiyāt, National Library, Cairo, f. 6r) wrote on the subject of al-Khwārizmī: "He was the first in the Islamic world to discover this science; he was recognized as the imam of arithmeticians, and master of that science." Lastly, Ibn Mālik al-Dimashqī (mss. 182 Riyāḍiyāt, National Library, Cairo, f. 272r) can be quoted: "You must understand that this science is the invention of the accomplished scientist Muḥammad Ibn Mūsa al-Khwārizmī." Evidence to this effect is abundant and could be continued.

5. Hajji Khalīfah notes that in a book by Abū Kāmil Shujā', *al-Waṣāya bi-al-jabr*, the author speaks of another book: "I have established, in my second book, proof of the authority and precedence in algebra and *al-muqābalah* of Muḥammad Ibn Mūsa al-Khwārizmī, and I have answered the impulsive Ibn Barza on the subject of what he attributes to 'Abd al-Ḥamīd, whom he mentions to have been his grandfather." Hajji Khalīfah, *Kashf al-ẓunūn*, 2 vols., ed. Sh. Yaltkaya (Istanbul: al-Ma'ārif, 1943) 2: 1407-8.
6. Nothing of great importance has emerged to clarify the history of mathematics in the first two centuries of the Hijrah. In a previous study of mine entitled "Algèbre et linguistique: l'analyse combinatoire dans la science Arabe" in *Philosophical Foundations of Science*, ed. by R. J. Seeger and Robert S. Cohen (Boston: D. Reidel; Boston Studies in the Philosophy of Science, vol. 11, 1974), pp. 383-99, it has been shown that linguists, lexicographers, and notably al-Khalīl Ibn Aḥmad (d. ca. A.D. 786) possessed several combinational rules. It should not, however, be concluded that they were familiar with the combinational analysis as analysis. The rules are applied but neither stated nor demonstrated. According to the late evidence of Ibn Khaldun in his *al-Muqaddimah* (Prolegomena), some elementary progressions can be found. Analysis of other documents now available, by writers, philosophers, etc., in lieu of mathematicians, surrenders information too fragmented to produce a decisive conclusion. Entirely different are the now lost arithmetic works of mathematicians, like al-Khwārizmī himself, of the third century of the Hijrah. He had drafted a book, *Kitāb al-Jam' wa-al-tafrīq*, which is as yet untraced but is mentioned by Abū Kāmil in his *al-Jabr* (mss. Qara Muṣṭafa, 379f., 110). If the content of his work can be reestablished, through patient effort, the direction of mathematics at that time could be established. But this is a privilege for the future.
7. As when Solomon Gandz sees the origins of al-Khwārizmī's section on the "measurement" of surfaces and volumes in this book. Cf. Solomon Gandz, "The Miṣhnat ha-middot and the Geometry of Muḥammad Ibn Mūsa al-Khwārizmī," in *Quellen und Studien zur Geschichte der Mathematik, Astronomie und Physik*, Abt. A, Bd. 2 (Berlin, 1932); and G. B. Sarfatti, *Mathematical Terminology in Hebrew Scientific Literature of the Middle Ages* (Jerusalem: Magnes Press, 1968) (in Hebrew).
8. al-Khwārizmī, *Kitāb al-jabr*, p. 16.
9. Cf. A. P. Juschkewitsche, "Uber ein Werk des Abū Abdallah Ibn Mūsa al-Khwārizmī al-Magusi zur Arithmetik der Inder," in *Schriftenreihe fur*

Geschichte der Naturwissenschaften, Technik und Medizin, Beiheft zum 60 von G. Harig (Leipzig, 1964). This book of al-Khwārizmī should not be confused with *Kitāb al-jam'* cited by Abū Kāmil (see note 6). In the latter, al-Khwārizmī evidently deals with arithmetic problems also.

10. *Kitāb fī ma'rifat misāhat al-ashkāl* by Banū Mūsa. Cf. the (poor) transcription given in *Rasā'il al-Ṭūsi*, 2 vols. (Hyderabad: 'Uthmānīyah Press, 1940), 2:19f.

11. Sinān Ibn al-Fatḥ (mss. 260 Riyāḍīyāt, National Library, Cairo pp. 95-104) introduces the power of the unknown in a general way. He writes: "Let us call the first of these numbers, the second root, the third square (māl), the fourth cube (*maka'ab*), the fifth square-square, the sixth *madād*, the seventh square-cube, then you will have the eighth proportion, add the ninth, and thus all you need. It is permissible to change the names, once you have understood the intention. But as it is usual to use these names, we will conform."

This is an example to show what has been described, and it is in the order of Indian mathematics:

One ten hundred thousand ten thousand number root square cube square-square
a thousand thousand ten thousand thousand square-cube
eighth proportion
one hundred thousand thousand
ninth proportion

N.B.

(1) Sinān Ibn al-Fatḥ claims precedence for this generality; he writes: "Of those who have preceded me in this science, I have seen no one, nor heard of anyone, who has written a greater work in order to name the powers. I have been pleased to form this into a book in which it is shown how to develop these names."

(2) If the term *mitad* was of Arabic origin, it would derive from the root *md*, which signifies the elongation of something, or the extension of one thing by another. It can also indicate the plural of *mudd*, a kind of measurement which originally signified the holding out of the hands for food. The reason for such a choice to signify X, or the sixth position, is not clear. It is not impossible that it was borrowed from the Persian to indicate the sixth position.

(3) Ibn al-Fatḥ makes the nth power correspond to the power $n + 1$.

(4) Finally, the definition of d^6X is multiplicative, contrary to all the additive definitions known in Arabic.

12. al-Khwārizmī, *Kitāb al-jabr*, p. 17.
13. Ibid., p. 18; if equally one of his Latin translations in G. Libri, *Histoire des sciences mathematiques en Italie*, 4 vols. (Paris, 1838) 1:225; reprinted by G. Olms, Hildesheim, Germany, 1967.
14. al-Khwārizmī, *Kitāb al-jabr*, p. 19.
15. Ibid., pp. 18-19; and the Latin translation, Libri, p. 255.
16. Ibid., pp. 20-21; and the Latin translation, Libri, p. 257.
17. Ibid., p. 21.
18. Ibid., p. 27.

19. Ibid.
20. This is in the chapter concerned with the evidence encountered of this type of problem. Cf., for example, ibid., pp. 76f.
21. Aydin Sayili, *Logical Necessity in the Mixed Equations by 'Abd al-Hamid Ibn Turk and the Algebra of His Time* (Ankara: Türk Tarih Kurumu Press, 1962), notably the Arabic text, pp. 144f.
22. See Muḥammad Ibn 'Issa al-Mahāni's commentary on Book 10 of the *Elements* (mss. Paris 2425 pp. 180-187), where $39x^2 = x^4 + 225/4$ can be found. al-Khayyām reports that al-Mahāni "was led to use algebra in the analysis of the lemma used by Archimedes, considering it to be authorized in proposition 4 of the second book of his work *On the Sphere and the Cylinder.*" "Al-Mahāni," al-Khayyām continues, "arrived at cubes, squares, and numbers forming an equation that he did not succeed in solving." Cf. my *L'oeuvre algébrique d'al-Khayyām* (Aleppo: University of Aleppo, I.H.A.S., 1981), p. 11 (French section).
23. Cf. A. Youschkevitch, *Les mathématiques arabes: VIIIe-XVe siècle* (Paris: J. Vrin, 1976), pp. 52f.
24. Ibid.
25. Cf. my study, "Recommencements de l'algèbre aux XIième et XIIième siecles," in J. F. Murdoch and E. D. Sylla, eds., *The Cultural Context of Medieval Learning* (Boston: D. Reidel; Boston Studies in the Philosophy of Science, vol. 26, 1975); and "al-Karaji," in the *Dictionary of Scientific Biography*, vol. 7, pp. 240-246.
26. Cf. my forthcoming "Note sur la résolution des équations cubiques," a paper read at the Library of Congress, March 1985.
27. Cf. my "Résolution des équations numériques et algèbre: al-Tusi-Viete," *Archive for History of Exact Sciences*, vol. 12, no. 3:243, 290.

Ibn Khaldun, the Father of Economics

IBRAHIM M. OWEISS

In his *Prolegomena* (*The Muqaddimah*), 'Abd al-Raḥmān Ibn Muḥammad Ibn Khaldūn al-Ḥaḍrami of Tunis (A.D. 1332-1406), commonly known as Ibn Khaldun, laid down the foundations of different fields of knowledge, in particular the science of civilization (*al-'umrān*). His significant contributions to economics, however, should place him in the history of economic thought as a major forerunner, if not the "father," of economics, a title which has been given to Adam Smith, whose great works were published some three hundred and seventy years after Ibn Khaldun's death. Not only did Ibn Khaldun plant the germinating seeds of classical economics, whether in production, supply, or cost, but he also pioneered in consumption, demand, and utility, the cornerstones of modern economic theory.

Before Ibn Khaldun, Plato and his contemporary Xenophon presented, probably for the first time in writing, a crude account of the specialization and division of labor. On a nontheoretical level, the ancient Egyptians used the techniques of specialization, particularly in the era of the Eighteenth Dynasty, in order to save time and to produce more work per hour. Following Plato, Aristotle proposed a definition of economics and considered the use of money in his analysis of exchange. His example of the use of a shoe for wear and for its use in exchange was later presented by Adam Smith as the value in use and the value in exchange. Another aspect of economic thought before Ibn Khaldun was that of the Scholastics and of the Canonists, who proposed placing economics within the framework of laws based on religious and moral perceptions for the good of all human beings. Therefore all economic activities were to be undertaken in accordance with such laws.

Ibn Khaldun was cognizant of these ideas, including the one relating to religious and moral perceptions. The relationship between moral and religious principles on one hand and good government on the other is effectively expounded in his citation and discussion of Ṭāhir Ibn al-Ḥusayn's (A.D. 775-822) famous letter to his son 'Abdallah, who ruled Khurasan with his descendants until A.D. 872.[1] From the rudimentary thoughts of Ṭāhir[2] he developed a theory of taxation which has affected modern economic thought and even economic policies in the United States and elsewhere.

This paper attempts to give Ibn Khaldun his forgotten and long overdue credit and to place him properly within the history of economic thought. He was preceded by a variety of economic but elemental ideas to which he gave substance and depth. Centuries later these same ideas were developed by the Mercantilists, the commercial capitalists of the seventeenth century—Sir William Petty (A.D. 1623-1687), Adam Smith (A.D. 1723-1790), David Ricardo (A.D. 1772-1823), Thomas R. Malthus (A.D. 1766-1834), Karl Marx (A.D. 1818-1883), and John Maynard Keynes (A.D. 1883-1946), to name only a few—and finally by contemporary economic theorists.

Labor Theory of Value, Economics of Labor, Labor as the Source of Growth and Capital Accumulation

With the exception of Joseph A. Schumpeter, who discovered Ibn Khaldun's writings only a few months before his death,[3] Joseph J. Spengler,[4] and Charles Issawi, major Western economists trace the theory of value to Adam Smith and David Ricardo because they attempted to find a reasonable explanation for the paradox of value. According to Adam Smith and as further developed by David Ricardo, the exchange value of objects is to be equal to the labor time used in its production. On the basis of this concept, Karl Marx concluded that "wages of labour must equal the production of labour"[5] and introduced his revolutionary term *surplus value* signifying the unjustifiable reward given to capitalists, who exploit the efforts of the labor class, or the proletariat. Yet it was Ibn Khaldun, a believer in the free market economy, who first introduced the labor theory of value without the extensions of Karl Marx.

According to Ibn Khaldun, labor is the source of value. He gave a detailed account of his labor theory of value, presenting it for the first time in history. It is worth noting that Ibn Khaldun never called it a "theory," but had skillfully presented it (in volume 2 of Rosenthal translation) in his analysis of labor and its efforts.[6] Ibn Khaldun's contribution was later picked up by David Hume in his *Political Discourses*, published in 1752: "Everything in the world is purchased by labour."[7] This quotation was even used by Adam Smith as a footnote. "What is bought with money or with goods is purchased by labour, as much as what we acquire by the toil of our body. That money or those goods indeed save us this toil. They contain the value of a certain quantity of labour which we exchange for what is supposed at the time to contain the value of an equal quantity. The value of any commodity, therefore, to the person who possesses it, and who means not to use or consume it himself, but to exchange it for other commodities, is equal to the quantity of labour which it enables him to purchase or command. Labour, therefore, is the real measure of the exchangeable value of all commodities."[8] If this passage which was published in A.D. 1776 in Adam Smith's major work, is carefully analyzed, one can find its seeds in Ibn Khaldun's *Prolegomena* (*The Muqaddimah*). According to Ibn Khaldun, labor is the source of value. It is necessary for all earnings and capital accumulation. This is obvious in the case of craft. Even if earning "results from something other than a craft, the value of the resulting profit and acquired (capital) must (also) include the value of the labor by which it was obtained. Without labor, it would not have been acquired."[9]

Ibn Khaldun divided all earnings into two categories, *ribḥ* (gross earning) and *kasb* (earning a living). *Ribḥ* is earned when a man works for himself and sells his objects to others; here the value must include the cost of raw material and natural resources. *Kasb* is earned when a man works for himself. Most translators of Ibn Khaldun have made a common mistake in their understanding of *ribḥ*. *Ribḥ* may either mean a profit or a gross earning, depending upon the context. In this instance, *ribḥ* means gross earning because the cost of raw material and natural resources are included in the sale price of an object.

Whether *ribḥ* or *kasb*, all earnings are value realized from human labor, that is, obtained through human effort. Even though the value of objects includes the cost of other inputs of raw material and natural resources, it is through labor and its efforts that value increases and wealth expands, according to Ibn Khaldun. With less human effort, a reversal to an opposite direction may occur. Ibn Khaldun placed a great emphasis on the role of "extra effort," which later became known as "marginal productivity," in the prosperity of a society. His labor effort theory gave a reason for the rise of cities, which, as his insightful analysis of history indicated, were the focal points of civilizations.

Whereas labor may be interpreted from Ibn Khaldun's ideas as both necessary and sufficient conditions for earnings and profit, natural resources are only necessary. Labor and its effort lead to production, which is in turn used for an exchange through barter or through the use of money, that is, gold and silver. The process therefore creates incomes and profits which a man derives from a craft as the value of his labor after having deducted the cost of raw material. Long before David Ricardo published his significant contribution to the field of economics in 1817, *The Principles of Political Economy and Taxation*, Ibn Khaldun gave the original explanation for the reasons behind the differences in labor earnings. They may be attributed to differences in skills, size of markets, location, craftsmanship or occupation, and the extent to which the ruler and his governors purchase the final product. As a certain type of labor becomes more precious, that is, if the demand for it exceeds its available supply, its earnings must rise.

High earnings in one craft attract others to it, a dynamic phenomenon which will eventually lead to an increase in its available supply and consequently lower profits. This principle explains Ibn Khaldun's original and insightful analysis of long-term adjustments within occupations and between one occupation and another. However, this point of view was attacked by John Maynard Keynes in his famous statement that in the long run we are all dead. Nevertheless, Ibn Khaldun's analysis has not only proved to be historically correct but has also constituted the core thinking of classical economists.[10]

Ibn Khaldun succinctly observed, explained, and analyzed how earnings in one place may be different from another, even for the same profession. Earnings of judges, craftsmen, and even beggars, for example, are directly related to each town's degree of affluence and standard of living, which in themselves are to be achieved through the fruits of labor and the crystallization of productive communities. Adam Smith explained differences in labor earnings by comparing them in England and in Bengal[11] along the same lines of reasoning given by Ibn Khaldun four centuries earlier as he compared earnings in Fez with those of Tlemcen.[12] It was Ibn Khaldun, not Adam Smith, who first presented the contribution of labor as a means of building up the wealth of a nation, stating that labor effort, increase in productivity, and exchange of products in large markets are the main reasons behind a country's wealth and prosperity. Inversely, a decline in productivity could lead to the deterioration of an economy and the earnings of its people. "A large civilization yields large profits [earnings] because of the large amount of [available] labor which is the cause of [profit]."[13]

It was also Ibn Khaldun, long before Adam Smith, who made a strong case for a free economy and for freedom of choice.

> Among the most oppressive measures, and the ones most deeply harming society, is the compelling of subjects to perform forced work unjustly. For labour is a commodity, as we shall show later, in as much as incomes and profits represent value of labour of their recipients . . . nay most men have no source of income other than their labour. If, therefore, they should be forced to do work other than that for which they have been trained, or made to do forced work in their own occupation, they would lose the fruit of their labour and be deprived of the greater part, nay of the whole, of their income.[14]

To maximize both earnings and levels of satisfaction, a man should be free to perform whatever his gifted talents and skilled abilities dictate. Through natural talents and acquired skills, man can freely produce objects of high quality and, often, more units of labor per hour.

Demand, Supply, Prices, and Profits

In addition to his original contribution to the economics of labor, Ibn Khaldun introduced and ingeniously analyzed the interplay of several tools of economic analysis, such as demand, supply, prices, and profits.

Demand for an object is based on the utility of acquiring it and not necessarily the need for it. Utility is therefore the motive force behind demand. It creates the incentives for consumer spending in the marketplace. Ibn Khaldun had therefore planted the first seed of modern demand theory, which has since been developed and expanded by Thomas Robert Malthus, Alfred Marshall, John Hicks, and others. As a commodity in demand attracts increased consumer spending, both the price and the quantity sold are increased. Similarly, if the demand for a certain craft decreases, its sales fall and consequently its price is reduced.

Demand for a certain commodity also depends upon the extent to which it will be purchased by the state. The king and his ruling class purchase much larger quantities than any single private individual is capable of purchasing. A craft flourishes when the state buys its product. With his ingenious analytical mind, Ibn Khaldun had further discovered the concept known in modern economic literature as "derived demand." "Crafts improve and increase when the demand for their products increases."[15] Demand for a craftsman is therefore derived from the demand for his product in the marketplace.

As is commonly known, modern price theory states that cost is the backbone of supply theory. It was Ibn Khaldun who first examined analytically the role of the cost of production on supply and prices. In observing the differences between the price of foodstuffs produced in fertile land and of that produced in poor soils, he traced them mainly to the disparity in the cost of production.

> [In] the coastal and hilly regions, whose soil is unfit for agriculture, (inhabitants) were forced to apply themselves to improving the conditions of those fields and plantations. This they did by applying valuable work and manure and other costly materials. All this raised the cost of agricultural production, which costs they took into account when fixing their price for selling. And ever since that time Andalusia has been noted for its high prices . . . The position is just the reverse in the land of the Berbers. Their land is so rich and fertile that they

do not have to incur any expenses in agriculture; hence in that country foodstuffs are cheap.[16]

Besides individual and state demand and cost of production, Ibn Khaldun introduced other factors which affect the price of goods or services, namely, the degree of affluence and the prosperity of districts, the degree of concentration of the wealthy, and the degree of customs duties being levied on middlemen and traders. The direct functional relationship between income and consumption as presented by Ibn Khaldun paved the road to the theory of consumption function as a cornerstone of Keynesian economics.[17]

Ibn Khaldun also made an original contribution in his concept of profits. In economic literature, a theory of profit as a reward for undertaking risk in a future of uncertainties is generally attributed to Frank Knight, who published his ideas in 1921.[18] There is no doubt that Frank Knight substantially advanced a well-established theory of profit. Nevertheless, it was Ibn Khaldun, not Frank Knight, who originally planted the seed of this theory: "Commerce means the buying of merchandise and goods, storing them, and waiting until fluctuation of the market brings about an increase in the prices of (these goods). *This is called profit* (*ribḥ*)."[19] In another context, Ibn Khaldun stated again the same idea: "Intelligent and experienced people in the cities know that it is inauspicious to hoard grain and to wait for high prices, and that the profit (expected) may be spoiled or lost through (hoarding)."[20] Profit is therefore a reward for undertaking a risk. In the face of future uncertainties, a riskbearer may very well lose instead of gain. Similarly, profits or losses may accrue as a result of speculation which is carried out by profitseekers in the marketplace. To maximize profits, Ibn Khaldun introduced a gospel for traders, "Buy cheap and sell dear,"[21] which has been widely quoted ever since. In his translation of the *Muqaddimah* of Ibn Khaldun, Franz Rosenthal stated in a footnote, "In 1952 a book by Frank V. Fischer appeared, entitled *Buy Low—Sell High: Guidance for the General Reader in Sound Investment Methods and Wise Trade Techniques.*"[22]

If Ibn Khaldun's gospel is applied to cost analysis, it becomes obvious that profit may be increased, even for a given price of a final product, when one reduces the cost of raw material and other inputs used in production by buying them at a discount or, in general, at a low price even from distant markets, as he indicated in his account of benefits of foreign trade. Nevertheless, Ibn Khaldun concluded that both excessively low prices and excessively high prices are disruptive to markets. It is therefore advisable that states not hold prices artificially low through subsidies or other methods of market intervention. Such policies are economically disastrous because the low-priced goods will disappear from the market and there will be no incentive for suppliers to produce and sell whenever their profits are adversely affected. Ibn Khaldun also concluded that excessively high prices will not be compatible with market expansion. As the high-priced goods sell less in the market, the policy of excessively high pricing becomes counterproductive and disrupts the flow of goods in markets. Ibn Khaldun had thus laid down the foundations of ideas which later led to the formulation of disequilibrium analysis. He also cited several factors affecting the upward general price level, such as increase in demand, restrictions of supply, and increase in the cost of production, which includes a sales tax as one of the components of a total cost. After his analysis of what stimulates overall demand in a growing economy, Ibn Khaldun stated the following:

> Because of the demand for (luxury articles), they become customary, and thus come to be necessities. In addition, all labor becomes precious in the city, and the conveniences become expensive, because there are many purposes for which they are in demand in view of the prevailing luxury and because the government makes levies on market and business transactions. This is reflected in the sales prices. Conveniences, foodstuffs, and labor thus become very expensive. As a result, the expenditures of the inhabitants increase tremendously in proportion to the civilization of (the city). A great deal of money is spent. Under these circumstances, (people) need a great deal of money for expenditures, to procure the necessities of life for themselves and their families, as well as all other requirements.[23]

As to the impact of restricted supply on the price level, Ibn Khaldun summed it up thus: "When goods are few and rare, their prices go up."[24]

By carefully reading the above two passages, it becomes obvious that Ibn Khaldun discovered what is now known as cost-push and demand-pull causes of inflationary pressures. In fact, he was the first philosopher in history who systematically identified factors affecting either the price of a good or the general price level.

Macroeconomics, Growth, Taxes, Role of Governments, and Money

In macroeconomics, Ibn Khaldun laid the foundations of what John Maynard Keynes called "aggregate effective demand," the multiplier effect and the equality of income and expenditure.[25] When there is more total demand as population increases, there is more production, profits, customs, and taxes. The upward cycle of growth continues as civilization flourishes and a new wave of total demand is created for the crafts and luxury products. "The value realized from them increases, and, as a result, profits are again *multiplied* in the town. Production there is thriving even more than before. And so it goes with the *second* and *third* increase."[26] People's "wealth, therefore, increases and their riches grow. The customs and ways of luxury *multiply*, and all the various kinds of crafts are firmly established among them."[27] The concept of the multiplier was later developed and expanded by several economists, in particular by John Maynard Keynes. However, it was discovered for the first time in history by Ibn Khaldun.

Modern national income accounts were also developed and expanded using the equality of income and expenditures. Expenditures of one citizen are income to others; therefore total expenditures are equal to total incomes. This equality was first discovered by Ibn Khaldun. In fact, he used both terms as synonymous to one another after having established the equality between them.[28] "Income and expenditure balance each other in every city. If the income is large, the expenditure is large, and vice versa. And if both income and expenditure are large, the inhabitants become more favourably situated, and the city grows."[29]

Ibn Khaldun introduced the pioneering theory of growth based on capital accumulation through man's efforts.

> (Man) obtains (some profits) through no efforts of his own, as, for instance, through rain that makes the fields thrive, and similar things. However, these things are only contributory. His own efforts must be combined with them, as will be mentioned. (His) profits will constitute his livelihood, if they correspond to his necessities and needs. They will be capital accumulation if they are greater than (his needs).[30]

Ibn Khaldun gave his account of the stages of economic development, from nomadic to agricultural to more "cooperation in economic matters" which occur through an expansion of a town to a city, where demand increases and skilled labor congregates and expands production both in quantity and in "refinement." Economic growth continues so long as there is an extra effort which creates capital accumulation, which in turn, combined with effort, leads to more production and the development of crafts in the cities. As was presented earlier, wealth expands through labor and its efforts, whereas with less human effort there may occur a reversal to stagnation, followed by a downward trend in people's standard of living.

Governments play an important role in growth and in the country's economy in general through their purchases of goods and services and through their fiscal policy of taxation and expenditures. Governments may also provide an environment of incentives for work and prosperity or, inversely, a system of oppression which is ultimately self-defeating. Even though Ibn Khaldun regards governments as inefficient, "not so much calculation" is carried out by them of what is contemporarily known as cost and benefit, they still play an important role in the country's economy through their big purchases. Government expenditures stimulate the economy by increasing incomes, which are further hiked through a multiplier effect. However, if the king hoards the amount he collects in taxes, business slackens and the economic activities of the state are adversely affected through the multiplier effect.[31] In addition to its welfare program for the poor, the widows, the orphans, and the blind, provided there is no overburden for the treasury, the government should spend its tax revenue wisely to improve conditions of its "subjects, to safeguard their rights and to preserve them from harm."[32]

Ibn Khaldun was the first major contributor to tax theory in history. He is the philosopher who shaped the minds of several rulers throughout history. More recently his impact was evident on John F. Kennedy and later on Ronald Reagan. "Our true choice is not between tax reduction on the one hand and avoidance of large federal deficits on the other. An economy stifled by restrictive tax rates will never produce enough revenue to balance the budget, just as it will never produce enough jobs or enough profits." John F. Kennedy said that back in 1962, when he was asking for a tax decrease, a cut in tax rates across the board. But when John Kennedy said those words, he was echoing the words of Ibn Khaldun, a Muslim philosopher back in the fourteenth century, who said the following: "At the beginning of the dynasty taxation yields large revenues from small assessments. At the end of the dynasty taxation yields small revenue from large assessments. . . . This is why we had to have the tax program as well as the budget cuts, because budget cuts, yes, would reduce government spending."[33]

According to Ibn Khaldun, tax revenues of the ruling dynasty increase because of business prosperity, which flourishes with easy, not excessive taxes. He was therefore the first in history to lay the foundation of a theory for the optimum rate of taxation, a theory which has even affected contemporary leading advocates of supply-side economics such as Arthur Laffer and others. The well-known Laffer curve is nothing but a graphical presentation of the theory of taxation developed by Ibn Khaldun in the fourteenth century.[34]

"When tax assessments and imposts upon the subjects are low, the latter have the energy and desire to do things. Cultural enterprises grow and increase, because the low taxes bring satisfaction. When cultural enterprises grow, the number of individual imposts and assessments mount. In consequence, the tax revenue, which is the sum total of the individual assessments, increases";[35] whereas with large tax assessments, incomes and profits are adversely affected, resulting, in the final analysis, in a decline in tax revenue. Ibn Khaldun made a strong case against any government attempt to confiscate or otherwise affect private property. Governments' arbitrary interferences in man's property result in loss of incentives, which could eventually lead to a weakening of the state. Expropriation is self-defeating for any government because it is a form of oppression, and oppression ruins society.

In macroeconomics Ibn Khaldun also contributed to the theory of money. According to him, money is not a real form of wealth but a vehicle through which it can be acquired. He was the first to present the major functions of money as a measure of value, a store of value and a "numeraire." "The two mineral 'stones,' gold and silver as the (measure of) value for all capital accumulations . . . [are] considere[d] treasure and property. Even if under certain circumstances, other things are acquired, it only for the purpose of ultimately obtaining [them]. All other things are subject to market fluctuations from which (gold and silver) are exempt. They are the basis of profit, property and treasure."[36] The real form of wealth is not money, however; wealth is rather created or otherwise transformed through labor in the form of capital accumulation in real terms. It was, therefore, Ibn Khaldun who first distinguished between money and real wealth, even though he realized that the latter may be acquired by the former. Yet money plays a much more efficient role than barter in business transactions in a society where man exchanges the fruits of his labor, whether in the form of goods or of services, with another to satisfy the needs which he cannot fulfill alone on his own. Money also facilitates the flow of goods from one market to another, even across the border of countries.

Foreign Trade

Ibn Khaldun also contributed to the field of international economics. Through his perceptive observations and his analytical mind, he undoubtedly shed light on the advantages of trade among nations. Through foreign trade, according to Ibn Khaldun, peoples' satisfaction, merchants' profits, and countries' wealth are all increased.

The merchant who knows his business will travel only with such goods as are generally needed by rich and poor, rulers and commoners alike. (General need) makes for a large demand for his goods . . . it is more advantageous and more profitable for the merchants' enterprise . . . (that he will be able to take advantage of) market fluctuations, if he brings goods from a country that is far away . . . merchandise becomes more *valuable* when merchants transport it from one country to another.[37]

The underlined word, *valuable*, indicates Ibn Khaldun's perception of the gains of trade. If a good becomes more valuable by being transported from country A to country B and still sells at a profit in B after the cost of transportation and all other costs are taken into account, then it is (1) cheaper than the same good produced internally, (2) of better quality, or (3) a totally new product. If the foreign good is cheaper than that produced internally, foreign trade will serve to economize labor and other resources by having them diverted from the high-cost good which cannot face competition to other low-cost products. The resources which are saved from this process of diversion may be used to produce other goods or may add another layer of capital accumulation. Foreign trade may therefore contribute positively to the country's level of income as well as to its level of growth and prosperity. If the foreign good is of a better quality than that produced internally, the imported good will add to the level of satisfaction of those who purchase it. In the meantime, internal producers facing the competitive high-quality product must attempt to improve their production or accept a reduction in their sales and revenues. There will be a welfare gain in either case: a rise in the quality of internal products or a diversion of resources from the production of a high-cost good to a low-cost good, as in the first case. In the last case, when the imported good is a totally new product, the welfare gain from foreign trade may be expressed in terms of an increase in the level of satisfaction of those who purchase it or in terms of an increase in quantity or quality of production of other goods if the imported item is a new tool or a modification of an existing one. Furthermore, an introduction of a totally new product through foreign trade may attract internal producers, if it is feasible, to produce it once they are capable to compete with the foreign product.

Ibn Khaldun was conscious of what was later termed the "opportunity cost." Applying *valuable labor* to improving poor soils means that the labor could have been better used in the production of other goods. Resources in general should be put to the best possible use. Otherwise there will be a cost which will surface in a loss in value. Foreign trade provides further incentives in the attempts to optimize the use of labor and other natural resources.

Ibn Khaldun's originality in his perceptive observations and analysis of foreign trade deserves proper recognition in the field of international economics. The subject of gains from trade has been substantially developed and expanded, in particular, since the publication of *Political Discourses* by David Hume in 1752. But the first original seed of the subject was planted by Ibn Khaldun four centuries earlier.

Ibn Khaldun and Adam Smith

In spite of Ibn Khaldun's overall contribution to the field of economics, it is Adam Smith who has been widely called the "father of economics." Schumpeter's view of Smith's economics is more critical than admiring.[38] Personally, I do not share such a view, for I still consider Adam Smith one of the great philosophers who has significantly contributed to the field of economics even by having been a mere collector of previous economic thoughts. He eloquently presented these ideas in detail in an excellent new form and style. Nevertheless, by comparison, Ibn Khaldun was far more original than Adam Smith, in spite of the fact that the former had also restructured and built upon foundations laid down before him, such as Plato's account of specialization, Aristotle's analysis of money, and Ṭāhir Ibn al-Ḥusayn's treatment of government's role. Still, it was Ibn Khaldun who founded the original ideas in numerous areas of economic thought.

Despite Ibn Khaldun's contributions, some economic ideas as well as some economic philosophy of the freedom of choice, as presented above, were later attributed to Adam Smith without giving due credit to the original thinker Ibn Khaldun. "Smith's great economic treatise contains both his 'preaching' of the 'gospel' of economic liberalism, i.e., economic freedom for all individuals."[39] Since there is such a striking similarity in the economic thought of Ibn Khaldun and of Adam Smith, it must be left to the economic historian to ascertain direct or indirect links between these two great thinkers who were four centuries apart. However, I would like to suggest some possible and likely points of contact. Even though Adam Smith did not explicitly refer to Ibn Khaldun's contributions, it may well be argued that there were several channels through which he may have encountered the latter's pioneering and original economic thought.

Adam Smith graduated from Glasgow University, where he was influenced by his teacher Francis Hutcheson, who was in turn affected by Antony Ashley Cooper,[40] known as Lord Shaftesbury in the late seventeenth century and early eighteenth century, and other philosophers who were concerned with "liberal enlightenment," all of whom may have been directly or indirectly affected by Ibn Khaldun's thought. After his graduation, Adam Smith devoted six years to research at Oxford University's library, where he may have been exposed to Ibn Khaldun's contributions even without having been aware of the author's name. It was not uncommon in early times that ideas were circulated, discussed, and delivered from one generation to another without the name of an author. Furthermore, ever since the Crusades, which lasted from the eleventh to the thirteenth centuries, most Western philosophers attempted to discount the impact of Muslim scholars through a multiplicity of approaches, which included using Muslim ideas without mentioning the name of a Muslim author. The protracted war waged by the Crusaders to capture the Holy Land from the Muslims created a strong antagonistic feeling, well embedded in the Western mind, from which Western scholars were not immune and which lasted for centuries, probably until modern times. Another possible channel through which Adam Smith may have been directly or indirectly exposed to Ibn Khaldun's economic thought was through his tour of Europe. During this tour he encountered Quesnay, other Physiocrats in Paris, and other European intellectuals who may have been influenced by Ibn Khaldun in one way or another.

Adam Smith could also have been exposed to the economic contributions of Ibn Khaldun through the dominant influence of the Ottoman Empire. Ever since the Ottoman Empire rose in the fourteenth century—and vastly extended its boundaries at its peak in the sixteenth century to include much of southeast Europe, southwest Asia, and northern Africa—a new bridge was erected linking intellectuals in the Continent with their counterparts in the vast territories of the empire, of which Egypt became a part in 1517. It was in Egypt that Ibn Khaldun spent the latter part of his life revising manuscripts of his works which he had originally completed in Tunis in November of 1377. His thoughts were then transmitted from one generation to another, from one century to another, and from one country to another. Influenced by Ibn Khaldun's idea that craftsmen and industrialists play a significant role in a country's growth, prosperity, and power, Sultan Selim I, after having successfully extended his domain of influence over Egypt in 1517, took back with him from Cairo to Constantinople the best-known artisans at that time. In modern terminology, this was a case of a "transfer of technology."

The impact of Ibn Khaldun was extensive and profound, not only in the minds of some rulers and statesmen, but also among intellectuals and educators long before his books were even translated into other languages. In response to great interest in his works, his books were finally translated to the Turkish language in 1730,[41] exactly forty-six years before the publication of Adam Smith's *The Wealth of Nations.*

Concluding Remarks

Even if Adam Smith was not directly exposed to Ibn Khaldun's economic thoughts, the fact remains that they were the original seeds of classical economics and even modern economic theory. Ibn Khaldun had not only been well established as the father of the field of sociology, but he had also been well recognized in the field of history, as the following passage from Arnold Toynbee indicates:

> In his chosen field of intellectual activity [Ibn Khaldun] appears to have been inspired by no predecessors . . . and yet, in the Prolegomena . . . to his *Universal History* he has conceived and formulated a philosophy of history which is undoubtedly the greatest work of its kind that has yet been created by any mind in any time or place.[42]

Through his great sense and knowledge of history, together with his microscopic observations of men, times, and places, Ibn Khaldun used an insightful empirical investigation to analyze and produce original economic thought. He left a wealth of contributions for the first time in history in the field of economics. He clearly demonstrated breadth and depth in his coverage of value and its relationship to labor; his analysis of his theory of capital accumulation and its relationship to the rise and fall of dynasties; his perceptions of the dynamics of demand, supply, prices, and profits; his treatment of the subjects of money and the role of governments; his remarkable theory of taxation; and other economic subjects. His unprecedented contributions to the overall field of economics should make him, Ibn Khaldun, the father of economics.

Notes

1. Charles Issawi, *An Arab Philosophy of History, Selections from the Prolegomena of Ibn Khaldun of Tunis (1332-1406)* (London: John Murray, 1950), p. 80.
2. Ibid., p. 89. The letter appears in the third chapter, section 50, of the *Prolegomena.* See Ibn Khaldun, *The Muqaddimah, an Introduction to History*, tr. by Franz Rosenthal, 3 vols., 2nd ed. (Published for the Bollingen Foundation by Princeton University Press, 1967); hereafter, *The Muqaddimah.*
3. Joseph A. Schumpeter, *History of Economic Analysis*, edited from manuscript by Elizabeth B. Schumpeter and published after his death (New York: Oxford University Press, 1954), pp. 136, 788.
4. Joseph J. Spengler, "Economic Thought in Islam: Ibn Khaldun," *Comparative Studies in Society and History*, vol. 6, no. 3 (April 1964).

5. Karl Marx, *Zur Kritik der Politischen Ökonomie*, p. 45, as quoted in Erik Roll, *A History of Economic Thought*, 4th ed. (London: Faber and Faber, 1978), p. 266.
6. *The Muqaddimah*, 2:311ff.
7. David Hume, *Political Discourses* (Edinburg: Printed by R. Fleming for A. Kincaid, 1752), p. 12.
8. Adam Smith, *An Inquiry into the Nature and Causes of the Wealth of Nations*, ed. by Edwin Cannan (New York: Random House, 1937), p. 30.
9. *The Muqaddimah*, 2:313.
10. John Maynard Keynes, *General Theory of Employment, Interest and Money* (New York: Harcourt, Brace and Co., 1936), pp. 4-22.
11. Adam Smith, *An Inquiry*, pp. 67-73.
12. *The Muqaddimah*, 2:273-274.
13. Ibid., p. 282.
14. Ibn Khaldun, *An Arab Philosophy of History* (Issawi's translation), p. 85.
15. Ibid., p. 72.
16. Ibid., pp. 73-74.
17. Cf. Milton Friedman, *A Theory of Consumption Function* (Princeton: Princeton University Press, 1957).
18. Frank H. Knight, *Risk, Uncertainty and Profit* (New York: Houghton Mifflin, 1921).
19. *The Muqaddimah*, 2:340.
20. Ibid., 2:339.
21. Ibid., 2:337.
22. Ibid., 2:337 (see footnote 52).
23. Ibid., 2:279-280.
24. Ibid., 2:338.
25. Keynes, *General Theory*, pp. 23-34, 113-131, 52-61.
26. *The Muqaddimah*, 2:273.
27. Ibid., 2:287.
28. Ibid., 2:274.
29. Ibid., 2:275.
30. Ibid., 2:311-12.
31. *The Muqaddimah*, 2:92.
32. Ibn Khaldun was mostly influenced in government expenditures by the letter of Ṭāhir Ibn al-Husayn. See Issawi, *Arab Philosophy*, p. 89. See also *The Muqaddimah*, 2:140-141.
33. President Reagan quoted Ibn Khaldun twice, on September 2, 1981, and on October 1, the same year. See *Public Papers of the Presidents of the United States, Ronald Reagan* (Washington D.C.: U.S. Government Printing Office, 1981), pp. 745, 871.
34. Arthur B. Laffer and Marc A. Miles, *International Economics in an Integrated World* (New York and London: Scott, Foresman and Co., 1982), pp. 157-158.
35. *The Muqaddimah*, 2:89-90.
36. Ibid., 2:313.
37. Ibid., 2:337-338.

38. Joseph A. Schumpeter, *History*. pp. 185-94, 474.
39. Overton H. Taylor, *A History of Economic Thought* (New York: McGraw-Hill Book Co., 1960), p. 78.
40. Antony Ashley Cooper (3rd Earl of Shaftesbury), *Characteristics of Men, Manners, Opinions and Times*, vol. 2, *Inquiry Concerning Virtue and Merit*, 6th ed. (London: J. Purser, 1737).
41. Spengler, "Economic Thought," p. 305.
42. Arnold J. Toynbee, *A Study of History* (London: Oxford University Press, 1935) 3:322.

A Mamlūk "Magna Carta"

AZIZ SOURIAL ATIYA

I

The charter, or royal decree (*Marsūm sharīf*), which is the subject of the present study was discovered by Muḥammad Ibn Qāsim Ibn Muḥammad al-Nūwairy al-Iskandāranī while preparing the encyclopedic work entitled *Kitāb al-ilmām*. Originally intended to be a record of his observations on the disastrous Cypriot crusade of A.D. 1365 against the city of Alexandria, this work was extended by the insertion of all manner of materials gleaned from a vast array of manuscripts which he must have possessed. By vocation, the author described himself as a copyist of old manuscripts for the rich merchants of Alexandria. In the course of his work he apparently was in the habit of saving excerpts from treatises, some known and others unknown to us, for use in his own future writings. Hence the explanation of the title of his work as a book of gleanings, which rendered it rather encyclopedic in character. In one section on world and Mamlūk history, al-Nūwairy describes the third reign of Sultan al-Nāṣir Muḥammad Ibn Qalāwūn (A.D. 1309-40), for whom he had great admiration. He paints a portrait of that sultan as a mystic figure who spent his evenings in his palace (al-Oaṣr al-ablaq) in the Cairo citadel looking at the stars in meditation and pious consideration of the good that he could render toward his subjects. Oppressed by his third reign, the sultan conceived the idea of issuing a global decree to rectify all the evils of his forebears.

Evidently al-Nūwairy, in his wanderings in the Arabic manuscripts, must have found an original copy of the charter in question, and he decided to include its text in toto as a supplement to al-Nāṣir's biography for the glorification of his hero. Because of the importance and the comprehensive constitutional nature of the charter, it became known to the chroniclers of late medieval Egypt, such as the towering al-Maqrizī,[1] as well as Abū al-Maḥaṣin Ibn Taghrībirdī[2] and Ibn al-Dawādārī.[3] But nowhere did it appear in full except in the work of al-Nūwairy. All the others simply referred to it as a major document of the later Middle Ages in Egypt or else quoted briefly from it. In form and content, it was reminiscent of the English *Magna Carta* of A.D. 1215 during the reign of King John, but with a major difference. Whereas the British document, which has served as the basis for the British constitution over the ages, was imposed on the monarch by the aristocracy, our document owed its issuance not to the rapacious Mamlūk amirs (princes), but solely to Sultan al-Nāṣir without any external pressure for the establishment of justice in the country and the rectification of numerous economic evils imposed on the people by his forebears. It is hoped that the publication of this unique document will furnish future historians of medieval Egypt with basic material for the further study of economic, social, and constitutional conditions in Egypt under the Mamlūk regime.

The charter appears in only one manuscript of *Kitāb al-ilmām*, the Bankipore XV, 1066. Curiously, it is completely absent from both the Berlin (W. 359 and 360) and the Cairo (Hist. 14490) manuscripts, which were copied from an original by al-Nūwairy himself. The charter is dated in the year A.H. 715/A.D. 1315, that is, exactly a century after the ratification of the British *Magna Carta.* al-Nāṣir's decree was issued after the completion of a general survey of the country for a fair assessment of the land tax system in a register known as "al-Rūk al-Nāṣiri." Although the text as presented in that manuscript suffers from a few lacunae, the bulk of the document is intact and offers a rare analytical inventory of the national problems which the sultan aimed at resolving for the good of his subjects and the solace of his own soul. The language used by the scribe who composed the decree for the sultan is typical of that era and could stand prolonged linguistic studies, which are outside our limited scope, in the establishment of its historic text.

As will be seen from the body of that text, it begins with a protocol, or prelude, in which the scribe glorifies al-Nāṣir's sultanate and makes special mention of the sultan's charitable motives in granting the charter to his subjects in order to eliminate the evils imposed on the country by previous legislation and by former rulers. The complete Arabic text of this scarce document is presented in the following pages, together with a few additional footnotes of an explanatory nature. Afterwards, I shall attempt a brief analysis of the substance of the charter in twenty-two items, each one representing a new legislative measure addressing a particular problem. These problems cover practically every phase of economic, social, and military practice prevailing in the country. Thus the document offers a solid basis for extensive studies in the history of Egyptian medieval civilization, studies of which this brief attempt is only a modest beginning.

The text of this important and unique document is presented without any improvement in style, terminology, or idiom, which sometimes borders on the colloquial usage of the time.

(مرسوم شريف)

رسم بالأمر الشريف العالى المولوى السلطانى الملكى الناصرى مثال العلامة الكريمة محمد بن قلاون، لا برح إحسانه يرعى بحسن نظره مصالح الرعية، وامتنانه يسعى بأنواع السماح والبر إلى البرية، وتوالى فضله على الأمة المحمديه، يخجل بكرمه وسمى[1] (كذا) وليه أن يخلد المرسوم الشريف فى الأعمال البهنسايه[2]، بما شمل الرعايا، وأهل البلاد وكافة البرايا، من صدقاتنا التى عمت، ومعداتنا التى نمت وتمت، وبما سامحناه وأبطلناه عنهم من المكوس والمظالم والحوادث والرسوم التى كانت تستأدى منسوبة للحقوق الديوانيه، بالجهات التى ذكرها فى هذا المرسوم المكتّب من نسخة المرسوم. . .[3]. والمقررات والمراسيم الشريفة التى اقتضتها آراؤنا العاليه، وذلك عند رَوْك[4].

(١) كذا فى الأصل وجائز قراءة الكلمة «ويسمى» وربما كان المقصود «وسمو».

(٢) كذا فى الأصل ولعل الكلمة «البهنساويه» نسبة إلى منطقة البهنسا بمصر الوسطى، وقد آثرنا الابقاء على صيغة المرسوم كما هى دون تعديل أو تصحيح لفظى إلا فى أضيق الحدود التى يقتضيها السياق باعتبار أن النص كما هو يمثل اللغة الديوانية الشائعة فى ذلك العصر.

(٣) هنا كلمة لا يستقيم بها السياق ويمكن قراءتها «لسامع» أو «بمسامع».

(٤) إشارة للروك الناصرى وهو عبارة عن عملية مسح الأرض وتقدير الضريبة وتوزيع الإقطاعات على مساحتها، وقد خصص المقريزى (الخطط، طبعة مصر ١٣٢٤هـ ص ١٤ ــ ١٤٧) فصلاً لذلك تحت عنوان «ذكر الروك الأخير الناصرى».

الديار. فأول ما ابتدأنا به تَعْفية آثار مظلمة قد أذلهم ليلها، وعم ويلها، واندفع سيلها. وهى المقررات التى كانت تستأدى، منسوبة لحقوق سواحل الغلال والعرصات، وتسقط هذه المظلمة وتعفا آثارها من القاهرة ومصر المحروستين والأخصاص والفروع المنسوبة إلى ذلك جميعها، ولا يتعرض إلى تنمية الدرهم الفرد عن الغلة الواصلة ولا المبيعة ولا شىء من [مخطوط بانكى يور ١٧٩ : أ] الرسوم، ولا الوجوه التى كانت تستأدى منسوبة لعلامات سواحل الغلات بالجهتين المذكورتين. وكذلك رسمنا بإبطال نصف السمسرة وضمانها وهو الكسر الذى يستأدى من السماسرة والمناديين، ويساهمون فيه من أجرة بيعهم وشرائهم. ونحو هذه المظلمة وإسقاطها من بطون الأوراق والدفاتر والدواوين، وتعفية آثارها نظراً فى حالة الضعفاء الذين امتحنوا بهذه المحنة إلى أن يسر الله تعالى لهم هذه المحنة على أيدينا ومنَّ بإسقاطها، وأمَّنا الرعايا والضعفاء والمساكين من تناولها منهم وتوفّراً لخاطرهم على كسبهم ومعايشهم، والأدعية الصالحة لنا يقبلها الله تعالى من كل داع مخلص. وكذلك بإبطال المقدمين ومقرراتهم وبدولهم وما يضم إلى ذلك من الحوايص والبغال، وإبطال للرسل والمترددين من البلاد وتعفية آثارهم لتطمئن الرعايا بأمانكم. وقررنا أن يكون نواب الأمراء الذين يقررونهم ببلادهم نواباً عن مجلس الحرب السعيد. . . . . .(1) واحد من أهلها لحق من الحقوق، فيخلصه الوالى ممن يتعين في جهته ويوصله لمستحقه ويتصدَّى لإزالة التعدى عن أحد منهم على الآخر. وإن اتفق فى البلاد أمر كبير مثل قتيل أو ظهور فساد فيها أو حضور واحد من المفسدين إليها، فيكون والى الناحية ومشايخها وخفراؤها ملتزمين بالدرك فى ذلك وإحضار الغرماء والمفسدين إلى والى الحرب، ولا يمكّن أحداً (كذا) من الفساد، ولا يستحسنوا لأحد فعله عندهم، ولا يجمعوا أحداً عن شىء يتعين عليه، ولا يحمى بلد على بلد أخرى، ومن حضر إليهم من المقبحين أو المتحيدين فلا يؤوه ولا يقربوه، بل يمسكوه ويعيدوه إلى بلده، ويسلموه إلى أهل تلك البلد، ويشهدوا عليه وعلى شيوخها بتسليمه لهم، أو يسلموه لوالى الحرب من غير حماية، ولا يمكّن من إقامته يوماً واحداً عندهم ولا يؤوه ساعة

(1) العبارة هنا مطموسة بالأصل.

واحدة. ومن ارتكب (خرو)جاً[١] عن مرسومنا هذا أوحمى أحداً أو مكّن أحداً من الإقامة عنده من المفسدين أو المسلحين[٢]. . . . وفعل[٣] خلافه أو نقض حكماً واحداً من أحكامه فى أى بلد كان، فالوالى بتلك البلد وشيوخها وخفراؤها وأرباب الدرك يقومون[٤] بحكم سيوفنا بالتوسيط والشنق والتسمير على نخيل تلك البلدة. وإن اتفق فى سنة من السنين حصول شراقى، وقصد بعض الفلاحين أن ينتجع من بلده إلى بلد ريّ ليزرع فيها مؤنته فيتوجه برضى مقطعى بلده ويكون حطه معهم بالرضى بذلك، وعند ضمّ المغل يرجع إلى بلده ووطنه بحيث لا يحصل فى ذلك منازعة ولا يدعى أخذ[٥] فلاح غيره لكونه زرع زرع عنده، فيعمل كل منهم بما شمله من إحساننا وصدقاتنا ومعروفنا وبرّنا. وكذلك رسمنا بإبطال رسوم الولاية وعدم استيدائها، ولا يُمكَّن أحد من الولاة ولا نوابهم ولا المتحدثين عندهم من جباية رسم ولا مشاهرة ولا إحداث حادثة عليـه[٦]، وكذلك كتّاب الولاة ودواوينهم ومباشروهم فلا يتعرض أحد منهم إلى تناول رسم ولا جامكية على البلاد، فقد رسمنا بإبطال جوامكهم على البلاد وأسقطنا ذلك عن الرعية، فلا يتعرض أحد بعد مرسومنا هذا من كُتَّاب الولاة ولا مباشريهم إلى تقرير جامكية [بانكى يـور ١٧٩:ب] على البـلاد ولا رسم ولا مقرر ولا مشاهرة ولا مياومة، ولا يستأدى من ذلك الدرهم الفرد ولا شىء قلّ ولا جلّ، فقد أبطلنا هذا الحادث وعفينا آثاره، فليحذر كل منهم من تناول شىء من ذلك. رسمنا بإبطال حقوق السجون ومقرراتها وضمانها ومنع التعرض لأخذ الدرهم الفرد منها، وأن لا يجمع على المسجونين بين ضيق السجن وضيق العسر، فأنه ما بقى عند المسجونين إطلاقة بمقدار تعويقة على

---

(١) الكلمة مطموسة جزئياً، وقد أكملناها من السياق.

(٢) فى الأصل «المسجين» وقد تكون «المساجين».

(٣) جاءت الكلمة بأول السطر، وجائز أن يكون مطموساً منها حرف ألف فتصبح قراءتها «أو فعل».

(٤) فى الأصل «يموتون» وهو خطأ قلمى واضح.

(٥) الكلمة فى الأصل «أحد» بدون نقط، وقد آثرنا نقطها كذلك للسيـاق.

(٦) فى الأصل «على عليه» وتقع كلمة «على» بين السطرين وهى زائدة.

الضمان المذكور. فرأينا أن تكون هذه الحسنة مسطرة فى صحائف حسناتنا وتقرّبنا إلى الله تعالى بتعفية آثارها. ثم أنعمنا النظر فى مصالح البلاد والأعمال الراتبة، فوجدنا أهم أمورها مصالح جسورها وإتقانها، وأن لا تدخل الأيدى بجباية مبلغ، فرسمنا بأن تعمل جميع الجسور والترع بالجراريف والأبقار والرجال على قدر مصلحة كل بلد من غير أن نطلب عن ذلك دراهم ولا دخول ولا خروج، بل كل بلد تعمل (بأهلها)[1] وتعفا من الطلب بالدراهم عن القش والمدامسة وعن رسوم الخولة والمهندسين، وإبطال استخراج الدراهم عن جميع ذلك، ويستقر العمل دون جباية مبلغ، وتوفر على الرعايا صدقة عليهم، ونظراً فى حالهم، ويمحا ذكر طلب يطالب للجراريف والجمع والرسوم السدود بحيث لا يكون لسد ولا مهندس، ولا خولى رسم ولا بدل ولا استيداء الدرهم الفرد، بل كل بلد يلتزم مقطعها بعمل ما يجب عليه عمله من غير رجوع إلى العوائد القديمة. وكذلك رسمنا بإبطال طرح بالفراريج، بل يكون بيعها وشراؤها بالسعر الخاص أسوة بقية الأصناف من غير جبر ولا إكراه. ولا تُرمى فراريج بلد على أهلها. ولا يُلزم أحد بمشترى شىء منها اغتصاباً، ولا يُقرّر شىء منها بضمان ولا رسم ولا غيره، وتنقض العوائد السيئة التى كانت فى ذلك من غير رجوع إليها، ونكون أسوة المبيعات التى تباع وتشترى من غير طرح ولا رمى ولا تقرير. وكذلك رسمنا بإبطال مقرر الفرسان ومقرر الخيل الذى كان يستأدى وقت حركات الجيوش المنصورة إلى البواكير، وكذلك قود[2] الخيل، وأبطلنا هذه المظلمة[3] ابتغاء لثواب الله تعالى، والله لا يضيع أجر المحسنين، ووثوقاً بكرم الله تعالى، وإمداد[4] نصره للمؤمنين[5]. وكذلك رسمنا فى أمر الأفراح بأن لا يؤخذ مقرر ملاهى ممن يعمل فرحاً، ومن أعرس أو كتب كتابه أو أملك أو كان عنده ختان، أو ولد له ولد، أو غير ذلك من الولائم، ولم يعمل فرحاً فلا يُلزم بالقيام بشىء من المقررات المثبوتة للملاهى وللأفراح،

---

(١) العبارة هنا مطموسة ولكن أغلبها يقرأ إلا هذه الكلمة اقتبسناها من سياق الكلام.

(٢) والمقصود بالكلمة «أود».

(٣) الكلمة مطموسة جزئياً ولكنها واضحة من السياق.

(٤) فى الأصل «والأمداد».

(٥) فى الأصل «المسئولين» وهو خطأ قلمى واضح.

ولا يطلب مقرراً للملاهى إلا ممن يعمل عنده فرحاً بملاهى، ومن لم يكن عنده أحد من الغوانى (والملاهى)[١] فلا يطلب عن وليمته شىء قلّ ولا جلّ من المقررات التى كانت تستأدى أولًا. وكذلك رسمنا بالمسامحة بثمن العبى[٢] التى كانت تقررت وأبطلناها، فلا يتعرض أحد لاستخراجها بعد مرسومنا هذا. وكذلك رسمنا بإبطال المقرر من الأتبان التى توجد لمعاصر الأقصاب[٣]، وأن لا يتعرض أحد إلى أخذ تبن من بلد من البلاد إلا بثمنه ورضى أصحابه، ويستمر الحكم في ذلك عاماً شاملاً لمعاصر الخاص الشريف والأمراء وغيرهم من الجهات، وتستقر أتبان المعاصر الجارية في الخاص الشريف على بلاد الخاص الشريف من جملة ما يؤخذ منها، ولا يتعرض إلى غير بلاد [نفس المخطوط ١٨٠ : ألف] الخاص الشريف إلا بالثمن المرضى والقيمة العادلة، ولا يُجبر أحد من أهل البلاد على بيع تبنه بغير رضاه، ولا يقرر عليه شىء من التبن حسب ما رسمناه. وكذلك رسمنا بإبطال حماية المراكب وأن لا يعود أحد من الأمراء وأرباب الجهات يحمى مركباً لا يستأدى عن الحماية حقاً ولا مقرراً من المقررات التى كانت تستأدى فيما قبل مرسومنا هذا، ولا يتعرض أحد إلى المراكب بغير حق يشهد به الديوان المعمور من غير حماية. وكذلك رسمنا بالرفق بالرعايا، وأن لا يطالب الحىّ عن الميت، ولا المقيم عن النازح، ولا الحاضر عن الغائب، ما لم يكن ضامناً أو كفيلاً أو ملتزماً. وكذلك قد رسمنا بالمسامحة بما انساق للأمراء والمقطعين من البواقى في بلادهم من الخراجى والضمان وغير ذلك، وإلى آخر مُغَل سنة أربع عشرة وسبعمائة، ولا يطالب أحد من الرعية والمزارعين إلا بحق شرعى يكون الغريم قد قبض العوض عنه، ومهما كان باقياً من خراج أو ضمان وما يجرى مجرى ذلك فيسامح. ولا يطلب منهم بالجملة لكافيه، ويستمر الحكم على ما رسمنا به فى المسامحة إلى آخر مُغْل سنة أربع عشرة وسبعمائة، ولا يتعرض أحد من نواب الأمراء والمقطعين إلى استخراج شىء من الباقى المختص بالسنة المذكورة وما قبلها. وكذلك رسمنا أن تعفا

---

١) الكلمة مطموسة بالأصل، ولكنها واضحة من سياق الحديث.

٢) الكلمة واضحة بالأصل، وأغلب الظن أن المقصود بها جمع كلمة «العباءة».

٣) في الأصل «الاقتصاب» والكلمة غير منقوطة، ولكنها واضحة من السياق.

جماعة الفلاحين من ضيافة القدوم عند انتقالات الإقطاعات فى سنة الرّوك المبارك. وكذلك رسمنا بإبطال عداد النحل[١] حسب ما يشهد به الديوان المعمور من جملة ذلك، وتفصيله الحكم فى ذلك فى بلاد الخاص الشريف والأمراء والمقطعين، ولا يستخرج بعد هذا المرسوم الشريف، وكذلك رسمنا بإبطال زكاة الرجال بالديار المصرية بالوجهين القبلى والبحرى، ثم أنعمنا النظر فيما عدا الملّة المحمدية من الطوائف ليكون عدلنا جامعاً لجميع الملل والطوائف، فرسمنا فى أمر الجوالى بالديار المصرية وأعمالها تؤخذ من اليهود والنصارى أن لا تؤخذ منهم جالية إلا على حكم التصقيع، ورسمنا بالمسامحة بما كان يستأدى[٢] (مـ)ـنهم[٣] منسوباً للعجز حسب ما يشهد به الديوان المعمور. وكذلك رسمنا بإبطال جميع البدول من الولاة والنظار (والمـ)ـستوفين[٤] وأرباب الوظائف[٥] جميعاً من أرباب وغيرهم. فليستقر حكم هذا المرسوم الشريف لاستقبال تاريخه بعمل[٦] الروك المبارك وخروج المناشير الشريفة. وهو من استقبال شهر صفر سنة ست عشرة وسبعمائة، بلغ الله تعالى إليها وختمها بالصالحات. وتبطل هذه الحوادث والمظالم التى رسمنا بإبطالها من القاهرة ومصر المحروستين وسائر أعمال مصر بجميع الولايات والأعمال بالوجهين القبلى والبحرى حيث ما شهد الديوان المعمول بجمله ذلك وتفصيله، وتفريقه وتأصيله، لا يختص بذلك بلد من البلدان، ولا مدينة من المدن، ولا قرية ولا كفر ولا جهة ولا منيل كبيراً كان أو صغيراً، ولا استثناء فى هذا المرسوم الشريف ولا رجوع ولا تعقيب. وسبيل كل واقف على مرسومنا هذا من النواب والأمراء

---

(١) جائز أن تكون الكلمة «النخل» لأن النقطة الأولى ساقطة والنقطة الثانية قد تتبع الخاء أو ما قبلها، ولكننا آثرنا استعمال «النحل» لوجود كلمة «استخراج» فيما بعد مما يتصل بعسل النحل.

(٢) فى الأصل «يستددى».

(٣) الكلمة مطموسة جزئياً بأول السطر وهى واضحة من السياق.

(٤) الكلمة مطموسة جزئياً ولكنها واضحة من السياق.

(٥) فى الأصل «الوضائف».

(٦) الكلمة مطموسة جزئياً وهى واضحة من السياق.

والولاة والنظار والمستوفين والشادين والمتصرفين وسائر ولاة الأمور فى ممالكنا الشريفة العمل بحسبه من غير تأويل فى ذلك ولا تبديل. ومن نقض شيئاً من ذلك أو استحل حرمته أو أحيا مظلمة أماتها عدلنا الشريف فعليه لعنة الله والملائكة والناس أجمعين، لعنة باقية إلى يوم الدين. والعلامة الشريفة أعلاه حجة به. وقد كتبنا مثالها فى الأول إن شاء الله تعالى. كُتب ثامن عشر ذى الحجة [مخطوط بانكى يور ١٨٠ : ب] سنة خمس عشرة وسبعمائة حسب الأمر الشريف. الحمد لله وحده وصلواته على سيدنا محمد وآله وسلامه وحسبنا الله ونعم الوكيل. إنتهى

III

What follows represents the sum total and purport of every problem that al-Nāṣir sought by laws to unravel for the good of his people.

1. The charter begins with a relatively long introduction glorifying the sultan and stating his good intentions to eliminate all injustices imposed on the people in the past, and this on the occasion of making a new survey (*rūk*) of the land for a benign assessment of taxes.
2. The first problem to be treated are the imposts previously decreed on what was sent by river to Cairo and its dependencies. These are to be lifted, and the recurrence of the levy of the single dirham at the disembarkation of cereals and the forced sale thereof at prescribed prices is prohibited.
3. Half the brokerage fee imposed on brokers and criers for sales is to be dropped and also deleted from the registers of the *diwāns* (government offices) in the interest of the feeble and poor subjects.
4. The offices of surveyors (*muqaddimūn*) are eliminated, together with their imposed allowances and the fodder extorted from people for their beasts of burden and their mules.
5. State messengers are prohibited from harassing the villages so as to assure the inhabitants of their own security. In cases of serious crimes, such as murder or pillage, the criminal is to be pursued everywhere, returned to his native village, and surrendered to its authorities and its police force (*Arbāb al-darak*), who will deal with him by hanging him or by crucifying him to a palm tree.
6. In cases of drought at one village, the farmers (*fallāhīn*) may go to another village with ample irrigation water to plant their crops, but only with the approval of the natives of the other village; they must return to their home village after the harvest.
7. Viceroys (*wālis*), their aides (*nā'ibs*), their representatives or secretaries (*kuttāb*), and tax collectors are prohibited from imposing a daily or monthly tax and from extorting provisions (*gamkīyah*) from villages, even the single dirham (*al-Dirhạm al-fard*).
8. Prisoners are to be exempted from extraordinary taxation or even ordinary taxes, including the single *dirham* (*al-Dirham al-fard*).
9. All levies for the preparation of dikes and the dredging of canals are to be eliminated, and there will be no more fees for the loan of agricultural implements, the supply of straw and cows, or for the employment of personnel, including overseers and engineers. Each village shall undertake these duties within its means and within its boundaries under the leadership of its feoffee (*muqta'*) or headmen, without recourse to the old customs.

10. There will be no more compulsion for anyone to purchase or sell chickens or any other articles at a prescribed price, but sales should be made in accordance with the rules of the free market and at a fair price.
11. The custom of requiring villagers to billet horsemen and provide fodder for their horses during troop movements is to be discontinued.
12. There are to be no amusement taxes on the celebration of weddings, engagements, or circumcision unless the celebrant hires a professional dancer-singer.
13. The tax on the purchase of cloaks, formerly levied from the public, is to be suspended.
14. The customary levies on state sugar mills are to be suspended for one year, and the remaining straw shall be offered for sale without compulsion at a fair price.
15. The monetary impost to protect river ships against piracy levied by the amir or local authorities is revoked, signifying thereby that protection would be furnished without charge. No one shall be permitted to intercept unprotected ships without authorization from the central administration.
16. Survivors should not be forced to bear responsibility for liabilities of the dead, nor should the settler bear responsibility for the immigrant, nor the present for the absent, unless he be a guarantor.
17. The remainder of *kharāj* (taxes) still owing from the A.H. 714 harvest will be overlooked.
18. The balance or remainder of levies or taxes still owed by farmers to the amirs and the feoffees until A.H. 714 shall be overlooked and excused.
19. Farmers should be relieved from billeting or forced hospitality imposed on them by itinerant functionaries in this year of land surveying (*rūk*).
20. Imposts on beehives by amirs or administrators are suspended.
21. Tithing imposts are suspended for Muslim males of Upper and Lower Egypt, and this rule is extended to Jews and Christians unless the imposts are for dues from rentals.
22. In conclusion, the enforcement of the articles of this charter (*marsūm*) is imperative and irrevocable in Cairo and all the provinces, cities, villages, estates (*kafrs*), etc., without exception and without favor for any town over another. Viceroys, amirs, governors, overseers, intendants, tax collectors, and all state authorities are bound by the terms of this decree literally and without interpretation or substitution of its contents. The sultan's sign at the beginning of the charter is its witness. This charter is ratified on the 18th of Dhul-Hijjah A.H. 715 by royal order.

This amazing charter of liberties, a veritable *Magna Carta* of Mamlūk times, must be considered a true landmark in the constitutional history of medieval Egypt. The fact that it was considered bona fide by Sultan al-Nāṣir Muḥammad in his third reign is a significant testament to the establishment of the rule of justice and clemency toward the common folk of that period and against former Mamlūk tyranny. It is doubtful, however, whether the noble spirit of this charter was maintained by al-Nāṣir's Burji or Baḥri successors. The old tyrannical ways appear to have been revived during the rest of the Middle Ages and persisted after the Ottoman conquest (A.D. 1517) of Egypt until the French Expedition (1798-1801) and the dawn of modern history.

Notes

1. Aḥmad Ibn 'Alī al-Maqrīzī, *al-Sulūk li-ma'rifat dūwal al-mulūk*, ed. M. Ziyadah (Cairo: Lajnat al-Ta'līf wa-al-Tarjamah wa-al-Nashr, 1941) vol. 2, pt. 1:150-52.
2. Abū al-Mahāsin Yūsuf Ibn Taghrībirdī, *al-Nujūm al-ẓāhirah fi mulūk Miṣr wa-al-Oāhirah* (Cairo: Dar al-Kutub al-Miṣrīyah, 1942) vol. 9:49-50.
3. 'Abdallah Aybak Ibn al-Dawādārī, *Kanz al-durar wa jāmi' al-ghurar*, ed. Hans Robert Roemer (Cairo: Sami al-Khanji, 1960) vol. 9:286.

Part Three

The Modern Age, Challenges and Responses

The Memoirs of Nubar Pasha as a Source for the Social History of Egypt

CHARLES ISSAWI

Nubar Nubarian (1825-99) was the most eminent of the remarkable group of Armenians who played a leading part in Egypt's political and administrative life during the nineteenth century. Born in Izmir and educated in Switzerland and France, he entered the Egyptian service in 1840, occupied increasingly important posts, and was prime minister in 1878-79, 1884-88, and 1894-95. He thus served under every ruler from Muḥammad 'Alī to 'Abbās II, inclusive.

Nubar owed his success to his high degree of intelligence, his knowledge of several languages, including Turkish, French, and English, and his thorough understanding of the workings of Western civilization, which was rushing in on Egypt from every side. Lord Cromer gives a vivid sketch of his personality.[1] In it he says: "Nubar Pasha was by far the most interesting of latter-day Egyptian politicians. Intellectually, he towered above his competitors." Characteristically, he adds, "Bearing in mind, however, the intellectual calibre of those competitors, he deserves more than such faint praise as this." He goes on to describe him as "statesmanlike" and as a "brilliant conversationalist" and a "skillful negotiator" and says: "I have never known any one more persuasive, or better skilled in the art of making the worse appear the better reason. I used often to half believe him, when I knew full well that he was trying to dupe me." But what seems to have impressed Cromer most was that, "unlike many Orientals, his foreign education had not resulted in his assimilating the bad and discarding the more worthy portions of European civilization." Realizing that Egypt was being Europeanized, he was anxious that this Europeanization would be done in the way most beneficial to the country, by introducing the "reign of law."

Other portraits are not so flattering, for example, that of Portal, the first secretary at the British Agency, who reported that Nubar was hated by the natives and Muslims, was thoroughly untrustworthy, and was an infernal liar.[2]

Nubar's memoirs, written in 1890-94 and recently published,[3] are an important source on Egyptian history in 1840-78. They deal mainly with the subjects that concerned him most closely: the establishment of the mixed courts and the events that led to Ismail's abdication and the British occupation. Nubar seems to have attached great hopes to the mixed courts. He thought that they would both curtail the Capitulations, whose harmful effects on Egypt he saw very clearly, and introduce the principles of modern justice in Egypt, thus gradually limiting the power of its monarchs and bringing about the rule of law. Few observers today would say that these hopes were realized or that the mixed courts greatly improved Egypt's judicial system, but their record was not undistinguished.

Nubar casts illuminating sidelights on Egypt's monarchs. There is Muḥammad 'Alī in the last year of his life. "He had kept his grand manner, his studied cleanliness bordering on elegance; his eyes were sharp and animated; he sat, his legs half folded, his sword always within an arm's reach" (p.39). While the British were driving his forces out of Syria, Muḥammad 'Alī saw to it that British trade and mails continued to pass through Egypt: "I am not at war with the English, it is their government which unjustly wages war against me; the English are my friends and it is up to me to safeguard their interests" (p.34). And "yet he was always haunted by the idea that England wanted to take Egypt," as Burckhardt realized in 1816 when he met the viceroy in Taif (p.36). As for founding an Arab empire: "Such a nonsensical idea never crossed the mind of Muḥammad 'Alī. To rule in Arabia as he governed Syria, yes; but as for creating an Arab empire, he was too much of a Turk and too jealous of his time to conceive a project of this kind; he knew, and said so himself, that the age of the prophets had passed" (p.36). Nubar's admiration for Muḥammad 'Alī is shown by what he claims to have told the emperor of Austria in 1869: "'Every time we deviate from the path he traced for us we go astray and take the wrong road.' And I could have added 'we ruin Egypt'" (p.56).

On the other hand, Ibrahim, whom Nubar also admired, would "under the influence of one or two glasses of champagne, declaim Arabic poetry, his eyes on fire" (p.202). There are some unexpected touches, such as Ibrahim weeping at the sight of the countryside along the Dordogne and explaining, "I weep to see this region so prosperous, while Egypt is so miserable; and yet Egypt's soil is more fertile than this." Ibrahim adds, I shall change all that, if God grants me life" (p.26). Or there is this incident in Liverpool, with Ibrahim leaning out of a window and saying: "You see those two men, half drunk? They were fighting, a policeman came and all he had to do was to show them his stick; they immediately broke off and are now quietly following him to jail. Therein lies the greatness of England, and not only in the factories we have visited" (pp.29-30).

Abbas I was considered by Europeans as "fanatical and retrograde—one should add that for them, then as now, the two terms are identical" (p.59). Nubar relates many stories regarding his cruelty and despotism but also notes his frugality and determination to cut public expenditures (pp.78-81). Under him officials were paid regularly, whereas under Muḥammad 'Alī they "waited fifteen or twenty months for their salaries" (p.113). "It is true that, during his reign, the people lived under a regime of terror; but they were not subjected to those unforeseen exactions" that had been common under Muḥammad 'Alī (p.80). At his death "the country lost its Oriental character, and it was because of its disorder that Europe implanted itself as sovereign in Egypt" (p.124).

Nubar has some liking but little esteem for Said: "He had too much wit, totally lacked self-respect and was too fond of shining" (p.127). A few examples of his prodigality fill a chapter (pp.137-42). Ismail he thoroughly disliked and held responsible for Egypt's ruin; hence, Ismail gets none of those sharp but friendly observations directed at his predecessors. But, speaking of the death of Prince Ahmad, the heir apparent, in a railway accident during the time when Nubar was director of the railways (see below), Nubar says he "was thrifty, wise, reserved; he had many of his father's qualities. If he had lived, Egypt would not have had Ismail, whom destiny blinded because his ruin and that of Egypt had been decreed" (p.182). Nothing is said about Tawfiq or Abbas. But he has this remark about Egypt's future ruler, Major Evelyn Baring: "He had been the secretary of his uncle, Lord Northbrook, when the latter was Viceroy of India. He was therefore steeped in the Indian spirit. As soon as he had heard my exposition of that idea he pushed it aside, without taking the trouble to examine it: 'This kind of institution is unknown in India,' he said" (p.507).

The memoirs are full of interesting observations on social matters, such as Muḥammad 'Alī's tenacious and successful efforts to improve the condition of Christians (pp.6-12), the methods of education in the Egyptian Mission in Paris (pp.31-34), the functioning of the mail service connecting Alexandria with Suez (pp.62-65), and the cholera epidemic of 1865 (pp.251-52).

There is also much useful information on economic affairs, such as the boom caused by the rise in cereal prices during the Crimean War (pp. 133-36) and the simultaneous buying of agricultural land by Greeks and Syrians (p.151), the construction of ports (pp.160-62) and railways (pp.245-46), cotton cultivation (p.336), and the use of forced labor in the construction of the Suez Canal and various irrigation works (pp.227-310, 410). "Strictly speaking, Egypt was only a factory of public works and water was the motive power of that factory" (p.496). As might be expected, there is much on land tenure (pp.68-74) and land taxes (pp.400-406,441).

I should like to dwell at greater length on an interesting episode: Nubar's service as director of the railways in 1857-59, at a time when traffic was unusually heavy because, in addition to the regular trains (which were generally four hours late), there were special boat trains for the ships from India and others carrying material for the Kafr al-Zayyāt bridge and Suez railways. His "personnel had the same mix as the population of Alexandria, where it had been recruited. In addition to the engineers and engine drivers who had come from England there were Greeks, Italians, and Frenchmen, all novices but all looking at their co-workers and supervisors with the spirit current in Alexandria, viz., that a European, simply because he was protected by his consul, deemed himself superior to the native who had no protection" (p.171). And indeed, a few days after he had assumed office, when he proposed to fine an engine driver who had caused an accident, he was told that he could not do so without the consent of the British consul.

Partly because the Egyptians were easier to manage, Nubar tried to substitute them for foreigners, for example, as telegraph and construction engineers. This situation led them to present exaggerated demands, but when some Egyptians, who had been trained in England, were asked to build railway cars, the results were so poor that they could not be used. The incident led Nubar to the following observations:

> I have always had to deal with mixed administration and I must declare that, in order to make them work, one must either let one element have the upper hand completely and use the other as the rider does his horse—which is dangerous, for such a situation can lead to an outburst—or else one must hold the balance evenly between the two; but, in the latter case it is necessary to have much tact and moderation and to pay continuous attention. It is also necessary to inspire both sides with respect. (p.174)

Because of their long shifts—sometimes twelve to fourteen hours—the European engine drivers went on strike. Nubar dismissed them and replaced them with others, including three Egyptians: "'Our life is in danger,' one heard everywhere. The British consul was agitated, as was to a lesser degree, the French consul; the Peninsular and Oriental Line and the Messageries Impériales protested; the Viceroy himself was anxious . . . They said they could not admit that trains carrying mails and passengers be entrusted to Arabs . . . It was evident that, in their minds, the word 'competent' could be applied only to Europeans" (pp.175-76).[4] Eventually the strikers were taken back and given overtime pay, but only on the condition that they would renounce their consular protection; instead they were to be tried, if need be, by a committee consisting of high officials in the railways. Once again Nubar makes the following observation:

Having *fallāḥīn* as engine drivers is now so much a matter of course, it seems so natural, it is even so economic, that I have often asked myself if I have not exaggerated the agitation provoked by the announcement that an Arab would be driving a train. I do not exaggerate, the agitation was great; it was real and, moreover, everyone was sincere, even the princes; the secret anxiety of the Viceroy was equally sincere. In European eyes an Arab was an incapable creature, who lacked foresight, was indolent and lazy. To entrust him with so many persons was folly. I did not share this opinion. I was convinced that, if he knew he was being supervised, an Arab would do his work as attentively as a European; I believed that he would drive his engine with the same prudence and skill. I would certainly not rely entirely on him for the upkeep of the machines; I know that, on that point, he is not careful. But I had warned the superintendant, who never let out a locomotive driven by an Arab unless he had previously inspected it. Once it is running, I used to tell myself, one can hesitate between a man who drinks wine and is often overwhelmed by heat. (pp.177-78).

Many of these observations apply to conditions in developing countries today. Reports by experts sent to Asia, Africa, and Latin America, which I read during my service at the United Nations, stress to the same degree the great mechanical aptitude and ingenuity of people in such countries and the very poor maintenance of machinery, which shortens its life to a fraction of what it should be.

This brief note concludes with a page from a master of English prose. In the course of his duties at the post office, Anthony Trollope was sent to Egypt in 1858 to conclude arrangements for the conveyance of British mails by railway. Here is his description of his negotiations with Nubar:

I found him a most courteous gentleman, an Armenian. I never went to his office, nor do I know that he had an office. Every other day he would come to me at my hotel, and bring with him servants, and pipes, and coffee. I enjoyed his coming greatly; but there was one point on which we could not agree. As to money and other details, it seemed as though he could hardly accede fast enough to the wishes of the Postmaster-General; but on one point he was firmly opposed to me. I was desirous that the mails should be carried through Egypt in twenty-four hours, and he thought that forty-eight hours should be allowed. I was obstinate, and he was obstinate; and for a long time we would come to no agreement. At last his oriental tranquility seemed to desert him, and he took upon himself to assure me, with almost more a British energy, that if I insisted on the quick transit, a terrible responsibility would rest on my head. I made this mistake, he said,—that I supposed that a rate of travelling which would be easy and secure in England could be attained with safety in Egypt. "The Pasha, his master, would," he said, "no doubt accede to any terms demanded by the British Post Office, so great was his reverence for everything British. In that case, he, Nubar, would at once resign his position, and retire into obscurity. He would be ruined; but the loss of life and bloodshed which would certainly follow so rash an attempt should not be on his head." I smoked my pipe, or rather his, and drank his coffee, with oriental quiescence but British firmness. Every now and again, through three or four visits, I renewed the expression of my opinion that the transit could easily be made in twenty-four hours. At last he gave way—and astonished me by the cordiality of his greeting. There was no longer any question of bloodshed or of resignation of office, and he assured me, with energetic complaisance, that it should be his care to see that the time was punctually kept. It was punctually kept, and, I believe, is so still. I must confess, however, that my persistency was not the result of any courage specially personal to myself. While the matter was being debated it had been whispered to me that the Peninsular and Oriental Steamship Company had conceived that forty-eight hours would suit the purposes of their traffic better than twenty-four, and that, as they were the great paymasters on the railway, the Minister of the Egyptian State, who managed the railway, might probably wish to accommodate them. I often wondered who originated that frightful picture of blood and desolation. That it came from an English heart and an English hand I was always sure.[5]

Notes

1. Evelyn Baring Cromer, 1st Lord of Cromer, *Modern Egypt* (New York: Macmillan, 1908) 2:335-42.
2. Quoted in Afaf Lutfi al-Sayyid, *Egypt and Cromer: A Study in Anglo-Egyptian Relations* (London: John Murray, 1968), p.60.
3. *Mémoires de Nubar Pacha*, Introduction and notes by Mirrit Boutros Ghali (Beirut: Librairie du Liban, 1983). Quotations from this source are indicated by page numbers in the text.
4. This situation provides a good illustration of Issawi's Factor of Error: "Experts in advanced countries underestimate by a factor of 2 to 4 the ability of people in underdeveloped countries to do anything technical. (Examples, Japanese on war planes, Russians on the bomb, Iranians on refineries, Egyptians on the Suez Canal, Chinese on everything.)" Charles Issawi, *Issawi's Laws of Social Motions* (New York: Hawthorn Books, 1973), p.24.
5. Anthony Trollope, *An Autobiography* (Berkeley and Los Angeles: University of California Press, 1947), pp.104-5.

The Neopatriarchal Discourse: Language and Discourse in Contemporary Arab Society

HISHAM SHARABI

Language is simultaneously a social institution and a system of values.[1] In its narrow sense, discourse is a form of language: "bodies of utterances or inscriptions larger than a simple sentence but smaller than a total language."[2] The sense in which I use the term *discourse* includes this denotation but goes beyond it to assimilate the objective realities emphasized in the above definition. In Frederic Jameson's precise terms, these objective realities refer to "'realities' or objects in the real world, such as the various levels or instances of a social formation: political power, social class, institutions, and, events themselves."[3]

The "language" of the neopatriarchal discourse is classical Arabic, in which the knowledge (beliefs, concepts, substantive information) and self-knowledge (modes of self-understanding and self-relating) of neopatriarchal culture become formulated and produced in the shape of discourse. One of the most striking characteristics of what we call classical Arabic (*fuṣḥā*) is the radical dichotomy it presupposes between everyday colloquial and formal language: on this level, the division is not merely one between the literate and the "vulgar" tongue, found in all class societies, but between two distinct "languages," essentially related but fundamentally different. The individual spontaneously absorbs the one from his environment in the process of growing up, but he has to appropriate the other as another language, much as he would a foreign language. The difference between spoken and colloquial Arabic and classical or literary Arabic involves something close to the difference between, say, modern French and medieval Latin. There is no society in the world today that uses its traditional classical language practically unchanged as its basic means of everyday communication and of formal discourse.[4] A major implication has been the reinforcement of social divisions and concealment of the material or class basis of cultural disparity: knowledge becomes a privileged possession and an instrument of power. Thus linguistic competence (familiarity with classical literature and the ability to use the classical language forcefully in public speaking) bestows status and power, and by the same token, the illiterate and the semiliterate are excluded from this knowledge (power), and their consciousness is formed largely outside the culture of the public educational institutions and the media (which are geared by their language to literate audiences).

In the process of socialization, the classical language plays an even more fundamental role in shaping orientation and attitude: it determines the form and content of the rearing and educational practices of society at large. Normally the child's first encounter with the classical or literary language is through the sacred text, which he is often made to learn by heart. From the very beginning the child thus experiences the dissociation between learning and understanding; his early spontaneous attempts at clarification (meaning, understanding) are aborted, and rote learning, based on memorization and the rejection of all questioning, becomes the normal way of acquiring ideas and internalizing values.[5] The mode of thought deriving from this practice, which is reinforced in the subsequent stages of socialization, is characterized by a peculiar capacity to resist external challenges either by rejecting them altogether or by absorbing them without experiencing change. Thus, as we shall see later, the European model of rational inquiry appropriated by the thought of the Awakening becomes largely a fetishized norm manipulated in support of its own particular "rationality" by the reformist, secular, nationalist, or fundamentalist position.

Reading as Interpretation

If language limits thought, classical Arabic limits it in a decisive way. This is not only because of the essentially ideological character of the classical, with its rigid religious framework, but also because of its inherent tendency to "think itself," that is, to impose its own patterns and structures on all linguistic production. It is a "received language," "a language of others," that favors, as Halim Barakat puts it, "literary over scientific writing and rhetoric over the written text and speech over writing."[6]

The sort of discourse this language produces mediates reality through a double ideology: the ideology inherent in the "trance of language,"[7] produced and reproduced by the magic of catchwords, incantations, verbal stereotypes, and internal referents, and the ideology supplied by the "encratic" language[8] produced and disseminated under the protection of political or religious orthodoxy. It is a discourse especially suited for the projection of a particular kind of being, for organizing the irrational, and for activating the imaginary.

Although, as Jacques Berque has rightly pointed out, this language can provide all the terminology of modernity, its connotations do not necessarily refer to modernity, as "lived and organized experience" (in Berman's terms). Or, as Berque wrote: "Who would claim that its connotations refer to . . . modernity? Does its true 'referent' not lie elsewhere?"[9] For its field is the rhetorical rather than the scientific, the metaphysical rather than the metonymic: "its fatherland is the general."[10]

The priority given speech over writing, noted by Barakat and Adonis, has far-reaching implications, to which I can here only briefly allude. This tendency should be assessed in itself, as an independent factor lying outside all considerations of literacy or education. In Europe, for example, the invention of printing had among its major effects making the Gutenberg Bible available on a wide scale, thus serving to spread and deepen the Protestant revolution. The individual act of reading the Bible constituted an intellectually revolutionary development in that it brought about a crucial transition: one which might be described as a transition from rhetoric to hermeneutics. Now traditional patriarchal culture never promoted the reading of the Koran, even after it became widely available after the introduction of the printing press in the nineteenth century. To this day it is still recited, chanted, and repeated by heart, but rarely read, if at all. Interpretation has remained the monopoly of specialists or religious officials whose exegesis derives not so much from readings of the sacred text as from commentaries upon it.

In this context, attention should be drawn to the subversive or liberating function of reading, and the primary concern of all established orthodoxy of protecting itself against all critical readings or interpretations, that is, those leading to understanding. Now subversion or liberation is attained by this sequence: reading (interpretation), understanding, criticism. So if reading is the path to innovation and change, speech, monopolized by orthodoxy and the status quo, is the condition of stability and continuity. Hence the centrality of the monologue in all forms of neopatriarchal discourse—not only in the modes of expression and interpersonal interaction, but also in terms of the values and relations validating and reinforcing these forms of expression and interaction.

The monological mode of discourse manifests itself, for instance, in the tendency of speakers persistently to exclude or ignore other speakers. But it is to be seen in the very structure of the discourse itself: the monological discourse is produced not just by force or authority, but also by the language itself, which, because it favors rhetoric, discourages dialogue.

In addition to the social and psychological implications of this aspect, there are important epistemological consequences as well, of which the most important, perhaps, is the way in which truth or validity is constituted: in insisting on agreement, all monologues exclude difference, questioning, reservation, and qualification. Hence monological speech and writing never exhibit hesitation or doubt—attributes that delimit or undermine monological authority—but rely on general and unqualified affirmation: the fundamental type of monological truth is absolute truth and its ultimate ground is revelation. Clearly the monological discourse is, by its very structure, a negation of the dialogue and of the assumption on which the dialogue is based: the assumption, for example, that no discourse is in itself final or closed, that only free questioning can yield true knowledge, and that truth is constituted not by authority but by discussion, criticism, and consent.

The monological discourse may be expressed in different forms and articulated in different voices, depending on its setting. Thus in the household it is the father's discourse which is the dominant discourse, the teacher's in the classroom, the sheikh's in the religious gathering or the tribe, the ruler's in the society at large, and so forth. It is from the structure of language itself rather than from the individual utterance that this discourse derives its perceived sense or signification. Although the structure is geared to reinforce authority, hierarchy, and the relations of dependency and subordination, it also produces oppositional forms typical of the neopatriarchal discourse: gossip, backbiting, storytelling, and silence—for discussion or opposition in these settings can only be carried out behind the back of authority, or underground.

Monological speech, in daily practice, rarely produces good listeners, for it aims not to enlighten or to inform but to dominate. The listener or recipient, the "other" of the monological relationship (the son, the student, the citizen), is reduced to silence; he or she may outwardly acquiesce, but inwardly could turn away. Hence the ambiguous relation of the illiterate masses to authority, or to orthodoxy, and to the high culture of the urban center. Colloquial, or oral, culture is in this respect like the culture of children or the counterculture of rebels, both of whom turn away, withdraw, and remain silent without engaging in overt or direct opposition.

It is not difficult to see why in the monological culture silence tends to reign; for, apart from the effect of censorship and intimidation, the social majority, that is, the poor, the young, and the women, is permanently reduced to listeners ("they listen [to] the word"): its world is inhabited by multiple single voices that command and legislate its life from above.

If in a monological culture validation rests, as it does in neopatriarchal society, on the spoken word ("so and so said that so and so said . . . "), then nonverbal proof (empirical evidence) is rendered secondary or even irrelevant. Thus the world of objects and events tends to be reduced to verbal presentations that possess their own system of validation. So the anecdote becomes the document and the evidence: to narrate is to reveal and to make intelligible.[11] Praxis becomes a function of narrative: the telling of the action is the action itself.[12] Indeed, events acquire their significance only in the telling. The ontological differentiation between the action and its verbal formulation is so blurred that its terms intermingle and often lose their separate identity.

In this kind of discourse the ideological component is no longer to be sought merely in the explicit content but rather in the presuppositions and assumptions implicit in its linguistic structure. This aspect becomes clear when we recall the ideological specificity of classical Arabic alluded to earlier. Thus ideology presents itself on two levels, the manifest level of the text and the underlying level of the linguistic categories. The ideological power function of the text can be easily grasped in its institutional and formal expressions, and will explain why in the neopatriarchal discourse ideological thinking is so far ahead of the critical. More difficult to pin down, however, is the effect of the unconscious and implicit categories. Roman Jakobson's characterization of speech-systems is of special relevance in this instance: a speech-system should be defined less by what it permits us to say than by what it compels us to say.[13]

One way of dealing with this aspect of the monological discourse is to analyze its cultural context, that is, to account for variations in meaning and interpretation resulting from changes in linguistic context. By *linguistic context* I mean, for example, the process of coding and recoding which takes place in translation from one mode of expression to another or from one "language" to another. In translations from a foreign language, the richness of classical Arabic makes it seem easy to overcome the problem of translating terminology and of recoding. But this does not take into account the shift in context and the way categories and terms are grounded in specific meanings and experiences. Nor is this difficulty in translating or understanding superseded merely by adequation of language, that is, by gaining linguistic competence without, however, having an inner grasp of the cultural context, the unified structure of concepts, categories, and linguistic codes. Failure to overcome this difficulty, and total unawareness of this failure, is evident in the (unconscious) recoding which occurs in the Arabic translation of Western texts (both linguistic and cognitive), which are transformed in the process into new (Arabic) linguistic forms. An extreme but illuminating literary example is Mustafa al-Manfalouti's popular novel *Majdouline*, the Arabic translation of *Paul et Virginie*. Here the transposition of character, plot, meaning, and motivation into the context of the classical Arabic and Egyptian culture is so complete as to render the original work virtually unrecognizable: the result is an exemplary neopatriarchal literary product. Here as elsewhere adaption is the mechanism whereby the process of shifting from one context to another is carried out, a process of *ta'rīb* (literally, Arabization), through which the original text is *transformed* into Arabic.

This failure to penetrate the alien Western cultural text from the "inside" and to appropriate it comprehensively as a translated meaning or content sheds some light on another phenomenon involving a movement of interpretation between different contexts or cultural backgrounds. It is the parallel failure of transferring scientific and technological knowledge despite exposure to European science as early as the first student missions to Paris in the 1820s. Neopatriarchal culture still sends out student missions to acquire basic scientific knowledge in the West over a century and a half later.[14]

On the other hand, one of neopatriarchy's most notable successes has been in evolving effective defenses against failure: an apologetic doctrine based on a vision of the Arab past which, in its more vulgar forms, reduces Western civilization to a product of Arab or Islamic civilization. The success of this maneuver, in turn, points up the central shortcoming of the Arab Awakening: its failure to confront Europe on its own terms (as did the Japanese), to recognize the terms of modernity, and to attempt an epistemological or paradigmatic break with its patriarchal past.[15] In this light even the linguistic, or "language," problem would no longer appear as a serious problem of adequately transposing meaning from one context or culture to another, but would revert to one of a structural dysfunction occurring within the framework of the awakening consciousness itself. Thus neopatriarchy, while consenting to the modernization of its material life by accepting the concepts and products of "science" and "progress," repressed the radical questioning which briefly appeared at the beginning of the Awakening. From the very start, the traditional patriarchal discourse, with its closed reading of history and society, was thus never seriously questioned or challenged; on the contrary, it was preserved intact and placed alongside the emerging "scientific" or "modernist" discourse. With this initial compromise or surrender, there could be no radical divergence from orthodox ideology. From the start the new, neopatriarchal culture necessarily took the form of an affirmative rather than a critical culture in its discourse, which was developed by the rising literati in the three centers of neopatriarchal intellectual life (Beirut, Cairo, and Damascus) for the next three generations (1880-1950).

In concluding this section, I must underscore a point which the earlier discussion should have made clear, namely, that the impossibility of making the epistemological break under the conditions in which the Arab Awakening took place was a foregone conclusion. I am referring here to the conditions created by the extension of European hegemony by the early nineteenth century, constituting the crucible within which the neopatriarchal discourse was born.

The Different Languages of Neopatriarchy

If we were to map out in a schematic way the development of the neopatriarchal discourse, from its early stages in the late nineteenth century—from the suppresson of questioning and skeptical impulses and their replacement by an affirmative paradigm—to its final stage in the 1970s and 1980s, the following ideological pattern would emerge:

Ideological Phases of the Neopatriarchal Age

Orientation	*(Islamic) reformism*		*Secularism*
(1880-1918)	"Progress," "reform"		"Democracy," etc.
Doctrine	*Salafīyah*	*Nationalism*	*Socialism*
(1918-1945)	Islamic revival	Unity, independence	Revolutionary movement
Political practice	*Islamic radicalism*		*Modern sultanate*
(1945-1980)			Emergence of the multistate system
(1980-)	*Militant fundamentalism*		*Secular criticism*

Again, it is important to note that the neopatriarchal paradigm which developed over a hundred years was not simply the product of a philosophical failure but rather of social and historical realities, on which I will elaborate further.

In its early phase, the development of the reformist and secular paradigm must be seen against a context characterized by the development of trade, the expansion of cities and towns (for the first time since their decline in the thirteenth and fourteenth centuries), and the rise of a commerical and compadore bourgeoisie, a period ending with World War I. During this phase the mass of society was out of the social picture. Mass movement into the cities only begins after World War I, and the political and social integration of the proletarian and semiproletarian majority does not take place until after 1945, and in some countries much later.

In the past hundred years, neopatriarchal discourse may be said to have expressed itself in three languages, each with its own vocabulary and its own concepts, each grounded in a world, or a subculture, different yet connected to the others. There is, first, the world of the peasant and tribal countryside, which is divided from the other two not only by social and economic differences but also by culture, psychology, and outlook, the linguistic difference between classical and colloquial, the difference between literate and illiterate, and so on. The other two worlds are urban. Within the city there are two different worlds: that of the urban proletariat and lower petty bourgeoisie, which is an extension of the countryside, though now differentiated from it; and that of the middle and upper bourgeoisie, the world of well-being, wealth, and high culture. It should be noted that these three worlds are neither self-sufficient nor self-contained, and although their constitution is based on class division they cannot be accounted for solely by category of class. Socialization, particularly in the last two or three decades, has blurred the division between rural proletariat, urban proletariat, and urban petty bourgeoisie, and has increasingly separated them from the urban upper-class minority, based on wealth and power.

Recall that the language of the countryside, the colloquial dialect of the prodominantly illiterate tribal peasant and village population, is still (in the late 1980s) that of over three-quarters of neopatriarchal society, that the rural discourse, enclosed in the local vernacular, is the product of the oral culture of the countryside—the beliefs, legends, and traditional practices of village and desert life. It is thus the most traditional or patriarchal discourse of neopatriarchal society, for in the oral culture of the rural world the horizon of the spoken language and traditional values and beliefs coincide in frozen and unchanging symmetry. Indeed, the silence and passivity of the rural proletariat, the backbone of neopatriarchal society, is grounded in its illiteracy. Here the problem of illiteracy/literacy is not simply a question of reading and writing. Seen in the context of the literate language (classical

Arabic), of the division between a written and an oral culture, illiteracy constitutes both a linguistic and a psychological disability without parallel in any other Third World society. For to make the transition into literacy is not merely to learn a system of signs, but to learn a system of values which has no relevance to the daily existence of the rural population. In the literacy campaigns, the process of learning the written (classical) languages becomes a kind of ritual in which the profane (the everyday) has to be suppressed and subordinated to the sacred text. Instead of intellectual windows being opened for the newly literate, the latter are brought closer to authority and its controls. Functional illiterates, the invariable product of all anti-illiteracy campaigns—men and women who can perhaps sign their names and read the headlines of a newspaper and make out the drift of a newscast—are, strictly speaking, still unable to read. The classical language by its very character produces or reinvents the very same mental obstacle which the attempts at overcoming illiteracy presumably seek to remove: autonomous awareness. Even as literacy spreads, illiteracy is preserved and compounded, for the power of the language is such as to inhibit the appropriation of any kind of alternative paradigm; literacy only reinforces the power of the monological discourse. For the rural proletariat, breaking the vicious circle occurs by other, unintended means—by being conscripted into the army, by moving into the city, by gaining regular access to urban culture through improved communications, and so forth, developments which over the last two or three decades have been responsible for the spontaneous breakdown of the isolation of rural life, though they have not led to bridging the social and psychological gap separating city from countryside.

The literate language of the neopatriarchal city naturally divides into two kinds of discourse, one expressed in the language of the traditionalist, patriarchal language of the sacred texts, the other in the language of the progressive reformist and secular ideologist, the neopatriarchal language of the daily newspaper. However, although the two discourses and their linguistic modes may differ in form as well as content, they are not essentially antagonistic, for in both their agreements and their oppositions they share the same basic paradigm.

The Traditional Discourse

Let us first address the traditional (Islamic) discourse. The power of this type of discourse, and the language through which it comes to expression, derives from an authoritative origin or text on which it bases its claim to truth and validity, a claim which serves to achieve two things simultaneously: to consolidate the hegemony of the text (source) and to block the possibility of its criticism or replacement (that is, of expressing what has not been already expressed in or through it). Here not only are certain domains of thought (such as modern paradigms) automatically sealed off, but the method of thinking itself is disarmed by strict restriction to traditional modes: commentary, exegesis, recitation, and so forth. Thus the role of language in the traditional discourse is not so much to communicate or to clarify as to command and to impose obediences both in its theoretic and social use or form. In other words, the aim of the traditional discourse is not to bring about awareness, understanding, or self-consciousness, but their opposite: to reinforce an affective (noncritical) state rooted in external dependence and inner submission. Whence the necessity of a system of knowledge based on learning by rote (including learning the modern academic text) and the cultivation of intellectual passivity and uncritical submission to the printed page. Thus, to borrow a familiar phrase, here too, the text is everything and nothing exists beyond it; and that is not because of a linguistic theory but as a result of a metaphysical assumption: the traditional discourse in whatever form it is expressed excludes every other discourse, for it not only contains the only true knowledge but also the solution to all problems. The only problem with which this position concerns itself is the social reinstatement of true Islam, the sole condition for the salvation of the individual and of society.

The cognitive system in which the traditional discourse is grounded is designed to insure the supremacy of the religious perspective and automatically to delegitimate different or opposing positions. It does this by stressing a mode of presentation for which only a certain kind of knowledge is possible and in which all other types are excluded. It cultivates certain forms of cognitive dissonance and corresponding forms of social ignorance, partly by direct ideological censorships, partly by reducing all questioning to the self-evident, and partly by making social reality appear "natural" and fully transparent. This system of knowledge develops its own logic and ways of interpretations which are often impervious to evidence and persuasion and function only in accordance with their own absolute or total categories. (One wonders, for example, what would be the effect if the sacred text were translated into the common tongue and its cognitive categories, so that it became immediately intelligible the way the Bible was at the beginning of the European modern age.)

It is important to note, however, that this inflexible opposition to doubts, questionings, and change (toward modernity) derives not only from doctrinal or ideological considerations but mainly from practical, political concerns. Indeed, the traditionalist Islamic discourse in its various forms (reformist, conservative, fundamentalist) is concerned as much with religious purity as it is, if not more, with political power. I will have occasion, later, to deal with this central theme.

The Reformist-Secular-Ideological Discourse

Alongside the traditional text stands the "newspaper" text of the reformist-secular-ideological discourse of bourgeois and petty bourgeois sectors. In this discourse the classical language is no longer tied to the sacred texts, but is "modernized," that is, simplified to fit the requirements of the times. Still, this modernized version of classical Arabic is in structure and tone essentially the same as the classical language of medieval Islam. Its modernization is a superficial, nonstructural change which took place under the influence of the literary revival of the late nineteenth century and the sudden exposure to Western knowledge. "Modern" classical Arabic evolved into "newspaper" Arabic, an easier, suppler language than the traditional classical, in which the new literature and learning as well as the new popular media now found expression. It coexisted harmoniously and without contradiction with the traditional discourse, but not with the colloquial, or oral, discourse of the common masses, as we shall see presently. The claim that the "newspaper" Arabic of neopatriarchal society constitutes a synthesis between the colloquial and the classical as does, for example, modern French between medieval Latin and the spoken language is an exaggeration, more wishful thinking than reality. This simplified classical Arabic, like the social formation it reflects, is neither fully traditional nor really modern, but an uneven combination of the two. It is the product of forces and developments over which there existed no conscious or self-directing controls, with the result that the essential division or opposition between the colloquial and the classical (both in its traditional and "newspaper" forms) remained unchanged. This fact has been instrumental in preserving the social and cultural divisions of neopatriarchal society and in maintaining the epistemological compromise of the Arab Awakening over a period of two or three generations, thus blocking the possibility of a genuine epistemological break with traditional patriarchal discourse. No breakthrough toward full modernity was possible.

This fact may be seen throughout three of the phases marking the cultural and political formation of neopatriarchal society in the last hundred years: from the late Ottoman phase (to the end of World War I) through the period of European domination (to the end of World War II) to the age of independence (post-World War II to the present).

Phases of Neopatriarchal Development, 1880-1980

Ottoman phase (1880-1918)	*Reformism and secularism* Islamic reform, science, democracy
European phase (1918-1945)	*Nationalism, Islamism, socialism* Liberalism, Arab unity, Islamic revival, socialist theory
Independence phase (1945-1980)	*Multistate system, capitalist, noncapitalist development* Nationalism, socialism, Islam
Postindependence (1980-)	*Islamic radicalism, secular criticism* Militant fundamentalism, liberal and socialist secularism

The Ottoman phase, which saw the rise of the first class of intellectuals who tended to identify with the emerging urban bourgeoisie, brought a new vocabulary into use which was culled from the great Arabic classics, laced with the concepts and terminology of European thought.[16] It was the newly discovered Arabic classics, now printed for the first time in Beirut and Cairo as well as in Europe, that projected the image of the "glorious Arab past," obscured until the Awakening by Ottoman oppression and cultural backwardness. For Muslim reformists as well as for secular intellectuals living in the late Ottoman Empire, the revival of society and the restoration of the Arab cultural and national identity implied above all breaking away from Ottoman political and cultural domination.[17] But the cultural problematics, unlike the political, received, as we have seen, no clear-cut resolution: the issues implicit in the process of cultural revival were not as simple and were neither clearly formulated nor fully confronted. The sacred and literary texts were inscribed in the new discourse of the Awakening without any critical awareness as the finished models of reformist and secularist consciousness. In retrospect, the four hundred years of "decline" were seen as somewhat accidental, so that the movement toward change was now to be directed more to correct or to purify society than to critically determine the content and goal of the movement toward change. Thus the need to question the past and to reassess its values and categories from a critical standpoint did not arise, or if it did was swept aside as unnecessary or irrelevant. It is therefore not surprising that the classical (traditional) paradigms were merely refurbished and "modernized" rather than reformulated or replaced, and were adopted enthusiastically by the educated strata—whose interest, in any case, lay not in questioning tradition or established authority but in reforming society "to catch up with the caravan of progress and civilization."

The next period, the period of European domination, saw the expansion of the secular and liberal bourgeois intelligentsia. Now, following the end of the First World War, Europe became politically and culturally a direct and pervasive presence in the Arab world. The system of education was rapidly Europeanized and an increasing number of students traveled to Europe to study. But, despite its more modern education, this interwar generation of intellectuals did not go beyond the epistemological boundaries set by the previous one; it exhibited the same docility toward the established order and world view. Thus the two dominant ideological currents of this period, Islamic reformism and liberal secularism, were the ones that dominated the previous (Ottoman) phase, with only this difference, an enhancement of the secular liberal currents reflecting Europe's dominance and the spread of European-style education.

The period of independence, the era of ideological struggle and the multistate system, witnessed the eclipse of the reformist, liberal, nationalist and socialist modes of the neopatriarchal discourse and the spread of Islamic fundamentalism, first as a defensive reaction, then increasingly as an aggressive and militant political movement.

In sum, during the last century or so, the discourse of neopatriarchal society has never in any of its phases or aspects taken a genuine or consistent critical position in addressing the social, political or ideological issues of this age of transition. Its political thought has remained essentially utopian in orientation, serving more to reinforce the established order and the affirmative culture dominant in it than to question their political and ideological foundations, and has remained totally inhibited in the face of the traditional religious discourse.[18]

An important social development during the independence period is the structural transformation of the educated stratas resulting from the spread of education and the emergence of a position of social dominance of the petty bourgeoisie. It should be recalled that the terms *education* and *culture* are synonymous in Arabic; "*educated* (*muthaqqaf*, intellectual) describes practically anyone with a college degree or one who has achieved a certain amount of formal education. A definite or clear class correlation of intellectuals was no longer possible; education and being educated now embraced individuals from all classes including to some extent the proletarian masses. The educated, (intellectual) class was no longer confined, as it had been until the 1950s, to an elite composed of a relatively small group of writers, teachers, artists, professionals, and educated individuals. It now meant being part of a large, continually growing body of a literate and vocal group dominated by the petty bourgeois class. The intelligentsia in the classical age of Islam—the poet's, the ulemas, the scholars—was largely dependent on the sultan's largess for its well-being. Now, in the age of independence, a similar situation obtained: the intelligentsia was again the servant of the state, and from its ranks came the state ideologues as well as the top civil servants and technocrats.

The three phases in which neopatriarchal discourse developed in its various forms may be characterized by the mode of conceptualization distinctive of each phase. For example, in the Ottoman period, during which it can be maintained that the dominant mode of neopatriarchal thought was shaped, the view of science was fundamentally ideological, with little if any awareness of its methodological character. The Awakening's ideology was based on scientism, while its *epistemology* remained bound to patriarchalism. This fact was expressed in the slogan, now revived by fundamentalism, *science and faith* (*al-'ilm wa-al-imān*), the combined ground of insuring simultaneously ideological purity and social strength.

Unlike Japan, which at that very moment was systematically importing European science and technology and converting them into effective conceptual and instrumental possessions, Arab neopatriarchy was cultivating a literary and religious attitude toward Europe and modernity. From the start it robbed itself of the opportunity to develop, as did the Japanese with amazing consistency, an autonomous and self-directing position which would, as it absorbed the shock of Europe, pave the way to scientific understanding. A curious, persistent blindness seemed to prevent this early generation (but also the two following generations) from grasping the fundamental opposition between science and ideology at the heart of Western thought and being—the implications of which the Japanese seemed to have clearly understood from the very beginning—with the result that its consciousness may be described as an *arrested* consciousness, poised as it was on a prescientific or literary-ideological level: a naive thought.

Nor was the mode of conceptualization of the following period of European domination radically different, only that the generation of this period learned to speak a European language, English or French, through the modernized educational system. Thus a *fourth* language makes its appearance alongside the other three—the colloquial, the traditional classical, and the "newspaper" classical—as a medium of expression and communication.[19]

Perhaps the single greatest failure of this first foreign-language-speaking generation of intellectuals is its utter inability to bridge the ideological or epistemological gap inherited from the previous generation (which the Japanese had by now, 1920-1945, long transcended). These intermediate intellectuals, too, remained torn between tradition and modernity, between naive thought and scientific thought—and between the worlds posited by this opposition. The causes of failure are not hard to point out: on the level of comprehension it may be seen in the shortcomings of the new tool, their linguistic grasp. Although bilingual intellectuals of this generation could speak, read, and write a foreign language, most of them had only a tenuous grasp of its idiomatic or paradigmatic structure. An English or French speaker, for example, might speak the language fairly fluently, but his or her discourse would still be a naive discourse, a word-for-word rendering comprehensible only by reference to the paradigms of the written (traditional or modern) classical language. Translation into the Arabic illustrates the paradigmatic imprisonment of the naive and prescientific or literary thought of these neopatriarchal intellectuals. Though some of them—for example, Taha Hussein, Tawfiq al-Hakim, Abbās al-'Aqqād, and some of the younger generation of European- and American-trained professors and scholars of the 1930s and 1940s—wrote and spoke with a new voice, particularly in the fields of literature and history, their ideas and techniques were based largely on wholesale haphazard and uncritical borrowing. European thought, in the process of its "translation" into the language of the Arab secular liberal or leftist intellectuals of the interwar period, underwent significant distortion. Caught in the terminology and structures of "newspaper" Arabic, the translated views and concepts emerged in hardly recognizable forms.

What I have characterized as naive thought or discourse is ideologically variable, defined less by concrete content than by form or structure. For example, if the dominant discourse of the European period upheld the ideas and ideologies of liberalism, humanism, socialism, reason, progress, and so forth, it had little significance for the way in which intellectuals conceptualized these doctrines or their concrete expressions. Their abstract and largely idealistic approach to social reality rendered the intermediate intellectual generation an objective supporter of the status quo represented by both European domination and, later, by bourgeois rule of the early years of independence. The one-dimensional character of the liberal discourse of the reformist and secular intellectuals may be seen in the way it formulated the relation of thought to action:

preaching or rhetoric, identifying the word with the deed, was the mode of social action.[20] This tendency comes out clearly in the manner of writing prevalent in the 1920s, 1930s and 1940s. Whatever its specific content, the writing of this period tended toward formal principles and reinforced the dominant monological discourse. By its naive or utopian vision, it obscured the social context of material reality and helped to cover up the tragedy and horror of everyday life. It is not surprising that social practice in the period of independence reflected not only a sharp divorce between ideology and practice but also an abandonment of the prescriptions of theory or ideology (now reduced to pure rhetoric or realpolitik) toward naked activism and, finally, after the collapse of the ideological political parties (beginning in the 1950s) and the rise of the modern sultanate state, toward pure Machiavellianism.

Notes

1. See Roland Barthes, *Elements of Semiology*, trans. Annette Lavers and Collin Smith (London: Cape Editions, 1967), p. 14.
2. D. Davidson as paraphrased by Alex Callinicos, *Marxism and Philosophy* (New York: Oxford University Press, 1983), p. 147.
3. Frederic Jameson, *The Political Unconscious: Narrative as a Socially Symbolic Act* (Ithaca: Cornell University Press, 1981), p. 297.
4. One exception is Israel; but Hebrew was intentionally introduced to provide a single language to replace the various languages of Jews emigrating from various countries to Israel, and to secure national unity by reverting to the traditional language. It should be noted, however, that Israeli Hebrew has been consciously transformed in its vocabulary and use into a modern language.
5. The implications of this practice have been carefully noted by Adonis ('Ali Aḥmad Sa'id), *al-Thābit wa-al-mutaḥawwil* (*The Permanent and the Changing*) (Beirut: Dar al-'Awdah, 1974), 1:29.
6. Halim Barakat, *Contemporary Arab Society* (in Arabic), (Beirut: Center for Arab Unity Studies, 1984), p. 246. All quotations from Arabic are my translation.
7. Adonis ('Alī Aḥmad Sa'id), 1:29.
8. Roland Barthes' term in *The Pleasure of the Text*, trans. Richard Miller (New York: Hill and Wang, 1975), p. 40.
9. Jacques Berque, *Arab Rebirth: Pain and Ecstasy*, trans. Quintin Hoare (London: As-Saqi Books, 1983), p. 27.
10. Ibid.
11. This, for example, is how the truth of the Ḥadīth (collective sayings of Prophet Muḥammad) and that of the *tā'rīkh* (history) are constituted: their reality is the text, itself the reflection and repository of the oral

narrative chain.

12. In the patriarchal setting, as Claude Levi-Strauss has shown, narrative fulfills a social and a psychological function, by verbally, "in the imaginary," reconciling socially irreconcilable contradictions; as such, narrative is an act through which the patriarchical individual seeks to resolve crucial problems. In the neopatriarchical setting, however, where the character of the real has been transformed, narrative becomes a form of escape or of wishful thinking.
13. Quoted by Roland Barthes, "Inaugural Lecture, Collège de France," *A Barthes Reader*, ed. Susan Sontag (New York: Hill and Wang, 1982), p. 460.
14. In the case of Japan, the transfer was virtually completed in a generation and a half, between 1866 and 1900.
15. The notion I have in mind follows Michel Foucault's epistemic orders, Thomas Kuhn's theory of paradigms, and Louis Althusser's "epistemological rupture" in Marx.
16. The earliest and one of the best examples of the language and discourse of the *Nahḍah* is provided by Faris al-Shidyāq in his remarkable book, *al-Sāq 'ala al-sāq* (Beirut: Maktabat al-Ḥayāt, 1967), in some respects the most original Arabic work of the Age of Awakening.
17. The political side of how this was accomplished has been fully narrated by George Antonius, *The Arab Awakening* (Philadelphia, 1938), and the cultural and ideological side by Albert Hourani, *Arabic Thought in the Liberal Age, 1798-1939* (London: Macmillan Press, 1962), and Hisham Sharabi, *Arab Intellectuals and the West: The Formative Years, 1875-1914* (Baltimore: Johns Hopkins University Press, 1970).
18. There were some exceptions, particularly in the period of European domination: for example, Ṭahā Ḥusayn and Ali Abdul Raziq, in their criticism of the prevailing perspective on pre-Islamic civilization and Islamic law, respectively. See Ṭahā Ḥusayn, *Concerning Pre-Islamic Poetry* (in Arabic) (Cairo: Dār al-Kutub al-Miṣrīyah, 1925); and Ali Abdul Raziq, *Islam and the Foundation of Government* (in Arabic) (Cairo: Maktabat Miṣr, 1925). It is noteworthy that Ḥusayn was a graduate of the Sorbonne and Abdul Raziq of Oxford; both, however, once over a brief period of youthful defiance, settled into conventional careers, at peace with the status quo. See Hourani, *Arabic Thought*, pp. 216-18, 327.
19. The full social and intellectual consequences of the new linguistic possession does not, however, become apparent until later, with the rise of the critical or radical intellectuals of the 1970s and 1980s.
20. For an interesting account of Arab liberalism and its intellectual roots, see 'Alī Umlīl, *The Arab Reformist Movement and the Nation State* (in Arabic) (Beirut: Dār al-Tanwīr, 1985), pp. 87-106, 153-68. For the younger generation which grew up in the next, postindependence period, this confusing dualism, in which thought seemed to enjoy a separate and autonomous existence, led to a pattern of behavior based on pure action: militancy in the discourse of the period of ideology took the form of violence and terror, not of democracy and human relations.

The Interplay Between Social and Cultural Change: The Case of Germany and the Arab Middle East

BASSAM TIBI

Even in scholarly debate there exists confusion with regard to the widespread loose usage of the terms *culture* and *civilization.* It seems difficult to define what culture is. Clifford Geertz tells us that there are a number of ways "to escape this—turning culture into folklore and collecting it, turning it into traits and counting it, turning it into institutions and classifying it, turning it into structures and toying with it. But they *are* escapes."[1] The analysis of *civilization* is no less incomplete than that of *culture.* Moreover, the interplay between culture or civilization and social structures is not always clear. Many social scientists and anthropologists adhere to reductionist approaches. Culture is seen as the motor of social change or, the other way around, as the mirror of social change.

This paper seeks to clarify these issues in a conceptual way. Empirically the Arab Middle East and Germany are the focus of a comparative analysis. It lies beyond the scope of this paper to discuss broadly the prevailing concepts of culture and civilization. I adhere to Geertz's concept of culture, which is free of multiple referents and of ambiguity. He says that culture "denotes an historically transmitted pattern of meanings embodied in symbols, a system of inherited conceptions expressed in symbolic forms by means of which men communicate, perpetuate, and develop their knowledge about and attitudes toward life."[2]

Civilization has a different meaning and should not be used loosely as a synonym for culture. Norbert Elias, the great theorist of civilization, discusses the different French, Anglo-Saxon, and German traditions of the meaning of culture and civilization. In his view civilization denotes the historical process of change of human behavior, as well as of social and political structures. Whereas the concept of culture concentrates on the specific character of the different traditions, the concept of civilization focuses on the process of the change of patterns that all cultures share.[3] It has two components: *sociogenesis* and *psychogenesis*, that is, the process of change in both structure and human behavior.

Geertz's concept of culture and Elias's concept of civilization could be combined and used as a framework for the analysis of the interplay between social and cultural change in the process of civilization. Historically, there have been different processes of civilization, one of which was Islamic. Since the rise of industrial civilization in Europe, and the accompanying Western and European invasion of the whole world, there has been one prevailing civilization process. Our world could be defined as a world society, and in this sense I developed the term *world-societalization* of the civilization process. Notwithstanding this universalization, different cultures still exist. Today, although we can witness one civilization process based on modern science and technology, we cannot find a world culture, or any *culture universelle.* The various cultures that are exposed to this universalized process of civilization must each cope in its way with this new pattern of civilization. Moreover, the interplay between social and cultural change in our times is complicated through this new phenomenon: social change is no longer domestically generated because it is externally induced and hence very rapid.

How do people in the Arab Middle East cope with these new circumstances?

The culture of the Middle East is based on the religion of Islam. In our context we are interested in Islam within the framework of the cultural dimension of religious analysis. The study of religion as such is not within the scope of this inquiry. In this sense, I refer to the *crisis of Islam*, a phrase I used as a title for one of my major books. It is the crisis of a nonindustrial culture in a historical period dominated by a universal process of industrial civilization based on modern science and technology.[4]

The leading Arab scholar Constantine Zurayk, to whom this volume pays tribute, is one of the keen analysts of this new phenomenon. Our age is for us, in his words, a *'aṣr mutafajjir* (explosive time).[5] In a volume of collected essays, *Nahnu wa-al-tārīkh* (Facing History), he emphasizes that "the Arabs are not isolated from the world that surrounds them . . . The violent trends that have agitated the great powers have had their great effect on Arab society . . . in our age that we call modern times."[6] In his memorial lecture given at the Center for Contemporary Arab Studies, Georgetown University, Zurayk referred to the tensions between Islam and the modern science that is based on reason: "The traditional tension between faith and reason is now unprecedentedly widespread and significant."[7] It is his hope that the Arabs will make the "effort to overcome and learn from the singular challenges and tensions of our times."[8] This is a crucial hope that we share with him, for to such efforts also belongs the effort of scholarly analysis. The interplay between social and cultural change, or, in other words, the ability of a people to cope culturally with social conditions in a rapidly changing world, is my primary focus. The first part of this paper deals with the general framework of this topic. The second part is devoted to analyzing the cultural attitudes of the Arabs in this *'aṣr al-mutafajjir.* In both parts a comparison is made with Germany.

Cultural Innovation in the Development Process

During the past decade, social scientists have concentrated on the problem of economic growth in Third World societies. They have overlooked the fact that social change also includes cultural innovations. Analysis of the whole societal context frequently went by the board in the study of the development process. Scholars concentrated on partial aspects of society and the changes occurring there, without placing these microinvestigations in their overall social context.[9]

Lately there have been signs of heightened awareness among social scientists that cultural innovations must be studied in the framework of macrosociological analysis. Some revisionist American modernization theorists have recently adopted a macrosociological approach, in the European tradition, towards problems of social change. Macrosociological analysis, central in classical sociology, has been suppressed, especially in the United States, in favor of microsociological research. Only since the fifties and sixties can one observe a rapidly increasing interest in macrosociological inquiry. Undoubtedly this change is related to the new significance of those preindustrial regions known today as the Third World.[10] Sociological analyses of a whole social context tend to be found more frequently in the sociology of development. Sociological analyses of industrial societies are still predominantly microsociological.

The sociologist Eisenstadt[11] employs macrosociological analysis to investigate social change. He finds that the development studies today are closely related to this approach. From the modernization theory paradigm, he borrows the concepts of 'tradition' and 'modernity' and attempts to use them as analytical concepts with which to explain social change. His criticism of the earlier modernization theory paradigm is principally that it affords no explanation of how modern societies can emerge from premodern societies, particularly since the preconditions for such emergence are described precisely with the concepts and features of those same societies.

The notion of transitory society, a transitional phase between modern and traditional society, does not solve this question. The paradigm operates with ideal types, all of which are oriented towards a particular type of society, namely, industrial society; it is incapable of explaining social change as a process. In Thomas Kuhn's theory of science[12] this analytical gap might be described as a central *anomaly* in the modernization theory. Unsolved anomalies lead, in this view, to a crisis of the paradigm during which its adherents think up numerous clarifications and ad hoc modifications of their theory to get rid of any apparent conflict.[13] Some modernization theorists proceed in similar fashion. They try to save the paradigm by building into it a variety of forms and differences in modernization as well as possible breakdowns.

Backward societies have underdeveloped social structures. Even critical modernization theorists think that this underdevelopment is caused by the prevailing tradition, which may be overcome by modernization. In this way they remain true to the traditional modernization theory. They only doubt whether unilinear development is possible after the initial phase. In their opinion the decisive problem of these societies does not lie in the relatively low level of modernization; it lies, rather, in the inability to develop a new cultural framework and in the lack of regulating mechanisms and modern norms.

The analysis of the sociocultural dimension of traditionality remains central. Yet to investigate it alone as the substance of underdevelopment means mistaking a single, albeit important, dimension of a social phenomenon for the whole.

The major concern of this paper is therefore to investigate the interplay between the cultural and the socioeconomic components in the process of social change. Since comparative researches have proved to be fruitful, I have chosen to trace some similarities and differences in both German and Arab cases to show the interrelations between cultural and socioeconomic constraints of development. I will focus my inquiry on the Reformation in German Christianity and the lack of such cultural innovation in Islam. The underlying concern of this focus is this: since Islam and Christianity are substantial elements, respectively, of the Arab and the German cultures, I will investigate the innovations within Arab Islam and German Christianity in order to single out their relevance for the societal change under discussion.

One particularly interesting aspect of this question is *to what extent a culture may hinder or promote cultural change.* This inquiry lies at the heart of my most recent book on the capability of Islam to cope with the rapid social change that Arab and other Islamic societies are now undergoing.[14] Here I would like to discuss the thesis that the Protestant ethic is economic and to examine the argument that it alone determined social change. An extensive examination of Weber enables me to conclude that the Protestant ethic coincided with other social conditions and that this fact explains why it produced the changes that it did; Weber quite clearly discards the thesis that the Protestant ethic alone could have taken effect as a modernization movement.[15] This debate is of particular interest for the Islamic cultural area and is worth elucidating further. Social scientists should be wary of reductionism in their study of any society and especially in their work at the macro-sociological level of analysis.

The relationship between culture and processes of social change has been studied from two opposing standpoints: they both, however, share a tendency towards reductionism. Whereas scholars trained in the old human sciences tradition or today's modernization theorists relegate the religious phenomenon to the world of ideas, some Marxist authors question the autonomy of the normative and simply reduce religion to the economic.[16]

For the leading Orientalist Gustav von Grunebaum, religion as a cultural normative system possesses a distinct ideal power; he refers to the special attitude "of a religious movement to bring about a cultural change" and attributes this attitude to the fact "that a religious change often aims to revise or even replace fundamental value judgements and is thus in a position to alter the whole order pertaining in a cultural system more radically than any other set of ideas."[17] The opposite viewpoint can already be found in Engels, who, unlike Marx, always had reductionist tendencies. In spite of being "Europe-centric" in approach, von Grunebaum at least concedes that Islam has produced a great civilization, whereas for Engels, Islamic history is merely circular and static, supposedly manifested in a "periodically recurring clash" between nomads and tradesmen from the towns: the Bedouins defeat the townspeople; then they, too, turn into city dwellers in the course of historical development. "A hundred years later they are in exactly the same position as the earlier rebels; a new religious purification is needed."[18] According to Engels, this "periodically recurring clash" is disguised as a religious dispute and fails to lead to a higher level of development because the conquering nomads "leave the old economic conditions untouched. *So everything remains the same and the clash becomes periodic.* In contrast, in the popular uprisings of the Christian West, the religious disguise serves merely as a banner and a mask for attacks on a decaying economic order, which is finally overthrown, giving way to a new one, and the world progresses."[19]

The emergence of Islam is visualized by Engels in this context of circular processes of social change: "Islam is a religion for Orientals, in particular for Arabs, hence for tradesmen and craftsmen in the towns, on the one hand, and nomadic Bedouins on the other."[20] Engels's interpretation of European history as dynamic and of Islamic history as circular matches the classification of peoples into those who are dynamic (Europe and America) and those who are static (non-Western), which can be found in Europe-centric ideologies. Thanks to research carried out by the French sociologist of religion and Islam scholar Maxime Rodinson, we now know that Islamic history was not a circular process. When describing his work as a Marxist, Rodinson took care to add, "This does not mean, as many people might like to believe, that I subordinate my research to dogmas of dubious value and suspect origin."[21]

In his biography of Muḥammad, Rodinson describes the complex process of the emergence of Islam as a "mobilizatory ideology" and shows how a vast empire with a highly developed culture arose within this framework. Here our interest is restricted to the interpretation of the religious phenomenon, that is, of the relationship between culture (Islam) and the social process. To me, there is no easy reductionist link between the normative and the idealist direction of a reduction of history to the world of ideas, nor in the vulgar materialist direction of a reduction of culture to the economy. Islam, as a culture, could not have emerged without the requisite social and structural framework. The presence of this framework alone would not, however, have sufficed to bring about the developments which did, in fact, take place.

I dispute the value of schematic interpretations of history; no specifically European predictable path of development exists, any more than a specifically Islamic evolution exists. The history of the Middle East is not circular; Islam helped the Arabs progress from primitive Bedouins to exponents of a highly developed culture. This historical achievement is not, however, due to Islam alone. The emergence of Islam is the result of a complex social evolution, of the interplay between culture and the social and structural framework. We know from Geertz that "culture patterns have an intrinsic double aspect: they give meaning, that is, objective conceptual form, to social and psychological reality both by shaping themselves to it and by shaping it to themselves."[22]

Having emphasized this methodological requirement of being wary of reductionism and keeping the underlying interplay between cultural and social and structural constraints of development in mind, I want to discuss the question of whether the Protestant Reformation was the major element of the German cultural innovation. My findings could then affirm or deny the assertion that the lack of such a reformation in Islam itself is the explanation of underdevelopment. This part of the paper deals with culture and society within a national framework, and could be considered as a historical perspective. I also feel the need to deal with some current issues related to the societal context of the contemporary world.

Because of its interwoven structure and its dense transportation and communication networks, the world today, as mentioned before, may be defined as a world society. Within this framework one could discuss the question of cultural authenticity and intercultural communication as constraints for cultural innovations in our contemporary world, for cultural change in our age does not take place within a national framework. All national societies of our world are integrated into the existing international, that is, world societal, structure.[23]

In this paper, my point of departure is that in contemporary world society the countries of the Islamic Middle East form part of the underdeveloped regions of the Third World. I will inquire into the type of change required for these countries to develop their structures. The salient feature of these cultures is their predominantly religious, nonsecular character. Hence the congruence between culture and the religious setting is doubtlessly clear.[24] We look at religion as a "cultural system" in the already introduced sense of Clifford Geertz.[25]

Religious organizations and the relationship between politics, society, and religion play a central part in modern social sciences as a cultural setting. Weber's interpretation of the Protestant ethic and the related discussion of it by historians and sociologists of religion are the main concern of many scholars—a revival to be explained by the renewed importance attributed to Weber in the sociology of social change. From this point of view sociologists have brought the value of the Weberian framework for the study of Islam and other non-Western cultural settings into focus. Eisenstadt, for instance, points out the following: "As interest grew in the past fifteen years in the development and modernization of non-European countries, so also did Weber's thesis regain people's attention. In the presence or lack of an equivalent to the Protestant ethic, many people saw the key to understanding the success or failure of modernization in non-European countries."[26]

Here I should like to stress that Muslim thinkers explain the backwardness of the Islamic Middle East by the lack of such an ethic. Only in a religious movement like that of the Reformation, and in a reformer like Luther, who could find a new Islamic ethic, do Islamic modernists of the nineteenth century see a way out of backwardness into modernity. Afghānī (1839-97),[27] the *rector spiritus* of contemporary Islamic modernism whose influence began in the second half of the nineteenth century, argues as follows in one of his early writings: "When we reflect on the causes of Europe's revolutionary transition from a barbarian state to civilization, we can see that this change was only possible through the religious movement initiated and led by Luther. . . . He managed to move Europeans to adopt a new reformed outlook."[28]

Eisenstadt's references to the relationship between religion and social change strike me as valuable because they contain strands of highly successful analysis. Particularly worth quoting is one paragraph which acts as a corrective to Afghānī's Islamic modernist view, just cited, that the traditionality of the Islamic Middle East might be overcome by a religious revival movement along the lines of the Lutheran model:

> The reformation was originally, of course, not a modernization movement. It had no modernizing impulse but was concerned rather to set up a new, purely medieval socio-political-religious order. Originally Protestantism was indeed a religious movement which, as such, sought to restructure the world. However, since Protestantism contained at the same time strong impulses related to this world, *these impulses mingled from the start with the main socio-political, economic and cultural trends of European . . . societies* towards the end of the seventeenth century, namely with *the development of capitalism, the Renaissance states, absolutism, secularity and science.*[29]

Properly speaking, this paragraph ought also to be a corrective to Eisenstadt's own assessment of cultural value orientation as the motor of social change. The text established quite clearly that *a religious ethic can only have a decisive effect on social change when it coincides with other sociopolitical and socioeconomic conditions.* The interrelation between prevailing cultural outlooks and socioeconomic development in a given totality has to be examined by the macrosociologist if any substantial conclusions are to be drawn. One example of a successful attempt to accomplish this is the analysis of Islam's foundation by Maxime Rodinson, noted earlier. Eisenstadt hints at the way an economic ethic can take effect in society, but always allows cultural value orientations to predominate in his principal statements.

Eisenstadt's cultural determination of traditional society as one which defines itself and is conditioned by tradition strikes me as useful, although this is clearly only one dimension of the phenomenon of underdevelopment and one which does not grasp the whole issue. If one remains on this sociocultural level of the debate, then religion can be seen to be one of the central ingredients of traditionality.

In traditional societies religion has not yet been secularized: it is a part of the sociocultural and political order. Religious leaders see their task as one of "formalizing and formulating their beliefs and their tradition in such a way that they can be fully articulated and organized on a relatively differentiated cultural level."[30] Part and parcel of this embodiment in organizational forms is both the forestalling of any kind of intellectualization of religiosity and the binding of religion to the state as the legitimization of the powers that be. Traditional religious leaders saw "in free religious activity . . . a threat to political loyalty."[31] Eisenstadt realizes how difficult it is to arrive at universally valid statements through generalization and for that reason adduces modifying empirical illustrations of this thesis.

At this stage in the course of our analysis we may conclude that cultural change is not autonomous and merely constitutes one important dimension of the process of social change. Cultural innovation always takes place within socioeconomic constraints, although it cannot be reduced to them mechanically. It could be perceived as a political threat by those ruling political elites who need a religiously articulated political legitimacy. Cultural innovation could be suppressed politically to maintain the traditional order. Many examples could be used to illustrate this thesis. The German Reformation movement, starting with Luther and the radical theology of the German theologist Thomas Munzer, was welcomed neither by parts of the ruling elites nor by their allies, the clergy. Similarly, the reaction of traditional ulema, the Islamic clergy, to cultural efforts towards changing Islam exerted by Islamic modernists like Afghānī and his disciples was extremely hostile. In sum, it is important to stress the relationship between religion as a cultural setting, and between society and political rule for a proper understanding of social change and its requirements in nonindustrialized societies.[32]

These reflections lead to the conclusion that cultural innovations are a key to social change, even if alone they cannot cause a society to be transformed into a higher level of development. To take full effect, they have to coincide with other social and economic conditions, as we have seen in the case of the Lutheran Reformation and the emergence of the Protestant ethic. The Reformation movement in Germany was an important contribution to modernity in German history, but, as I have pointed out, it cannot be understood properly within an isolated cultural framework. Cultural change was a prerequisite of modernization in Germany, but it alone could not have brought about the social change that has taken place. As to the Islamic Middle East, we can conclude that some observations of the modernization theorists are applicable to current problems in that area, but only after a certain amount of modification.

The modern Middle East is structurally underdeveloped and its culture is traditional. Nevertheless, it is not the cultural traditionality which is the cause of underdevelopment, which in turn is not reducible to a socioeconomic structure. In other words, the Islamic Middle East today, like other parts of the Third World, needs cultural renewal, a process which involves, among other things, a modern understanding of the local culture. It could mean the separation, as in modern societies, of religion from politics, with the former continuing to exist as a religious and social ethic.[33] But cultural innovation alone is not sufficient to overcome underdevelopment. Cultural innovations must fit into a development strategy embracing all spheres of society. Islam's contribution to this process could lie in its liberation from cultural traditionality while being preserved as the Muslim ethic. Unfortunately, Islamic cultural revival within the framework of the currently prevailing Islamic resurgence does not meet this urgent historical need.[34] This problem has been stated in the findings of my most recent book, *Der Islam und das Problem der kulturellen Bewältigung sozialen Wandels* (see note 14), to the effect that the religious culture of the Middle East, being its cultural system, does not, at this stage of development, provide the people with the capability of culturally coping with the problems of rapid social change that this part of the world is now undergoing.

Cultural Innovation and Defensive Cultural Responses

In the introductory remarks to this paper an effort was made to straighten out the prevailing confusion in the use of the concepts of 'culture' and of 'civilization.' To this effort belongs the combination of Geertz's concept of culture, which merely refers to a domestic framework, with Elias's concept of civilization, which alludes to the *universalization of the European process of civilization* in the wake of the Industrial Revolution of modern times. In resorting to this framework we become aware of the fact that no single culture in our times can be treated for its own sake and on its own terms. It is clear that cultural as well as social and political change in all non-Western societies takes place under constraints stemming from the international, or world-societal, environment. For this reason I want to shift away in this second part from the problem of cultural change as an inner-societal issue to focus on the phenomenon of intercultural interaction as the subject matter of this part of the inquiry. The question to be raised is how cultures react when they are penetrated by another culture. The reaction of German culture toward the French penetration and similarly the reaction of the Arab culture toward the Western influences within the framework of the universalized process of civilization will be the cases in point.

It seems to me appropriate to outline the employed framework and to make its terms of reference clear. *Acculturation* is used to denote the processes of *interaction among cultures.* Human cultures have always been influenced by each other—this is not a new phenomenon. But the international system, or, as we say in the language of my discipline in Germany, the World Society (*Weltgesellschaft*), of which we are members, is, in our modern age, the global arena of each intercultural interaction. In this sense the cultural differences between the North and the South, that is, between the industrialized and the nonindustrialized parts of our world, shape the process substantially. Each culture has its own world view, that is to say, the shared cultural assumptions concerning the nature of the social world. Cultural values are socially produced, and they change historically in relation to political and economic circumstances. Any accounting of the shared assumptions of peoples, of their cultural values, must historically take into consideration the patterns of these social, economic, and political variations.

In the modern age, the more advanced European societies have developed their own world views, or cultural values, domestically. Even during the radical shift to modern industrial society, their scope of development was restricted to their own boundaries. Later they started to conquer the whole world under the colonial framework. Today, beyond the colonial age, we can observe that the industrial European conquest has given our world a certain, I would say, world-societal shape, one in which transportation and communication networks connect all cultures and intensify their interactions. Cultural constraints of societal change are no longer nationally determined because national boundaries merely refer to legal sovereignty, not to the constraints of development themselves in an intensely interdependent world.

One might be inclined to argue that this analysis merely refers to the pattern of development of Third World societies and has no relevance to a comparative inquiry into German and Arab societies. But students of German history are acquainted with the effects of the challenge of the French Revolution upon Germany and its development. Compared with France or England, the still ununified Germany of the eighteenth and most of the nineteenth century was structurally much less developed. Before the French invasion of Germany during the Napoleonic War, German intellectuals used to admire and glorify French culture and feel inferior to it. This Francophilia turned into Francophobia after the French invasion in 1806. Fichte, the German cosmopolitan philosopher and a great admirer of the French Revolution, turned into a passionate German nationalist after the invasion and wrote the flaming *Address to the German Nation* (*Reden an die Deutsche Nation*)[35] urging his countrymen to resist the French penetration.[36]

Arab nationalists who in the course of their French education before World War I had been great admirers of France and who even became its political allies against the Ottoman Empire never expected to be colonized by France. They became enemies of France after the French occupation of Greater Syria by the end of the war. The French challenges to Germany and the German response to them during the early nineteenth century became a reference point to many Arab nationalists. In *Arab Nationalism: A Critical Inquiry*, I have provided detailed research on this issue, to which I would like to refer briefly, although the historical situation in the German and Arab cases clearly differs.[37]

Early Arab nationalism, like early German nationalism, was a cultural nationalism and actually the response to an external challenge. German cultural nationalism, as it was examplarily articulated in the writings of Herder, transcended the emancipation that had been awaited in vain and was an escape from the misery of contemporary conditions in Germany. The politicized pattern of this cultural nationalism became, during the so-called Napoleonic wars of liberation, an ideological weapon against foreign rule. The cultural revival in Germany emerged as an ideological response to an exogenous challenge. It put forward a legitimate historical demand, namely, liberation from foreign rule. The German romantic movement, as a cultural revival, is historically ambivalent. The Francophobia of German romanticism was a disguised form of an articulated will for national emancipation, in the same way as the nationalism of the colonial countries was a disguised form of anticolonialism. But German romanticism had no innovative future view in the sense that the society which it strove to create was a utopia of the past. This was also true of the Arab nationalists, who wanted to restore the glorious Arab past and to try to conjure up its values as a future perspective for facing the colonial challenge.

But neither German romanticism nor its evoked cultural revival were able to unify Germany and to make it strong enough to face the challenge. By contrast, political action under Bismarck and the unfolding of socioeconomic structures linked with an innovative cultural world view oriented toward the future were leading to a politically, structurally, and culturally renewed Germany. Adherents of *Arab Germanophilia* during the period between the two world wars were lacking an appropriate understanding of the interplay between the cultural, political, and socioeconomic constraints of development. Moreover, they did not understand that a utopia oriented toward the past, such as the utopia of German romanticism, could not be conducive to a proper understanding of a present which was crying out for change and which could not be directed toward the past. For the past cannot be restored.

Germanophilia no longer exists in the Arab region of world society. Since the 1970s one can observe a pervasive tendency of a new cultural revival which is clearly hostile toward everything foreign coming from outside: it is disguised as an Islamic resurgence.[38] It seems obvious that the disruptive effects of the rapid social change taking place in the Middle Eastern societies and the resulting structural transformations require the search for firmer foundations of society than has been offered by dominant political ideologies adopted from the West and from the East as well. Scholars acquainted with the Arab region are aware that Islam, as a prevailing faith, has never been questioned. In drawing attention to Islamic resurgence, I merely refer to the current understanding of Islam as a culturally exclusive normative system, and also to the repoliticization of the sacred.

Any cultural exclusiveness can be considered as a sign of cultural ghetto formation, especially in our culturally interdependent world. In order to understand this tendency of detachment from the world societal structure, a short historical review is necessary. Contemporary world society is a result of the spread of European influence at all levels throughout the world, not only in the economic and cultural spheres, but also in the area of modern communications and transportation, which produced an international system of interaction, what we call "international relations." This is the universalized process of civilization to which I have repeatedly alluded in this paper.

Not only in the Middle East, but also in most of those geographical areas described as Third World, we have been able to observe since the 1970s a protest movement taking place against the West's cultural and consequently economic dominance. The movement derives its strength from the very social classes that can be considered Westernized, that is, that have received a Western education. While European influence was spreading around the world, it was accompanied by a cultural penetration that has been given the name *acculturation*, which means cultural contacts. There have always been cultural contacts between different races, but acculturation has been the only phenomenon that covers the whole world, thus creating a world society. The return to cultural origins and the protest against European domination that have been in evidence since the 1970s are opposed to acculturation and therefore are called *counteracculturation*.

For a better understanding of this contemporary phenomenon, I would refer to the three points described in *Die Krise des modernen Islam* (The Crisis of Modern Islam).[39] The three phases given below are a reconstruction of the European penetration of the rest of the world.

1. The first phase extended until the second third of the nineteenth century. In this phase native populations attempted to ward off penetration and redoubled their own cultural activity to resist the foreign intrusion.
2. The resistance weakened during the second phase, because *economic penetration was successfully followed by cultural penetration.* The result was the adoption of Western ideas and the rise of a modern elite who spoke and thought like Westerners. Arab Francophilia and Arab Francophobia linked with an Arab Germanophilia can be historically encountered in this period.
3. Meanwhile, as the North-South conflict intensified and as the Westernizing phenomenon became limited to the purely cultural sphere, that is, only to the elite of the concerned nations and not to the other social structures, there was a renewed process of returning to cultural origins to put fresh life into national cultures instead of foreign ones. These are the tendencies we have been able to observe in the Third World areas since the 1970s.

The Islamic region of our world society is a good illustration of the developments that have become apparent since the first "Iran shock." These developments will not be set forth again here, since they are described at length in my book on Islam. I will restrict myself to inquiring whether the process of Islamization is a return to cultural origins or leads to the formation of a ghetto. This question is important to any discussion of international understanding, which today can be diagnosed as seriously disturbed since the Islamic region of world society includes no fewer than forty nation states and a population of over seven hundred million. Islamic resurgence aims to make Islam a political force; that is, in addition to being a religious creed, it is to be considered primarily as a political ideology to be used for rejecting any foreign influence.

The notable feature of international understanding in world society in the past was that it occurred between Europeans and non-Europeans. However, it was carried on through the medium of a European language, both in form and content. In other words, it was one-sided and did not contain any intercultural communication. A return to cultural origins could encourage a true, reciprocal communication between peoples of different cultures, one that would go beyond the exclusive use of a European language. It could strengthen the cultural identities of non-European peoples and contribute to the development of their societies, particularly in the socioeconomic and political field.

But this return to cultural origins cannot be beneficial if it stirs up hatred against foreigners and extols chauvinistic sentiments. The current pattern of Islamic resurgence in various parts of the world calls for *al-Ḥall al-Islāmi* (the Islamic Solution)[40] as an alternative to all other ideologies; it insists on its exclusiveness and includes particularly strong tendencies toward the formation of cultural and political ghettos, in addition to returning to cultural origins.

The following question then arises: what can we do to diminish the ghetto tendencies and to improve intercultural communication in the sense of mutual understanding among the peoples belonging to the different cultures of our world society? It should be noted that ghetto tendencies are closely connected with the intensification of the North-South conflict. A development policy designed to resolve this conflict would, in turn, contribute to diminishing ghetto tendencies. But we have to face the truth that the future prospects are not promising.

As scholars, we have an obligation to question these ghetto tendencies and to assess them, for they might pose a threat to international peace since they do not contribute to the promotion of intercultural understanding. The merit of the comparative analysis I have provided in this paper is that it can lead to some conclusions concerning the interplay between social and cultural change. I have also dealt with cultural penetration and defensive cultural responses to it. Cultural penetration is a means of obtaining dominance. Politically, the defensive cultural response to it is legitimate, but history reveals that such patterns of rejection are always weak and not conducive to overcoming the conditions facilitating the penetration. Therefore cultural innovation should be promoted as an alternative to defensive cultural responses that draw on cultural revival and glorify the past. In addition, cultural innovation is compatible with reciprocal intercultural communication. It could also enable the people of nonindustrial cultures to cope more effectively with externally induced rapid social change. The people of the Middle East must make an effort to structurally change their societies and to adjust their culture to the changing world societal environment.

Notes

1. Clifford Geertz, *The Interpretation of Cultures* (New York: Basic Books, 1973), p. 29.
2. Ibid., p. 29.
3. See Norbert Elias, *Uber den Prozeß der Zivilisation*, 6th ed. (Frankfurt am Main: Suhrkamp Press, 1979), 1:1-26.
4. Bassam Tibi, *Krise des modernen Islams. Eine vor-industrielle Kultur im wissenschaftlich-technischen Zeitalter* (Munich: Beck Press, 1981). See the

review by Barbara Stowasser in *The Middle East Journal*, 37, no. 2 (1983): 284-285.

5. Constantine K. Zurayk, *Hadha al-'aṣr al-mutafajjir* (Beirut: Dār al-'Ilm lil-Malāyin Press, 1963).
6. Constantine K. Zurayk, *Naḥnu wa-al-tārīkh*, 2d ed. (Beirut: Dār al-'Ilm lil-Malāyin Press, 1963), pp. 205-206.
7. Constantine K. Zurayk, *Tensions in Islamic Civilization*, Center for Contemporary Arab Studies, Seminar Paper No. 3 (Washington, D.C.: Georgetown University, 1978), p. 17.
8. Ibid., p. 21.
9. See the book of Wolfgang Zapf, ed., *Theorien des sozialen Wandels*, 2d ed. (Cologne: Kiepenheuer und Witsch, 1970).
10. See the book of Dirk Berg-Schlosser, ed., *Die politischen Probleme der Dritten Welt* (Hamburg: Hoffman und Campe, 1972).
11. See S. N. Eisenstadt, *Tradition, Wandel und Modernität*, (Frankfurt am Main: Suhrkamp, 1973).
12. See Thomas Kuhn, *Die Struktur wissenschaftlicher Revolutionen* (Frankfurt am Main: Suhrkamp Press, 1967).
13. Ibid., p. 111.
14. See Bassam Tibi, *Der Islam und das Problem der kulturellen Bewältigung sozialen Wandels* (Frankfurt am Main: Suhrkamp Press, 1985).
15. See Bassam Tibi, "Unterentwicklung als kulturelle Traditionalität," *Soziologische Revue*, 3 (1980): 121-31. See also the respective chapter of Eisenstadt, pp. 236ff.
16. This criticism is elaborated in Bassam Tibi, "Islam und sozialer Wandel im modernen Orient," *Archiv fur Rechts- und Sozial-philosophie*, 54 (1979): 483-502.
17. Gustav von Grunebaum, *Studien zum Kulturbild und zum Kulturverstandnis des Islam* (Zurich: Artemis Press, 1969), pp. 483-502.
18. Marx/Engels, *Uber Religion* (Berlin/GDR; Dietz Press, 1958), p. 256.
19. Ibid. (italics added). All quotations from German and Arabic are my translation.
20. Ibid.
21. Maxime Rodinson, *Islam und Kapitalismus* (Frankfurt am Main: Suhrkamp Press, 1971), p. 13.
22. Geertz, p. 93.
23. This concept is elaborated in Bassam Tibi, "Kommunikationsstrukturen der Weltgesellschaft und der interkulturelle Konflikt. Das islamische Exempel," *Beiträge zur konflikt-Forschung*, 11, no. 3 (1981): 57-77.
24. For more details, see Dale Eickelman, *The Middle East: An Anthropological Approach* (Englewood Cliffs, N.J.: Prentice-Hall, 1981), esp. pp. 175ff. and pp. 201ff.
25. See Geertz, pp. 87-125.
26. Eisenstadt, p. 237.
27. On Afghānī, see the biography of N. Keddie, *al-Afghani* (Berkeley-Los Angeles: University of California Press, 1972).

28. al-Afghānī, *al-'A'māl al-kāmilah*, ed. M. 'Imārah (Cairo: Dār al-Kātib al-'Arabi, 1968), p. 328.
29. Eisenstadt, pp. 242ff.
30. Ibid., p. 206.
31. Ibid., p. 208.
32. In regard to Islam, see the collection of papers (case studies) of John L. Esposito, ed., *Islam and Development: Religion and Sociopolitical Change* (Syracuse: Syracuse University Press, 1980), and of James P. Piscatori, ed., *Islam in the Political Process* (Cambridge: Cambridge University Press, 1983).
33. The author had made this suggestion in his paper delivered to the First International Islamic Conference. See Bassam Tibi, "Islam and Secularization," in Mourad Wahba, ed., *Islam and Civilization. Proceedings of the First International Islamic Philosophy Conference, 19-22 November 1979* (Cairo: 'Ayn Shams University Press, 1982), pp. 65-80.
34. See Bassam Tibi, "The Renewed Role of Islam in the Political and Social Development of the Middle East," *The Middle East Journal*, 37, no. 1, (1983): 3-13.
35. Johann Gottlieb Fichte, *Reden an die Deutsche Nation*, new ed. (Hamburg: Felix Meiner-Verlag, 1955).
36. More details and references may be found in Bassam Tibi, *Arab Nationalism: A Critical Inquiry* (New York: St. Martin's Press, 1981), pp. 101ff.
37. Ibid., pp. 70ff, 90ff, 123ff.
38. See Tibi, "The Renewed Role of Islam."
39. See Tibi, *Krise des modernen Islam*, pp. 59ff.
40. Yūsuf al-Qurdāwī, *al-Ḥall al-Islāmī* (Beirut: Mu'assasat al-Risālah Press, 1974).

Criticism and the Heritage: Adonis as Advocate of a New Arab Culture

MOUNAH A. KHOURI

I

Among contemporary Arab writers on the problems of cultural orientation and the crisis of Arab intellectuals, the poet-critic Adonis (ʻAlī Aḥmad Saʻīd) occupies a leading position. His critical works,[1] especially his monumental study of Arab Islamic culture entitled *al-Thābit wa-al-mutaḥawwil: Baḥth fī al-ittibāʻ wa-al-ibdāʻ ʻind al-ʻArab* (The Static and the Dynamic: A Study of the Imitative and Innovative in Arab Culture),[2] are an intellectual tour de force which comprehensively and radically shake the structures of the old heritage and chart the future directions of the new one.

In this three-volume scholarly work, Adonis focuses his critique on the problem of determining why and in what ways Arab Islamic culture, as manifested in various intellectual disciplines from their emergence in the early Islamic period down to modern times, declined from the glorious achievements of certain early periods to its present state of petrification in which it desperately cries out for revival. Briefly stated, Adonis's diagnosis of Arab culture stresses what he calls the "static" and the "dynamic" as the two main currents of thought and directive forces which shaped that culture. Adonis sees the present stagnation as a result of the victory of traditionalism over the forces of change within the Arab mind. Moreover, in his judgment, Arab culture is fundamentally religious and therefore clings to fixed absolutes, rejecting creativity and condemning innovation; its evolution has thus been confined to a closed circuit whose parameters are determined by tradition.

Adonis, with his exceptional literary sensibility and dialectical skill, uses this static-versus-dynamic critical framework to describe, evaluate, and judge the whole of Arab culture, including all of Arabic literature. By doing so he hopes to destroy the static within it and reconstruct the dynamic, to use his own words, "with the aim of understanding Arab culture as it is, in order to change it into what it ought to be."

Having chosen phenomenology as his method of inquiry, Adonis divides each volume of his work into two major parts, one dealing with the static and the other with the dynamic. Volume 1, *al-Uṣūl*, first discusses the origins of the static or traditional world view and then proceeds to the origins of the dynamic, or innovative one. Volume 2, *Ta'ṣīl al-uṣūl*, follows the same procedure but shifts the emphasis from the origins of the two opposing currents to the process by which they became firmly established. The first volume thus deals with the period from the death of the Prophet (A.D. 632) to the end of the Umayyad caliphate, while the second proceeds from the rise of the Abbasid dynasty (A.D. 750) to the end of the tenth century. Using the static-dynamic framework in both volumes, Adonis deals with the political, ideological, and literary aspects of Arab Islamic culture. Volume 3, *Ṣadmat al-ḥadāthah* (The Shock of Modernity), after a brief recapitulation of the conclusions of the first two volumes, depicts the same two opposing currents as manifested in modern Arabic poetry. Though much more limited in scope and field of inquiry than the first two volumes, this supplementary work is important in that it provides an inside view of contemporary Arabic literature. Moreover, this last volume (along with his more recently published collection of essays, *Fātiḥah li-nihāyat al-qarn*) further illustrates Adonis's argument that both the classical and the most influential modern expressions of Arab Islamic culture, with only a few exceptions, are opposed in almost every particular to liberal culture. By rejecting the static values of the prevailing cultural and literary traditions, by redefining poetry as a vision to change the world, and by creating a new mode of literary expression, Adonis aspires to restore to the Arab poet his vital role of spokesman of his age, and to the Arab man the position at the center of the universe which has been denied to him, thus allowing him to regain his new identity and build a new culture based on freedom, creativity, and enlightened change.

This essay will attempt to analyze Adonis's critique of Arab Islamic culture as expounded in his major works on the subject. It is divided into two parts: the first a brief account of Adonis's basic views, and the second my evaluation of his critique.

The predominance of the static current manifests itself in (1) the triumph of *naql* (traditional or authoritative transmission) over *'aql* (reasoning) in the religious thought which has shaped the whole of Arab Islamic culture; (2) the emergence of coercive political power in the hands of the caliphs, who in due time assumed divine authority and exerted it over the Muslim community with the passive acquiescence of most religious leaders; (3) the condemnation in literature of poetry for its own sake, and the attempt to make literature the handmaiden of religion by emphasizing its didactic function and moralistic aspect at the expense of its esthetic or artistic value; and (4) the reverence for the past and for tradition, which has led Arabs to look upon pre-Islamic poetry as an ideal model to be imitated and upon the Arabic language as essentially Koranic and thus not subject to change or figurative interpretation.

The leading traditionalists are al-Shāfi'ī, in the fields of law, politics, and religion; and al-Aṣma'i and al-Jāḥiẓ, in the literary sphere. Of the static norms formulated by the former, Adonis says, "Al-Aṣma'i's principle of poetic excellence is another form of what we may call the priority (*awwalīyah*) of the pre-Islamic"—that is, its antecedence, which becomes "a symbol of soundness, because it is a symbol of the natural," of what is inherently great. He then turns to al-Jāḥiẓ's views on poetry and quotes him as saying the following: "All acquired knowledge is imperfect in comparison to that knowledge which is innately acquired. The knowledge of the Arabs is poetry—an innately acquired knowledge. It is a natural instinct of the Arabs."[3]

Adonis further locates al-Jāḥiẓ's views on rhetoric (*balāghah*) within the context of his ethnocentrism: "Rhetorical eloquence is not merely communication, but communication according to the dictates of pure Arabic style and its principles." For al-Jāḥiẓ, language and style are matters relating to form: "Hence al-Jāḥiẓ distinguishes between form (*lafẓ*) and content (*ma'na*) and gives primary importance to form, because ideas (*ma'ānī*) are lying in the road and recognized by everyone . . . What is important is establishing the meter and choosing the words, ease of articulation, fluency, soundness of expression, excellence of style: for poetry is a craft, a kind of weaving, or painting."[4]

As for the dynamic current of change, overshadowed throughout Islamic history by the static, it is manifested (1) in religion, by the dominance of *ta'wīl* (rational interpretation) of religious texts and by the rise of the Mu'tazilite, Batini, and Sufi movements; (2) in politics, by the extension of political power to non-Arabs and by the rebellious struggles of the Kharijites, the Qarmatians, and the Zanj for socio-economic justice for all; and (3) in literature, by the assault against the pre-Islamic poetic norms, the emphasis on poetry's artistic values as opposed to its moralizing function, and by reliance on fidelity to life rather than on conformity to social standards as the source of poetic creation.

The leading literary figures of this creative trend are Abū Nūwās and Abū Tammām. Adonis believes that the urban esthetic sensibility found its most significant expression in the poetry of these two modernists, who share in the rejection of the traditional, but each of whom followed his own innovative path: "Abū Nūwās observed the world around him as it is, lived it as it is, and drew a vivid picture of it with words, correlating poetry with life; Abū Tammām observed the world around him as it is, but went beyond it to create [another] artistic world. Thus with him modernity acquired a dimension of pure creativity without a preexisting model (*al-khalq lā 'ala mithāl*), whereas with Abū Nūwās it acquired a metaphoric, symbolic dimension."[5] Moreover, in Adonis's view the change in emphasis from oratory (*khaṭābah*) and improvisation (*irtijāl*) to writing (*kitābah*) as a conscious creative art marks the beginning of a fundamental change in the structure of Arab Islamic culture.

Adonis points out four basic features of the tradition-bound mentality responsible for the retardation of the prevailing culture. The first, on the existential plane, is theocentricity (*lāhūtīyah*), by which he means the tendency to exaggerate the separation between man and God and to make the religious concept of God the main principle and objective; the Arab mentality emphasizes the abstract uniqueness of God in absolute transcendence (*al-ghaybīyah al-muṭlaqah*).[6] The second feature, on the psychological plane, is passéism (*al-māḍawīyah*, orientation toward the past), by which he means attachment to the known and rejection, or even fear, of the unknown.[7] The third characteristic, on the plane of expression and language, is separation of speech from meaning, with meaning as antecedent to speech, which is nothing but its form or decorative representation. This view is illustrated by historical experience: the Arab prefers oratory to writing. The former is extemporaneous and is largey mechanistic in its dependence on memory, and the latter is the product of sophisticated thought and creative imagination.[8] The fourth, on the plane of the development of civilization, is opposition to modernity. The Arab views the past as a source of his general and particular concepts, not only in regard to his person but also in regard to the world and his relationship with it. He seems to have an innate distaste for the new, the innovative, and the explorative.[9]

The third volume of *al-Thābit wa-al-mutaḥawwil* assesses the responses of a select group of modern Arab poets to the concept of modernity as understood by Adonis, and studies their poetic achievements. This group includes six poets or groups of poets: al-Bārūdī, al-Ruṣāfī, Muṭrān, the Diwān and Apollo groups, and Jubrān Khalil Jubrān of the Mahjar movement. The volume concludes with a description of Adonis's own concept of modernity: his *Bayān al-kitābah*, or Manifesto on Writing (that is, of modern poetry). In view of this document's importance, I quote its major themes here:

Creativity means embarking upon the unknown, not upon the known, for the writer is neither thinking in a way differing from what is familiar to him . . .

The boundaries which have traditionally divided "writing" into various genres must be abolished . . . our criteria for the evaluation of a work's excellence will be based not on the distinction between genres, but rather on the work's intrinsic creative quality.

The relationships within the creative process . . . will no longer be between the creative writer and a preexisting heritage, but rather between the creative writer and the act of creation . . . The heritage is not what makes you; it is you that creates the heritage. The heritage cannot be imitated, only created.

The creative act is more important than what is created . . . The primary purpose of the creative writer is not to bring forth his work, but rather to bring forth himself.

Culture is not what we have created, but what we are creating.

In poetry . . . [the] point of departure used to be as follows: Writing is the by-product of meaning . . . Today the point of departure is: Meaning is the by-product of writing . . . In the past understanding was an end in itself, but today it must become a means.

Form is not a mode of expression; rather, it is a mode of existence.

The poet does not transmit in his poetry clear or ready-made thoughts as was the case in all classical poetry. Instead, he sets his words as traps or nets to catch an unknown world.[10]

In assessing the poets mentioned above, Adonis applies his concept of poetry as a vision transcending the established forms, concepts, and values. He seeks evidence of radical change in the rhythmic structure, in the use of words and images, and in the semantics of the language. On the basis of these criteria he dismisses all of them except Jubrān as revivalists who had made only minor contributions to the true modernization of Arabic poetry. As for Jubrān, Adonis describes him as

modern and classical, realistic and mystical, nihilistic and revolutionary. He was modern when he viewed man in his ordinary, daily life and immersed himself in that level of existence . . . yet he was classical because he saw man as the zenith of perfection and power.

He was realistic because he criticized reality as no contemporary of his did, yet he was mystical because he aspired to the infinite unknown and directed himself toward it, while criticizing reality as it is and transcending it. He was nihilistic because he screamed out his anguish over the conditions of modern man, and he was revolutionary because he regarded man . . . as the source for the New Man of the future.[11]

Adonis's critique of today's prevailing Arab Islamic culture is based on his belief that the static current is still dominant and that the so-called renaissance in contemporary Arabic poetry is basically imitative in almost all its major characteristics. In his view, Arab heritage extends beyond those elements which the majority of Muslims accept but which he sees as one-dimensional and embodying only static values. It also includes more dynamic elements which should be stressed in modern times in order to insure progress. These dynamic elements have been suppressed by the traditionalists for many centuries. The group has always been more highly valued than the individual, and stability has been sought at the expense of risky change and creativity. Innovators have been silenced, while static values and attitudes have been preserved. Thus the Arabs will not be able to build a new culture without first criticizing and challenging the structures of the old one.

Adonis identifies specific obstructions to progress which must be overcome, notably the nature of the Arab regimes. Both "traditional" and "progressive" regimes share essentially the same oppressive and coercive characteristics. Economic growth is designed to benefit particular classes and groups. Political parties have conflicting ideologies and strive to control rather than to liberate, to gain power rather than to use it for progress and change.

The key idea in Adonis's vision is that the Arab world must overcome these problems and establish a new culture based on freedom, creativity, and change. For this to happen, the Arab intellectual elite must reject the prevailing culture. Reconciliation and acquiescence on their part perpetuate the old culture, with its pattern of suppressing change and innovation. They must stress diversity and individuality, and above all freedom. In fact, it is freedom in all spheres that Adonis sees as the most essential element of the new Arab culture.

The Arabs must reevaluate their heritage and learn to separate the valuable from the outdated, the dynamic from the static. They must preserve, without imitating, not only the vital elements in the heritage, but more importantly the flame (*lahab*) which has kindled all that is dynamic in that heritage. While retaining its own identity, Arab culture must be open to other cultures and must resume making the kinds of significant contributions to civilization which it has made in the past.

II

These are, in broad strokes, some of Adonis's main critical views on the Arab heritage. What follows is my own analysis of his thought on the subject.

Although a considerable number of works have been written by Arab authors in the last two decades about the crisis of the prevailing Arab

Islamic culture and the Arab predicament in modern times, Adonis's writing on this subject, especially his *al-Thābit wa-al-mutaḥawwil*, has been singled out by most critics as outrageously provocative in its attempt to purge Arab culture of its traditional religious thought. The violent opposition with which it was met may be compared with the critics' vehement reaction in the 1920s to the publication of Ṭahā Ḥusayn's controversial book *Fī al-shi'r al-jāhilī* (1926) (On Pre-Islamic Poetry) and 'Alī 'Abd al-Rāziq's *al-Islām wa-uṣūl al-ḥukm* (1925) (Islam and the Bases of Political Authority), as well as to the more recently published work of Ṣādiq Jalāl al-'Aẓm, *Naqd al-fikr al-dīnī* (1970) (Critique of Religious Thought).

Regardless of the fact that these authors deal with different aspects of the Arab Islamic heritage (the question of the authenticity of pre-Islamic poetry or the problem of the relationship between religion and politics or more generally between religious thought and the Arab cultural heritage), regardless of the differences in their treatments of these issues, and regardless of the validity or inconclusiveness of their findings, they essentially share a common critical approach to the study of certain aspects of their culture. It is basically a philosophical attitude rooted in their belief—a belief shared by a few other Arab intellectuals—in freedom of inquiry and of expression. Ṭahā Ḥusayn, as a champion of the Arab world's first determined battle for that freedom, describes it as the fundamental guiding principle of the writing of creative literature, history, science, philosophy, art, and the whole range of intellectual concerns. In contrast with this, he says, the study of literature in the Arab world has historically been considered a mere handmaiden of religion, the Arabic language, and the study of the Koran. This has made those things both sacrosanct and profane. By sanctifying them, the dogmatists set them above true scientific inquiry, which demands criticism, denial, or at least doubt.[12]

In principle it is the spirit of this skeptical Cartesian methodology, acclaimed in the West from the seventeenth century onwards as the apotheosis of scientific knowledge and historical consciousness, which to a greater or lesser extent pervades the works of the modern Arab intellectuals mentioned above and shapes their reappraisal of certain aspects of the Arab Islamic heritage. Nothing in their works has aroused more protest and hostility than their common attempt to question the ready-made historical knowledge which some traditional "authorities" held to be sanctified postulates within the structure of Islamic thought, thus excluding any challenge or questioning of their established judgment.

Granting that the real significance of these intellectuals' controversial works lies not in the undisputed soundness of the findings but rather in the legitimacy of their right to adopt the methods of modern critical scholarship and to apply them to the reinterpretation of certain fundamental principles of Arab Islamic culture, the question which we must now address regarding Adonis's critique of that culture is this: How sound is his methodology, and how sound or disputable are his conclusions? The criticism leveled against Adonis's reappraisal of the prevailing Arab Islamic culture centers for the most part around three main points: his methodology, his characterization of the "Arab mentality," and his concept of modernity, which is at the root of his ideas for building a new Arab culture.

In describing his methodology, Adonis says: "I have used what may be called a phenomenological history of Arab culture as it is revealed by the events and ideas the authenticity of which is agreed upon by all parties concerned. I emphasize here phenomenologism, because I have restricted myself to studying cultural phenomena in themselves in isolation from their material basis."[13] The reasons which he gives for this exclusion from his study of "the economic infrastructure and the relations of productions which predominated in the first three centuries of the *Hijra*," the period treated in the first two volumes of *al-Thābit wa-al-mutaḥawwil*, are the lack of reliable primary sources for the economic history of this period and his own incompetence to treat the subject even if such primary sources had been available. He further adds: "My main purpose is to study the Islamic revelation as it manifested itself in day-to-day practice and in the method of thought. For this reason I have restricted myself to studying the ideological superstructure of Islamic society as it appeared in practice and theory, beginning with the death of the Prophet."[14] The reason he gives for choosing this date as a starting point is his desire to proceed from events and ideas upon which all those concerned are in agreement, be they religious, social, literary, intellectual, or political. As for the scope of his study, which evolved from his initial special interest in Arabic poetry, it was determined by his conviction that "the study of Arab culture as a whole alone permits us to understand the Arab vision of man and the world."[15] It is therefore to the investigation of this vast cultural domain in its totality that Adonis has applied his phenomenological method of analysis. This approach has been criticized on two grounds: the inadequacy of the methodology itself, and its misapplication to the study of such a complex phenomenon as the whole of Arab Islamic culture.

The assumption of this methodology is that what is known is known only to consciousness, and it is in consciousness alone that evidence is weighed and its force determined. For consciousness to apprehend the phenomena under investigation and to achieve knowledge which can justly be regarded as necessary and certain, it must be purified of its intentionality, or previous beliefs and presuppositions. Such mental activities and all kinds of thoughts and feelings must be suspended or "bracketed." This neutralization process is called "phenomenological reduction." This phenomenological standpoint appeals to an entirely different type of experience than does the natural way of relating to the world—that is, to pure or transcendental experience. This is the direct, immediate, intuitive grasp of the essential traits of any object or datum investigated. It disregards the particular and incidental about the facts to be known, and achieves through "pure seeing" the absolute knowledge of essences. The knowledge thus gained is self-evident and free from error.

Critics are generally agreed that some of the aims of phenomenology are plausible and attractive, especially its attempt to reconcile the classical opposition between absolute knowledge and experience—making the latter, in its pure form, the basis of the former, and emphasizing the role of "immediate seeing" in achieving necessary knowledge. Nevertheless, they challenge the validity of several of its basic contentions. What, some critics ask, guarantees the self-evidence of phenomenological essences, and what insures that "pure seeing" is perfectly pure and clear? Is it ultimately true that we cannot be seriously mistaken about the direction of our consciousness and about what we mean, no matter how critically we set up the conditions? Are we ever able to ascertain that the presuppositions, beliefs, thoughts, and feelings which we have "bracketed" have been effectively neutralized? Can the intentionalities of consciousness ever be fully separated from the natural, historical experience of things that shapes the development of consciousness? These are, on the theoretical level and stated in the broadest terms, some of the serious questions raised in connection with the shortcomings of phenomenology as a theory of knowledge and as a method of historical analysis. Perhaps more important than this theoretical argument about the methodology itself is the way Adonis has understood it and practically applied it to the study of Arab Islamic culture.

As he states in the introduction to *al-Thābit wa-al-mutaḥawwil* quoted earlier, Adonis emphasized phenomenology as his chosen methodology because of his declared intention to restrict himself to the investigation of cultural phenomena in isolation from their material basis. This approach obviously meets with strong opposition from his Marxist critics. They object to what they consider a kind of Hegelian idealist interpretation of Arab Islamic culture, that is, to his view that religious thought was the primary factor (*al-muḥarrik al-awwal*) shaping the distinguishing features of that culture: theocentricity, passéism, separation of form from content in literature, and rejection of innovation. One of these critics has pointed out that the different aspects of a society's life at any one time are organically related in the sense that its political, economic, and cultural phenomena constantly interact with each other, and also that the economic factor, which Adonis basically disregarded in his study of Arab Islamic culture, is so important that it exerts a decisive influence over all the rest. Thus Adonis's attempt to investigate phenomena in themselves to the exclusion, for whatever reason, of the economic conditions in terms of which all states of affairs must finally be understood is as futile and misleading as his characterization of the Arab mentality.[16]

In this connection it must be noted that Adonis, contrary to his declared intention to isolate phenomena from their material basis, applies his understanding of Marx's historical materialism to the study of class struggle and its impact on religious thought during the period of the first four caliphs and of the Umayyads, and considers the economic factor to have been the primary cause of the conflict which arose during that formative phase of Arab Islamic culture between Sunnism and Shi'ism and between Batinism and Zahirism, as well as of what he calls the "static-dynamic conflict" within the structure of the culture. However, while it cannot be denied that Adonis does provide this partial treatment of the material basis of that particular phase of the Arab heritage, his work's shortcoming lies in his failure to follow it up more thoroughly and consistently throughout his study. For any interpretation of phenomena must be inadequate if it leaves out one of the most basic and pertinent factors involved: the material basis of society's life.

This search for a subjective knowledge of essences in contradistinction to an objective knowledge of facts has led some to evaluate Adonis's historicism or idea of history, however challenging and illuminating it may be, as that of a reductionist who often overlooks the complexities of the phenomena under investigation when he uses simplified constructions or neat patterns to arrive at general conclusions which can have no more than relative validity. In his attempt to grasp the essential structures of the phenomena of Arab Islamic culture, Adonis has been even more sharply criticized for failing to be equally concerned with the discovery of general concepts, as well as with the necessary evidence provided by the objective entities which correspond to them.

As was pointed out in the first part of this paper, Adonis distinguishes two main streams of thought in his interpretive study of Arab Islamic culture. The first is static, which has been upheld by the dogmatists of the orthodox systems, whose rigid adherence to the fundamental principles of religious culture admitted of no significant change or development and eventually led to the stagnation of thought in medieval Islam, as well as in the prevailing contemporary Arab culture. The second is dynamic, which aims at the radical transformation of the Islamic intellectual tradition. In Adonis's view, the dynamic is associated with certain movements of rebellion (*khurūj*) against the established order, including the Kharijite movement, the major offshoots of Shi'ism, the Zanj revolt, Mu'tazilism, the rational philosophical movement, and the Sufi movement.

Underlying this distinction between the two currents are the following assumptions, on which Adonis bases his critique of the existing Arab Islamic culture and his evaluation of the prospects for building a new one:

1. He believes that the two currents have always run in opposite directions without ever flowing into each other, and that the relationship between them has been confrontational rather than dialectic.
2. He sees the static current as rooted in the Islamic religious world view, which according to him has pervaded the whole of Arab Islamic culture and has shaped its major characteristics, and which therefore has enabled the static current to crush the dynamic one.
3. He identifies traditionalism with imitativeness and utter lack of change, in contradistinction to liberalism and innovation, which he invariably identifies with the dynamic current of thought.

One can scarcely deny that these two streams of thought are discernible in the course of religious culture, and that Adonis deserves credit for making this general observation. However, the concept's positive value lies in the fact that, whether as a general assumption or as an abstraction of some kind, it served him as part of the process of acquiring historical knowledge. All intellectual histories are compartmentalized in the sense that they look at the past from a certain perspective and concentrate on limited aspects of it. Even granting this, however, I myself doubt that Adonis's phenomenological conclusions based on such assumptions are also derived from the certainty of historical facts.

The contention that the two currents never flowed into each other merits a closer look. We might perhaps find it plausible to classify under the static category a dogmatist theologian like al-Shāfi'ī (d. A.D. 819), who asserted that a ḥadīth, even an "isolated" one transmitted through only a single chain of transmission, had to be accepted as binding—and that no application of reasoning which contradicted it could be allowed. But how are we to classify such an extraordinarily important religious figure as al-Ghazālī (d. A.D. 1111) without taking into account the dialectic process of thinking which he generated between religion and philosophy or between the religious sciences (*'Ulūm shar'īyah*) and the rational sciences (*'Ulūm 'aqlīyah*)? How can we disregard the fact that when he questioned the tenets of Islamic philosophy as expounded by al-Fārābī (d. A.D. 950) and particularly by Ibn Sina (d. A.D. 1037), he was opposed not to rational thinking per se but rather to what he considered metaphysical speculation lacking the certainty or demonstrative force of scientific reasoning—and that his method of questioning was, within the dogmatic field, a rational one? Moreover, how can we ignore the fact that it was his influence that enabled Sufism to attain a firm and secure position within Islam? If al-Ghazālī's thought had such range, flowing in all directions and transcending strict compartmentalization, how can we classify him within one stream of thought and exclude him from the other without being rightly accused of gross reductionism and oversimplification?

Similarly, the reduction of varied and complex movements to what Adonis believes to be their essential traits (such as the identification of the Kharijites with egalitarianism and social justice, the Qarmatians with communism or libertinism, the Mu'tazilites with rational thinking, and the Sufis with pantheism) cannot be accepted without reservation. To do so would be to ignore the doctrinal and practical excesses of the Kharijites, the fanatical interpretation of the Koran, the socioeconomic bases of both the Zanj and the Qarmatian revolts, and especially the diversity and complex structures of the Mu'tazilite and Sufi doctrines and belief systems.

In a statement intended to correct the general tendency to describe the Mu'tazilites as "rationalists or even as freethinkers," H. A. R. Gibb says the following:

> This is now recognized to be a serious misrepresentation . . . In its beginnings, the leaders of the Mu'tazila were rigid puritans; their teachings were perfectly compatible with (and indeed based upon) the Koran, and we shall probably not be far wrong in regarding them as the most active and vigorous section among the orthodox Sunni teachers in Iraq. It has, indeed, sometimes been a source of embarrassment to later orthodox opponents of the Mu'tazila that both the great saint al-Ḥasan of Basra (d. A.D. 728) and the great jurist Abū Ḥanifa (d. A.D. 767) show more than a hint of what were later called Mu'tazilite leanings in their doctrine.[17]

In this connection it must be added that even al-Ash'ari (d. A.D. 935), the founder of the Sunni theology dominant throughout medieval Islam, was able to reinforce orthodox Islam by putting its theology on a logical basis precisely because he had been a Mu'tazilite, and that al-Ghazālī, having been an Ash'arite theologian, was able to reestablish theology on a basis of personal mystical experience. He was thus able to combine what had hitherto seemed separate and conflicting scholastic, philosophical, and mystical systems of ideas.[18]

As for the special emphasis which Adonis places on Sufism's anti-transcendentalist and pantheistic belief in the unity of Being, aimed at altering the nature of the relationship between God and man, it is only valid in the case of certain extreme forms of Sufism, such as that of Ibn 'Arabi in the thirteenth century. Even in this case, one wonders if such an alteration of the relationship actually took place, since Ibn 'Arabi affirmed that there was in reality one and only one Existence—namely, God—and he regarded all else as illusion, shadow, or appearance.

In the sphere of Islamic law, it is tantamount to serious misrepresentation to classify as static or dynamic the formal legal doctrines and definitions of the four major schools which recognized the Koran, Sunnah, *ijmā'*, and *qīyās* as their sources, allowed several formal differences to exist among themselves, and gave every believer throughout the Muslim world the right to belong freely to the school of his choice.

Even in the literary sphere, where Adonis's exceptional sensibility and sound critical judgment could scarcely be questioned, the distinction he makes between the norms, values, and attitudes of the traditionalists and those of the modernists is so categorical that it admits no interaction between the two. This is clearly shown in his treatment of two major representatives of the two trends. The first is al-Jāḥiẓ, whom Adonis regards without reservation as an advocate of traditionalism because of his emphasis on innate talent, moral commitment, immediacy, and clarity as the principal criteria for the creation and appreciation of authentic Arabic poetry. The second is Abū Tammām, whom Adonis considers the modernist par excellence because he used his poetic language in such a fresh and original way as "to create after no other model" (*al-khalq lā 'ala mithāl*)—creating a new type of poetry.

There is a measure of truth in associating al-Jāḥiẓ with the mainstream of the literary tradition and in viewing Abū Tammām as a leading modernist. But the classification of these two prominent figures under two separate literary categories, with the implication that al-Jāḥiẓ was merely imitative while Abū Tammām was purely innovative, is a misrepresentation not only of the nature and intrinsic merit of their individual works and achievements, but also of the nature and significance of the dialectical relationship which existed between the current of continuity and that of change within the Arab literary heritage.

A close examination of Abbasid literature reveals that it inherited two interrelated traditions. One was the Arab cultural and ethical tradition of the Jāhilīyah (pre-Islamic) with which the majority of Arab Abbasid poets and critics and a number of non-Arabs (such as al-Jāḥiẓ, who was born to a family of *mawāli* of Abyssinian or Nubian descent) were associated. The other was the Islamic historical tradition, which formed the basis of the Islamic religion and of the Abbasid state, and which was shared by Arabs and non-Arabs alike. In their efforts to counter the Arabs' claim to superiority on the basis of their lion's share both of the Jāhilī cultural tradition and of the Islamic religious tradition, the majority of the non-Arabs (such as Bashshār, Abū Nūwās, and many other poets and critics) supported the Shu'ūbiyah movement which emerged in literary and intellectual circles. This movement glorified the older Persian civilization at the expense of the Arabs, claiming for Persia "the origin of nearly everything of value in Muslim culture."[19] The movement's claim found articulate expression in Mihyār's famous poem in which he boasts of inheriting his culture from Persia and his faith from Arabia, and of thereby possessing the glories of both legacies: the religion of the Arabs (Islam) and the civilization of the Persians:

> I inherited culture from the noblest of ancestors
> And took my religion from the best of prophets.
> Thus I gathered the whole of glory:
> The Persians' greatness and the Arabs' religion.

In my opinion it was this struggle to establish cultural superiority and to assert national identity that underlay both the Shu'ūbīyah and the anti-Shu'ūbīyah movements. On one side the struggle led the Arabs to form a strong attachment to the Jāhilī poetic tradition, idealizing it as the canon of their cultural and esthetic values. On the other side it led the Shu'ūbī poets and critics to ridicule and reject that tradition as outmoded. It must be noted in this connection that the Prophet's change of attitude toward poets and poetry, as shown by his acceptance of Ka'b Ibn Zuhayr as an Islamic court poet,[20] must have reinforced the belief of the Arabs and of those who were fully identified with them that the two traditions to which they were heir and which had their roots in the Arab heritage—the Jāhilī and the Islamic—were fully compatible.

When Adonis condemns al-Jāḥiẓ as a traditionalist 'advocating essentially Jāhilī poetic norms and values, he commits several errors. First, he overlooks the fact that a tradition-bound "Arab mentality" was not al-Jāḥiẓ's only motive for returning to the distant past and defending the Jāhilī cultural heritage. al-Jāḥiẓ had been strongly drawn to that cultural heritage as a non-Arab of obscure ethnic origin who was educated in the traditional culture by the most learned men of his day (al-Aṣmaʻī, Abū ʻUbaydah, and Abū Zayd). He came to identify himself fully with that tradition and culture, and thus defended it passionately. Second, Adonis associates the norms upheld by al-Jāḥiẓ—such as spontaneity, immediacy, and clarity—with Bedouinism and orality. He then condemns these concepts in favor of excessive artistry, ambiguity, and difficulty, which he views as characteristics of "sophisticated," "urban," and "creative writing" and therefore alien to al-Jāḥiẓ's literary taste and traditional outlook. Passing such a judgment means not only replacing what he considers a set of outmoded "fixed absolutes" (such as orality, immediacy, and clarity) with another set of "modern" fixed absolutes (such as structural complexity and inexhaustible ambiguity), but also to use what is essentially his understanding of twentieth-century poetic criteria and sensibility to evaluate the norms and values of an Arab classical tradition which emerged and developed some fourteen centuries earlier.

More important than these extrinsic considerations are the intrinsic qualities of al-Jāḥiẓ's own work, which Adonis misjudges as traditionalistic. Charles Pellat, in his scholarly study of al-Jāḥiẓ, provides a more adequate appraisal of the great Basran writer. Speaking of the innovativeness, originality, and contribution of this man who lived and died by the written word, Pellat says, "He gave literary prose its most perfect form, as was indeed recognized first by politicians who made use of his talents for the Abbasid cause and then by Arab critics who were unanimous in asserting his superiority and making his name the very symbol of literary ability." Praising the spirit of criticism and systematic doubt with which al-Jāḥiẓ approached every subject (except, of course, for the foundations of the Islamic faith), Pellat adds: "He takes for granted the right to submit to scrutiny accepted attitudes to natural phenomena, ancient history and legends handed down as truths, to restate problems and skillfully suggest rational solutions. Nor is that all; for at a time when medieval Arabic culture was taking shape, he brought together what seemed of most value to him, drawing either on the Arab heritage of which he was a passionate defender or on Greek thought." This, essentially, is the image of al-Jāḥiẓ, whose "tone of irony, reasoned doubt, exuberant delight in all phenomena and casual precision of his Arabic diction and style cannot fail to impress us today as it impressed his ninth-century readers."[21]

I believe that enough has been said to show that Adonis's classification of al-Jāḥiẓ under the static category of traditionalist writers is an error, since it blurs the creative dimension of his vital contribution to the development of Arabic letters.

All the cherished qualities which Adonis found lacking in the traditionalist al-Jāḥiẓ he found embodied in their perfect form in the innovative poet Abū Tammām, the figure in whom he confers pride of place among the modernists. What underlies Adonis's judgment of Abū Tammām's poetry is his belief in the latter's ability to "create after no other model," to transcend the norms and values of the ancient poetic and cultural tradition, to seek the new and original, and to discover, through fresh use of the language, "a world constantly in need of exploration."

One can hardly dispute that Abū Tammām deserves the highest respect for the esthetic merit of his poetry. What is open to doubt is Adonis's claim that his poetry was created afresh, without being influenced in its new mode of existence by any earlier model. It must be added that this central assertion by Adonis about Abū Tammām's innovativeness is based not on textual analysis of his poetry, but rather on discussion of the controversial *mūwāzanah*, or "comparison" (of the merit of his verse and that of his contemporary al-Buḥturī), which was carried out by al-Āmidī, al-Ṣūlī, and other classical critics. Although I acknowledge that this important controversy can significantly help us to appreciate the sensibility of the poet's age and what it expected from poetry, it might be more appropriate for our purposes to focus on Abū Tammām's poetry itself and to make a few critical remarks about its distinguishing features as they relate to the question of continuity and change raised by Adonis.

To begin with, newness in poetry, unlike newness in the other arts, is merely relative. This is because language, poetry's necessary medium of expression, is by definition tradition-bound in that it cannot be emptied of its referential connotations or intentionality, however unconventionally or figuratively it may be used by the individual poet. In other words, the poet's language cannot be reduced to the kind of abstraction that a painter's colors or a musician's melody fundamentally are, and which possibly enables the painter or musician to create a completely new or absolutely original work of art. Thus, at least theoretically, Adonis's claim that Abū Tammām created his poetry "after no other model" can have only relative validity.

More important than this theoretical consideration is the question of newness in Abū Tammām's poetry. I will address this issue by analyzing two of his best poems: "Madḥ Mālik Ibn Ṭawq"[22] and "Fatḥ 'Ammūrīyah." In the former poem Abū Tammām intercedes with the Taghlibite chief Mālik Ibn Ṭawq on behalf of the Banū Usāmah, who had rebelled against him, and asks that he pardon them. The poet begins with the traditional Jāhilīyah *nasīb* or *ghazal* prelude, asking if "time would give an answer to a question" about the wasted "ruins at Amrah, of Zaynab and Rabāb"—two maidens like "two moons" or "two white gazelles." He then turns to attributing to his patron the virtues of the heroic Jāhilīyah, such as generosity, courage, justice, clemency, and forgiveness. This is followed by a long eulogistic section in which he praises Jawaāb, one of Mālik's ancestors, for forgiving in times past a tribe which had rebelled against him, and urges his patron to follow the noble tradition of his forefathers. Abū Tammām concludes the poem by offering it to Mālik as if it were, in his own metaphor, the daughter of his creative mind, a virgin bride of ever fresh youth and beauty.

Despite the poet's claim to have presented his patron with a virgin composition which he had created, in Adonis's words, "after no other model," it is clear that the Jāhilīyah tradition has supplied him with the fundamental constitutive elements of his eulogy: the heroic virtues which adorn his master Mālik, as well as the literary material underlying his desert metaphors and imagery. Moreover, apart from a brief reference to the "Messenger of God" as having provided—in the Koran and the Sunnah—the greatest example of returning the spoils of an enemy, the poem is predominantly secular.

Abū Tammām's second poem, *"Fatḥ 'Ammūrīyah,"*[23] celebrates the victory of the caliph al-Mu'taṣim over the Byzantine emperor Theophilus and the capture of the Byzantine city of Amorium in A.H. 223/A.D. 838. The astrologers had warned the caliph against trying to conquer it at that time, but he ignored their advice, attacked the city, and won for Islam one of its most glorious battles. Without trying to provide here a detailed analysis of this long (seventy-one-line) panegyric, it may suffice, obviously at the risk of oversimplification, to focus on some of its basic formal and referential features which seem relevant to the question under discussion: the "relative newness" of Abū Tammām's poetry.

Five interrelated sections may be discerned in this poem, which exalts the heroic image of the Arab Muslim Abbasid caliph. Lines 1-10 denounce the false predictions of the astrologers, and set the tone for the whole poem by declaring that "true knowledge" lies in the "edge of the sword" and not in the reading of the gleaming stars. Lines 11-24 depict Amorium as a "virgin whom the hand of fate had not deflowered," thus paving the way for her *fatḥ* (the word means both conquest and deflowerment) by the "sword" of Islam. Lines 25-36 describe in epic terms the battle (the ceremony of *fatḥ*) in which the honor of the Byzantine imperial forces is violated by the caliph's Muslim armies. Lines 37-66 make a sharp contrast between the triumph of the "believers" under the leadership of their holy war commander al-Mu'taṣim (lines 37-49) and the shameful rout and defeat of the "unbelievers" and their fleeing emperor (lines 50-66). Finally, lines 67-71 complete the poem by comparing the victory of God's caliph (al-Muʻtaṣim) over his Byzantine Christian enemies on the day of the Battle of Amorium to the victory of God's Messenger (Muḥammad) over his Meccan opponents on the "Day of Badr":[24] two glorious days for the Arabs and Islam.

Throughout the poem one can clearly discern elements drawn both from the Jāhilīyah tradition (metaphors of desert warfare, *nasīb*, the deserted campsite, and concepts of honor and vengeance) and from the Islamic tradition (the whole concept of al-Muʻtaṣim's holy war against the Byzantine unbelievers), which Abū Tammām fuses together into the complex structure of his epiclike *qaṣīdah* (rhymed poem). Moreover, when he blends all these disparate elements together, he uses the traditional *basīṭ* meter and overloads the poem with ornamental devices such as *jinās* (assonance), *talmīḥ* (allusion), and double entendre.[25]

This poem, with its complex structure of thought and excessive ornamentation, is highly representative of Abū Tammām's verse. Medieval critics were divided in their reactions to it. Some greatly admired the work, while others severely condemned it, a situation which seems likely to continue in the present. Such a divergence of views is legitimate and perfectly justifiable, but although the two poems just discussed are exceptionally ingenious and highly expressive, we cannot accept Adonis's claim that they (along with the rest of Abū Tammām's poetry) are virgin compositions created "after no other model" and thus deserving, by virtue of their absolute originality and newness, of being classified in the dynamic (*mutaḥawwil*) category.

To complete this analysis of Adonis's views, I must turn to the question of religion. First, however, I must repeat here that the predominantly secular nature and function of Abū Tammām's *"Madḥ Mālik Ibn Ṭawq"* does not necessarily make it a better poem than his *"Fatḥ 'Ammūrīyah"*— which is, as we have shown, very Islamic in character. In fact, were it not for the heightened religious feelings that permeate the poem's structure, its excessive rhetorical ornamentations would have reduced it to sheer verbal virtuosity and dry intellectualism. It was precisely this kind of mechanical dryness that led, in the hands of the lesser poets of the post-Abbasid period, to the ossification of Arabic poetry until the rise of al-Bārūdī and of Shawqi's neoclassical school in modern times.

So far I have argued that neither the secularization of poetry nor its Islamization is what makes it dynamic or static, and that one therefore cannot draw up two separate lists—one of great innovators and the other of those who fail to innovate as Adonis does. I am also tempted to ask here under which category Adonis would have listed poets of diverse interests, values, outlooks, and techniques, such as al-Mutanabbī, al-Ma'arrī, and Ibn al-Fāriḍ, had he decided to include them in his study. I suspect that, when we call them "great poets," we do not do so on the basis of their religiosity or atheism or their morality or immorality, which would amount to making an extraliterary (social or ethical) evaluation of their works. Instead, we judge them according to purely literary criteria. Their greatness (like that of Abū Nūwās, whom Adonis very insightfully discussed) is hard to define except by saying that each of them gave us his vision of life and of the world around him as seen from his own perspective at a particular age. Just as we do not have to be royalist in politics, Catholic in religion, or puritan in temperament to appreciate T. S. Eliot's poetry, we do not have to share Abū Nūwās's libertinism, or al-Mutanabbī's idealization of Bedouin life and Arab virtues, or Abū al-'Alā's skepticism, or Ibn al-Fāriḍ's mysticism, in order to appreciate their poetry. None of them may be said to have become truly alienated from the literary tradition of the past. On the contrary, each one of them, in proportion to the excellence and vigor of his poetry, kept up the continuity of our living Arabic literature.

As I pointed out above, Adonis believes that the lack of change in Arabic poetry is mainly due to the religious nature of Arab culture, which allowed static values to become major characteristics of the "Arab mentality." His view is a valid critical judgment of Arab Islamic thought at certain stages in its history, especially during the long period of decline which has extended down to modern times. What is certainly contestable is his claim that those characteristics are essential traits not only of Arab Islamic culture in the period of decline, but also of that culture in other periods and of the hypothetical entity he calls the "Arab mentality." However, an exploration of what is purely Arab and what is mainly non-Arab in the Arab Islamic heritage would take up much space and lead us far afield from our subject.

In one of his concluding statements, Adonis asserts that the relationship between the literary heritage and the religious heritage became so close that these two legacies "constituted an indivisible entity." Father Paul Nwyia shares Adonis's view that Islamic religious thought has played an important role in the history of Arabic poetry, but he also believes that this role was much more complex than Adonis thinks.[26] In his opinion there must have been other factors which deepened the impact of the pre-Islamic mentality on the Arab mind and caused Islam to reclaim the Jāhilīyah and reintegrate it into its own structure, so that Muslim Arabs looked upon the Jāhilī poetry as an ideal model even after rejecting its outlook and values. Explaining how the notion of time cannot be applied in the same way to religion and literature, Nwyia wrote the following in his introduction to Adonis's *al-Thābit wa-al-mutaḥawwil:*

If religion had a negative influence on literature, it is because the Arabs applied the same concept of time to both religion and literature instead of having two different concepts. This manifests itself in the examination of the relationship of both religion and literature to the future. When religion speaks about resurrection, the last judgment, Heaven, and Hell, it signifies that the future is actually present. For we cannot ignore the fact that it is of the essence of religion to claim knowledge of the future. Such a claim cannot be made by literature. The future is the "coming," and the "coming", for religion, is known before it "comes"; but for literature it is unknown because it is new with regard to the "existing"... As for the relationship of religion and literature to the past, in religion, we cannot deny the fact that the past has great importance, for the time of the revelation or appearance of the Prophet is the essential time in which everything new on Earth is born. It is therefore necessary that the "time of appearance" should assume a special meaning in the sense that the relationship of the present to that time has its own special nature which does not exist in any other historical time. From this standpoint we could say that the past of religion is not a religious time except insofar as it is present in the present. All this is not possible in the sphere of literature. For the man of letters who attempts to repeat the experience of his predecessors is no more than an imitator.

To these illuminating observations Nwiya adds his psychological interpretation of the "*māḍawīyah*" problem by asking, is not "the return to the distant past an expression of the longing of man for the lost paradise, or his yearning for the bosom of the mother, or as Carl C. Jung says, a reemergence of primordial archetypes in the depth of the collective consciousness so that [the poet's halting] at the deserted encampment is not a return to the Jāhilīyah inasmuch as it is a return to the deepest symbols in the history of the Arab collective unconscious?" He then points out that the deserted encampment is an image linked to the desert, and that the desert is a primordial symbol in the depths of the Arab psyche. Thus returning to the past and imitating it are not phenomena peculiar to the Arab mind. Adonis wrongly attributes it to religion when it is actually a basic human attribute whose suppression or elimination would be disastrous for our mental equilibrium. Nwiya closes his argument by recognizing the role played by the religious vision in the dominance of traditionalism in poetry, but he rightly asserts that such a vision could not have imposed what it did impose unless it encountered a need for the continued return to the past.

More serious than Adonis's criticism of passéism and imitativeness is his condemnation of theocentricity as a major characteristic of the Arab mentality. Theocentricity, as defined above, is the tendency to place the religious concept of a transcendental God at the center of thought, thus reducing man to a marginal, submissive creature with almost no will or freedom. He enlarges on this concept as follows: "Just as the religious person no longer thinks for himself but it is the religion which thinks for the religious person . . . and the individual no longer acts for himself but it is God who acts for the individual, so the poet no longer writes for himself but it is the poetry which writes for the poet."[27]

Adonis's view of Islam is important for our understanding not only of how he sees the relationship between religion and literature, but also (and more importantly) of his critical perspectives on Koranic Islam, one of the most fundamental principles of which is theocentricity. His treatment of this issue thus requires special consideration.

We need not go into a detailed discussion of such ultimate questions as the doctrines of God's uniqueness (*fardanah*), of His absolute transcendence (*al-ghaybīyah al-muṭlaqah*), and of men's accountability to Him on the Last Day. It will be enough to say here that these doctrines, as stressed in the Koran and practiced by true Muslims, are not merely abstract metaphysical concepts of no positive value. Rather, they are basic guiding principles which have played a vital functional role in the social and ethical life of the Muslim community in the past and which are still doing so today. It has been rightly noted that "just as in Kantian terms no ideal knowledge is possible without the regulative ideas of reason (like first cause), so in Koranic terms no morality is possible without the regulative ideas of God and the last judgment . . . God is (for genuine Muslims) the transcendent anchoring point of attributes such as life, creativity, power, mercy, and justice and of moral values to which human society must be subject if it is to survive and prosper."[28]

Furthermore, alongside the majestic and transcendental aspects of God as the High and Mighty One, the Judge and the Avenger, the Koran also stresses belief in Him as the Compassionate, Merciful, Provider, Proector, Clement, and intensely real, for He "is closer to man than his neck-vein."[29] Thus a closer look at Adonis's statement about the theocentricity of the Arab Muslim mentality reveals two interrelated errors. The first is to misinterpret the true nature of the relationship between God and man as reflected in the Koran itself. The second is to claim, quite unconvincingly, that a particular mode of thought such as al-Ḥallāj's or Ibn 'Arabī's mysticism, or the flame (*lahab*), which kindled their pantheistic theosophy, could resolve the theocentricity problem and restore to the Arab Muslim man his rightful place at the center of the universe. As a result of his attempt to humanize God, Adonis goes to the other extreme and tends to deify man. This may be in harmony with some secular philosophies, but it is certainly in disharmony with Koranic Islam.

All this leads us to raise a key question about Adonis's position on Koranic Islam: Does the change which he advocates throughout his study of Arab Islamic culture in general and of Arabic poetry in particular have any radical effect on his view of the Koranic revelation itself?

Adonis states at the beginning of *al-Thābit wa-al-mutaḥawwil* that his "main purpose is to study the Islamic revelation in day-to-day practice and in the method of thought."[30] However, the fact that he exceeds the limits of his stated objectives in his treatment of certain issues (such as prophecy and the concept of God) leads him to reiterate his original statement and clarify his position by declaring the following:

> My position vis-à-vis Islam is very clear; there is no harm in repeating it briefly in order to eliminate any confusion. I distinguish between three levels: Koranic Islam, Islam as historically practiced, and Islam as [lived] by Muslims today. The first is the origin and foundation; there is no Islam without it. It is an indivisible whole which must either be accepted in its totality or not at all. This, I believe, is the opinion of the true Muslim. As for the other two levels, it is possible to divide and criticize them, thereby allowing each individual to exercise his own personal judgment.[31]

Candid, emphatic, and suggestive as it is, Adonis's statement, like most of his poetry, challenges us to look behind its outward meaning and to try to grasp its inner truth by asking, in this particular case, just what is this Koranic Islam which he views as an indivisible whole and seems to embrace with such unquestioning acceptance? Adonis gives us no clear definition. We cannot tell exactly where, or on what basis, he would set the border between that which must be accepted and that which may be criticized. Yet unless we can more clearly define Koranic Islam and spell out a sound methodology with which to interpret its general principles and adapt them to the imperative needs of the modern world, there is no visible way to judge clearly the conformities and deformities of historical Islam.[32]

These criticisms notwithstanding, and although Adonis had an ambiguous attitude toward normative Islam, in my judgment the overall validity of his critique of the prevailing Arab culture, of his criteria for building a new one, and of the new direction he provided both theoretically and practically for the creation of a truly Arabic poetry all make him the most eloquent spokesman for enlightened cultural change in the Arab world today.

Notes

1. Given the limited space available here for this essay, which centers primarily on Adonis's critique of Arab Islamic culture, it is impossible to furnish adequate bibliographical material for the study of his other major achievements or to provide biographical information on him. For more extensive information, see 'Alī Aḥmad al-Shar', "An Analytical Study of the Adonisian Poem," Ph.D. thesis (NES Department, University of Michigan, Ann Arbor, 1982), pp. 1-28 and 287-94. The critical works of Adonis used in this paper include *al-Thābit wa-al-mutaḥawwil: Baḥth fī al-ittibā' wa-al-ibdā' 'ind al-'Arab*, 3 vols. (Beirut: Dār al-'Awdah, 1974-1979), hereafter referenced as al-Thābit; *Fatiḥah li-nihāyat al-qarn; Bayānāt min ajl thaqāfah 'Arabīyah jadīdah* (Beirut: Dār al-'Awdah, 1980); and *Zamān al-Shi'r* (Beirut: Dār al-'Awdah, 1972). 'Alī Aḥmad Sa'īd is entered under *Adūnīs* in the Library of Congress.
2. In addition to Adonis's works on the subject, other important studies include Tahā Ḥusayn, *Mustaqbal al-thaqāfah fī Miṣr* (Cairo: al-Ma'ārif, 1938); C. Zurayk, *Naḥnu wa-al-tārīkh* (Beirut: Dār al-'Ilm lil-Malāyin, 1959); L. 'Awad, *al-Thawrah wa-al-adab* (Cairo: Dār al-Kātib al-'Arabī, 1967); Mahmud A. al-'Alim, *al-Thaqāfah wa-al-thawrah* (Beirut: Dār al-Adāb, 1970); 'Abdallah al-'Arawi, *al-Idyulūjīyah al-'Arabīyah al-mu'āṣirah* (Beirut: Dār al-Ḥaqīqah, 1970), *al-'Arab wa-al-fikr al-tārīkhī*, (Beirut: Dār al-Ḥaqīqah, 1972), and *Azmat al-muthaqqafīn al-'Arab* (Beirut: al-Mu'assasah al-'Arabīyah lil-Dirāsāt wa-al-Nashr, 1978); Muḥammad 'Imārah, *Naẓrah jadīdah ila al-turāth* (Beirut: al-Mu'assasah al-'Arabīyah lil-Dirāsāt wa-al-Nashr, 1974); Zakī N. Maḥmūd, *al-Ma'qūl wa-al-lāma'qūl fi turāthina al-fikrī* (Beirut: Dār al-Shurūq, 1975); 'Abd al-Raḥman Sharqāwī, *Qira'āt fī al-fikr al-Islāmī* (Beirut: Dār al-Waṭan al-'Arabī, 1975); Ṭarīf Khalidī, *Dirāsāt fī tārīkh al-fikr al-'Arabī al-Islāmī* (Beirut: Dār al-Ṭalī'ah, 1977); and Naṣīf Naṣṣār, *Naḥwa mujtama' jadīd* (Beirut: Dār al-Ṭalī'ah, 1977).
3. *al-Thābit*, 2:48-49.
4. Ibid., 2:51. For Adonis's detailed discussion of al-Jāḥiẓ, see pp. 46-58. (All translations are by the author.)
5. Ibid., 115. For his assessment of Abū Nūwās's and Abū Tammām's contribution to the modernity of classical poetry, see pp. 109-20.
6. Ibid., 1:27.
7. Ibid., 7:28.
8. Ibid., 1:29.
9. Ibid., 3:303-4.
10. Ibid., 3:312-15.
11. Ibid., 2:210.
12. See Ṭahā Ḥusayn, *Fī al-shi'r al-jāhilī* (Cairo: Dār al-Kutub, 1926), pp. 11-14. For a discussion of Ṭaha Ḥusayn's views on this subject, see Muḥammad al-Nuwayhi's article, "Towards the Reappraisal of Classical Arabic Literature and History: Some Aspects of Ṭahā Ḥusayn's Use of Modern Western Criteria," *International Journal of Middle East Studies* 2, no. 1 (1980): 189-207.

13. *al-Thābit*, 1:17, 24.
14. Ibid., 1:18.
15. Ibid., 1:20.
16. On this point, see S. J. al-'Aẓm's article, "Adūnīs wa-al-naqd al-munfalit min 'iqālih," *Dirāsāt 'Arabīyah*, 18th year, no. 4 (February 1982): 47-74. Other reviews of *al-Thābit* include Y. al-Yūsuf, "Hal al-Ummah al-'Arabīyah mu'ādiyah lil-Ibdā'?" *al-Mawqif al-adabī* (Damascus), no. 81 (January 1978): 107-13; A. 'Abd al-Dā'īm, "Ḥawl Risālat Adūnīs: Al-turāth al-'Arabī bayn al-ittibā' wa-al-ibdā'," *al-Adāb*, 21, no. 8 (August 1973): 9-12, 75-81; Rif'at Salām, "'An al-manhaj al-mithālī fī *al-Thābit wa-al-mutaḥawwil*," *al-Adāb*, 26, no. 12 (December 1978): 30-34; and M. al-'Abdullah, "Fī kitāb *Ṣadmat al-ḥadāthah*," *al-Aḥad* (November 6, 1978). See also T. al-Khalidi, "Nahnu thalāth qabā'il: Islāmīyah wa-'Arabīyah wa-Marksīyah," *al-Nahār al-'Arabī wa-al-dawlī* (August 19, 1978): 28.
17. See H. A. R. Gibb, *Mohammedanism* (London: Oxford University Press, 1973), p. 77.
18. Ibid., p. 95.
19. H. A. R. Gibb, *Arabic Literature* (Oxford: The Clarendon Press, 1963), p. 48.
20. On this point, see Irfan Shahid's article, "A Contribution to Koranic Exegesis," in *Arabic and Islamic Studies in Honor of H. A. R. Gibb*, ed. G. Makdisi (Cambridge: Harvard University Press, 1965), pp. 563-80. See also M. Zwettler's study, "The Poet and the Prophet: Towards Understanding the Evolution of a Narrative," in *Jerusalem Studies in Arabic and Islam*, 6 (1984): 313-87.
21. See Charles Pellat's article on al-Jāḥiẓ in the *Encyclopedia of Islam*, new ed., 2:385-87. See also M. Zwettler's essay on al-Jāḥiẓ in *The Genius of Arab Civilization*, ed. J. Hayes, 2d. ed., (Cambridge: Massachusetts Institute of Technology, 1983), pp. 48-49.
22. For this poem, which begins "law anna dahran," see *Diwān Abū Tammām*, ed. M. A. 'Azzām, (Cairo: Dār al-Ma'ārif, 1964), 1:75-91.
23. For this poem, which begins with "*al-Sayfu aṣdaqu anbā'an*," see *Diwān*, 1:40-74. See also A. J. Arberry's translation of this poem in *Arabic Poetry* (Cambridge: Cambridge University Press, 1965), pp. 51-62. For a perceptive study of Abū Tammām's poetry, including the two poems mentioned above, see Susan P. Stetkevych's article, "The Abbasid Poet Interprets History: Three Qasidas by Abū Tammām," *Journal of Arabic Literature* 10 (1979): 49-64.
24. A reference to the Prophet's celebrated victory over the Meccan forces in A.D. 624.
25. These and many other *badī'* (science of metaphors) devices are readily recognizable in Abū Tammām's poem.
26. *al-Thābit*, 1:11.
27. Ibid., 1:66.
28. See Fazlur Rahman, *Islam and Modernity* (Chicago: University of Chicago Press, 1982), p. 42.
29. *Koran* 1, vol. 15.

30. *al-Thābit*, 1:23.
31. Adonis, "Bayn al-thābit wa-al-mutaḥawwil: Khawāṭir ḥawl al-thawrah al-Islāmīyah fī Irān," *Mawāqif*, no. 34 (1979): 151.
32. For an inside view of this question, see Fazlur Rahman, *Islam and Modernity*, pp. 13-22, 141-45. Professor Fazlur Rahman persuasively demonstrates that for normative Islam to be what Muslims claim it to be—comprehensive in scope and efficacious for every age and place—Muslim scholars and educationists (the latter were scarcely discussed by Adonis) must reevaluate their methodology and hermeneutics. Islam's modernity, he argues, cannot be achieved through a mechanical juxtaposition of old and new, or through a piecemeal, ad hoc interpretation of the Koran, but rather "by studying the Koran's social pronouncements and legal enactment in the light of its general moral teaching and particularly under the impact of its stated principles on the one hand and against the background of their historical milieu on the other" (p. 141).

Aḥmad Amīn and ʻAbbās Maḥmūd al-ʻAqqād Between *al-Qadīm* and *al-Jadīd:* European Challenge and Islamic Response

IBRAHIM IBRAHIM

In Egypt the modern intellectual as both a historical phenomenon and a social concept has been intrinsically connected with the process of Westernization which Egypt has been undergoing from the beginning of the nineteenth century. Indeed, he has come into being as a by-product of that process.

Until the turn of the eighteenth century, Egyptian society lived under a distinct Arab Islamic civilization, which embraced and determined every sphere of life. In the sphere of law, for instance, the *Shari'a*, the sacred law, was the "regulative principle"[1] according to which society was conducted. In education the Azhar and the religious schools were the sole centers of learning, with the classical Arab Islamic culture the only recognized culture. And finally, the ulema, men of religion, were not only the revered men of learning but also the spokesmen of the *ummah* (Islamic Community) in political matters; the people looked up to them as their leaders in their relations with the ruler.[2]

But from the beginning of the nineteenth century, a fundamental change—indeed, a transformation—in many aspects of life began to occur, one which resulted in the disruption of the prevailing traditional culture, as the European challenge led in turn to an Islamic response. The introduction of European positivist laws had shaken the predominance of the *Shari'a*, which was the instrument by which the social ethic of Islam was consolidated.[3] The most profound effect, however, resulted from the educational policy pursued by the rulers of Egypt throughout the nineteenth century. By establishing modern schools based on Western models[4] and by sending educational missions to Europe, they, consciously or unconsciously, not only opened society to new modes of thought and ideas or demonstrated the superiority of Europe and their need to assimilate from its civilization, but also gradually created a new nontraditional intelligentsia: civil servants, technicians, jurists, and journalists, a stratum which was not guided by the rule of tradition.

Thus, by the end of the nineteenth century, Egyptian society was no longer the "traditional society" with its traditional institutions, culture, and outlook, but a disrupted society reflecting all the contradictions which influences, from outside as well as from within, create. In it we find the old existing beside and competing with the new: the modern judge of the civil courts beside the traditional *qāḍī* at the *Shari'a* court, the *'ālim* of the Azhar beside the professor at the secular institutes.[5] In other words, there was a schism in society. And none were affected by the change more than the ulema, the guardians of the *Shari'a* and the traditional centers of learning.

Having lost the material foundation of their power, the ulema lost their standing as intellectual leaders, and their views—even if they still found favorable response from the majority—could not find acceptance among the leaders of modern Egypt. This change was inevitable, for once education and law were removed from their hands, their political influence waned. It was the modern intelligentsia which the modern state needed. This stratum became the nucleus of a class of government officials who were eventually to become the leaders of the people, a function which the ulema used to fulfil.[6] Intellectually, the views of the ulema became obsolete and out of date. For with the extension of Western education and the increasing intellectual intercourse with Europe, the traditional views of life were giving way to new ideas about society and culture.

Influenced by the French Enlightenment, nineteenth-century positivism, and utilitarianism, the modern intellectuals came to ignore tradition and began to orient themselves toward European culture and thought. Islam seemed to them no longer capable of meeting problems created by modern civilization. Neither the *Shari'a* nor traditional culture could conform or fit with the spirit of the age. It was European civilization which could lead to the welfare state and the creation of the virtuous society.[7] Aḥmad Luṭfī al-Sayyīd wrote in 1914:

> The wave of civilization has come to us with all its virtues and vices, and we must accept it without resisting it. All that we can do is to Egyptianize the good that it carries and narrow down the channels through which the evil can run. We must possess that civilization as it is, but not try to control it.[8]

Aḥmad Luṭfī al-Sayyīd and his modernist associates—the brothers Fatḥi and Sa'd Zaghlūl, Qāsim Amīn, Muṣṭafa 'Abd al-Rāziq, and other members of the *Ummah* group—came from big land owning families, and most were trained at Western schools of law. From their vantage point as members of the leading elite, they were convinced that Egypt must become a part of the modern world; to progress, Egypt had to accept the laws and ideas that led to European ascendency. The leading young intellectuals, in the interwar period, came also to acknowledge the superiority of European culture to their own and to believe that European political and social values were higher than those prevailing in their own country. The secret of this superiority, they thought, lay in the freedom of men and women, in respect for individual rights, particularly freedom of speech and of the press and, above all, in the scientific spirit. Throughout the interwar period, the Wafd, the leading political party, formally adopted and fought with great vigor for these modern and somewhat revolutionary ideas—in particular, for a freely elected parliament to which government should be accountable.[9]

These ideas were embraced by a number of gifted writers, two of whom were Aḥmad Amīn, who gained prominence as a historian and scholar, and ʻAbbās Maḥmūd al-ʻAqqād, a poet and gifted literary critic and essayist and the biographer of the Egyptian leader Saʻd Zaghlūl.

Aḥmad Amīn (1886-1954) was born in Cairo into a pious Muslim family from the village of Sumukhrat in the province of al-Buḥayrah. Like Ṭahā Ḥusayn and other members of his generation, he was sent to the Azhar, where he was greatly impressed by two lessons given by Shaykh Muḥammad ʻAbduh. He writes: "I heard his beautiful voice, saw his venerable appearance, and understood from him what I had not understood from my Azharite shaykhs. I regretted not having been an earlier student of his and I decided to continue attending his lessons. But these two lessons were his last, may God have mercy on him."[10] Amīn soon left the Azhar, taught at various government schools, and later enrolled at Madrasat al-Qaḍā' al-Sharʻī, the Muslim Judicial School established in Cairo in 1907 thanks to the efforts of Saʻd Zaghlūl; following his graduation, Amin was appointed to teach at that same school.

Amīn did not like the Azharite teachers at the school; he was impressed, however, by those teachers who were influenced by Muḥammad ʻAbduh because "they did not rely on the old books" and by others who had been educated in England, France, and Germany. It was here that he read John Stuart Mackenzie's *Manual of Ethics* and John Stuart Mill's *Utilitarianism*, and attended outstanding lectures—for example, one on Herbert Spencer, another on Pestalozzi. He was particularly enamored of lectures given by renowned Orientalists invited to teach at the newly created Egyptian University: "I liked most the lectures of Nallino on the history of Arab astronomy, the lectures of Professor Santillana on Islamic philosophy, and the lectures of Professor Guidi on Arab geography . . . I saw here a new kind of education which I had not known: thoroughness in research, depth in study, patience in referring to various sources, comparison between what the Arabs and the Europeans said and quite serious deductions made from all that."[11]

'Abduh and his disciples—and the new knowledge he acquired at their hands—deeply affected him at the time, and were destined to influence his outlook on culture and society and his writings for years to come. While still at school, he contributed to the daily newspaper *al-Jarīdah*, founded in 1907 by Aḥmad Luṭfī al-Sayyīd, leader of the *ummah* group, and moved within its circle of young thinkers. Amin was very much impressed by al-Sayyīd and *al-Jarīdah*, which he saw as a training ground for the intellectuals of the day.

His [Aḥmad Luṭfī al-Sayyīd's] office at the newspaper building was a club where a group of young intellectuals met. From time to time, political lectures were delivered in the courtyard of the house and were followed by debate . . . I benefited from this contact in gaining some political and social education, thanks to the lectures of our Professor Luṭfī and others, and my contact with a select group of the best intellectuals.[12]

While teaching at the Judicial School, Amīn felt the urge to learn a foreign language and opted for English, not only to enrich his scholarship but also to enhance his social standing. With the help of an English woman, he began to study the language, reading with her Plato's *Republic* and books on the principles of philosophy, logic, and Islamics written by Orientalists. As he so eloquently reminisced in his autobiography, *Ḥayātī:*

I used to live in the past but now I live in the past and the present . . . I used to believe things had one color and one taste but when other colors and tastes were placed alongside, my eye was opened to comparison and my mind to criticism. If I had not passed this stage but become a man of letters, I would have been a reactionary man of letters concerned with embellishing words not with seeking excellence in thought; I would have depended on the literature of the ancients and excluded that of the moderns; I would have turned in thought towards the former not the latter. If I became a writer, I would have been a compiler who compiled separate materials or separated compiled materials without investigation or criticism. For my humble production in translation, composition, and writing, I am indebted to this stage following the early stages, and to this new flower which made a bouquet when added to the old flowers.[13]

He knew Shaykh Muṣṭafa 'Abd al-Rāziq, who was to become Shaykh al-Azhar in 1945 and to serve until he died in 1947, and 'Āṭif Barakāt, dean of the Judicial School, which was fast becoming the stronghold of the Wafd. He was also attached to Aḥmad ʻAbd al-Raḥmān Fahmī, secretary of the Wafd, and Kāmil Bey Salīm, Saʻd Zaghlūl's secretary, who introduced him to the Egyptian leader with whom he would later develop a strong relationship.

During the revolution of 1919, Aḥmad Amīn was entrusted with the preparation of discourses for use in the mosques; he also took part in the demonstrations to assert Muslim-Copt solidarity. "I used to seek a demonstration, and wearing my turban, climb into a carriage to accompany a priest wearing his clerical cassock and carrying a flag bearing the cross and the crescent."[14]

Because of his upbringing and temperament, Aḥmad Amīn was more inclined toward scholarship and education than politics. Thanks to Ṭahā Ḥusayn, he was invited in 1926 to join the faculty of arts and sciences at what is now the University of Cairo. There he gained great prestige as a renowned scholar in Islamic history, and eventually became the dean of that same school.

Like Ṭahā Ḥusayn and others, Amīn was deeply interested in the overriding concern of Egyptian intellectuals at that time: how to reconcile Islam with Western civilization. What most interested him was discovering how Egyptians and Muslims could assimilate Western ideas and values and at the same time retain their own identity. On the one hand, Amīn realized—as did others—that Islamic civilization was in decline and could not rise on its own to challenge and compete with Europe; but he believed, on the other hand, that its weak indigenous culture could be revived—through careful, selective assimilation from the West and, above all, through the adaptation of Islam to the modern world. The problem lay, however, with the opponents of the *tajdīd:* the narrow-minded traditionalists and men of religion who believed in the *taqlīd.* They could not understand the new, either because they lacked the spirit of inquiry and questioning, which is the essential characteristic of the new, or because they, as men of the old civilization, had a vested interest in backing the old.[15]

To Amīn, Western civilization was the embodiment of the new: through its political and scientific revolutions it had become the most powerful civilization in the world; it had unified the world into a single body, dominated it, and made it impossible for any other civilization to exist and develop outside its sphere. Even those, like Gandhi, who rebelled against it and tried to resist its penetration into their countries failed and were compelled to surrender to it.[16] Because of its demonstrated prowess, Muslims had no alternative but to accept Western civilization.

Consciously or unconsciously we are linked to Western science, literature and civilization; all of these are deeply influencing our life. This is irresistible . . . because Western civilization has narrowed the gap between different parts of the world . . . The East has thus become linked to the West and influenced by it in all aspects of life: in political movements; in scientific, literary and artistic matters; in material as in intellectual matters; indeed in everything. Muslims must therefore understand that they have become a part of this unified world, which is subject to common patterns and a uniform civilization. Hence the only way for Muslims to progress is to follow the path that Europe has travelled.[17]

It can be maintained, Aḥmad Amīn argues, that Islamic civilization is diametrically opposed to Western civilization, in that the former is characterized by its spirituality and humane outlook, whereas the latter is rational and materialistic. Although this is true, a reconciliation between both is possible because Western civilization does not rest on religion: were it resting on a religion which is in opposition to Islam, assimilation would become impossible, "but fortunately this is not the case . . . It does not rest on religion but on science."[18] Hence there is no objection to borrowing from it. "Indeed, it is their [the Muslims'] duty to adopt Western science," without which there can be no progress.[19]

This should not imply, however, that the new should replace the old; the new has to adapt itself to the indigenous civilization, to build on it in order to take root in society and become acceptable to the community. The reformer should therefore take into consideration the social conditions of his country: "What suits this nation would not suit the other, and what suits the West would not suit the East."[20] Accordingly, the assimilation of Western civilization should go hand in hand with religious learning and the intensification of the spirit of Islam.

At the same time, Amīn is always critical of the Azhar's method of teaching and of the Azharites: Egypt, he believes, needs a new type of learned man; neither the Azharites nor the graduates of European universities are capable of leading the reform movement. The outlook of the former has become obsolete, and their thought is alien to the spirit of the age. Western-educated men are also alien to their society; they are not sympathetic to the Islamic spirit of their fellow countrymen.

By contrast, then, the new reformer should be conversant with both the traditional culture and modern civilization, for his task is to synthesize the new with the old, the East with the West. This is not a novelty for Muslims, he stresses; the Abbasids, for instance, assimilated much from Indian, Persian, Greek, and Roman civilizations, synthesized those civilizations with their own, and created a new Islamic culture. The same, Amīn believes, could be done now by Muslim reformers.[21]

Amīn's sympathies, as clearly revealed by his autobiography and by his interpretation of Islamic history, were more with the new and the reformers, who emphasized the role of reason and freedom as a prerequisite for progress. What was needed now was a new definition of tradition and religion in general, and of the *Shari'a* in particular. This problem was not new for him—Muḥammad 'Abduh had already paved the way in his attempt at reconciling Islam with modern civilization.

'Abduh accepted the change which Egypt was undergoing and showed great admiration for the achievements of modern Europe, but he insisted on Islam as the guiding principle in society. He believed, however—and here is the crucial turning point from the traditional view—that Islam, as it is, could not meet the problems created by modern civilization. Islam must therefore be reformed and reinterpreted to fit with the new reality. Hence his rejection of the uncritical acceptance of tradition and his plea for a rational interpretation of the Koran as well as the *Shari'a:*

> There is a general agreement among Muslims that in case of conflict between reason and what has been given as tradition, the conclusions of reason are to be given preference. Two possibilities remain with regard to the tradition: either to acknowledge its genuineness while confessing inability to understand it and resigning the matter to God's knowledge or to interpret it so that it would, in a sense, agree with what reason has established, without, however, doing violence to the rules of the language.[22]

The significance of 'Abduh lies in the fact that he marks the breach with the scholastic structure of dogma as elaborated in the Middle Ages. His views were disputed by the ulema; he was, however, influential in the circles of the "modern" intellectuals. What attracted them to his ideas was the spirit in which he approached questions of dogma and practice and especially his rejection of the traditional teaching that the doctrines of the Koran had been authoritatively expounded once and for all by the doctors of the first three centuries of Islam and that no free investigation of the sources could be tolerated.[23]

Generally speaking, 'Abduh understood the *Shari'a* in the traditional sense, in that it derived from revelation. Nevertheless, he introduced a new concept based on the European theory of natural law and utilitarianism. Thus, although he adopted the distinction made by Muslim thinkers, such as Ibn Taymīyah, between acts directed towards *'ibādāt* (the worship of God) and those directed towards *mu'āmalāt* (society), he went on to teach that the Koran and Ḥadīth laid down specific rules about worship but very general rules about society. Therefore, it was the task of human judgment and reason to guide society and regulate the affairs of men in that society. "The true Muslim is he who uses his reason in the affairs of the world and of religion; the only real infidel (*kāfir*) is he who closes his eyes to the light of truth and refuses to examine rational proofs."[24]

Like 'Abduh, Aḥmad Amīn adopted the division between *'ibādāt* and *mu'āmalāt*. But in light of the newly acquired knowledge of social evolution and the idea of the environment, and under the influence of his Orientalist masters, he went beyond 'Abduh's arguments by stressing the historical and environmental conditions that affected the *Sharī'a*, which he saw as subject to changes that occur in society, thus undermining the link between *'ibādāt* and *mu'āmalāt* which 'Abduh had attempted to establish.

Generally speaking, Amīn believed that all religions are alike, for "truth is the aim of all religions." Thus, he saw no divergence between the prophets, as there is between the philosophers, because revelation stems from one God. However, the difference between religions lies in their rules, which should be ascribed to the variety of natural and social environments in which they originated.[25] This is normal, for each religion has to understand and adapt itself to the conditions of its environment, which is always changing and evolving. Any religion must therefore have, inherent in itself, a certain kind of flexibility in order to adapt itself as new conditions arise; this spirit of flexibility lies in *ijtihād*.[26] The absence of it in other religions led to their decline; the rise of Islam, which was a necessity in order to correct and complement them, was inevitable.[27]

But, from its early days, Islam could not avoid the impact of the new environment it encountered outside Arabia. Once the Arabs expanded beyond their Arabian Peninsula borders, they began to assimilate and adopt some of the laws, values, ideas, and beliefs they encountered: the legacies of pre-Islamic Persia, of the Christian Syrians, and of Egyptian Copts, who were later converted to Islam. "Do you think," Amīn asks, "that when Persians, Syrians, Copts, became Muslims, their religious dogmas, which were inherited for centuries from their fathers and ancestors, were wiped out? . . . Never; this would be impossible and psychology would refute it."[28]

Amīn is aware of the primacy of the *Sharī'a* in the life of the *ummah*. Nevertheless, in the course of his studies he began to question its exclusively Islamic character. For him, the birth and development of the *Sharī'a* was not merely a result of deduction from the Koran but also the by-product of the environment. "From the time of the *Umayyads*, Muslim jurists had begun to assimilate and 'Islamicize' the customs and laws prevailing in the conquered countries."[29] Since then, *al-'urf* (customary law) had become one of the important sources of the

Shari'a,[30] a fact which Amīn attributed to two factors. First, many of these customs were not known at the time of the Prophet—hence the absence of *naṣṣ* (Koranic text) concerning them, either in the Koran or in the Sunnah. Secondly, it was not easy for the conquered people to turn their backs on their customs, which had been passed down from one generation to another. Therefore, Muslim jurists accepted and Islamicized many of these laws and customs.

The *Shari'a* should not, therefore, be interpreted in modern times as it was interpreted in the past; instead, to interpret it properly, a new kind of *ijtihād* is needed—*al-ijtihād a-muṭlaq* (independent reasoning).[31] This position is not inconsistent with Islam; in fact, it is preached by it, since God Himself glorified reason and invested it with the power to interpret and legislate whatever new conditions might arise. "A God who exalts reason could not reveal rules and then render them invalid," wrote Amīn in criticizing contemporary Muslims who had abandoned reason, closed the door of *ijtihād*, and continued to look at the new in light of the old.[32]

How must one carry out the *ijtihād*? Amīn follows the traditional schools: it must rest on the four sources, the Koran, Ḥadīth, *ijmā'* (consensus), and *qiyās* (analogy). But he lays emphasis on *ijmā'* rather than on the Koran or the Sunnah. The Koran is looked upon as the source of general rules on faith and worldly matters. Concerning the Sunnah, Amīn agrees with Ignaz Goldziher that many laws in the *Shari'a* were taken from the *Jāhilīyah* traditions and were accepted by Muslims because they fit into the environment of early Islam. The most important principle, however, is the principle of *ijmā'*, which he identifies with modern parliaments. "If the representatives of the people in parliaments [in whom he sees *ahl al-ḥall wa-al-'aqd*] in modern times agree on an issue, then this must become binding as law."[33]

Social life, argued Aḥmad Amīn, is in constant flux. Moreover, modern civilization has created thousands of problems in social, economic, and international matters; all of these problems require new legislation. Here, it is the function of reason to create laws. God did not reveal to the Prophet rules concerning matters of the future; this is understandable, for the validity of a law is dependent on time, which changes, and if these rules do not suit their age they become irrelevant even if they were essentially correct. To substantiate this position, Amīn quotes the jurists, saying, "*'Urf* is the judge, and rules change as times change. Necessities make what was forbidden permissible; hence what Muslims consider good is good enough for God."[34]

Therefore, *al-ijtihād al-muṭlaq* is not only legitimate but has become imperative. This should not imply, however, that Muslims should blindly accept Western civilization; on the contrary, they should open their eyes and minds and try to adapt their laws and make them fit it. Thus has arisen the need for a new type of *mujtahid*, one who is solidly grounded in both Islamic tradition and modern thought, a *mujtahid* who can understand the *Shari'a* and adapt it in the full light of reason to modern conditions.[35] Amīn takes Jamāl al-Din al-Afghāni and Muḥammad 'Abduh as models. He attributes their success to their acquaintance with Western thought as well as their deep knowledge of Islam. By contrast, the eighteenth-century reform movement, Wahhabism, could not find followers and flourish outside of the Arabian Peninsula because it restricted itself to traditional interpretations of Islam and thereby closed its eyes to modern civilization. Indeed, its perception of Islam was constrained by the conditions of life prevailing in the peninsula; hence its limited success.[36]

This liberal interpretation becomes clearer in Aḥmad Amīn's attempt to reconcile religion with science. For him there is no conflict between the two: faith should be linked to the heart and science to reason. Each must restrict itself to its own field and refrain from questioning the other. Danger arises, however, when both the men of religion and those of science try to intervene in the sphere of the other. "If this ceases to take place, there will be no conflict, but cooperation. For science complements religion as religion complements science: Each of them reveals a part of the truth." The difference between science and religion lies in their methods: the tool of science is reason, whereas the tool of religion is passion.[37] Hence Amīn's critique of the Mu'tazilah for their subjection of divine questions and matters of dogma to reason. "This can be helpful in philosophical matters," he writes. "In religious matters, however, it is the feeling which counts rather than logical principles. This is so because religion is not analogous to mathematical formula."[38]

As is evident from the foregoing interpretation, Aḥmad Amīn's ideas were formulated in the light of modern thought. He recognized that the process of change was irresistible and that the impact of Western ideas was deeply felt in Egypt as well as in other Islamic countries. Generally speaking, he welcomed and urged change because he saw in it the means to progress. But, taking 'Abduh as his master, he wanted to link the change to Islam; thus, his advocacy of independent *ijtihād* was primarily aimed at "Islamicizing" the new. However, Amīn remained vague and confused about the laws which would emerge from *al-ijtihād al-muṭlaq*.

Amīn was never able to define his concept of the modern *Shari'a* or the Islamic authority which should exercise it. He did once argue that Islam should not be separated from politics because it included religion and the state, just as he also disputed the views of "'Ali 'Abd al-Rāziq on Islam as a spiritual, nontemporal mission, and sympathized with the Muslim Brothers in their call for the establishment of an Islamic order."[39] Nevertheless, this single statement, which came toward the end of his life, was made in such a confusing context that it should not mislead interpreters into maintaining that Amīn was in favor of the restoration of the caliphate or an Islamic state, as one critic has maintained.[40] Rather, Amīn's view was a sort of *schwarmerei* for a Muslim movement that could reform the depressing state of affairs in Egypt resulting from a severe economic crisis reinforced by the continuing British occupation. Indeed, it is doubtful if Amīn was ever aware of the contradiction between his concept of Islam and that of the Muslim Brothers. Thus, his idea of independent *ijtihād*, which was in fact nothing but the adaptation of the *Sharī'a* to modern conditions, his concept of authority, which rests on *ahl al-ḥall wa-al-'aqd*, whom he identifies with representative government, and finally, his concept of the *Sharī'a* itself as the outgrowth of environmental and historical conditions all show how far he deviates from the traditional doctrine and from 'Abduh, not to mention the Muslim Brothers.[41]

Although it is true that Amīn introduced in *Yawm al-Islām* some Islamic elements, such as the *taḥlil* and *taḥrīm* as revealed by God, it is also true that these same rules lost their validity after he introduced, coincidentally, the independent *ijtihād*, whose task is to interpret the *naṣṣ* anew, and which can, in light of the *maṣlaḥah* (general interest), neglect it. For, as we have seen above, "what Muslims consider good is good enough for God."[42]

Aḥmad Amīn's political system is the parliamentary system in the best sense of the word. As he clearly puts it: "The rule has become the people themselves, who choose their representative to conduct their affairs. And, if any government hopes to survive, it must then embody the will of the people, provided that they (the people), in their turn, are aware of their rights." Democracy, he concludes, should be adopted, particularly by Easterners, because the East has suffered much under a variety of despotic governments and is thus in need of it more than other nations.[43]

Like Aḥmad Amīn, 'Abbās Maḥmūd al-'Aqqād (1889-1960) was born into a lower-income conservative Muslim family in Aswān. He attended the only government primary school there, where he met two schoolmates and brothers, Aḥmad and 'Alī Māhir, who would become leading figures in Egyptian politics in the interwar period.

al-'Aqqād's father admired 'Urābī and his rebellion, so the young 'Aqqād read avidly such journals as *al-Ustādh, Abū Naḍḍārah*, and *al-'Urwah al-wuthqā*, to which his father subscribed. He finished primary school in 1904, but since he was not able to begin his secondary education, he started to work for the government as a civil servant in the provinces. In 1905 he moved to Cairo, a city that was bursting with the excitement of modern trends and new ideas, where he continued with the government for two more years. He then moved into teaching and journalism. He worked for *al-Dustūr* under editor Muḥammad Farīd Wajdī, a disciple of Muḥammad 'Abduh; but he also contributed to *al-Jarīdah*, under Aḥmad Luṭfī al-Sayyīd, and to *al-Mu'yyad*, edited by Shaykh 'Alī Yūsuf.[44] At the same time, he began an interesting process of self-education: well-selected readings in classical Arabic literature, Islamic philosophy and history, and English literature and German thought. Through continuous self-education, discipline, and hard work he read widely in English and became acquainted with such works as Darwin's theory of evolution and Nietzsche's theory of the "Superman" and was able to compose his first *diwān*. During World War I he launched, with his friend Ibrahim 'Abd al-Qādir al-Māzinī, the movement for the renewal of Arabic literature, and they began in their writings to introduce new literary concepts and to discuss esthetic problems.[45] It was then that al-'Aqqād's name as an *adīb*, an intellectual, started to appear in the literary circles of Cairo. Later he met Sa'd Zaghlūl and became the ideologue of the Wafd and the relentless critic of its opponents: the king and the *al-Aḥrār al-Dustūrīyūn* (Liberal Constitutionalists).

In 1930 al-'Aqqād was sentenced to nine months in jail because of his attacks against the king and Ismā'īl Ṣidqī's dictatorship.[46] Around 1937, when the split took place within the Wafd, he joined the Sa'dist front and became a staunch enemy of the Wafd and its leadership, particularly al-Naḥḥās, the leader of the party.

Like other members of his generation, al-'Aqqād was influenced by the ideas of Muḥammad 'Abduh.[47] The impact of those ideas led him to plead for a reconciliation between the old and the new, between Islam and modern civilization. He saw this as not only imperative but also legitimate, for every civilization has to borrow from another; the Greeks, for instance, had borrowed from the Near East and the Arabs from Persia.[48] For al-'Aqqād, Western civilization was not merely the civilization of Europe, but the outgrowth of various civilizations as well; it had as much of an inheritance from Baghdad as from Rome, Athens, or Byzantium; indeed, it was influenced in many aspects by the Arab Islamic civilization.[49] Thus, the West was indebted to the East, and now it was time to pay back the debt. Europe, even if indirectly and against its will, did borrow; therefore, its merits, which he assessed positively, lay in the fact that it introduced the Easterners to the real basis of *nahḍah.*

Europe taught the East that without scientific thinking there could be no progress. Furthermore, it purified the mind of superstitions and vanities and finally released the tension between religion and progress in such a way that it satisfied the mind and conscience of the Muslims. Thus, the new concepts—of religion, of nationalism, of the relationship between man and God and between the individual and the state—which had become current in Egypt were the result of the impact of Europe.[50]

al-'Aqqād's favorable assessment of Western culture and his enthusiastic welcome for its impact on Egypt would be evident later in the 1930s, when the debate over East versus West took place among a group of Egyptian intellectuals. Once again, he—with Ṭahā Ḥusayn—derides those who praised the spirituality of the East and attacked the materialism of the West. Western civilization for him is neither materialistic nor in decline, as its opponents claimed. On the contrary, the West is still leading in the spiritual, intellectual, and creative spheres, and is an example which the East should attempt to follow. Easterners should therefore be critical of those Europeans who belittle spirituality in Europe and America.[51]

Against those who pointed to the decline of the West and the fall of its civilization, al-'Aqqād argues that it was erroneous to desire the fall of such a civilization. Western civilization, he emphatically repeats, is no longer the civilization of Europe, but belongs to the world, including the East; it is not the civilization of one generation or of one particular nation, but the quintessence of past human creativity and endeavor. He warns, therefore, against those who embrace Oswald Spengler's pessimistic views in *The Decline of the West* and reminds them that, thanks to Western civilization, the world has become one: that is to say, there is no room for a new Eastern civilization. al-'Aqqād finds the "secret" behind Europe's progress in part in the scientific spirit, but above all in the freedom that generates culture and social morality. It is harmful, therefore, for the East to strive to adopt science and freedom on the one hand, while wishing, on the other, for their decline in the West.[52] Indeed, if the West were to decline, the whole of the world would regress and fall back to conditions prevailing in prehistoric times.[53]

The future, al-'Aqqād concludes, lies not in antagonism between East and West but in cooperation. This cooperation, he cautions, is dependent on the victory of democracy and the destruction of the racialist regimes in the West as well as of the despotic ones in the East.[54]

According to al-'Aqqād, history, with its aim to extend the freedom of the individual, is progressing: in the past, individual rights did not exist; the individual was merged into the collectivity and his rights and responsibilities were marginal. But through the process of evolution individual freedom was realized. Thus, the advancement of a nation can only be measured according to the degree of freedom the individual enjoys. Indeed, freedom, which al-'Aqqād identifies with life itself, has priority over science and national strength, because neither can be attained without freedom.[55]

On these grounds, the evaluation of different social and political ideologies depends on the degree of freedom preached by them. Hence all political ideologies, despite their varying labels, can be reduced to two categories: either liberal ideologies, which respect the freedom of the individual, or totalitarian ideologies, which glorify the state over the individual. The future, however, lies with the former, because history is on its side, and al-'Aqqād worked to further it.[56]

Hand in hand with political freedom should be freedom of thought and culture. This is essential, stresses al-'Aqqād, "for freedom of culture is the expression of the sum total of human life." It is the real proof of free society and just government.[57]

These views were expressed by al-'Aqqād during the 1930s and World War II, when, under the influence of Fascist regimes and wartime propaganda, democracy was being questioned in Europe—a state of affairs that echoed in Egypt as well as in the Arab East. It was at that time that al-'Aqqād began his severe attacks on totalitarian ideologies, defending democracy against the assaults of its critics and presenting it as the highest value in life. In one of his speeches in parliament, where he was a member of the Senate, he stood firmly by the cause of the democratic West and urged Egyptians and Arabs to take sides with it. There is nothing nobler for Egypt," he said, "than aiding democracy, and there is no evil equal to that of the Nazis winning the war."[58] In spite of their grievances against the West and their struggle for national independence, the Arabs should not trust Nazi promises, but should remain faithful to the Western democracies. For the evil of the Nazis is much greater than that of the West, as is best seen in their barbaric rule of occupied Poland, Austria, Holland, and other countries. It is true, he argues, that the West is suppressing the East; nevertheless, there is a categorical difference between those who deny freedom in essence, that is, the Nazis, and those who recognize it but put off the granting of it, meaning the democratic West. Indeed, it would be impossible to live in a world dominated by totalitarian regimes, whereas there would still be hope of living freely and happily so long as democracy survives.[59]

Contrasting the evils of totalitarianism with the merits of democracy, al-ʻAqqād asserts that Nazism denied progress in history and thus robbed the individual of his freedom and responsibility, as could be seen in Nazi Germany. Once the Nazis seized power, the German intellect, which was leading the world in all branches of human knowledge, went into decline. Democracy, on the other hand, encourages free thought and helps the human intellect to develop and advance; the discoveries of the last century, which had surpassed all that man had discovered in the course of a hundred thousand years, were the best evidence of this fact.

Furthermore, whereas dictatorship is, by nature, militant, aggressive, and war seeking, democracy is peace loving. This, too, can be seen in history: militarist Sparta launched wars against democratic Athens, the racist states of the South (U.S.A.) warred against the liberal states of the North, and Napoleonic France battled democratic Britain.[60] In modern times, the Nazi movement in Germany rested on militarism and could not, therefore, survive without wars.[61]

But there is another merit in democracy: it leaves the door open for development and can, over the course of time, improve itself by its own efforts. This is because power rests with the majority. Power in totalitarian regimes, however, rests with a tyrant who glorifies physical power, a concept overthrown by the force of humanity long ago.

In his conclusion, ʻAbbās Maḥmūd al-ʻAqqād warns Egyptians and Easterners that the decline of the East was due to the tyranny of its rulers, which had impinged on the freedom of the individual for thousands of years.[62] The East, however, began its resurrection in the twentieth century by establishing democracy, "which [society] should regard as its greatest issue." It is the duty of Easterners, therefore, to restore to the individual his rights and to cement and defend democracy, which, despite its shortcomings, is still "the cave of peace and refuge of human kind and the only system which can assist progress,"[63] since all signs show that democracy is proceeding triumphantly and will, in the future, become the only valid system in the world.[64]

As a firm believer in democracy, al-ʻAqqād strongly believed in the separation of religion and politics. To be sure, Islam was always honored, held in high esteem, and defended, especially when attacks were leveled against it by foreigners and others. Nevertheless, his concept of Islam was the most enlightened of that time.

Like Aḥmad Amīn, al-ʻAqqād accepted the division ʻAbduh had established between *ʻibādāt* and *muʻāmalāt*. However, he went beyond them both in his emphasis on reason as the final arbiter in social and political matters. In his view, Islam laid down certain general rules according to which society should be conducted. But in light of the spirit of the age and the interest of the community, it left to society itself the task of reconciling these rules with the conditions that might emerge. For "there is, in the last resort, no conflict between the interest of the community and religion." It is, rather, the spirit of the rules, and not the words themselves, which should be taken into consideration. Hence there is no objection in Islam, for instance, if at any time there exist different political and economic systems in various countries, or, indeed, if these existed in the very same country in two different periods. This attitude recognizes the development of socioeconomic conditions, which are bound to change from time to time and from nation to nation. "What suits this age was not acceptable fifty or sixty years ago and will not be acceptable in the next fifty or sixty years."[65]

For al-'Aqqād, the task of religion is to provide men with general ideals and moral values and to purify their souls to help them become virtuous human beings. To this end, the conscience should become the regulative principle. "If the conscience were purified, society would find its way to perfection." It is the conscience which counts, and "the real revelation has to be in the souls of men, not in books."[66]

On the grounds of this interpretation, al-'Aqqād narrows down the function of religion to a very limited sphere. In his view, religion should interfere neither in politics nor in social matters. Thus in 1939, when the idea, propagated by the palace, of establishing the caliphate in Egypt, was in the air,[67] it was he who opposed and attacked it in strong terms, using language similar to that of 'Ali 'Abd al-Rāziq in *al-Islām wa uṣūl al-ḥukm* (1925). For him, the establishment of a caliphate would be harmful to Egypt, for "it [would] create a religious priesthood, which is in opposition to the instructions of Islam."[68]

These radical views were worked out later in his book *al-Tafkīr farīḍah Islāmīyah* (Thinking is an Islamic Duty), written in 1962. The date is important. At that time, when the state was proceeding with secularization and socialism, the idea of Islam, as preached by the Muslim Brothers, was hotly disputed by the state. (In May 1962, President Nasser introduced the charter in which he outlined the secular-socialist policy of Egypt.) Although it is not easy to assert that al-'Aqqād's book was written as an attack on the Muslim Brothers' concept of Islam, the arguments presented and the themes discussed in this book justify such an assertion.[69]

In *al-Tafkīr farīḍah Islāmīyah*, al-'Aqqād glorifies Islam as the greatest religion ever known to man. Its greatness, however, should be seen in its respect for reason. Throughout the book are found arguments exalting the role of reason as the guiding principle in society;

it also contains repeated attacks against traditional thinking and men of religion. Its starting point is that reasoning is a *farīḍah* (religious duty) in Islam, a religious duty like other religious duties (*ṣalāt* [prayer], *zakāt* [alms giving], and so forth). Hence, there can be nothing more evil to Islam than the restriction of reason. al-ʻAqqād identifies reasoning with *ijtihād*, which should be carried out within the limits of the traditional categories of duties, such as *qīyās, istiḥsān* (preference), and *maṣlaḥah mursalah*. However, he goes well beyond traditional *ijtihād* and claims that reason, although still obliged to take into consideration the Koran, the Sunnah, and *ijmāʻ*, should be left free to interpret the *naṣṣ*. Indeed, the *naṣṣ* cannot be taken as a substitute for reasoning, that is, *ijtihād*, because the latter is a religious duty, which was laid down by God, and is necessary both for its own sake and as a means of comprehending the other rules.[70]

Turning to men of religion, al-ʻAqqād questions their authority. For him, men of religion are alien to Islam, which neither allows a priesthood nor tolerates the existence of any intermediary between man and God, as is emphasized in the Koran. "Such a religion, without temple or priesthood, can appeal to nothing but human reason, untrammeled by any authority that might prevent man from full comprehension or meditation."[71] In fact, the end of divine revelation meant that reason had reached maturity and had become capable of managing society without prophets or priests.[72] "Anybody who takes reason as his guide has no course before him but to do good and avoid doing wrong."[73]

Reason is therefore the only guide in this world; and yet there are certain profound obstacles which paralyze reason: *ʻibādat al-salaf* (attachment to ancestral ways), which he identifies with total adherence to the past; blind belief in men of religion; and submissiveness to political authority. Islam is opposed to all of this: it does not approve of the Muslim closing his mind and continuing to live according to his forefathers; it does not approve of him abandoning his reason and becoming submissive to those who, in the name of religion but in opposition to reason and faith, exploit him.[74] These obstacles can make a Muslim lose his faculty of reason, which is the source from which man derives "his noblest human aspirations, namely, the righteousness of his conscience."[75]

Despotism is another danger to the freedom of reason, but, compared with *ʻibādat al-salaf*, or the deceit of the men of religion, despotism is a lesser threat to human dignity. This is because despotic rule exerts its pressure on the conscience from the outside, and can in the long run stimulate both conscience and reason to revolt.[76]

After defending the authority of reason as *farīḍah*, a duty in Islam, and disputing the very basis of the claim of men of religion to the right to interfere between man and God, al-'Aqqād goes on to argue that Islam approves of modern civilization. European philosophy, social and political science, and fine arts (including sculpture, painting, and drama) are not only accepted by Islam but also encouraged. In philosophical matters, for instance, Islam is the most liberal and tolerant religion; throughout Islamic history, Muslims have embraced and assimilated all philosophies they have encountered. The fact that some philosophers, such as al-Ghazālī and Ibn Rushd, were suppressed should be attributed to political reasons, not to Islam. Islam also encouraged science and made it a duty of Muslims to acquire it.[77]

al-'Aqqād claims that Islam is not opposed to the appearance of women on the stage. Echoing Muḥammad 'Abduh's view,[78] he maintains that Islam allows "embellishment, rebukes those who forbid it and attributes beauty to God."[79] Furthermore, "the general rule in Islam is that there shall be no prohibition as long as there is no harm . . . ; should there be real benefit, then there should be no prohibition . . . because this would hinder the *maṣlaḥah*, general interest." Accordingly, all fine arts are in accordance with Islam, "the religion that preache[s] the love of life and the rule of reason."[80]

The most far-reaching and influential of al-'Aqqād's ideas is his justification of modern intellectual trends and political ideologies. He proves that Islam embraces and accepts modern thought by examining its attitude to the theory of evolution and to existentialist philosophy, as well as to democracy, socialism, and the idea of the United Nations.

As for democracy, he asserts that, in the true meaning of the word, it was proclaimed by Islam fourteen centuries ago, and in practice rested on responsibility of the individual, *shūra*, equality of rights, and the rule of law.[81] In another of his books, *al-Dimūqrāṭīyah fī al-Islām*, he even accepts the political theories of John Locke and declares them to be compatible with Islam, for Islam approves of all liberal doctrines except those "which give the ruler divine authority or one which cannot be withdrawn."[82]

Nor is socialism alien to Islam, since it prohibits the accumulation of wealth by one class and entitles the poor to share in public wealth.[83] The same can be said of Islam's attitude toward the United Nations, for, in contrast to other religions, which preach distinctions between races and men, Islam preaches the brotherhood of men. "The Muslim believes that the generality of men constitutes one family; for God, the noblest man is the most pious, and the most pious is he who does the most good to mankind." Indeed, Islam proclaims and furthers the unification of the different nations, in order to realize universal unity.[84]

al-'Aqqād's most radical and controversial ideas, however, appear when he discusses the theory of evolution. He boldly states that Islam is not opposed to it; Islam approves of the struggle for existence and the survival of the fittest, which al-'Aqqād considers the essential principles of the theory. Darwin's theory on the evolution of the species, he says, is even compatible with the Koran, as evidenced by several verses which he quotes from the Koran. In conclusion, he advises Muslims, in his typically eclectic manner, to reconcile themselves to Darwin's theory:

> If the Muslim believes in the rise of man from a finer sort of clay, if he believes that man grew from the earth as a plant, that he underwent various stages of development, then it is legitimate for him to accept what true science confirms about the evolution of the species from earthly matter such as clay and water to this harmonious, well-proportioned creature. All this is irrespective of the literal meaning of *species*, as he [the Muslim] is not concerned about taking its meaning in the literal, fundamental sense.[85]

From among modern philosophical trends, al-'Aqqād selects existentialism for closer scrutiny. Even though he shares some reservations about it, he nevertheless accepts it as compatible with Islam because of its emphasis on the freedom of the individual. Existentialism, he writes, preaches that "the individual must not yield to any power save that of conscience, which judges his acts and intentions," and which cannot be replaced by the commands of the community or that of the ruler. For this is the right and duty of reason.

Finally, al-'Aqqād draws a line between reason and faith: religion should leave worldly matters to social philosophy, whereas philosophy should respect the right of religion in its own domain, namely, revelation.[86]

As is clear from this interpretation, the views of both 'Abbās Maḥmūd al-'Aqqād and Aḥmad Amīn on religion in general and on the *Sharī'a* in particular, and on reason and revelation, reflect the tremendous shift away from Muḥammad 'Abduh's thought. The *Sharī'a* was deprived of its preeminence and was considered as the outgrowth of the historical condition. In its stead, reason alone became the regulative principle according to which society should be conducted.

Although Islam was honored and treated with great veneration and respect, it was nevertheless assigned a place on a scale and thus weighted against something other than itself, Western civilization. Although it is true that both Amīn and al-'Aqqād praised many aspects of Islamic civilization, still, consciously or not, they took Europe as a model to be followed, and the Islam they presented was imbued with the spirit of European liberal political ideas and institutions, secular and ethical values, socialist principles, and even economic theories and practices.

Notes

1. Albert Hourani, *A Vision of History* (Beirut: Khayat, 1961), pp. 145-60.
2. H. A. R. Gibb and H. Brown, *Islamic Society and the West*, (London: Oxford University Press, 1969), pt. 2, p. 110.
3. See H. A. R. Gibb, *Modern Trends in Islam* (Chicago: University of Chicago Press, 1947), p. 89; Joseph Schacht writes: "The sacred law of Islam is an all-embracing body of religious duties, the totality of Allah's commands that regulate the life of every Muslim in all its aspects; it comprises on an equal footing, ordinances regarding worship and ritual, as well as political and [in the narrow sense] legal rules . . . Islamic law is the epitome of Islamic thought, the most typical manifestation of the Islamic way of life, the core and kernel of Islam itself." *An Introduction to Islamic Law* (London: Oxford University Press, 1964), p. 1.
4. See J. Heyworth-Dunne, *An Introduction to the History of Education in Modern Egypt* (London: Luzak, 1938).
5. The dual character of Egyptian society is best illustrated in the work of M. al-Mūwaylihī, written in the late nineteenth century, *Ḥadīth 'Isa Ibn Hishām* (Cairo: al-Dār al-Qawmīyah lil-Ṭibā'ah, 1964).
6. Afaf Luṭfi al-Sayyid, "The Role of the 'ulema' in Egypt and in the Early Nineteenth Century," in P. M. Holt, ed., *Political and Social Change in Modern Egypt* (London: Oxford University Press, 1968), pp. 278-80.
7. See Albert Hourani, *Arabic Thought in the Liberal Age: 1798-1939* (Cambridge University Press, 1983), pp. 178-80.
8. *al-Jarīdah*, January 10, 1914, cited in Jamal M. Ahmed, *The Intellectual Origins of Egyptian Nationalism* (London: Oxford University Press, 1960), p. 97.
9. Hourani, *Arabic Thought*, pp. 324-25.
10. Aḥmad Amīn, *Ḥayātī*, 4th impression (Cairo: al-Naḥah al-Miṣrīyah Bookshop, 1961); *My Life*, trans. by Issa J. Boullata (Leiden: E. J. Brill, 1978), p. 48.
11. *My Life*, pp. 72-73; see also *Ḥayātī*, p. 109.
12. Ibid., p. 90; see also *Ḥayātī*, p. 133.
13. Ibid., p. 106; see also pp. 160-61.
14. Ibid., p. 133; see also *Ḥayātī*, pp. 202-3.
15. Aḥmad Amīn, *Fayḍ al-khāṭir*, 2nd ed. (Cairo: al-Nahḍah al-Miṣrīyah Bookshop, 1958), 8:21-23, 126.
16. "al-Muslimūn sabab min asbāb al-ḥarb" *al-Thaqāfah* (April 25, 1939), p. 75; also *Fayḍ al-khātir*, 9:6-8; also *al-Sharq wa-al-Gharb* (Cairo: Lajnat al-Ta'līf wa-al-Tarjamah, 1955), p. 20.
17. "al-Muslimūn," pp. 7-8.

18. *Fayḍ al-khāṭir*, 8:23.
19. "Bayn al-māḍī wa-al-mustaqbal," *al-Thaqāfah*, no. 759 (Jan. 30, 1950), p. 7.
20. *Fayḍ al-khātir*, 9:18.
21. Aḥmad Amīn, *Yawm al-Islām* (Cairo: Dār al-Maʻārif, 1952), pp. 226, 269-70; and "Ḥalaqah mafqūdah," *al-Risālah*, 1, no. 1 (January 15, 1933), p. 6.
22. Cited in N. Safran, *Egypt in Search of Political Community: An Analysis of the Intellectual and Political Evolution of Egypt, 1804-1952* (Cambridge: Harvard University Press, 1961), p. 66.
23. See Gibb, *Modern Trends*, p. 43.
24. Cited in Albert Hourani, *Arab Thought*, p. 148.
25. *Fayḍ al-khātir*, 6:52; see also *Yawm al-Islām*, p. 42; see also by Aḥmad Amīn, *Fajr al-Islām*, 8th ed. (Cairo: al-Nahḍah al-Miṣrīyah Bookshop, 1961), p. 72.
26. *Fayḍ al-khātir*, 3:173.
27. *Yawm al-Islām*, p. 42.
28. *Fajr al-Islām*, p. 94.
29. Aḥmad Amīn, *Ḍuḥa al-Islām* (Cairo: al-Nahḍah al-Miṣrīyah Bookshop, 1962), 2:165.
30. Ibid., pp. 239-40.
31. This concept of *ijtihād* corresponds to *ijtihād al-raʼī* as opposed to *taqlīd*. See Schacht, *Introduction to Islamic Law*, pp. 69-75.
32. *Yawm al-Islām*, pp. 45, 46, 187.
33. Ibid., pp. 196, 197.
34. Ibid., pp. 200, 228.
35. Ibid., pp. 191-92. In his studies on the Muʻtazilah, Amīn showed great sympathy and identified with their view of reason; he related the disaster that befell Islam to their suppression: "In my view the elevation of reason and free will, even if this was done with some exaggeration, is far more beneficial than the elevation of their opposite . . . Indeed, had the Muʻtazilah's teachings on reason and on free will prevailed, the present Muslims would have had a different and better understanding today." Cf. *Ḍuḥa al-Islām*, 3:70.
36. *Yawm al-Islām*, p. 194.
37. *Fayḍ al-khātir*, 4:155, 5:12.
38. *Ḍuḥa al-Islām*, 3:70-73.
39. *Yawm al-Islām*, pp. 154-57.
40. N. Safran, *Egypt in Search of a Political Community*, p. 227.
41. Muṣṭafa al-Sibāʻī, the late head of the Muslim Brothers in Syria, disputes the views of Aḥmad Amīn on the Sunnah and the Ḥadīth and accuses him of presenting to the Muslims the views of Western Orientalists, in particular those of Goldziher, which al-Sibāʻi attacks. See *al-Sunnah wa makānatuha fī al-tashrīʻ al-Islāmī* (Cairo: Dār al-ʻUrūbah, 1961), pp. 213-15.
42. *Yawm al-Islām*, p. 228.
43. "Fann al-ḥukm," *al-Risālah*, 5, no. 218 (September 6, 1937), p. 1442.
44. ʻAbbās M. al-ʻAqqād, *Ḥayāt qalam* in *al-Sīrah al-dhātīyah* (Beirut: Dār al-Kitāb al-Lubnāni, 1982), pp. 371-82.
45. See David Semah, *Four Egyptian Literary Critics* (Leiden: E. J. Brill, 1974), pp. 3-19.

46. See Rajā' al-Naqqāsh, *'Abbās Maḥmūd al-'Aqqād bayn al-yamīn wa-al-yasār* (Beirut: al-Mu'assasah al-'Arabīyah lil-Dirāsāt wa-al-Nashr, 1973), pp. 79-85.
47. He wrote a book full of praise, calling him a man of genius. See *'Abqarī al-iṣlāḥ wa-al ta'līm: al-Ustādh Muḥammad 'Abduh* (Cairo: Dār al-Qalam, n.d.).
48. al-'Aqqād, *Athār al-'Arab fī al-ḥaḍārah al-Urūbbīyah*, 2nd. ed. (Cairo: Dār al-Ma'ārif, 1963), pp. 29-30; also "al-Nahḍah al-sharqīyah al-ḥadīthah," *al-Muqtaṭaf*, no. 751 (July, 1927): 10.
49. al-'Aqqād, "al-Ḥarb al-ḥadīthah wa mā tulqīh 'ala al-sharq min durūs," *al-Hilāl*, 48, no. 9. (June 1, 1940): 972.
50. *Athār al-'Arab*, pp. 156-57, 123, 178.
51. "al-Baḥth 'an ghad," *al-Risālah*, 6, no. 253 (May 9, 1940): 763.
52. "al-Mustaqbal ba'd al-ḥarb, hal hūwa lil-Sharq aw lil-Gharb?" *al-Hilāl* 49, no. 1 (December, 1940): 14.
53. "al-Ḥarb al-ḥadīthah," p. 972.
54. "al-Mustaqbal ba'd al-ḥarb," pp. 14-16.
55. al-'Aqqād, *Ruḥ 'aẓīm, al-Mahatmā Ghāndī* in *al-Majmū'ah al-Kāmilah* (Beirut: Dār al-Kitāb al-Lubnāni, 1981) 20: 277; see also "al-Fard wa-al-dawlah," *al-Risālah* 11, no. 509 (April 5, 1943): 263-64.
56. *Fī baytī* (Dār al-Ma'ārif: Iqrā' series, no. 33, 1955), p. 41.
57. "Ḥurrīyat al-fikr hiya ḥurrīyat al-ḥayāt," *al-Hilāl* 45, no. 1 (November 1, 1936): 22; see also "Adab al-mūwāfaqah," *al-Risālah* 5, no. 211 (July 19, 1937): 1164-1165.
58. al-'Aqqād, *Hitlar fī al-mizān* (Cairo: n.p., n.d.), p. 214.
59. al-'Aqqād, *Hitlar*, p. 155.
60. Ibid., pp. 175-78, 191-92; also "Ayn al-kultūr," *al-Risālah* 7, no. 327 (October 9, 1939): 1929-30.
61. "al-faylasūf al-ḥakīm," *al-Risālah* 5, no. 222 (October 4, 1937): 1605.
62. al-'Aqqād, *Hitlar*, p. 193.
63. "al-Faylasūf al-ḥakīm," p. 1605; see also "al-Siyāsah wa-al-akhlāq," *al-Kitāb* 8 (February, 1952): 143.
64. 'Abbās M. al-'Aqqād, *al-Ḥukm al-muṭlaq fī al-qarn al-'ishrīn* (Cairo: al-Balāgh al-Usbū'ī Press, n.d.), pp. 10-14. al-'Aqqād's firm belief in freedom would manifest itself when Shaykh 'Alī 'Abd al-Rāziq aroused violent uproar with the publication of his book, *al-Islām wa uṣūl al-ḥukm* [The Principles of Government in Islam] in 1925. 'Abd al-Rāziq, a member of al-Aḥrār al-Dustūrīyūn, al-'Aqqād's bitter enemies, was condemned by al-Azhar, dismissed from office, and declared unfit to hold a public office. It was al-'Aqqād who stood by him, defended him in the press despite the fact that Sa'd Zaghlūl took an opposite view, and condemned the book and its author. Similarly, and in defiance of his leader Sa'd Zaghlūl, al-'Aqqād stood by another member of al-Azhar, Dr. Ṭahā Ḥusayn, whose book *Fī al-Shi'r al-jāhilī* [On Pre-Islamic Poetry], which infringed on some Islamic dogmas, also aroused violent condemnation from the ulema. See al-Naqqāsh, pp. 99, 103-4.
65. al-'Aqqād, *al-Tafkīr farīḍah Islamīyah* (Cairo: Dār al-Qalam, 1962), p. 195.
66. al-'Aqqād, *Ma yuqāl 'an al-Islām* (Cairo: Dār al-'Urūbah, 1963), pp. 232-33.

67. al-'Aqqād, *Haqā'iq al-Islām wa abāṭīl khuṣūmih* (Cairo: Dār al-Qalam, 1957), pp. 129-30, 136-38.
68. See E. Kedourie, "Egypt and the Caliphate 1915-1946," *Journal of the Royal Asiatic Society*, pt. 324 (October, 1963): 208-48.
69. "Miṣr wa-al-khilāfah," *al-Hilāl* 47, no. 5 (March, 1939): 483.
70. According to Lūwis 'Awaḍ, the leftist contemporary writer, al-'Aqqād's works on Islam were written with the intention of undermining the views of the Muslim Brothers, whom al-'Aqqād attacked as a sect alien to Islam. Cf. *Dirāsāt 'Arabīyah wa Gharbīyah* (Cairo: Dār al-Ma'ārif, 1965), p. 32.
71. *al-Tafkīr*, pp. 142-49.
72. Ibid., pp. 19-20.
73. Abbās M. al-'Aqqād, *al-Insān fī al-Qur'ān al-karīm* (Cairo: Dār al-Hilāl, 1962), pp. 24-25.
74. *al-Tafkīr*, p. 22.
75. Ibid., pp. 23-24; see also *al-Insān*, p. 24.
76. *al-Tafkīr*, p. 30.
77. Ibid., pp. 68-69, 86-100.
78. See Muḥammad 'Abduh, "al-Ṣūwar wa-al-tamāthīl wa fawā'iduhā wa ḥukmuhā," in M. R. Riḍa, *Tārīkh al-Ustādh al-Imām al-Shaykh Muḥammad 'Abduh* (Cairo: al-Manār Press, n.d.), 2: 498-502.
79. *al-Tafkīr*, pp. 102-3.
80. Ibid., pp. 106-17.
81. Ibid., p. 196.
82. al-'Aqqād, *al-Dimūqrāṭīyah fī al-Islām* (Cairo: Dār al-Ma'ārif, 1952), p. 70.
83. *al-Tafkīr*, p. 199.
84. Ibid., pp. 101, 221; see also *al-Insān*, pp. 10, 51.
85. *al-Tafkīr*, p. 201.
86. Ibid., p. 205-6.

Amīn al-Rīḥānī and King 'Abdul-'Azīz Ibn Sa'ūd

IRFAN SHAHID

I

The Arab American writer Amīn al-Rīḥānī was the first to write fundamental works on the late King 'Abdul-'Azīz: namely, the relevant part in *Mulūk al-'Arab*,[1] which he finished in 1924, and *Najd wa mulḥaqātuh*,[2] written three years later, which was devoted exclusively to King 'Abdul-'Azīz and to the Saudi state. Soon after, he turned into English the part on the king in *Mulūk al-'Arab*[3] and published it simultaneously in both Great Britain and the United States in 1928 under the titles *Ibn Sa'oud of Arabia* and *The Maker of Modern Arabia*,[4] respectively. The distinguished and influential Arab American writer was also the first to take the measure of King 'Abdul-'Azīz, for whom he had great admiration, as the dominant power in the Arabian Peninsula. He strove long and hard to bring this assessment to the attention, first, of the Arabs and then to the Western world, particularly Great Britain and the United States. His works gave the outside world, both in the Arabophone East and the Anglophone West, its first glimpse of the founder of the modern Saudi state.

This paper will address itself to a discussion of the uniqueness of al-Rīḥānī's encounter with, and account of, King 'Abdul-'Azīz and its implications for the Saudi-American relationship. Before al-Rīḥānī made his journey to Arabia in 1922, he had addressed a letter to Henry P. Fletcher, then American undersecretary of state, on October 18, 1921. In that letter he asked the undersecretary to facilitate for him the issue of a passport and explained the nature of his mission in Arabia.

Two elements in this letter are relevant to the theme of this paper.[5] First, he makes it clear that he is not going as a tourist but on a serious mission to catch up with the course of events in Arabia and that his interest in Arabia "is that of a friend who desires to see her go forward hand in hand with European civilization." He sums up his mission by saying, "And I have no axe to grind—except the axe of civilization." Second, he assumes that the U.S. government "is no doubt interested in the development of conditions in the Near East, particularly in Mesopotamia and Arabia," and he promises to furnish a report on Arabia and later write a book.

Thus, al-Rīḥānī appears in this letter as a good Arab and a good American who is trying to do justice to the fact of his ethnic origin and at the same time to the interests of his adopted country, which he apparently served earlier during World War I in Mexico, as he mentions in the first paragraph of his letter.[6]

In the following year al-Rīḥānī made his historic journey, during which he traveled far and wide in the peninsula and met its rulers. When he started on his journey from the United States, he apparently had not heard of King 'Abdul-'Aziz. But no sooner had he set foot on Arabian soil than the name and fame of the king began to reach him, and the two finally met in Najd. The results of this encounter and later contacts are seen in al-Rīḥānī's books.

The dominant foreign power in Arabia at the time was Britain, and al-Rīḥānī's journey in Arabia and his encounters with its rulers took place under the long shadow of the strong British presence. Yet the United States is not entirely absent from *Mulūk al-'Arab*. President Wilson had become known to the Arabs through his Fourteen Points, especially the principles of self-determination on the part of oppressed nationalities; and King 'Abdul-'Aziz had heard of these principles and expressed great respect and admiration towards the American president.[7]

After the conclusion of his journey in 1922, al-Rīḥānī began to write about Arabia and did his translation. The excerpted *Mulūk al-'Arab* was the first authoritative English book of the twenties on King 'Abdul-'Aziz, and it set him in the context of the international politics of the postwar period.[8] al-Rīḥānī had thus fulfilled the promise made in 1921 in his letter to the American undersecretary of state that a book would come out of his journey in Arabia.

al-Rīḥānī's motives in issuing an English version for Americans can only be conjectured. But it is practically certain that he would have liked to have seen an American involvement in the destinies of Arabia in the twenties and thought that an account of the Saudi state under King 'Abdul-'Aziz, spreading knowledge about the king and his state in the United States, would contribute to that end. In this context, he also must have remembered how dissatisfied the king was with the British for having surrounded him with hostile dynasts in Ḥijāz, Transjordan, and Iraq.[9] What is more, by then he must have been aware of the part played by President Wilson in sending the King-Crane Commission to the Arabs in Syria and Palestine in 1919 to ascertain, on the spot, the wishes of the peoples of the Fertile Crescent as to their political future.[10]

The odds, however, were decidedly against the fulfillment of such hopes on the part of the Arab American writer, who was at one and the same time a dreamer and a realist. First, *The Maker of Modern Arabia* was a translation from the Arabic *Mulūk al-'Arab*, and of a portion of it at that. Originally, it had been written and addressed to an Arab, not a British or an American, readership; hence, with the change of readership it could not have its full effect. Books on Arabia in that decade were dwarfed by T. E. Lawrence's *Seven Pillars of Wisdom.* Although not about Ibn Saud specifically, this was a literary classic with which al-Rīḥānī's book could not compete. Soon it was followed by St. John Philby's books, *Arabia of the Wahhabis* in 1928 and *Arabia* in 1930, written by a colorful Englishman who belonged to the establishment and, what is more, was a civil servant in the employ of the British government, however intermittently, and an unofficial consultant to the king.[11]

Second, the image of the Arabs in America in the twenties and the thirties may also have been a factor in discouraging American involvement in Arabia, especially since it was in this period that public opinion made its "active intrusion . . . into the realm of public affairs."[12] These were the decades that witnessed the appearance of those motion pictures that did not create a favorable climate of opinion concerning the Arabs and Arabia. The celebrated film *The Sheik* was produced in the twenties and was followed by others in the twenties and the thirties. They all projected an image of the Arabs as villains as well as romantic lovers.[13]

The most important factor, however, which militated against American involvement in Arabian affairs was the political mood of the country in the twenties. This was the postwar period, during which the United States turned inward with a wave of isolationism and a return to "one hundred percent Americanism."[14] Hence the spirit of internationalism receded and with it any possible involvement with an Arabia that at best was opaque and at worst a desert region which presented no challenge to American enterprise.[15]

Thus, al-Rīḥānī could not bring his country of adoption to a serious involvement with his larger Arab homeland. The beginning of the Saudi-American relationship was thus delayed till the forties, when President Roosevelt met King 'Abdul-'Aziz aboard the U.S.S. Quincy in the Great Bitter Lake of the Suez Canal in 1945, five years after the death of the Arab American who had dreamed about it some twenty years before. That his British counterpart, St. John Philby, was able to stay in Saudi Arabia as a friend and unofficial counselor to King 'Abdul-'Aziz made it even more certain that Great Britain, and not the United States, was to be the dominant power in the region for a few more decades. When oil was discovered in commercial quantities in Arabia, the United States took over many of the responsibilities of Britain for the defense of the region after World War II.

II

Who was this Arab American figure who dreamed of this historical possibility twenty years before it finally happened? The facts are not unknown to historians of modern Arabic literature, and it is in this context that he is remembered rather than as a voice and a force in the politics and the political ideology of the emergent Arab world in the first half of the twentieth century. It is time that al-Rīḥānī be remembered in this light. In this paper only what is relevant to its theme can be discussed, such as the making and the cultural transformation of this remarkable Arab American and his unique vision of the maker of modern Arabia and the Saudi-American relationship.

In a moving autobiographical account in the introduction to *Mulūk al-'Arab*, al-Rīḥānī describes the stages of his cultural metamorphosis from a Maronite in a struggling hamlet in the Lebanese countryside to an Arab nationalist promoting the interests of the Pan-Arab movement.[16] The catalyst that stimulated his conversion was the American transcendentalist Ralph Waldo Emerson, through whom he became acquainted with Thomas Carlyle. The latter's *On Heroes, Hero-Worship and the Heroic in History* introduced him to the glories of Arab Spain. And finally, the New York Public Library, with its wealth of English travel literature on Arabia, introduced him to the lure of the unknown and the urge to cross the Arabian frontier.[17] Thus, the search for identity ended with al-Rīḥānī's discovery of his Arabness in the distant West.

al-Rīḥānī was the father of Arab American literature, but unlike many of the Arab American literati, he was a man of action who walked in the corridors of power,[18] a dynamic personality, and a spell-binding orator. Short of stature, frail of constitution, with a nervous disorder that plagued his right shoulder,[19] he nevertheless traversed hundreds of miles in the Arabian Peninsula, often on camel. Even more remarkable than all these disabilities is the fact that the new traveler in Arabia was an Arab coming from the New World. Arabia had been the preserve of romantic Englishmen whom the desert beckoned, but it never attracted Arab travelers in modern times. Its only Arab visitors were the Muslims who traversed its length and breadth on their way to perform the pilgrimage in Ḥijāz. This was indeed a most unusual travel adventure, unique in the annals of the Arabian Peninsula, by a Christian Arab who discovered his identity in Manhattan and who decided to make the pilgrimage—a cultural one—to the cradle of the Arabs and Islam.

al-Rīḥānī's journey to Arabia and his travels within its confines brought him in touch with the rulers of the Arabian Peninsula. But at the conclusion of his journey, it was clear that the ruler who riveted his attention was the Sultan of Najd. The various passages in *Mulūk al-'Arab* in which al-Rīḥānī records his impressions of King 'Abdul-'Aziz are penetrating, and they are the impressions of a highly intelligent observer of the Saudi scene in the twenties.[20] It is clear from what al-Rīḥānī wrote that the Arab American writer quickly realized that the peninsula had given birth to a hero who was larger than life. The various dimensions of the king's towering personality were also recognized by the writer closest to al-Rīḥānī as a biographer and admirer of King 'Abdul-'Aziz, namely, Philby, but there is no doubt that al-Rīḥānī was closer to the Arab king by virtue of his Arabness and the fact that he spoke the king's Arabic. Consequently, his appreciation of the king in the twenties was sounder and more profound.[21]

The climax of al-Rīḥānī's vision of 'Abdul-'Aziz and the Saudi state comes not in *Mulūk al-'Arab*, which discussed the Arabian Peninsula in its entirety in 1922, but his book which appeared in 1927, *Najd wa Mulḥaqātuh* which was devoted exclusively to the Wahhabi movement and the Saudi state from its inception in the eighteenth century. Its climax was the reign of King 'Abdul-'Aziz in its various states, from the time he made his historic march from Kuwait as a *ghāzi* and captured his ancestral capital, Riyāḍ, in 1901, to the year 1926, which witnessed his entry into Mecca and the union of the two regions, Najd and Ḥijāz—in other words, a quarter of a century of war and achievement which resulted in the creation of the modern Saudi state. It is the epic of the rise and triumph of the maker of modern Arabia.

al-Rīḥānī was the first to tell the story of these moving events that convulsed the peninsula and was the first to advertise the genius of King 'Abdul-'Aziz to the outside world. He was also the most perceptive interpreter of Arab and Islamic history. al-Rīḥānī was not a professional historian; he was a visionary and an acute observer of men and events. He could relate the massive accomplishment of King 'Abdul-'Aziz to that of other heroes of Arab and Islamic history, something his English colleagues who wrote on the king and the Saudi state did not do. In his introduction to *Najd*, he drew some telling analogies between King 'Abdul-'Aziz and these heroes—Mu'āwīyah, al-Ma'mūn, and Saladin—and how they failed to assert their authority over the Arabian Peninsula.[22]

al-Rīḥānī points out that since the days of the caliph Omar, this was the first time that the peninsula was effectively controlled by a stable central power, the Saudi state in Riyāḍ. He then gives recognition to the role of the king in the sedentarization of the Bedouin and the establishment of the *hujar.* He further calls on the king to spread literacy among them (the Bedouin) and propagate education. Thus, al-Rīḥānī emerges as a concerned Arab and a warm and admiring friend of the nascent Saudi state. He spares no effort to put at the disposal of the king the experience of a fellow Arab who was coming from the technologically most advanced state in the Western world.

III

These, then, are the distinctive features of al-Rīḥānī's works and achievements. They qualify him for a privileged place among those who made Arabia their concern in the first half of the twentieth century. His travels in Arabia, his encounters with King 'Abdul-'Aziz, and his books on Arabia naturally invite comparison with Philby, who made Arabia exclusively his concern. Both were admirers of the king and both made important contributions, each in his own way, to interpreting Saudi Arabia to the West and the Western reader. But Philby was a Britisher, a wanderer, a great explorer, and an enigmatic figure. al-Rīḥānī, on the other hand, was a romantic and a man of letters, an idealist who discovered his identity in a foreign land and who was driven by nostalgia for the original home of the Arabs and Islam to visit Arabia, where he met the hero who represented for him the incarnation of the chivalrous and heroic Arab of classical times. In spite of his American and his apparently British connections, he remained a sincere Arab nationalist working for the people he discovered to be his own people. And there was no question about his sincerity and loyalty as there was about Philby's, whether rightly or wrongly.[23] But al-Rīḥānī did not explicitly articulate his conception of the Saudi-American relationship in concrete, expansive terms.[24] It is therefore important to recover the elements of this conception, how it grew and matured. They may be summed up and presented as follows.

First, of all the Arab American writers, al-Rīḥānī was the only one who was not alienated by his experiences in the United States, but, on the contrary, was attracted to his adopted country. He had participated actively for two decades in American cultural life, assimilating what he thought was wholesome and transmissible to the literature and culture of his people in the Arab homeland.[25] In the twenties he wanted the American influence and connection to be extended to the political sphere. The Arabian adventure, and his desire to see America involved in Arabia's future with himself as the apostle of the new relationship, was characteristic of al-Rīḥānī's self-image as the bridge between two countries and cultures—the interpreter of the Arabs and Islam to the West, especially America, and vice versa.

Second, unlike European powers such as Britain, France, and Italy, the United States had no colonial record in the Arab world, which therefore knew it as the country of physicians, educators, and philanthropists, who had established an excellent rapport with the Arab peoples among whom they worked. al-Rīḥānī admired the forms of American political life, and in one of his essays addressed a spirited apostrophe to the Statue of Liberty, hoping that it would turn its face to the East, whence he hailed.

Third, the opportunity to bring about an American connection, for better or worse, seemed to him to come after the conclusion of World War I, when President Wilson not only enunciated the principle of self-determination for oppressed nationalities but also saw to it that the King-Crane Commission was sent to the Arab Near East. al-Rīḥānī, it is practically certain, hoped that the American giant would express interest in the fortunes of the Arabian, just then awakening after World War I, and would be aroused by the electrifying personality of King 'Abdul-'Aziz, and that the two complementary resources would make for a harmonious, fruitful, and mutually beneficial cooperation.

Towards that end, al-Rīḥānī translated his books on Arabia into the language of his country of adoption, hoping that they would spread knowledge about Arabia and thus prepare the ground for some involvement by the United States in the fortunes of the Arabian Peninsula. But his hopes foundered on the rock of American isolationism. He must have been aware of the mood of the country; nevertheless, he published his books in English and tried to project an image of the new Arabia to the American public.[26] His dream had to wait twenty years for its fulfillment—for another cataclysm, another world war, and a new America that was committed to the ideal of internationalism and global involvement.

Amīn al-Riḥānī's Letter to Undersecretary of State, Henry P. Fletcher

Ameen Rihani
43 East 27th Street
New York
325 East 68th St.

October 15, 1921

Hon. Harry P. Fletcher
Under-Secretary of State
Washington, D.C.

File MB October 27, 1921

Dear Sir;

I did not have the pleasure of seeing you in Mexico City when I was there in the winter of 1918 doing some work for our Government and the Allies and getting, as you perhaps remember, "thirty-three-ed" for it.

I am now planning a trip to Arabia, not for "recreation" or as "a tourist", but on a business of high importance. The enclosed list of questions, which are of vital interest to the whole world to-day and which I shall not answer until I have gone over the ground thoroughly, will give you an idea of what I propose to do. I have many friends among the Arabs; and one of them, who is an official of the Government of Hejaz, is going to accompany me through the Peninsula. I shall probably get at sources of information, without running any danger, that are hardly accessible to a European or an American writer. And I have no axe to grind except the axe of Civilization. Local politics will not concern me. I shall go through the country as an observer only and I shall be very careful, as a good American, not to do anything that might embarrass the Government.

Now, I write you about this matter for two reasons: First, our Government is no doubt interested in the development of conditions in the Near East, particularly in Mesopotamia and Arabia; and I shall be pleased to furnish it, from no other than a purely patriotic motive, a report on the subject. There will be a book, of course, which I shall publish later. My interest in Islam, in Arabia rather, is that of a friend who desires to see her go forward hand in hand with European Civilization. Is this possible? That is what I would like to find out.

If our Government's interest goes even beyond this, and there are other questions which you or whoever is in charge of the Near East Department would add to the list, I shall thank you for so doing. I will come to Washington for the purpose if it is preferred.

Secondly, I am now writing to ask you to facilitate the matter of obtaining a passport. I want to go to Djeddah first, where my friend is, thence, either through the Peninsula or around it, up to Basra and Baghdad. I shall return from Baghdad to Damascus and Beirut, to be able to visit my mother and sisters who are still in the old country in Mt. Lebanon.

I shall not make an application for the passport until I hear from you. I want to leave next month. With the hope that you will be so kind as to let me have an early reply, I am, sir

Very truly yours,
[signed]
Ameen Rihani

Notes

1. *Mulūk al-'Arab*, 2 vols. (Beirut: Dār al-Rīḥānī, 1960), reprinted many times since 1926.
2. The full title is *Tārīkh Najd wa Mulḥaqātih* (Beirut: Dār al-Rīḥānī, 1964), reprinted several times since 1927.
3. *Ibn Sa'oud of Arabia* (London: Constable, 1928).
4. *The Maker of Modern Arabia* (Boston and New York: Houghton Mifflin, 1928).
5. This letter is included at the end of this chapter.
6. For an account of his activities in Mexico, see Albert Rīḥānī, *Ayna tajid Amīn al-Rīḥānī* (Beirut: Dār al-Rīḥānī, 1979), pp. 42-43.
7. On his admiration for Wilson, see *Mulūk al-'Arab*, 2:44.
8. St. John Philby's *The Heart of Arabia* and *Arabia of the Wahhabis*, respectively. It was not until 1930, when Philby published his *Arabia*, that he wrote a comprehensive history of the Wahhabi movement and the Saudi state from its beginnings in the eighteenth century, and in so doing he relied partly on al-Rīḥānī's *Najd*, which he describes as "an admirable popular summary by a Christian Arab of American nationality." *Arabia* (London: Benn, 1930), p. ix.
9. See *Mulūk al-'Arab*, 2:58.
10. The report of the commission was not made public immediately but by 1928 it was. For this commission and its recommendations, see G. Antonius, *The Arab Awakening* (London: H. Hamilton, 1938), pp. 294-98; for the text of the recommendations, see appendix H, pp. 443-58.
11. For a full bibliography on reviews of the English version in Britain and the United States, see Albert Rīḥānī, *Ayna tajid*, pp. 92-95.
12. See Selig Adler, *The Uncertain Giant* (New York: Macmillan, 1965), pp. 22-23.
13. See Sari J. Nasir, *The Arabs and the English* (London: Longman, 1976), pp. 146-51.
14. On the strong isolationist mood of the United States in this period, see Adler, *Uncertain Giant*.
15. American consular reports from the region on the mission of al-Rīḥānī in Arabia did not help either, since they were sending conflicting signals. The consul in Baghdad, Thomas Rowens, was for him; the consul in Aden, Raymond Davis, was against him, according to photocopies of these reports in my possession.
16. *Mulūk al-'Arab*, 1:5-9.
17. Of English travel literature that influenced him, he lists the works of W.G. Palgrave, J.L. Burkhardt, Richard F. Burton, and Charles M. Doughty.
18. The number of influential leaders he met with was legion. Just before his death in 1940, he met with King Hassan in Morocco and with Generalissimo Franco in Madrid. For a description of his talks with these two leaders, see his book, *al-Maghrib al-Aqṣā* (Cairo: Dār al-Rīḥānī, 1952).
19. His English counterparts, Lawrence and Philby, were athletic and robust.

20. See *Mulūk al-'Arab*, 2:40-41, 49-50.
21. Philby's knowledge of Arabic in the twenties cannot have been very deep.
22. See *Najd wa mulḥaqatuh*, pp. 8-9.
23. See Khayrī Ḥammād, *'Abdallah Filbī* (Beirut: al-Maktab al-Tijārī, 1961).
24. al-Rīḥānī's views on Arab nationalism and the Arab political scene are scattered here and there in the vast corpus of his writings, and this scattering has operated to his disadvantage as a theorist and has obscured his place in history of modern Arab thought. Hence he does not appear in Albert Hourani's classic, *Arabic Thought in the Liberal Age* (London: Macmillan, 1970).
25. He was also critical of many aspects of American life and culture.
26. In keeping with his motto, *Qul kalimatak wa imshī.*

A Reinterpretation of the Origins and Aims of the Great Syrian Revolt, 1925-1927

PHILIP S. KHOURY

The breakup of the Ottoman Empire and the European partition of its Arab provinces into smaller administrative units after World War I stimulated the development of new, more broadly-based, and better-organized movements of protest and resistance than had previously been known in the Arab East. Political movements could no longer remain localized, atomized, and isolated. They had to embrace a new style of politics linked to new systems of ideas and to operate on a much larger territorial scale. Broadly constructed alliances linked together different political elites, social classes, confessional groups, and urban and rural forces against direct European intervention. These movements also sought moral and material support across new artificially erected administrative borders from neighboring independence movements, and even assumed international dimensions.[1]

One example of the changing character of political movements of protest and resistance was the Great Revolt of 1925-27, a major watershed in the history of modern Syria and in the national independence struggle against the French Mandate. In its style, intensity, duration, scale, and methods, the Great Revolt compared favorably with other resistance movements that were beginning to leave their mark on the countries of the Arab East after World War I, in particular the Egyptian Revolution of 1919 and later the Arab Revolt of 1936-39 in Palestine. The Great Revolt was popular insofar as its active participants were drawn from nearly all walks of life in Syria—urban and rural, Muslim and Christian, rich and poor. Its leadership framed its aims and appeal in the new nationalist idiom of the times. And the revolt itself let this new sentiment of nationalism spread faster, wider, and deeper than ever before, enabling it to become the dominant organizing principle of Syrian political life during the mandate. Moreover, the Great Revolt sought and won attention and support from parallel independence movements in the Arab countries, from the Muslim world at large, and from Syrian emigré communities in the West. Its sheer size and scale insured it international headlines, especially in France, where it had a disruptive impact on domestic politics and contributed to a serious change in French perceptions about how best to govern Syria.[2]

Many of the new features introduced into the political life of the interwar period had their origins in the changes that swept the Ottoman Empire in the nineteenth century—in administration and law, in commerce, industry, and agriculture, in the movement of goods, peoples, and ideas, and, above all, in the empire's relations with Europe. The integration at this time of the Middle East into a world market dominated by Europe meant that, with different speeds and rhythms, old local economies broke apart as pastoral and subsistence agriculture gave way to settled market-oriented farming. Meanwhile, the economic and legal framework was established for the appropriation and extreme concentration of private property, and provincial capitals were able to radiate their influence far beyond their immediate countryside, creating larger, better-integrated regional economic and political units.[3]

In many ways, these sweeping changes left their deepest imprint on the traditional elites of the Ottoman Empire. After the mid-nineteenth century, a new social class of landowners and bureaucrats was forged out of disparate and socially differentiated urban forces with independent influence in the Arab provinces. This same class was to dominate political life in Syria and Palestine down to World War II and even beyond. It not only became more closely identified with a reformed and reinvigorated Ottoman state, which its politically active members came to serve as a provincial aristocracy of service. In order to achieve its goal the new class used the marriage bed, new commercial ties, and economic influence in the countryside among rural notables, tribal shaykhs, and the peasantry.[4]

The growth of the Ottoman state apparatus, the introduction of new secular laws, the spread of modern secular education, and the widening of the Middle East's links with the outside world not only created new social forces but also altered the intellectual and political climate of the region. Traditional ideas—historically the monopoly of the religious establishment—began to lose their attraction to the educated elites. At the same time, the religious establishment's traditional activities as interpreters of the law and as educators and heads of the mystic orders declined in social value. Less and less significance came to be attached to control of posts in the religious institutions, while greater wealth, power, and status accrued to those holding offices in the new modern branches of the provincial administration, and to large landowners.[5]

This is not to suggest that religious solidarity among Arabs had vanished; it still existed, as did other loyalties to family, tribe, ethnic, and confessional group, neighborhood, and village. But all these ties had been corroded by the rise of new loyalties that accompanied the general structural changes of the nineteenth century. The most dynamic and significant of these loyalties was modern nationalism.

Two types of nationalism emerged—one territorial and the other ethnocultural—and both types coexisted in all political movements of the interwar period. And although nationalism was not a thoroughly secular idea because no interpretation of Arab history and culture—on which nationalism rested—could deny the contribution of Islam, it nevertheless was expressed increasingly in secular terms. Those who were to infuse modern nationalism into political movements of protest and resistance in the early twentieth century—members of the urban-absentee landowning-bureaucratic class—eventually rejected the idea propounded by Muslim reformers and activists of the period that Islam could provide the principles for governing the modern independent nation state. For them, Islamic law was too outmoded as a governing system. Their attitude reflected their position in the social hierarchy. After all, they now provided the bulk of the recomposed political elite which had been educated in modern schools, employed in the new secular branches of the Ottoman government, and hence had no strong attachment to the weakened religious institutions.[6]

It is against this background of structural change that historians must explain the evolution of movements of protest and resistance in the interwar Arab East and, in particular, the Great Revolt in Syria. Unfortunately, the historiography of the Syrian Revolt is conspicuously underdeveloped, even more so than that of the 1919 Revolution in Egypt or the Arab Revolt in Palestine,[7] itself a reflection of the impoverishment of historical scholarship on Syria during the mandate.[8] The purpose of this article is to provide a reinterpretation of certain features of interwar political movements by correcting two general misconceptions about the Great Revolt. Both concern the nature of the contributions made by the Druze leadership which sparked the revolt in 1925 and the nationalist leadership in Damascus which assumed its control soon afterwards.

The Great Revolt is fascinating for several reasons, but perhaps most strikingly because it did not first break out in Syria's nationalist strongholds, the great towns of the interior, but in the remote Jabal Druze (Jabal al-Durūz) among a compact religious minority with no apparent attachment to the nationalist sentiments radiating from towns like Damascus. Not surprisingly, then, the handful of historians who in recent years have made efforts to systematically investigate the origins of the Great Revolt begin by looking at the Druze uprising that initiated it.[9] They generally concur that the movement in the Jabal was internally motivated, a violent reaction to excessive French interference in Druze affairs. Their emphasis is on the uniqueness of the Druze uprising and on its isolation from developments elsewhere in Syria. These historians begin with how Druze religious beliefs and social customs combined with the physical inaccessibility of the Jabal to differentiate Druzes from the Sunni-Muslim Arabs of the towns. They emphasize that all Druzes stood against outside interference in the Jabal. Then they turn their attention to how the French tampered with the local Druze power structure, upsetting the traditional balance of power and severely reducing Druze political autonomy.

At first glance, this interpretation of the Druze uprising seems plausible. The French did interfere excessively in local Druze affairs, and those who launched the rebellion certainly did so to protect their vested interests and power in the Druze community. But it also suggests that the Druze uprising of 1925 was nothing more than a local rebellion to satisfy local aims; any larger implications were merely circumstantial. It is here that historians have either overlooked or ignored certain critical aspects of the Druze uprising, an omission which has distorted their appreciation of the overall revolt and the Druze contribution to it. They have viewed the Druze uprising as merely the latest in a long series of uprisings against external interference in the Jabal that date from Ottoman times.[10] They also recognize that in 1925 the Druze outburst was against French and not Ottoman rule and that it was more explosive. Although these historians indicate how unpopular the French, like the Ottoman's before them, were in Jabal Druze, they attach little significance to the Druze uprising in the larger scheme of Syrian history and the national independence movement.[11]

A more careful exploration of the Druze rebellion, the character of its leaders, and their relations to the outside world suggests the need for a more nuanced interpretation of the Druze contribution to the Great Revolt. We discover, for example, that the Druze elite was divided into factions and along kinship, status, and, increasingly, ideological lines. As for the leaders of the Druze rebellion, they did not perceive it as an isolated phenomenon, nor did they intend to restrict it to a local theme. In fact, these leaders were in direct and regular contact with nationalist circles in Damascus and were as responsible for the transformation of their uprising into a nationwide revolt as was the nationalist leadership in the Syrian capital. Thus, the 1925 rebellion does not conform to the traditional pattern of Druze resistance to external interference in its communal affairs that some historians have emphasized. The Druze leadership's objectives may have been old and familiar—the retention or restoration of its power in the Jabal—but the tactics they adopted were clearly new. Druze leaders had a much wider vision of political realities than historians have previously acknowledged. They actively sought alliances beyond the Jabal that cut across regional, class, and religious lines and that, in the process, helped to give political movements in Syria greater dimension and force. The failure of historians to appreciate that the Druze uprising was directly connected to the development of nationalism in Syria has caused them to underestimate the contribution of the Druze rebel leadership to the spread and prolongation of the Great Revolt.

Conversely, these same historians have had a tendency to give undue weight to the contribution of the nationalist leadership in Damascus to the revolt. This emphasis comes out clearly when they try to explain how and why a seemingly isolated, local Druze uprising blossomed almost overnight into a nationwide revolt with revolutionary implications. At this stage, they suddenly shift their attention from the Jabal Druze to Damascus, locating the motor force behind the spread of the revolt in the Syrian capital among the nationalist elite. Their argument is that more sophisticated Damascene nationalists—armed with a powerful new idea and in search of a catalytic agent to realize their "revolutionary" objectives—persuaded a pliant, inarticulate Druze rebel leadership to link up with them by propelling their rebellion down the slopes of the Jabal toward Damascus. Without marshalling convincing evidence to support their argument, these historians assume that Druze leaders were passive actors, merely pawns in the bigger, more evolved nationalist game being played out in Damascus and other Syrian urban centers.[12] Instead of searching for ties between the Jabal Druze and Damascus that might have allowed for the construction of a more broad-based alliance of city and countryside, urban and rural elites, and different confessional groups, historians have treated the Druze role in the revolt in nearly complete isolation from the political changes sweeping Syria after World War I.

Just as historians have underestimated the contribution of the Druze leadership to the Great Revolt by not placing the Druze uprising more squarely in the stream of Syrian political life, so too they have exaggerated the contribution, not to mention the objectives, of the nationalist elite in Damascus. Therefore, a serious reassessment of the Great Revolt, its origins and evolution, and the complex role of its leadership is required.

Druzes in the Context of pre-1920 Syrian History

Since the early eighteenth century, when large numbers of Druzes fled Mount Lebanon and took up residence in an equally rugged and isolated mountainous region southeast of Damascus, the Druze community in Syria was engaged in a perpetual struggle to preserve its independence and individuality from more powerful external forces.[13] The Ottoman governors of Damascus, unable to extend their authority over the Jabal Druze, were forced to acknowledge the de facto authority of the Druze community's paramount clan, first the Ḥamdani and, after 1869, the Aṭrash (Ṭurshān).[14] But by the end of the nineteenth century a reinvigorated Ottoman government seriously threatened the semiautonomous status of the Jabal by seeking to place it more securely in the orbit of Damascus.

To a certain extent, the Jabal Druze was already opening up to the outside world under the pressure of agrarian commercialization and modern transportation. Increasingly strong commercial ties between the Jabal and Damascus drew members of the Druze elite into the city and into contact with its Ottomanized elite.[15] Nevertheless, the corporate consciousness of the Druze community, with its esoteric religious beliefs,[16] feudal social structure, and physical isolation, was still insular and defensive and maintained by the fear of subjugation at the hands of the Ottoman authorities in Damascus. Whenever the Druze community felt that the state was impinging upon its autonomy, the usual impulse was to revolt. Between 1899 and 1910, when Ottoman efforts to impose direct control over the Jabal were strongest, the Druze mounted six armed insurrections.[17] But despite continued resistance, the Jabal Druze was irretrievably lured into the political and economic orbit of Damascus by World War I.

Druze clan leaders welcomed Sharif Husayn's call for an Arab revolt in 1916 because it diverted the attention of the Turks from the Jabal, enabling them to reassert Druze political autonomy. The Druze leadership, however, like the local Arab leadership in Damascus, was conscious of its vulnerability. It therefore approached the Arab revolt cautiously, preferring to await its final outcome. The Jabal Druze served, however, as a contact point between the Ḥijāz and Damascus, and some younger Druze notables with ties to Damascus took up arms against the Turks, joining Amir Fayṣal's northern army. Among them was Sulṭān al-Aṭrash, a thirty-year-old chieftain and a veteran of the last major Druze uprising against the Turks in 1910, during which the Turks captured his father and hanged him in Damascus.[18] Under the short-lived Arab government in Damascus, relations between the Jabal Druze and Amir Fayṣal were amicable. Damascene nationalist leaders, with ties to the Jabal, made political overtures to Druze leaders on behalf of Amir Fayṣal. Fayṣal recognized the popular Druze chieftain Salīm al-Aṭrash as *mutaṣarrif* (governor) of the Jabal. Other Druze notables also played prominent roles in Hashimite politics and in the administration in Damascus. Most active was Nasīb al-Aṭrash, an uncle of Sulṭān Pasha, who was a deputy from the Jabal Druze to the Syrian Congress in 1919-20. Sulṭān al-Aṭrash himself held a post in the Sharifian Army.[19]

But with the collapse of Fayṣal's nationalist government and the imposition of French rule in Syria in 1920, Druze leaders became preoccupied with the French military occupation of the Jabal. And although a number of Druze leaders had been infected by the ascendent idea of Arab nationalism radiating from Damascus, that idea radiated less vigorously after the French seized control of the city.

The French made their first diplomatic inroads in the Jabal Druze in the late nineteenth century, despite Ottoman efforts to prevent European involvement there. Before the 1880s the British had been the only European power with influence among the Druzes, largely because they had protected the Druze community in Mount Lebanon in the aftermath of the civil war of 1858-60. But continued British support of the Ottoman state led some Druzes to seek French support. In the Jabal Druze the French seized this opportunity but chose to develop their ties with the major rival of the Aṭrash clan, the 'Amr ('Awāmrah).[20]

It was not until France occupied Syria in 1920 that she began to develop an important base in the Jabal Druze. In fact, the French strategy for governing the Jabal was a microcosm of the general imperial strategy for Syria. It was three-pronged and focused on setting rural areas against the nationalist towns, on isolating Syria's compact regional minorities from the mainstream of Syrian Arab political culture, and on playing elite against elite. This grand design, a derivative of Marechal Lyautey's imperial strategy in Morocco, seemed ideally suited to the Jabal Druze.[21] The Druzes inhabited a remote, inaccessible, mountainous agricultural area. They constituted a compact minority; 90 percent of the Jabal's population were Druzes with religious and social customs sufficiently distinct from the Sunni-Muslim Arabs of the plains and towns.[22] And local authority in the Jabal was divided between rival clans prone to intense factionalism.

The formula adopted by the French governing Jabal Druze concentrated on the development of a special and direct relationship with the Druzes that would recognize local customs and at the same time would circumvent Damascus. The first French high commissioner, General Henri Gouraud, a veteran of Morocco, chose a trusted aide, Colonel Georges Catroux, another veteran of Morocco, to reach an accord with the Druze community.[23] In November 1920, Catroux initiated negotiations with the ruling families of the Jabal which led to a Franco-Druze Treaty in March 1921. Its terms stated that the Jabal Druze was to form a special administrative unit, distinct from the Damascus state,[24] with an elected Druze governor and a representative council (*majlis*). Administration was to be under Druze control. In return, the Druzes had to recognize the French Mandate and accept the usual array of French advisers (*conseillers*) and the garrisoning of French troops at Sūwaydā', the Jabal's capital.

The first governor to preside over this new arrangement with the French was Salīm al-Aṭrash, still the acknowledged paramount chief of the Druze community. Whereas Salīm Pasha had been one of the first Druze chiefs to recognize Amir Fayṣal's authority in 1918, now with the French occupation he felt he had to strike a balance between Druze aspirations and French needs. His elevation, however, from a position in the Druze power structure of primus inter pares to that of governor of a separate Druze state gained Salīm al-Aṭrash little more than verbal recognition from other Druze leaders.[25] For Aṭrash chieftains, the French-imposed system of constitutional office holding threatened to erode the tradition of familial paramountcy that had characterized the structure of power in the Jabal since the eighteenth century. It enabled those Druze chiefs who managed to gain control of the new political institutions to isolate their rivals more easily than before, since traditional channels to political office and benefits were now blocked. A *majlis* of Druze notables served as a counterweight to the governorship, and French influence with its members was a check on the Aṭrash governor, if they found him undesirable.[26]

There was bound to be deep resentment in certain Druze quarters against the new administrative system which sanctioned foreign intervention in the Jabal. Violent altercations between Druzes and the French authorities followed the March 1921 treaty. The first significant Druze uprising against the French rule started in July 1922. Its catalyst was the arrest in the Jabal Druze of a certain Adham Khanjar, a Lebanese, whom French authorities accused of belonging to a rebel band that had tried to assassinate General Gouraud thirteen months earlier while he was on tour in the Qunaytra region. In that ambush, Gouraud escaped unharmed. An outraged High Commission believed that a member of Amir 'Abdullah's entourage in Amman had planned the attack, and that the assailants had escaped across the Transjordanian frontier, where they received 'Abdullah's protection. The French applied heavy pressure on the British in Transjordan to force 'Abdullah to hand over the assailants. 'Abdullah could not conceal his ambitions for a Syrian throne and surrounded himself with Syrian advisers in hopes of furthering his credibility in Syria as a desirable ruler. Although poor by royal standards, 'Abdullah distributed money and arms to Syrian rebels in this period.[27] And although the French successfully used the incident to get the British to curb 'Abdullah's activities, no progress had been made in the search for Gouraud's assailants until Khanjar's arrest on July 21.

Khanjar's interrogation revealed that he had been on his way to visit Sulṭān al-Aṭrash, the Druze chieftain most feared by the French. When Sulṭān Pasha learned of Khanjar's arrest, he immediately requested the senior French official in Sūwaydā', Commandant Trenga, to place the prisoner in his custody, since Druze custom dictated this minimal hospitality. When Trenga did not reply, Sulṭān al-Aṭrash went to Sūwaydā' to deal with the matter personally. There he learned that the French were transferring Khanjar to Damascus. He quickly organized a recovery party and attacked the armored convoy escorting the prisoner. The French responded by sending troops to destroy Sulṭān al-Aṭrash's home. The first French raid failed, but a second succeeded at the end of August. Intent on teaching Sulṭān Pasha an unforgettable lesson, the French not only plundered his home, but afterwards aerially bombarded it.

Sulṭān al-Aṭrash had been looking for an opportunity to rally Druzes against French interference in the Jabal, and the Khanjar incident in the summer of 1922 created the opportunity. For nearly a year, Druze rebels wages guerrilla warfare throughout the Jabal. Sulṭān Pasha, however, was forced to seek refuge across the border in Transjordan at the end of the summer. Under renewed pressure from the French, the British agreed to oust him from Transjordan in April 1923. Soon afterwards, Sulṭān al-Aṭrash surrendered to the French, who, not wanting to prolong the rebellion, reached a truce with him, which neither party expected would last.[28]

During the first major Druze uprising against the French, Sulṭān al-Aṭrash was in contact with and received the backing of nationalists in Damascus and Amman. Their own precarious situations, however, prevented them from offering his movement much more than moral support. At the time of the Druze uprising in July 1922, the nationalists' own political organization in Damascus, the Iron Hand Society, was politically defunct; the French had infiltrated and suppressed it that spring, jailing or exiling its most important leaders.[29] Nevertheless, Sulṭān Pasha proclaimed his revolt in the name of Syrian independence and the reunification of the Jabal Druze with Damascus. Despite his limited formal education, he was familiar with the nationalist creed, as were his closest Druze allies. He was opposed to any form of French mandatory rule in Syria and considered himself a nationalist. His political leanings were toward the Hashimites, with whom he had been in contact since 1916.

After 1920, Sulṭān al-Aṭrash's contacts with Damascus came through two channels. One was Nasīb al-Aṭrash, brother of the governor of the Druze state, Salīm Pasha. Nasīb resided in Damascus, where he headed the Druze Agency, which functioned as a consulate for the Druzes in the town. Before Sulṭān Pasha launched his first revolt against the French, Nasīb al-Aṭrash had already publicly proclaimed that the Jabal Druze should be annexed to Transjordan, an indication of Nasīb Bey's pro-Hashimite proclivities. The other conduit was a popular thirty-year-old religious leader of the Maydan quarter, Muhammad al-Ashmar. He had strong ties to wealthy grain merchants of his quarter who traded with the Hawran and Jabal. Like Sulṭān and Nasīb al-Aṭrash, Ashmar was pro-Hashimite.[30]

In Amman, support for the Druze insurgents came from several Syrians in Amir 'Abdullah's entourage, most of whom had worked closely together during the Fayṣal era in Damascus as members of the ultra-nationalist Independence Party (*Hizb al-Istiqlāl al-'Arabī*). From their new base in Amman they worked for a united Syria, including Palestine and Transjordan. Unfortunately for Sulṭān al-Aṭrash, by the time he took refuge in Transjordan at the end of the summer of 1922, 'Abdullah, under British advice, had begun to mend his fences with the French. Still covetous of a Syrian throne, 'Abdullah sought to placate the French that summer by dismissing his most radical nationalist aides.[31] A second concession to the French was the tightening of security on the Syrian border, which the British arranged. This made the Transjordan side of the frontier an increasingly inhospitable refuge for Druze rebels. Indeed, the Franco-Transjordanian rapprochement meant disaster for Sulṭān al-Aṭrash's movement. The failure of his revolt, and his surrender, were directly tied to the British-engineered split between the radical Istiqlālists in Amman and radical 'Abdullah over Amir's attempt to improve his relations with the French. Druze politics were already intimately tied to the Arab nationalist movement and were affected by its emerging rivalries and divisions.[32]

The Druze Uprising: Causes

Even before Sulṭān al-Aṭrash's surrender, Salīm Pasha retired as governor of the Jabal Druze, leaving Commandant Trenga temporarily in control of his functions. One important reason for Salīm's resignation was that he had suffered an appreciable loss of influence among Aṭrash chieftains and with the *majlis*. Throughout his governorship, Salīm al-Aṭrash had quarreled with Sultan Pasha as well as with 'Abd al-Ghaffār al-Aṭrash, the most influential member of the *majlis* and the major stumbling block to French administrative reform in the Jabal Druze. Salīm Pasha's death in mid-September 1923, after a long illness, led to a fierce struggle within the Aṭrash clan over political succession. The clan's failure to agree on a candidate led the *majlis* to go outside not only the Aṭrash clan but the entire Druze community, and to appoint Trenga's replacement in the Jabal Druze, Captain Gabriel Carbillet, broke with Druze political tradition altogether and confirmed him as governor.[33]

Until the arrival of Captain Carbillet, the French strategy of isolating the Jabal Druze from Damascus and of creating a direct and special relationship with the Druze leadership had worked fairly well. Indeed, the French had allowed the Druzes a large degree of autonomy over local administrative matters. Commandant Trenga had shown flexibility in a very difficult situation and had also managed to initiate reforms and development projects of benefit to the Druze community. He established a regular budget and a Druze gendarmerie, he built roads for automobile traffic, and he began reconstructing the dilapidated system around Sūwaydā'. Organized political opposition to the French, although never insignificant, had yet to reach alarming proportions. For the time being, Sulṭān al-Aṭrash's movement had been successfully checked.

Captain Carbillet came to the Jabal Druze with previous experience as a native affairs officer in French West Africa. A young, energetic innovator, he proved to be an indefatigable but impertinent modernizer. He suddenly altered the delicate relationship Trenga had worked so hard to cultivate in the Jabal Druze by choosing to administer it directly and with a distinct flavor of personal demagoguery. His aim was to destroy the Jabal's ancient feudal system, which he considered retrograde.[34]

In the spirit of the Lyautey tradition of French rule in Morocco, Carbillet developed an efficient economic administration with few troops and trained native officials to carry out his plans.[35] In twenty months he completed Trenga's highway projects and added another 125 road miles for motor vehicles. He paved the streets of Sūwaydā' and built over 100 miles of irrigation ditches. He also rationalized the judicial system in the Jabal and established a court of appeals at Sūwaydā'. He increased the number of schools and improved the public sanitation system. However, Carbillet, the tireless reformer, the man whose love of the Jabal Druze was "second only to his love for France,"[36] imperfectly fit Marechal Lyautey's model of the elite French native affairs officer. Although he belonged to the elite Service des Renseignements, and thus spoke Arabic and was familiar with Druze religious and social practices, his method of rule was not at all subtle. Rather, it was the antithesis of rule along native lines (*association*) that Lyautey had favored, for Carbillet refused to operate within the framework of Druze political tradition.[37]

Carbillet's most ambitious project was to free the Druze peasantry from its historic economic insecurity by transforming the Druze feudal system, at whose top rested the Druze landowning clans. Communally held property was still prevalent in the agricultural areas of the Jabal, although a peasant revolt in 1889-90 had established property rights for Druze peasants in some districts. Common lands were redistributed on a triennial basis, but the Druze feudal elite normally received the most productive third of the lands of the previous rotation, which peasants generally farmed in addition to their two-thirds share. Carbillet—consistent with the early idealism of French agrarian policy in Syria, whose central idea was to create a nation of small peasant proprietors at the expense of the big landowning classes—eagerly offered Druze peasants individual ownership rights on lands planted with grapevines.[38]

Although some peasants became owners of small plots, the overall impact of Carbillet's land reform was slight. The conservative, suspicious Druze peasantry—still dominated by and dependent on the Druze clans—did not take advantage of his offering because it threatened a traditional way of life and because they were discouraged from doing so by their Druze lords. In fact, suspicion turned to alienation when Carbillet resorted to forced peasant labor, in lieu of taxation, to complete his various public works projects, particularly the road network, in record-breaking time. Peasants could not appreciate "the advantage of roads" designated for "wheeled vehicles they did not possess."[39]

Carbillet chose to adopt tactics in his game of divide and rule which pitted class against class, that is, French-backed peasants against their Druze lords. Yet he failed to secure the peasantry's support and, as a result, he reduced the potential of his other option: to exploit the division and antagonisms at the summit of the Druze power structure within the paramount Aṭrash clan and between it and its rivals on the *majlis*. Although Carbillet's attempt to destroy the power structure led to a diminution of the political authority and privileges of the Aṭrash chieftains, it eventually fanned Aṭrash discontent with his regime into another Druze revolt.[40]

Disenchantment with Captain Carbillet's reforms and autocratic administrative methods spread rapidly in the Jabal. He received a series of death threats in December 1923, and Aṭrash chiefs prepared a full-scale revolt against the French for April 1924. French intelligence, however, managed to catch wind of it beforehand, and successfully defused it. Nevertheless, by the end of 1924 Druze opposition to Carbillet was in evidence in all quarters, and the campaign against him began to build up steam. Peasants distrusted his land reforms and resisted his forced labor policy. Local functionaries were outraged by his direct one-man rule, which bypassed them. Rubbing salt in their wounds, Carbillet enforced a strict surveillance of administrative practices to obstruct functionaries from manipulating their offices for personal benefit.[41] Most important, however, was the intensely hostile reaction of the Druze clans, particularly the Aṭrash. Carbillet's land reforms and his personal rules were undermining their material base in land and the traditional system of political bargaining and decision making.

In the spring of 1925, the Aṭrash clan—temporarily laying aside its personal differences—sent a delegation to Beirut to complain about Carbillet to a new high commissioner, General Maurice Sarrail. These Aṭrash chiefs demanded that a Druze be made governor, as promised by the Franco-Druze treaty of 1921. Although Sarrail categorically refused to dismiss Carbillet, he did instruct him to take a leave of absence in France in mid-May.[42] In the interim, the high commissioner appointed Capt. Antoine Raynaud, who had been stationed in the Jabal Druze for some time, as provisional governor. Seemingly more in touch with the dynamics of Druze politics than Carbillet, Raynaud struck up cordial relations with Sulṭān al-Aṭrash at the expense of the *majlis*, which was mainly composed of lesser Druze dignitaries who had been Carbillet's only support in the Jabal. Perfectly aware of the seething dissatisfaction with Carbillet's rule, Raynaud reported to General Sarrail that one way to avoid such a disturbance would be to undertake a full-scale investigation of Druze allegations against the vacationing Carbillet.[43]

Raynaud's alarming report on the deteriorating situation in the Jabal Druze annoyed Sarrail, who suspected that Raynaud's criticisms of Carbillet's rule were motivated by personal ambition. Raynaud's close relationship with Sulṭān al-Aṭrash and the fact that the anti-Aṭrash faction on the *majlis* (which continued to express its preference for an independent Druze state) had already reelected Carbillet governor for another term the previous February, convinced the high commissioner to recall Raynaud at once.[44]

His replacement was Major Tommy Martin of the Service des Renseignements. After Martin reported a sudden increase in the number of violent incidents in the Jabal, Sarrail had a change of heart and instructed him to investigate the accusations against Carbillet. On July 11, Martin transmitted to Beirut his first impressions of the causes of trouble in the Jabal, which confirmed Raynaud's earlier warning: the

Aṭrash clan, which was opposed by most other clans and by the *majlis*, was preparing a major revolt. Evidence abounded that Sulṭān al-Aṭrash—backed by the united Aṭrash clan and joined by the influential ʻIzz al-Dīn al-Halabis,[45] a powerful clan of the northern Jabal thought to be the most cosmopolitan and educated of the Druze clans with the strongest ties to nationalists in Damascus—was rallying Druze bureaucrats and peasants. Martin's observations, however, either went unnoticed or were purposely ignored by the high commissioner, who had clearly begun to show the signs of crankiness and impatience of his seventy years.[46] Sarrail had already decided to take a tough stand against the Aṭrash leadership.

On the same day that Martin sent off his report, three Aṭrash chiefs arrived in Damascus at the invitation of the French high commissioner to discuss their grievances. Instead, they were arrested at their hotel and deported to Palmyra. A fourth Druze chief had been invited but never appeared; Sulṭān al-Aṭrash had anticipated the French tactics.[47]

General Sarrail's arrest of the Aṭrash chiefs was the immediate provocation for the massive Druze uprising a week later. Sulṭān al-Aṭrash knew that he was a marked man; past experience had taught him that resistance to the French was a better option than imprisonment. He also knew that he could tap the anti-French sentiments that had been brewing in the Jabal Druze for the past few years. Although arrest of his relatives was the catalyst for the once divided Aṭrash clan to close ranks around its now undisputed strongman, such a movement had been under way since 1923, when Captain Carbillet first tried to reduce Aṭrash primacy by playing the lesser dignitaries of the *majlis* against the Aṭrash clan and by attacking the material base of its power through land reforms. With his clan reunited and local rivals hamstrung by the absence of their French patron, Sulṭān Pasha faced little internal resistance to his call for a general revolt.[48] He could count on support from disaffected bureaucrats, who had suffered a significant loss of influence and income under Carbillet's one-man rule; from a group of young, educated Druzes with pronounced Syrian nationalist sympathies, who also saw the revolt as an opportunity to challenge the authority of the traditional Druze elite; and from an alienated peasantry whose lot had not perceptibly improved after the French governor's attack on the feudal privileges of the Jabal's landowning clans.

On July 18, 1925, Druze highlanders opened fire on a French airplane circling the Jabal. Two days later Sulṭān al-Aṭrash and a group of his armed horsemen attacked and occupied Salkhad, the second town of the Jabal, southeast of Sūwaydā'. On the 21st, Sulṭān Pasha's band ambushed 166 Algerian and Syrian troops under the command of Captain

Normand, who had been dispatched to rescue some airmen stranded six miles south of Sūwaydā'. Less than half the Normand column survived the assault. That same evening Sulṭān al-Aṭrash's forces laid siege to Sūwaydā'.[49]

In Beirut, General Sarrail was complacent. He was convinced that the uprising was limited in scope and thus could be contained and suppressed quickly. He was so confident that he even permitted an Algerian battalion to leave Syria on July 30 for Morocco, which was in the midst of the Rif rebellion.[50]

The initial success of the Druze rebels promoted an intense eagerness and enthusiasm in Sulṭān al-Aṭrash's camp. In the last week of July, Druzes from all over the Jabal rushed to his side, helping to transform his small band into an army of between eight thousand and ten thousand men in a region whose total population was only fifty thousand. In the neighboring Hawran, parts of which had been at the mercy of the Jabal for generations, panic spread among its mixed population of Christian, Muslim, and Druze peasants, who feared reprisals if they did not heed Sulṭān Pasha's call to arms. Some peasants fled to safer areas in the Ḥawrān or into Palestine. Others, mainly Christians, sought refuge in Damascus, bringing tales of massacre and pillage. Druze rebels had burnt at least five Christian villages toward the end of the month.[51]

At the end of July, a French relief column of three thousand troops under the command of General Roger Michaud set out from Izra' to break the siege of Sūwaydā' twenty miles away. On August 2, just seven miles shy of its destination, Druze horsemen led by Sulṭān al-Aṭrash surprised and routed the French column. French casualties were heavy: 14 killed, 385 wounded, and 432 missing. The French commander of a company of Madagascenes who had panicked and fled, committed suicide. Even General Michaud left the scene prematurely. The Druze rebels had also captured two thousand rifles.[52]

Back in Beirut, General Sarrail was shaken out of his complacence, although, as time would tell, it was too late to salvage his own career. In a desperate cable to Paris for reinforcements, he warned his superiors that the revolt was destined to spread.[53] This time his assessment was more accurate.

From Local Rebellion to National Revolt

Several other factors fueled the uprising in the Jabal and encouraged its spread throughout Syria and into the southern districts of Lebanon. One was the grave economic crisis of 1925. It so happened that the revolt coincided with one of the most severe droughts in recent years, the result of which was a miniscule wheat harvest in the Ḥawrān, the breadbasket of Damascus. In fact, the summer desiccation was the culmination of what had been an especially bizarre winter and spring throughout Syria. February and March had been two of the coldest months in memory, and an unusually late frost at the beginning of April had caused widespread damage to the gardens around Damascus, whose fruits were among the leading exports of the capital.[54]

The losses suffered by the tribes and villagers because of the severe winter, the subsequent drought, and the poor harvest in southern Syria created much economic insecurity. Whole villages had to be abandoned in the Ḥawrān as wells and springs dried up. In some areas the situation reached famine proportions. The penetration of Bedouins into the cultivated zones to the south and east of Damascus was deeper than in previous winters because of their own losses. In a vicious cycle, cultivators already hurt by bad weather suffered losses because of increased tribal raiding or the encroachment of tribal herds. In central Syria, crop production around Ḥama and Ḥoms, although not subject to the climatic crisis of the south, was well below average, because of an insect pest which destroyed a large proportion of the cereal crop.[55]

The worsening economic conditions in the Ḥawrān and around Damascus led to widespread disorder and brigandage, fanned on one side by the appearance of Druze rebels in these areas and on the other by the sight of French troops sweeping through the region in full marching order. Throughout August and most of September, however, the French were unable to halt the mounting unrest south of Damascus as Bedouins, peasants, deserters from the Syrian Legion, and unemployed artisans from large villages conducted daring raids near the Syrian capital. Often the villages around which these bands operated assisted in the attacks on French garrisons. French reprisals, when they were possible, took the form of burning and plundering cooperative villages, which only provided new recruits for the rebels.[56]

In the towns of the Syrian interior, which had never wanted nor accepted the imposition of the French Mandate, popular discontent quickly rose to a boiling point under the impact of the debilitating economic depression. Prices of foodstuffs and other necessities began to soar. Unemployment reached a new high, driving many artisans, casual laborers, and recently settled families on the outskirts of Damascus back to their ancestral villages and often into the roving bands of rebels and bandits that had become a common feature of the Syrian countryside.[57]

Merchants and moneylenders in Damascus were troubled by the poor harvests, which had forced Syria, traditionally an exporter of wheat and flour, to import both in great quantities from India and Australia. It was estimated that in 1925 they had advanced 200,000 Turkish liras to cultivators in the Ḥawrān and Jabal Druze on their crops, and they figured that a peace imposed by French bayonets would cause the total ruination of an already meager harvest, and thus a loss on their advances, at a time when commerce was stagnant. They therefore pressed for a negotiated peace. Bazaar moneylenders were strikingly inactive, and banks began to restrict credit, aggravating the commercial depression. The Chamber of Commerce frantically assembled in mid-August to determine how merchants could cut their losses. The French had already granted a moratorium on the payment of taxes, and some merchants, realizing that the chances of collecting their debts were slim, suggested that the chamber also call for a moratorium on loan repayments. This was met by a large opposition led by the biggest grain dealers of the Maydan quarter, who felt that such a measure would be disastrous to their future credit ratings with bankers. Meanwhile, rumors of impending bankruptcies began to spread, causing a financial panic.[58]

Apart from the general economic crisis of 1925, there were specific French policies which contributed to the rapid spread of the revolt. France was unable or unwilling to promote any recognizable financial and economic interests in Syria other than her own. French monetary policy, which tied the new Syrian paper currency to the continuously depreciating French franc, appeared to be melting away a considerable portion of Syria's national wealth. Individuals on fixed salaries, from ranking administrators to petty clerks, suffered the most from devaluation. Meanwhile, the drastic reorientation forced on the Syrian economy by the partition of geographical Syria in the aftermath of World War I and the continued erosion of Syrian industry in the face of European competition helped to create and maintain high unemployment and inflation. On one hand, the French supported a tightfisted fiscal policy in areas such as education, agricultural development, public works, and industry; on the other, they spent profusely on the repressive arms of the state—the army and police, and on unwieldy and overlapping state administrations.[59] On the political level, French policies were specifically tailored to weaken and isolate the forces of nationalism. Nationalist leaders were regularly frustrated in their efforts to assert an effective claim to adequate consideration from the ruling system in Syria. The French High Commission completely ignored nationalists, refusing to appoint them to the top posts in government they felt they deserved. They did, after all, have a high degree of independent influence, especially among the politically conscious and active populations in the large towns of the interior, where they were recognized as "natural" leaders.[60]

Syrian nationalists were always on the lookout for opportunities to shift the political balance of power back in their direction. In early 1925, the High Commission allowed them to organize their first legal political party in preparation for national elections later in the year. But this party, the People's Party (Ḥizb al-Sha'b), was little more than a loosely knit alliance of absentee landowners, merchants, and middle-class professionals. It had behind it only ideas and served mainly as an organ of anti-French and anticollaborationist propaganda, supported by the intelligentsia in Damascus and other nationalist strongholds. Indeed, the character of the People's Party reflected its leadership's real objective: not to overthrow the existing system by driving the French out but rather to convince the French to recognize the People's Party as the sole, legitimate representative of the Syrian people, and thereby to grant it a greater share of political power. This leadership focused on a two-stage strategy: first to convince the French that they would have to share power with this leadership in order to rule Syria, and then, once at the summit of politics, to gradually work to relax French control over Syria.[61] And the People's Party's bid for direct access to the French was reinforced by a judicious mix of diplomatic pressure and intermittent strikes and demonstrations. Nationalist leaders in 1925 were obviously not seeking a revolutionary solution to the Syrian question.

The Damascus Connection

The nationalist People's Party was not planning a major revolt at the time of the Druze uprising at the end of July 1925. It was not sufficiently organized for such an undertaking, nor was its leadership attracted to the idea of armed struggle against the French. Furthermore, Damascus was well fortified by the French, as were other nationalist towns. The effects, however, of a paralyzing economic depression and renewed signs of French inflexibility on the political front clearly suggested to the nationalist leadership that it should intensify its pressures on the French. This leadership had to make it clear once and for all that it not only enjoyed wide public support in towns like Damascus, but also commanded the allegiance of those districts in Syria, like the Jabal Druze, which the French planned to keep administratively isolated from the nationalist heartland. Thus, the outbreak of rebellion in the Jabal Druze created a new opportunity for the nationalist leadership to make its case more loudly heard at High Commission headquarters in Beirut.

Contacts between Damascus and the Jabal, which was only seventy-five miles southeast of the Syrian capital, were manifold. Merchants and moneylenders of the Maydan Quarter, where the grain trade was organized, were frequent visitors to the Ḥawrān and Jabal, whose cereal crops they financed. Similarly, Druze notables paid periodic visits to Damascus. Some spent the winter months in homes they owned or rented there. On the political level, the Aṭrash clan maintained formal links with Damascus nationalists through the Druze consular office in the Syrian capital.

Among Damascene nationalists, Nasīb al-Bakrī was clearly the most respected by Druze leaders and the most involved in Druze politics. He belonged to an aristocratic landowning family that claimed descent from the Prophet. He was the second of five sons of ʻAṭā al-Bakrī, who had been an influential member of the Damascus municipal and district councils from the 1890s until his death in 1914. Nasīb was a graduate of the elite preparatory school of Damascus, Maktab ʻAnbar, which had produced many early Arab nationalists.

The Bakrīs had lost their high offices after the Young Turk revolution of 1908 because of their close links to Sultan ʻAbd al-Ḥamīd II. They were also close to the branch of the Hashimite family headed by Sharīf Ḥusayn in Mecca, whom Nasīb's father had first met in Istanbul before Ḥusayn had assumed his post in Mecca. In 1909, when Sharīf Ḥusayn's son, ʻAbdullah, accompanied by his uncle, Sharīf Nāṣir, visited Damascus, they stayed at the Bakrī home. Later in 1915, when Amir Fayṣal visited Syria, he stayed at the Bakrī's country home in the Ghūṭa. By this time, Nasīb al-Bakrī and two of his brothers, Fawzi and Sāmi, had joined the secret nationalist society, al-Fatāt, of which Nasīb was secretary. Nasīb introduced Fayṣal to the party and he reportedly became a member.[62]

Nasīb al-Bakrī rushed to the Ḥijāz to offer his services to Sharīf Ḥusayn after he proclaimed his Arab revolt in 1916. His assignment was to return to Syria to organize a rebellion against the Turks in the Jabal Druze and Ḥawrān. In the Jabal, he found a party of Druze chieftains headed by Sulṭān al-Aṭrash willing to revolt against Ottoman rule. Nasīb al-Bakrī and Sulṭān Pasha led five hundred Druze horsemen into the Ḥawrān to occupy and control its main arteries in anticipation of the allied invasion from the south.[63]

Nasīb al-Bakrī's close relationship with Amir Fayṣal landed him the post of *chef de cabinet* in his government in Damascus in 1918. Not surprisingly, Fayṣal also chose Nasīb Bey to be his special emissary to the Jabal Druze, where Nasīb was to promote the unification of the Jabal with Damascus. His personal relationship with Sulṭān al-Aṭrash made him the logical choice for this delicate task. After the French occupation of Damascus in 1920, Nasīb al-Bakrī and his brothers maintained a conspicuously low profile, that is, until the summer of 1925, when he became the chief liaison of the People's Party with his former comrades-in-arms in the Jabal Druze.[64]

When news of the collapse and defeat of the Michaud column in early August reached Damascus, nationalist leaders began to meet secretly, moving from one home to the next, trying to plan a new course of action. Although excited by the news from the Jabal Druze, they were also apprehensive. Among the first series of meetings were ones held at the home of 'Uthmān al-Sharabāti, a wealthy tobacco merchant who had been heavily engaged in nationalist activities since the French occupation. In attendance were People's Party chiefs; political bosses (*qabaḍayāt*) from the quarters of 'Amara, Sūq Sarūja, Shaghur, and the Maydan; political leaders from Ḥama; and envoys from the Jabal Druze with information on the military situation there. At the same time, Nasīb al-Bakrī met regularly with 'Abd al-Ghaffār al-Aṭrash, the Sūwaydā' chieftain who was in Damascus to work out a joint plan for escalating the revolt.[65] For nationalist leaders in Damascus and other towns like Ḥama to encourage a full-scale uprising without guarantees that external support would be available was militarily and politically suicidal. These towns were still relatively well fortified by French garrisons and a gendarmerie, and the popular forces that the People's Party hoped to rally were not even equipped with small firearms. The Druze leadership's willingness to bring its revolt to the gates of Damascus, however, was just the assurance the People's Party needed to drop its preparations for upcoming elections and to intensify its pressures on the French in the nationalist towns.

The first nationalist delegation to confer directly with Sulṭān al-Aṭrash after he launched his uprising arrived in the Jabal Druze on August 19, just a month into the rebellion. It was headed by Nasīb al-Bakrī and included Shaykh Muḥammad al-Ashmar and Yaḥya al-Ḥayātī, the representative of a sizeable group of ex-Ottoman army officers who had served Amir Fayṣal and were prepared to contribute their talents to the revolt. The Damascus delegation and Sulṭān Pasha exchanged solemn oaths that the two parties would cooperate closely to drive the French out of Syria. The delegation promised the Druze leader that the people of Damascus were prepared to revolt if they received signs of encouragement from his rebel forces. Some nationalist leaders were skeptical about the revolt's prospects, but Sulṭān al-Aṭrash remained extremely optimistic. So far his forces had not suffered one setback, and armed tribesmen had just arrived from Transjordan to contribute to his revolt.[66] Three days later, on August 22, at a secret meeting at the Ghūṭa villa of Jamil Mardam, a wealthy young nationalist, Nasīb al-Bakrī reported to Dr. Shahbandar, the People's Party president, the results of his discussions with Sulṭān al-Aṭrash. Shahbandar decided to urge Aṭrash to make a surprise advance on Damascus to take advantage of the temporary absence of French troops tied down in the Jabal Druze and Ḥawrān. On August 24, rumors spread throughout Damascus that Sulṭān Pasha's army of Druzes and Bedouins was approaching. Panic spread as bazaar merchants started to move goods from their shops to their residences, and quarter bosses organized voluntary neighborhood guards. An uprising, however, never materialized; Sulṭān al-Aṭrash's rebel army had been stopped five miles southeast of Damascus by three squadrons of Moroccan *spahis* (native cavalry in the French army) supported by the French air force.[67]

After the abortive uprising, the French delegate (*délégué*) in Damascus initiated a house-to-house search for all suspected nationalist leaders. Many were apprehended and jailed without trial. However, the most important nationalist leaders, including Dr. Shahbandar and the Bakrī family, managed to escape the French dragnet, taking refuge in the Jabal Druze.[68] Damascus was thus stripped of its most important leaders and spokesmen. Meanwhile, French security dismantled the apparatus left behind by the People's Party. One important lesson had to be learned: the Damascus populace—regardless of how miserable and frustrated it had become under French rule—was unwilling to undertake a revolt without direct outside assistance. And this would not materialize for another seven weeks, until Druze and Damascene rebel forces finally managed to penetrate the Syrian capital. In the meantime the People's Party and the Druze leadership had set up a nationalist provisional government in the Jabal Druze (on September 9) with the stated goal of Syrian unity and independence from the Mediterranean coast to the depths of the Syrian interior. Nowhere in their program for action was the call to pan-Islamism or to revolution against the French based on the grounds of religion.[69]

This formal alliance was followed a month later by a massive uprising in Ḥama that had been ignited from outside that central Syrian town by a renegade Syrian Legion captain, in command of Mawālī tribesman, who was in direct contact with nationalist leaders in Damascus and with Sulṭān al-Aṭrash in the Jabal Druze. By the end of October, Syria was in full revolt. It was not a revolt consisting of several isolated local uprisings, but rather one whose component parts were intimately linked. A Druze-Syrian nationalist front had been forged, and with considerable ease. And even though the French eventually crushed the revolt and kept the Jabal Druze administratively autonomous from the Syrian state for another decade, the Druze leadership of the revolt remained actively involved in nationalist politics and committed to a "successful assimilation of the Druzes into a Syrian-Arab political community."[70] In fact, when the defeat caused a major rupture in the ranks of the national independence movement, Sulṭān al-Aṭrash and the emerging group of young, nationalistically oriented Druze intellectuals came down on the side of the Shahbandar-Hashimite faction with whom they had been tied from the start of the revolt. Druze leaders not only swam in the nationalistic stream; they also knew on which bank to pitch their tents.[71]

Conclusion

Although the Druzes revolted against French efforts to upset the traditional power structure in the Jabal Druze, it is no coincidence that the leaders of the uprising had political and social ties to Damascus. In fact, Druze rebel leaders were familiar with and sympathetic to the nationalistic creed of Syrian unity preached by the nationalist elite in the capital; many actually counted themselves as Syrian nationalists. They were attracted to a new system of secular ideas radiating from Damascus. And they also found nationalism a convenient instrument to counter French intervention and, in particular, the growing influence of the rival branch of the Druze elite, patronized by the French and predisposed to a separate Druze existence under French protection.

Druze rebel leaders were actually eager to extend their rebellion as widely as possible and therefore proclaimed it in the name of Syrian unity and independence from French rule. They fully realized that their movement had a greater chance of success if its scope could be widened. Thus, in the larger scheme of the Syrian independence struggle, Druze rebel chiefs were by no means passive actors taking their cues from nationalistic leaders in Damascus.[72]

This last point needs emphasis for two important reasons. First, it suggests that to understand the extent of the Druze contribution to the Great Revolt, it is necessary to place the Druze uprising more squarely in the context of Syrian political life. Second, it suggests that the contribution of the Syrian nationalist leadership in Damascus and other nationalist centers to the Great Revolt also needs reassessment. Because historians fail to see the Druze uprising as directly linked to the general development of nationalism in Syria, they misrepresent the actual objectives of the nationalist leadership and misclassify the Great Revolt. Their tendency is to exaggerate the contribution of the nationalist People's Party in Damascus. Indeed, one historian goes so far as to define the aims of the nationalist leadership in Damascus as "revolutionary," concerned with "the establishment of an independent, federated

Syrian state molded on a Western model," while those of the Druze rebel leaders were "counterrevolutionary," concerned with the retention of power and prestige in their own hands."[73]

It is more satisfactory to view the General Revolt and its component parts, like the mandate era itself, as belonging to a transitional stage in the political evolution of the Arab East.[74] Movements of protest and resistance in the interwar period should be seen as moving between the traditional and the modern, but at an uneven pace and with an uneven rhythm, not unlike the way economy and society were evolving at this time. As a consequence, such movements cannot easily be classified as either traditional or modern, because they reveal a complex mixture of traditional and modern features. Furthermore, as I have suggested, those features of interwar movements that have generally been viewed as traditional, or even retrograde, were something more evolved, while those generally thought to have been modern, or even revolutionary, tended to be something else.

In the case of the Great Revolt, its leaders clung to an older set of political objectives. Neither Damascene nor Druze leaders can be said to have adopted a revolutionary framework of ideas and objectives. They did not seek to overturn the French system of rule; rather, they sought something less: the modification of the existing system and the gradual relaxation of French control. Their real objective was to shift the balance of power between themselves and the French back in their own direction so as to restore their influence over local politics—an influence which the French had undercut both in the nationalist towns and in the Jabal Druze. Only from this position could they then work to ease the French out of Syria.[75]

But even if their objectives were not particularly revolutionary, they nevertheless had to employ new, more sophisticated methods to achieve them. The growth and spread of nationalism itself forged broader political alliances than had been previously known in Syria. Moreover, the disruptive effects of French rule, which by its very nature was perceived as illegitimate, required new, more highly developed mechanisms for resisting the French. Political movements of protest and resistance tended to be more intense and of longer duration; they no longer remained localized affairs but assumed national dimensions. They now embraced new patterns of political organization linked to new secular systems of ideas, and they operated on a much larger territorial scale than ever before.

The Great Revolt was, indeed, a signal event in the history of modern Syria and in the Arab world at large, for it revealed new broad-based alliances linking together different elites—like the Druzes and

Damascenes—as well as urban and rural forces, and social classes and religious communities. Its wider base and appeal also attracted moral and material support from neighboring countries simultaneously engaged in independence struggles against European rule. And the terms of the struggle, its broader appeal, and the fact that it was being waged against a foreign power made of the Great Revolt an international event with international implications.

Although the Great Revolt revealed objectives which were at once old and deeply rooted in Syria's Ottoman past, at the same time it revealed many modern features. Truly, the Great Revolt can be defined, with all its complexities and contradictions, as progressing between the old and the new.

Notes

1. Edmund Burke III, "Popular Protest and Resistance in the Arab World 1750-1925: A Research Agenda." Unpublished manuscript, Santa Cruz, 1980.
2. See my *Syria and the French Mandate: The Politics of Arab Nationalism* (Princeton: Princeton University Press, 1987), chap. 7; also see my "Factionalism Among Syrian Nationalists During the French Mandate," *International Journal of Middle East Studies* 13 (November 1981): 453; Jan Karl Tannenbaum, *General Maurice Sarrail: The French Army and Left Wing Politics* (Chapel Hill: University of North Carolina Press, 1974); Albert Hourani, "Revolution in the Arab Middle East," in P.J. Vatikiotis, ed., *Revolution in the Middle East and Other Case Studies* (London: Allen and Unwin, 1972), pp. 65-72; and Edmund Burke III, "A Comparative View of French Native Policy in Morocco and Syria, 1912-1925," *Middle Eastern Studies* 9 (May 1973): 173-86.
3. Hanna Batatu, "The Arab Countries From Crisis to Crisis: Some Basic Trends and Tentative Interpretations," in *The Liberal Arts and the Future of Higher Education in the Middle East* (Beirut: American University of Beirut, 1979), pp. 3-7.
4. See my *Urban Notables and Arab Nationalism: The Politics of Damascus, 1860-1920* (Cambridge: Cambridge University Press, 1983).
5. Ibid.
6. See my "Islamic Revivalism and the Crisis of the Secular State in the Arab World: An Historical Appraisal," in I. Ibrahim, ed., *Arab Resources: The Transformation of a Society* (London: Croome and Helm, 1983), pp. 217-19.
7. On the 1919 Revolution in Egypt, see Jacques Berque, *Egypt: Imperialism and Revolution* (New York: Praeger, 1972), part 3; and Marius Deeb, "The 1919 Popular Uprising: A Genesis of Nationalism," *Canadian Review of Studies in Nationalism* 1 (Fall 1973): 105-19. On the Arab revolt of 1936-39 in Palestine, see Y. Porath, *The Palestine Arab Movement 1929-1939* (London:

Cass, 1977), chapter 9; Tom Bowden, "The Politics of the Arab Rebellion in Palestine 1936-1939," *Middle Eastern Studies* 11 (1975): 147-74; and Ghassan Kanafani, *The 1936-39 Rebellion in Palestine* (Committee for Democratic Palestine, n.d.).

8. The standard studies of Syria during the French Mandate remain A. H. Hourani, *Syria and Lebanon: A Political Essay* (London: Oxford University Press, 1946) and Stephen H. Longrigg, *Syria and Lebanon Under French Mandate* (London: Oxford University Press, 1958). A recent study by a Syrian historian on politics during the mandate is Dhūqān Qarqūt's *Taṭawwūr al-ḥarakah al-waṭanīyah fī sūrīyā, 1920-1939* (Beirut: Dār al-Ṭali'ah, 1975). French scholars have so far failed to produce a systematic study of the mandate era in Syria. Perhaps the two most perceptive assessments by French historians are Pierre Rondot's "L'experience du mandat Français en Syrie et au Liban (1918-45)," *Revue de Droit International Publique*, Nos.3-4 (1948): 387-409; and André Raymond's "La Syrie, du royaume arabe a l'independence (1914-1946)," in André Raymond, ed., *La Syrie d'aujourd'hui* (Paris: Centre National de la Recherche Scientifique, 1980), pp. 55-85.

9. I refer to studies by scholars trained in Europe or North America who write principally in Western languages. Included among these are Joyce Laverty Miller, "The Syrian Revolt of 1925," *International Journal of Middle East Studies* 8 (1977): 545-63; Safiuddin Joarder, "The Syrian Nationalist Uprising (1925-1927) and Henri de Jouvenel," *Muslim World* 68 (July 1977): 185-205, and *Syria under the French Mandate: The Early Phase, 1920-27* (Dacca: Asiatic Society of Bangladesh, 1977); and Itamar Rabinovich, "The Compact Minorities and the Syrian State," *Journal of Contemporary History* 14 (1979): 693-712. We can add to the list David Buchanan McDowall, "The Druze Revolt, 1925-27, and its Background in the Late Ottoman Period," B. Litt. Dissertation (Oxford: University of Oxford, 1972). The first detailed study of the overall revolt of 1925-1927 is Elizabeth P. MacCallum, *The Nationalist Crusade in Syria* (New York: Foreign Policy Association, 1928). Narrative histories, documentary histories, and memoirs in Arabic on the "Great Revolt" and the Druze uprising are numerous. See Hanna Abi-Rāshid, *Jabal al-Durūz* (Beirut: al-Fikr al-'Arabi, 1961); Fakhrī al-Bārūdī, *Mudhakkirāt al-Bārūdī*, vol. 2 (Beirut/Damascus, 1951 and 1952); Ḥasan al-Ḥakīm, *Mudhakkirātī, ṣafaḥāt min tārīkh Sūrīyah al-ḥadīthah*, 2 vols. (Beirut: Dār al-Kitāb al-Jadīd, 1965-1966); Adham al-Jundī, *Tārīkh al-thawrah al-Sūrīyah fī 'ahd al-intidāb al-Faransī* (Damascus: Dār al-Kitāb al-Jadīd, 1965); Munīr al-Rayyīs, *al-Kitāb al-dhahabī lil-thawarah al-waṭanīyah fī al-mashriq al-'Arabī: al-Thawrah al-Sūrīyah al-kubrā* (Beirut: Dār al-Ṭalī'ah, 1969); Muḥyi al-Din Safarjālānī, *Tārīkh al-thawrah al-Sūrīyah* (Damascus: Dār al-Yaqẓah, 1961); Amīn Sa'īd, *al-Thawrah al-'Arabīyah al-kubrā* (Cairo: 'Isā al-Bābi al-Ḥalabi, 1934); Salāmāh 'Ubayd, *al-Thawrah al-Sūrīyah al-kubrā 1925-1927* (Beirut: Dār al-Ghad, 1971); and 'Abd al-Raḥmān al-Shahbandar, *al-Thawrah al-Sūrīyah* (Damascus: Dār al-Jazīrah, 1933).

10. Joarder adopts this view, as does Miller implicitly. On the other hand, most

Syrian historians writing in Arabic prefer to see the Druze uprising as a purely Syrian-Arab nationalist rebellion; however, they provide little evidence in support of this view. See note 9. An interesting interpretation of the relationship between modern Syrian historiography and Syrian politics can be found in I. Rabinovich, "Historiography and Politics in Syria," *Asian Affairs* vol. 9, pt. 1 (February 1978): 57-66.

11. Salāmah 'Ubayd and David Buchanan McDowall have broken new ground by tracing the development of economic, social, and political ties between the Jabal Druze and Damascus from the late nineteenth century. As a result, they attach a greater significance to the Druze uprising than other scholars. See note 9.
12. Miller, among other historians, creates this impression in "The Syrian Revolt of 1925," pp. 558-61. She has neglected to explore Druze-Damascus relations and especially the relations of the Druze rebel leadership with nationalist forces in Damascus. Rabinovich, on the other hand, is more cautious and his analysis more nuanced. Nevertheless, he concludes that the "alliance" of Druzes and Arab nationalists in Damascus "enabled the latter to graft the political super-structure of a Syrian nationalist revolt on a military effort invested primarily by the Druze community. The political programme of the Druze Revolt was couched in Syrian and Arab nationalist terms, but this should not be taken to mean that the Druze community or even an important segment of its leadership sought to amalgamate themselves into the Syrian state" ("The Compact Minorities," pp. 701-2).
13. K.S. Salibi, *The Modern History of Lebanon* (New York: Praeger, 1965), pp. 4-17.
14. See McDowall, "The Druze Revolt," pp. xxviii, 40.
15. Damascus was an important market center for the Druze cereal crop. See ibid., p. 131. By this time, there were signs of a conflict between small and large landowners in the Jabal Druze.
16. On the Druze religion, which was a splinter of Islam as of the eleventh century, see Antoine Isaac Silvestre de Sacy, *Exposé de la religion des Druzes* (Paris: L'imprimerie Royale, 1838); and M. G. S. Hodgson, "Duruz," *Encyclopedia of Islam*, new ed., vol. 2, pp. 631-34.
17. Commandant Hassler, "Les insurrections Druses avant la Guerre de 1914-1918," *L'Asie Française*, no. 239 (March 1926): 143-47; and Shakib Salih, "The British-Druze Connection and the Druze Rising of 1896 in the Hawran," *Middle Eastern Studies* 13 (May 1977): 251-57. These revolts were against increased taxation and conscription, and against efforts to halt the expansion of Druze influence in the Ḥawrān grain belt.
18. McDowall, "The Druze Revolt," p. 181. McDowall suggests, quite convincingly, that in times of political upheaval minorities like the Druzes seldom connected themselves to one of the main protagonists; rather, they tried their best to play Turk off Arab and vice versa. See also al-Jundī, *Tārīkh*, p. 233; Qarqūt, *Tatawwūr*, p. 62; and Hassler, "Les insurrections Druses," pp. 143-47. In 1910, hostilities between Druzes and the Bani Miqdād tribe of the Hawran brought in the Turkish army. Traditionally,

the Druzes were in a protector-client relationship with the peasantry of the Ḥawrān, but after 1900, peasants could no longer rely on Druzes for protection against the Bedouin and were forced to turn to Damascus and the Ottoman military for protection. See McDowall, "The Druze Revolt," p. 127.

19. *Oriente Moderno* 5 (1925); 466-67; Yūsuf al-Ḥakīm, *Sūrīyah wa al-'ahd al-Fayṣalī* (Beirut: Catholic Press, 1966), p. 92; al-Jundī, *Tārīkh*, pp. 240-41.
20. McDowall, "The Druze Revolt," pp. 153-68. Attempts to keep foreigners out of the affairs of the Jabal Druze were reinforced after the British consul in Damascus, Sir Richard Burton, became involved in intrigues in the Jabal in 1869-71. France: Ministère des Affaires Etrangères (hereafter, MAE), *Syrie-Liban 1918-1929*, Carbillet, "La paix avec les Druses," 10 February 1926, vol. 197, p. 2.
21. Burke, "A Comparative View," pp. 175-86.
22. Gabriel Baer, *Population and Society in the Arab East* (London: Routledge and Kegan Paul, 1964), p. 109.
23. McDowall, "The Druze Revolt," pp. 220-26.
24. By this time the French had divided Syria into several administrative units, including the separate states of Damascus and Aleppo. In 1922, the French proclaimed the Jabal Druze a separate unit under French protection. See also, MacCallum, *The Nationalist Crusade*, p. 105.
25. In fact, Salīm's loudest critics were his own relatives, particularly 'Abd al-Ghaffār and Sulṭān al-Aṭrash. Foreign Office (hereafter, FO) 371/6384, vol. 7847, Damascus Consul to FO, 8 June 1922.
26. MacCallum, *The Nationalist Crusade*, p. 106.
27. FO 406/46, Samuel to Churchill, 25 June 1921; FO 371/31, vol. 6373, French Ambassador to FO, 2 August 1921.
28. al-Jundī, *Tārīkh*, pp. 184-85; MacCallum, *The Nationalist Crusade*, pp. 108-09; Ẓāfir al-Qāsimī, *Wathā'iq Jadīdah 'an al-thawrah al-Sūrīyah al-Kubra* (Beirut: Dār al-Kitāb al-Jadīd, 1965), pp. 175-177.
29. See my *Syria and the French Mandate*, chapter 5.
30. FO 371/6457, vol. 13512, Damascus Consul to FO, 17 November 1921; FO 371/5762, vol 7847, Damascus Consul to FO, 22 May 1922. The family of Shaykh Muḥammad al-Ashmar (b. 1892) originated in Mecca. For 150 years they had lived in the Maydan quarter of Damascus, where they were prominent religious shaykhs. During the French occupation of Syria in 1920, Shaykh Muḥammad was one of the resistance leaders in the Ḥawrān. Later he returned to Damascus, where he joined the Naqshabandi *sufi* order, which had been active in anti-French demonstrations as of 1922. See al-Jundī, *Tārīkh*, p. 561; and George Faris, *Man hūwa fī Sūriyāh 1949* (Damascus, 1950), p. 21.
31. See my "Factionalism," pp. 447-54; and *Philby Diaries*, 30 July 1922, in *H. St. John Philby Papers*, Middle East Centre, St. Anthony's College, University of Oxford.
32. PRO, Colonial Office 733/44, pp. 71-72. "Report on the Political Situation in Palestine and Transjordan for the Month of March 1923"; see also my "Factionalism," pp. 441-69.

33. FO 371/5762, vol. 7847, Damascus Consul to FO, 8 June 1922. 'Abd al-Ghaffār came from the most important branch of the Aṭrash clan, the Joub Isma'il; however, he did not come from the same subbranch as Salīm Pasha, Nasīb Bey, and Sulṭān Pasha. 'Abd al-Ghaffār was thought to be close to the British and thus was held in great suspicion by the French. MAE, *Syrie-Liban 1918-1929*, "La paix avec les Druses," pp. 13-15; Capitaine G. Carbillet, *Au Djebel Druse* (Paris: Editions Argo, 1929), pp. 103-7; FO 371/9868, vol. 9054, Palmer (Damascus) to FO, 18 September 1923. One Syrian historian claims that Carbillet coerced the *majlis* into nominating him governor of the Jabal. See Hanna Abi-Rāshid, *Jabal al-Durūz*, pp. 190-92.
34. MAE, *Syrie-Liban 1918-1929*, "Enquête de M. Daclin: Djebel Druse," part 1, 7 September 1926, vol. 234, pp. 51-52; MacCallum, *The Nationalist Crusade*, p. 106.
35. See Sh. H. Roberts, *A History of French Colonial Policy 1870-1925* (London; P.S. King and Son, 1929); Burke, "A Comparative View," pp. 175-86; MAE, *Syrie-Liban 1918-1929*, "Enquête de M. Daclin," 7 September 1926, vol. 234, p. 52.
36. MacCallum, *The Nationalist Crusade*, p. 112.
37. MAE, *Syrie-Liban 1918-1929*, "Enquête de M. Daclin," pp. 53-55. The Beirut-based liaison officer of the British Air Ministry, who knew Carbillet quite well, described the French captain as a "rugged looking individual with a long, unkept beard," who "after so many years isolated in the wilds of the Jebel Druze country . . . has become almost a Druze himself." FO 371/4810, vol. 10835, Air Ministry to FO, 13 August 1925. Yet Carbillet was "totally incapable of understanding the native psychology, harsh and overbearing to his inferiors and heedless of local sentiment and prejudice." FO 371/5576, vol. 10851, Crewe (Paris) to Chamberlain, 15 September 1925.
38. MacCallum, *The Nationalist Crusade*, pp. 112-13; Miller, "The Syrian Revolt of 1925," p. 552, citing *Oriente Moderno* 4 (1924): 38; MAE, *Rapport a la Société du Nations sur la situation de la Syrie et du Liban* (Annual Report presented to the League of Nations) (1925), pp. 13-19. According to MacCallum, in 1924 one million vines were planted on land that had been "cleared of stones and enclosed by low stone walls to designate the boundaries of vineyards." *The Nationalist Crusade*, p. 111.
39. MAE, *Rapport a la Société du Nations, 1925*, pp. 16-19; MacCallum, *The Nationalist Crusade*, p. 113.
40. FO 371/5527, vol. 10160, Damascus Consul to FO, 16 June 1925; Tannenbaum, *General Maurice Sarrail*, p. 199; MAE, *Syrie-Liban*, "Enquête de M. Daclin," pp. 187-88.
41. FO 371/5527, vol. 10160, Damascus Consul to FO, 16 June 1925; Tannenbaum, *General Maurice Sarrail*, p. 199; MAE, *Syrie-Liban*, "Enquête de M. Daclin," pp. 187-88.
42. MacCallum, *The Nationalist Crusade*, p. 114.
43. Miller, "The Syrian Revolt of 1925," p. 552; Tannenbaum, *General Maurice Sarrail*, p. 200; MAE, *Syrie-Liban 1918-1929*, "Enquête de M. Daclin," p. 57.

44. There seems to be strong evidence of intrigue on the part of Raynaud. See Tannenbaum, *General Maurice Sarrail*, p. 202. Carbillet certainly thought so, accusing Raynaud of intriguing with the French assistant *délégué* to the state of Damascus. FO 371/4810, vol. 10835, Air Ministry to FO, 3 August 1925; MacCallum, *The Nationalist Crusade*, p. 116; Miller, "The Syrian Revolt of 1925," p. 552. By this time, the Aṭrash leadership was willing to settle for Raynaud as governor, but definitely not Carbillet. FO 371/4005, vol. 10850, Damascus Consul to FO, 23 June 1925.
45. Muḥammad 'Izz al-Dīn al-Ḥalabi (b. 1889) was one of the most important Druze leaders of the revolt, and was well connected in Damascus political circles. He had been active in Druze politics and military activities for some time. Educated at the military college in Istanbul, he led a party of guerrillas in the Jabal Druze and Ghūṭa (gardens of Damascus). During the Fayṣal era in Damascus, he was a member of the nationalist Arab Club (al-Nādī al-'Arabī) and the Indpendence Party (Hizb al-Istiqlāl al-'Arabī) and fought against the French invading forces at Khān Maysalūn in July 1920. Faris, *Man hūwa fī sūrīyah 1949*, pp. 129-30.
46. MAE, *Syrie-Liban 1918-1929*, "'Rapport' of Tommy Martin," 11 July 1925, vol. 234, p. 102; Tannenbaum, *General Maurice Sarrail*, p. 200.
47. FO 371/4810, vol. 10835, Air Ministry to FO, 13 August 1925; Joarder, "The Syrian Nationalist Uprising (1925-1927) and Henri de Jouvenel," p. 187.
48. Although there was no visible resistance to revolt in the Jabal, it seems that at first Druse religious leaders and "several tribal factions refused to join the rebellion." Tannenbaum, *General Maurice Sarrail*, p. 202.
49. al-Rayyīs, *al-Kitāb al-dhahabī*, pp. 165-67; General C. J. E. Andrea, *La revolte druse et l'insurrection de Damas, 1925-1926* (Paris, 1937), pp. 52-53.
50. Tannenbaum, *General Maurice Sarrail*, p. 201, citing "Les Affaires de Syrie," Fonds Painlevé, box 42, file *Syrie* (Notes Carbillet), pp. 34-35, located in the Archives Nationales, Paris.
51. One report claimed that by the end of July 1925 there were eight thousand to ten thousand Druze rebels. Another estimated that Sulṭān al-Aṭrash commanded fifteen to twenty thousand armed men. See FO 371/4475, vol. 10850, Smart to FO, 27 July 1925; MacCallum, *The Nationalist Crusade*, p. 118; FO 371/4475, vol. 10850, Colonial Office to FO, 28 July 1925; and FO 371/4739, vol. 10850, Smart to FO, 29 July 1925.
52. FO 371/5576, vol. 10851, Crewe (Paris) to Chamberlain, 15 September 1925; al-Rayyīs, *al-Kitāb al-dhahabī*, pp. 167-69; MacCallum, *The Nationalist Crusade*, p. 119; Tannenbaum, *General Maurice Sarrail*, pp. 202-3; al-Qāsimi, *Wathā'iq*, pp. 119-26.
53. Tannenbaum, *General Maurice Sarrail*, pp. 201-3.
54. FO 371/5252, vol. 10851, Smart to Department of Overseas Trade, 17 August 1925; United States National Archives, Record Group 59, *Syria*, 890d.00/284, Antoine Coudsi to Damascus Consulate, 28 October 1925. Apricot trees suffered considerable damage; apricots in their dried form and in dry paste were the leading fruit export of Damascus. The Aleppo region suffered from the same bad weather throughout 1924 and during the

winter of 1925, when fruits, barley, and wheat crops were damaged. MAE, *Syrie-Liban 1918-1929, Bulletin de Renseignements*, 7-14 February 1925, vol. 427B, p. 2.

55. FO 371/5252, vol. 10851, Smart.
56. Ibid.; FO 371/7297, vol. 10852, Damascus Consul to FO.
57. For instance, in Aleppo the French estimated that the price of goods of primary necessity rose 72 percent between February 1924 and February 1925. MAE, *Syrie-Liban 1918-1929, Bulletin de Renseignements*, p. 2; FO 371/5252, vol. 10851, Smart to Department of Overseas Trade, 17 August 1925; MAE, *Syria-Liban 1918-1929*, 10 September 1925, vol. 193, p. 65.
58. United States National Archives, *Syria*, 890d.00/284, Coudsi to Damascus Consulate, 28 October 1928; MAE, *Syrie-Liyban 1918-1929*, Henry de Jouvenel to Foreign Minister, 9 January 1926, vol. 214; FO 371/5252, vol. 10851, Smart.
59. See my *Syria and the French Mandate*, chapter 4.
60. On notables as "natural" leaders, see Albert Hourani, "Ottoman Reform and the Politics of Notables," in W. R. Polk and R. L. Chambers, eds., *Beginning of Modernization in the Middle East* (Chicago: University of Chicago Press, 1968), pp. 41-68; and my *Urban Notables and Arab Nationalism*, pp. 1-7.
61. Qarqūt, *Taṭawwūr*, p. 67; and my *Syria and the French Mandate*, chapter 7.
62. Muḥammad Adīb Taqī al-Dīn al-Ḥusnī, *Kitāb muntakhabāt al-tawārikh li-Dimashq* (Damascus: al-Maṭba'ah al-Ḥadīthah, 1928) 2: 819-22; *Salname*: *Suriye vilayeti, 1312 A.H./1894-95 A.D.* (Damascus, n.p, n.d), pp. 77-78; France: Ministère de la Defense (Vincennes), *Service Historique de l'Armée*, Serie 7N 2141, Akaba, 20 June 1918. See Index to Ẓāfir al-Qāsimi's *Maktab 'Anbar* ['Anbar School] (Beirut: Catholic Press, 1967); see also Faris, *Man hūwa fī Sūriyah 1949*, p. 67; Syria: Markaz al-Wathā'iq al-Tā'rīkhīyah (Damascus), al-qism al-khāṣṣ, *Nasīb al-Bakrī Papers*, "Biography of 'Aṭa b. Nasīb al-Bakrī."
63. *Oriente Moderno* 5 (1925): 462-63.
64. Ibid., pp. 466-67; al-Qāsimi, *Wathā'iq*, pp. 205-7.
65. Syria: Markaz al-Wathā'iq al-Tā'rīkhīyah, al-qism al-khāṣṣ, *Nazīh al-Mu'ayyad al-'Azm Papers*, "Notes on the Outbreak of the Revolt," no. 203, 1925; FO 371/5039, vol. 10851, Damascus Consul to FO, 2 August 1925; FO 371/4730, vol. 10850, Liaison Officer (Beirut) to FO, 10 August 1925; Hisham Nashabi, "The Political Parties in Syria 1918-1933," M.A. Dissertation (Beirut: American University of Beirut, 1952), p. 102; Ḥasan al-Ḥakīm, "Mūjaz tarjamat ḥayāt al-za'im al-khālid al-maghfūr lahu al-duktūr 'Abd al-Rahmān al-Shahbandar," unpublished biographical sketch of Dr. Shahbandar, the People's Party leader; FO 684/2/55/158, Smart to FO, 30 January 1925; conversation with Ḥasan al-Ḥakīm (Damascus, 17 July 1977). Both men were veterans of the Great Revolt of 1925.
66. Qarqūt, *Taṭawwūr*, p. 218. Actually, Nasīb al-Bakrī's nephew, Asad B. Fawzi, had been in the Jabal Druze with Sulṭān al-Aṭrash since 3 August 1925. See al-Qāsimī, *Wathā'iq*, p. 233; FO 371/5039, vol. 10851, Damascus

Consul to FO, 12 August 1925; FO 371/5571, vol. 10851, Crewe (Paris) to Chamberlain, 15 September 1925. Amir 'Abdullah's chief adviser, the Syrian 'Alī Riḍa al-Rikābī, allegedly funneled five thousand sterling to Sulṭān al-Aṭrash for the organization of the rebellion. There is no evidence to suggest that 'Abdullah approved of this support; later some Syrian leaders would accuse him of turning his back on their revolt. See Philby's *Stepping Stones in Jordan: 1922-24*, manuscript in *Philby Papers*, pp. 260-61.

67. Conversation with Ḥasan al-Ḥakīm (Damascus, 21 March 1976); MAE, *Syrie-Liban 1918-1929*, 4 September 1925, vol. 193, p. 56; al-Jundī, *Tārīkh*, p. 195; MAE, *Syrie-Liban 1918-1929*, (1 September - 9 October 1925), vol. 193, pp. 99-102; FO 371/5273, vol. 10851, Damascus Consul to FO, 25 August 1925; FO 371/5576, vol. 10851, Crewe to Chamberlain, 15 September 1925; FO 371/5252, vol. 10851, Smart, 21 August 1925; al-Rayyīs, *al-Kitāb al-dhahabī, pp. 190-92; al-Jundī, Tārīkh*, pp. 336-37.
68. FO 371/5273, vol. 10851, Damascus to FO, 25 August 1925; MacCallum, *The Nationalist Crusade*, p. 124. Other nationalist leaders who took refuge in the Jabal Druze included Nazīh al-Mu'ayyad al-'Aẓm, Ḥasan al-Ḥakīm, Jamīl Mardam-Beg, and Sa'īd Ḥaydar.
69. Ministère de la Defense, Service Historique de l'Armée, Renseignement, 20 Bureau, 15 May 1926, 7N 4171.
70. See Rabinovich, "The Compact Minorities," pp. 701-2.
71. MAE, *Syrie-Liban 1930-40*, vol. 477, pp. 12-18. Also my "Factionalism," pp. 441-69.
72. The impression that the Syrian nationalistic leadership in Damascus convinced Sulṭān al-Aṭrash and the Druze rebel leadership to extend their rebellion is grossly misleading. Miller's "The Syrian Revolt of 1925" creates this impression; see pp. 558-59.
73. Ibid., p. 561.
74. Although Miller seems to imply that the Great Revolt may be seen as a transitional stage in the development of political movements in Syria, she fails to see the Druze uprising in this light and thus misrepresents the character of the overall revolt (pp. 546-47).
75. I have argued elsewhere that Syrian nationalists participated in the revolt somewhat reluctantly, after making no progress on the diplomatic front for five years with the intransigent French. The point is that they did not perceive their participation as some revolutionary activity but rather as the most expedient way of convincing the French to recognize them politically and to accept at least some of their demands. Many nationalist leaders in Damascus had no interest whatsoever in a prolonged rebellion that might engulf the countryside around the Syrian capital and possibly jeopardize their most important material interests in the form of landownership and rents. There seems to be little doubt that revolutionary activity was not their favorite strategy; indeed, they were both inexperienced and uncomfortable with such activity. Limited and targeted urban political protests, such as demonstrations and strikes, were the preferred tactics, not full-scale rebellion. See my *Syria and the French Mandate*, chapter 7.

The Social and Economic Structure of Bāb-al-Muṣallā (al-Mīdān), Damascus, 1825-1875

ABDUL KARIM RAFEQ

Introduction

This paper deals with one of the most famous neighborhoods of Damascus located outside the Wall, namely, Maḥallat Bāb al-Muṣallā, which, under the original name of Mīdān al-Ḥaṣā (Pebbles Hippodrome), once constituted the main part of Lower Mīdān. Three other hippodromes were located north, east, and west of al-Ablaq Palace (present location of Takīyah Sulaymānīyah) built by al-Ẓāhir Baybars, the Mamlūk.[1] The Ayyubids and especially their successors, the Mamlūks, used the hippodromes to train their cavalry. Hippodromes had been increasingly used in Cairo, Aleppo, and other cities of the sultanate.

Mīdān al-Ḥaṣā, known simply as al-Mīdān, is characterized by its strategic location as a link between Damascus and the Ḥawrān. The Ḥawrān province (the main producer of cereals), had an important economic, military, and religious role to play throughout Syria's long history. It was a commercial hub linking Damascus to Palestine, the Ḥijāz, and Egypt; a crossing point for expeditionary forces coming from Egypt to Damascus (regular forces of the Mamlūk sultanate or rebels); and, during the Ottoman era, a crossing point for rebels coming from Egypt to occupy Damascus (like the military expeditions of 'Alī Bey the Mamlūk and Muḥammad 'Alī Pasha, in 1771 and 1831, respectively).

Because of its strategic location and its economic function, al-Mīdān played an important role in facilitating the journey of the Syrian Pilgrimage Caravan to the Ḥijāz and in providing the pilgrims with provisions and camels. Its southern end was called "al-Bawwābah" (the Gate), abbreviated from the expression *Bawwābat* (or *Bāb*) *Allah* (the Gate to God), because it led to the Holy Places in the Ḥijāz and Jerusalem; it still retains that name. Being so important, al-Mīdān attracted many people from neighboring and remote areas who came to do business or to seek refuge. Thus al-Mīdān extended toward the south so as to integrate the village of Qubaybāt, and it stretched from its southern end to Bāb al-Jābīyah (its link to Damascus). It was more than three kilometers long and extended on both sides. Because of the extent of this development, al-Mīdān was conventionally divided into three sections: Lower Mīdān, the section closest to Damascus; Middle Mīdān; and Upper Mīdān, ending at the Bawwābah.

The Bāb al-Muṣallā neighborhood constitutes the main part of Lower Mīdān.[2] This appellation is due to the presence of the Muṣallā Mosque; the mosque's area was formerly named "al-Muṣallā" (the place for worship). Indeed it was selected for this purpose by Abū 'Ubaydah after the Islamic conqust.[3] Being a spacious area, it was used to shelter various urban and rural groups of worshipers attending religious ceremonies like the prayer for rain and the prayers of the Two Feasts. For this reason, it was originally named the "Two Feasts Muṣallā" (Muṣallā al-'Idayn). We read in the book *Munādamat al-aṭlāl wa musāmarat al-khayāl* that "the righteous King Sayf al-Dīn Abū Bakr Ibn Ayyūb had built in the year 606 A.H. (1209 A.D.) a mosque dedicated to the prayers of the Two Feasts"; as mentioned by Abū Shāma, he (the king) "erected four elevated walls and placed doors to protect the Muṣallā from caravans; he built a *miḥrāb* [prayer niche] and a *minbar* [pulpit] with stones; he crowned it with a dome and built, in its southern section, two porticos and a wooden pulpit."[4] From the late period of the Mamlūk sultanate until the early period of the Ottoman sultanate, the name *al-Muṣallā* or *Muṣallā al-'Idayn* was widely used for this mosque in the writings of the Damascene chronicler Muḥammad Ibn Ṭūlūn (1476-1546). Later the neighborhood was named after the Mosque of Bāb al-Muṣallā and was known, in short, as Maḥallat Bāb al-Muṣallā.

In the registers of the Mīdān Religious Court, the Bāb al-Muṣallā neighborhood is defined as a suburb of Damascus and a part of Lower Mīdān, the latter being, during the nineteenth century, one of eight sections into which Damascus was divided in the "Government's Registers (Defters)"[5] for the purpose of tax collection.[6] In the court registers, the following designation is most frequently used in identifying the exact location of a place in Bāb al-Muṣallā: *ẓāhir Dimashq bi-maḥallat Bāb al-Muṣallā in zuqāq* . . . , that is, outside Damascus in Maḥallat Bāb al-Muṣallā in alley so and so. In fact, Bāb al-Muṣallā is the only *maḥallah* (neighborhood) mentioned under this designation in all of al-Mīdān. All other places in al-Mīdān are designated as located in *zuqāq* (alley) so and so in Maḥallat al-Mīdān, or simply al-Mīdān. The term *maḥallah* is used to name an entire area inside and outside Damascus. For instance, there are the *maḥallahs* of al-Sūwayqah, al-'Uqaybah, al-Qaymarīyah, Mi'dhanat al-Shaḥm, al-Kharāb, and Bāb Tūmā. But the boundaries of a given neighborhood may vary with time.

The prime location of Bāb al-Muṣallā on the southern outskirts of Damascus was a main factor in attracting active elements with various backgrounds (economic, military, and so forth), most of them from neighboring and southern areas and some from North Africa. The newcomers differed in their origin, their work, and their creed: there were villagers from the Ḥawrān and Jabal al-'Arab; immigrants from Wādī al-Tīm; peasants and grain merchants; Bedouins, Turkmans, and Kurds; Christians, Druzes, and Sunnites; and North Africans who came as mercenaries or as religious scholars seeking closeness to holy shrines or as immigrants fleeing the oppression of French and European colonialism. In spite of this ethnic variety, the strategic, economic, and human characteristics and interests of the Mīdān area have made its population a strong and cohesive group, ready to defy the oppressive civilian authorities throughout the ages. In this respect, Ibn Ṭūlūn mentions the resistance of the populace and thugs of Bāb al-Muṣallā to the Mamlūk's rule. The Muṣallā al-'Idayn was their rallying point, the place in which they gathered to pledge their collective resistance and fighting against the authorities. Conversely, since Bāb al-Muṣallā controlled the supply of provisions and military reinforcements from the south,[7] the rebels among the Mamlūks used it as a springboard for their rebellion against the state. In 1746, during the Ottoman era and the tenure of the governor of Damascus, As'ad Pasha al-'Aẓm, Bāb al-Muṣallā witnessed the biggest revolution staged by the local Janissaries against the Ottoman rule.[8] al-Mīdān also played a major role in many rebellions against the French rule, especially during the Great Syrian Revolt, in 1925. Subsequently, during the independence era, the local leaders defied the national government on many occasions.

This paper deals with the topography of the Bāb al-Muṣallā neighborhood, its socioeconomic structure, and the degree of integration between its social groups. Because of its special importance, the period 1825-75 has been selected for study. Important developments locally, in the Arab world, and in the Ottoman Empire at that time had influenced in various degrees the socioeconomic structure of Bāb al-Muṣallā and other neighborhoods.

First, the Janissaries were disbanded, in 1826, by Sultan Maḥmūd II. At that time, al-Mīdān was the headquarters of the local Janissaries; the majority (officers, rank and file) were Damascenes in military uniforms eager to preserve their economic and political privileges. Subsequently, Syria was occupied between 1831 and 1840 by the army of Muḥammad 'Alī Pasha, the governor of Egypt (1831-39). After his retreat, the Ottomans returned and tried to impose "from above" their authority and their new administrative organization. In the wake of the Industrial Revolution, Europe was also trying to impose, on all levels, its colonial influence on the Arab world.

The various political, economic, and social crises that plagued Syria had led to social disturbances which reached their apogee in the 1860 riots in Damascus. Although the Christians were numerous in Bāb al-Muṣallā, the population of this neighborhood, unlike that of Damascus, was able to avoid the deplorable consequences. In order to study the effects of the 1860 disturbances on the social and economic relationships of Bāb al-Muṣallā, I selected the period ending in 1875. In fact, these relationships grew in strength and cohesion and were able to meet the European challenge, which was endangering all social groups in an equal manner.

Five samples have been selected from the registers of the Mīdān Religious Court, which rules on legal matters concerning the people of Bāb al-Muṣallā. Each sample consists of data covering a whole year or so, with intervals of approximately ten years, depending on the availability of records. The first sample covers the period Rajab 7, 1240 - Rajab 7, 1241 (February 25, 1825 - February 15, 1826; Mīdān Court Register No. 307); the second covers the period Rajab 25, 1250 - Rajab 25, 1251 (November 27, 1834 - November 18, 1835; Mīdān Court Register No. 333); the third covers the period Rabīʿ al-Awwal 1, 1262 - Rabīʿ al-Awwal 1, 1263 (February 27, 1846 - February 17, 1847; Mīdān Court Register No. 392); the fourth covers the period Muḥarram 21, 1279 - Muḥarram 10, 1280 (July 19, 1862 - June 27, 1863; Mīdān Court Register No. 547); and the fifth covers the period Dhū al-Hijjah 16, 1290 - Dhū al-Hijjah 16, 1291 (February 4, 1874 - January 24, 1875; Mīdān Greater Court Registers Nos. 653, 654).

Topography of Bāb al-Muṣallā

Modern studies of some cities of the Arab world, including Damascus,[9] show that the center of the old city was determined by the merchants of the specialized markets, who relied partly on long-distance trade with products such as spices. The central location of these economic agents was reinforced by the presence of the Great Mosque, with its cultural role and the economic activities revolving around it. The headquarters of the governor and the citadel played a secondary role in determining the city's center, although they attracted special economic activities related to military needs. In Damascus, these needs were met by the markets Sūq Taḥt al-Qalʿah, Sūq Srūjīyah, and Sūq al-Khayl, in addition to coffeehouses as gathering places for soldiers. Because of the concentration of major economic and religious activities in the city's center, the homes of prominent merchants and religious scholars were located in the immediate vicinity, followed by the homes of craftsmen in the vicinity of their shops. People with limited incomes lived close to places of lucrative activities, near the city's wall and gates. To facilitate the transportation and marketing of goods, main roads were built across those areas converging towards the center. The suburbs, with their blend of urban and rural activities, were shaped according to their location and commercial operations. Having no major specialized markets, their various business activities focused on services. The non-specialized market was the *sūwayqah* (small market).

As in the case of the city, the shape of the suburbs was determined by the main economic factors. Therefore, Bāb al-Muṣallā, as well as other sections of Mīdān, was shaped by its location and the economic activities of its population, besides being an intermediary between rural producers and urban consumers.

The Bāb al-Muṣallā neighborhood was bounded to the north by the Murādīyah Mosque, the Sūwayqah Maḥrūqah market, and the quarter of the Maghāribah or Maghribīs (North Africans), where the "Maghāribah Khān" was located. On this side, according to one source, was a gate leading to the Bāb al-Muṣallā Law Court; a second gate opened on the main (Sulṭānī) street, in the neighborhood, and a third one gave access to its southeastern section.[10] These gates are not mentioned in the registers of the Mīdān Religious Court, perhaps because the records focus on landed property.

To the south, Bāb al-Muṣallā included the Mujtahid Alley, the southern end of the Tayāmina Alley, and the Qubbah al-Ḥamrā area. In hundreds of cases during the period under study, the records of the Mīdān Court mention the precise location of real estate properties; in two cases only, they mention a house of Bāb al-Muṣallā located in the Mūṣlī Alley[11] and another house of Bāb al-Muṣallā located in front of the tomb of Sayyidnā Ṣuhayb al-Rūmī.[12] Both locations were in Lower Mīdān, but directly south of the Qubbah al-Ḥamrā area, which constituted the southern end of the Bāb al-Muṣallā neighborhood.

The neighborhood stretched along Sulṭānī Street, which crosses al-Mīdān all along, the Bāb al-Muṣallā Mosque area being the hub of religious and economic activities. Other religious centers were also in the neighborhood: the Sayyīdnā Bishārah Mosque to the east of Sulṭānī Street,[13] the 'Umarīyah Mosque in the Arba'īn Alley,[14] and the tomb of Sīdī 'Asqalān close to the Muṣallā Mosque. But these centers were marginal compared to the Muṣallā Mosque and its pivotal role in the neighborhood's life.

Sulṭānī Street was the main economic artery of Bāb al-Muṣallā; on both sides, there were shops (entrepôts) for the sale of cereals (*bāykahs*) and other shops providing countrymen with services such as smithing, woodworking, cotton ginning, and the like. A slaughterhouse was located in an alley branching from Sulṭānī Street towards the east; its presence proves that there was a cattle trade going on between countrymen and the local population. In addition to this concentration of economic activities in Sulṭānī Street, other individual shops or clusters of shops were located in various alleys and squares providing the local population with all kinds of services.[15]

The residential alleys were on both sides of Sulṭānī Street and were concentrated on the west side between Sulṭānī Street and an almost parallel alley, the Mukhallalātī Alley. On the east side, the concentration decreased greatly and there were fewer residential alleys, since they were limited by gardens[16] around the Muṣallā Mosque to the east, other gardens in the Shāghūr neighborhood, and the Bāb al-Saghīr Cemetery.[17] On this side were located big cereal shops, which required big areas.

There was no need for each alley to have both ends joining Sulṭānī Street and Mukhallalātī Alley. An alley might end in another alley, which in turn might end in Sulṭānī Street or Mukhallalātī Alley in order to facilitate defense. Most alleys were parallel to each other and led to secondary alleys with dead ends. These were useful for security purposes and for the privacy of family life. No alley crossed Sulṭānī Street and continued to the other side.

In the samples selected for this study, the registers of al-Mīdān Court mention, in addition to the main Sulṭānī Street, twenty-eight alleys in the Bāb al-Muṣallā neighborhood: Abū al-Burghol, Abū Māylah, al-Arba'īn, 'Asqalān, 'Azzām, Bādir, al-Baqqārah, al-Bīṭār, al-Būshī, al-Ḥabbālah, Ḥamad, al-Ḥawārinah, al-Jūwwāni, al-Mazra'ah, al-Mujtahid, al-Mukhallalātī, al-Nashshār, al-Qamlah, Qawlabah, al-Qubbar al-Ḥamrā, Qūwayq, al-Sammān, al-Sha'rīyah, Sukkar, al-Tayāmina, al-Turkmān, al-Wasṭānī, and al-Zayn.

Some alleys were important and are still in existence; others were secondary and merged with other alleys. The location of a number of alleys and their other names are clearly mentioned in the records. For instance, the Arba'īn Alley (Alley of the Forty) was near the Tayāmina Alley, and the Bādir Alley was often named al-Muṣallā Alley because of its closeness to the Muṣallā Mosque.[18] In 1859, the Baqqārah Alley was designated as the Great Baqqārah Alley,[19] a designation used in a cadastral map prepared in 1934 (evidence of the expansion of the Baqqārah Alley). Close to the latter was the Bīṭār Alley. The Ḥamad

Alley branched from the Bādir Alley, and al-Zayn Alley was known as the Jūbān Alley,[20] named after the Jūbān family (whose importance is unknown). The 'Asqalān Alley received its name from the tomb of Sīdī 'Asqalān and was running to the east of Sulṭānī Street. The records mention, in the vicinity, the existence of the Sīdī 'Asqalān Fountain[21], and the Wasṭānī Alley (the Median Alley) was named the al-Maṣbanāt (Soap Works) Alley.

Some of these alleys are mentioned in one sample only: for instance, the Nashshār Alley and the Qawlabah Alley are mentioned only in Sample 5 (1874-75), and the Qūwayq Alley in the preceding sample (1862-63). Other alleys, like the Turkmān, the Sha'rīyah, the 'Azzām, and the Qamlah Alleys, in addition to some localities along Sulṭānī Street, were parts of the al-Qubbah al-Ḥamrā (Red Dome) area; but this dome has disappeared and the area's name is now al-Makhfar (the police station). Because of the lack of specialized topographic studies, it is difficult to know which alleys merged with each other and which new alleys were opened.

It is interesting to note that some alleys, like the Turkmān Alley, were named after a specific ethnic group; others were named after a specific region from which the people migrated, like the Tayāmina Alley for people from Wādī al-Tīm and the Ḥawārinah for the people from the Ḥawrān. Outside the city, several other alleys were named after the Ḥawārinah, as in the Shāghūr and Sinānīyah neighborhoods; this fact points to the great number of people who migrated from the Ḥawrān to Damascus. Some other alleys were named after families, like the Banī Sukkar Alley and the Banī al-Mujtahid Alley, in which each family owned many residential and commercial properties in addition to their family endowments (private *waqfs*). Without being comprehensive, the map in figure 1 includes many alleys; it does not indicate, however, any changes or modifications in them.

On average, an alley was three to five meters wide. As shown in the map, the number of houses located between two given alleys varied between two and six or more. The alleys, of course, were not identical in terms of population and number of houses.

Each alley had one or more blind alleyways on which the houses had their doors. Alleyways were named after alleys; for example, there was the Alleyway (*dakhleh*) of Abū Māylah, the Alleyway of al-Mujtahid, the Yābūsi Alleyway in al-Tayāmina, and the Mashā'ilī Alleyway in the Wasṭānī Alley.[22] The Zābūqa Alley[23] is also mentioned; it was narrow and long and probably had an open end. In some alleys there was a square, like the Lawzah (Almond Tree) Square in the Tayāmina Alley,[24] the square in the al-Qubbah al-Ḥamrā,[25] the Wasṭānī Alley

Square,[26] and the Ḥabbālah Square.[27] On the east side of Bāb al-Muṣallā, houses were surrounded on three sides by three different squares.[28] Some alleys had a hill; the Sūwayyim Hill in the Mukhallalātī Alley was named after the Abī Sūwayyim family and their house in that alley.[29] Sometimes an alley hill is mentioned, as in the case of the Jūwānī Alley (the Inner Alley).[30] It also seems that the alleys had gates; the registers mention the Ḥabbālah Gate near the alleyway of Abū Māylah.[31] No other information is recorded about these gates.

Quarters (*ḥarahs*) are mentioned as parts of the alleys, as in the following expression: "the house in the Tayāmina Alley in the Inner Quarter" (al-Ḥārah al-Jūwānīyah),[32] an indication that the quarter in this context is a derivation of the alley and perhaps that the alley in question is a big area. The registers mention "the house of the quarter's chief" (Shaykh al-ḥārah) north of a house being sold,[33] but we do not know if the quarter's chief was chief of an alley or of a quarter, that is, a part of an alley area. The registers also mention the title of "Chief of the Young" (Shaykh al-shabāb)[34] with no relation to a specific location; we do not know if this title belongs to a quarter, to an alley, to the Bāb al-Muṣallā neighborhood as a whole, or if it is merely a nickname.

Social Structure of Bāb al-Muṣallā

It is possible, from real estate sale and purchase contracts, to identify the various social groups that lived in Bāb al-Muṣallā. The house (*al-dār*) was the basic real estate unit, followed by the partition (*maqsam al-dār*), an independent part carved out from the house, and the square (*murabba'*), a large room within the house and an independent residence when sold separately. Being cheap, the *murabba'* was suitable to people with limited income. There was also the *farankah*, an upper room, and the *mashraqah*, a roof room, or simply a rooftop, used mostly during the summer; in some instances, each one of these was sold separately.

A review of individual real estate sale and purchase transactions (for a whole house or part thereof) that took place in Bāb al-Muṣallā during the period 1825-75 shows which social group was more or less active than other groups in selling or purchasing real estate properties. These differences are shown in the five samples selected from the registers of the Mīdān Religious Court (tables 1-5).

Table 1.
Residential Real Estate Transactions by Various Social Groups in Bāb al-Muṣallā, First Sample (Rajab 7, 1240-Rajab 7, 1241/February 25, 1825-February 15, 1826)

	Buyers						Sellers					
Social group	*Contracts*	*%*	*Total shares*	*%*	*Cost (piasters)*	*%*	*Contracts*	*%*	*Total shares*	*%*	*Cost (piasters)*	*%*
Shaykhs	1	2.50	24	3.25	565	1.79	—	—	—	—	—	—
Ḥājjis	15	37.50	273	36.99	10,741	33.94	13	32.50	242	33.52	11,009	33.21
Sharīfs	5	12.50	87	11.79	3,960	12.51	3	7.50	48	6.65	2,360	7.21
Military (*Aghas, Jorbajis*)	4	10.00	64	8.67	3,700	11.94	3	7.50	52	7.20	2,720	8.21
Ordinary people (no title)	6	15.00	110	14.91	3,195	10.10	6	15.00	95	13.16	2,940	8.87
Women	7	17.50	144	19.51	6,445	20.37	11	27.50	213	29.50	8,636	26.06
(Christians)	(3)						(1)					
Men (Christians)	2	5.00	36	4.88	2,960	9.35	4	10.00	72	9.97	5,480	16.44
(Christians, total)	(5)	(12.50)	(84)	(11.38)	(4,035)	(12.75)	(5)	(12.50)	(84)	(11.63)	(6,155)	(18.57)
Total	40	100.00	738	100.00	31,566	100.00	40	100.00	722	100.00	33,145	100.00

Table 2.
Residential Real Estate Transactions by Various Social Groups in Bāb al-Muṣallā, Second Sample (Rajab 25, 1250-Rajab 25, 1251/November 27, 1834-November 18, 1835)

	Buyers						*Sellers*					
Social group	*Contracts*	%	*Total shares*	%	*Cost (piasters)*	%	*Contracts*	%	*Total shares*	%	*Cost (piasters)*	%
Ḥājjis	1	14.28	24	16.67	500	9.00	—	—	—	—	—	—
Military (*Aghas, Jorbajis*)	1	14.28	24	16.67	1,300	23.42	—	—	—	—	—	—
Ordinary people	1	14.28	12	8.33	300	5.41	1	10.00	24	13.19	1,200	15.09
Women	3	42.88	60	41.66	2,850	51.35	7	70.00	128	70.33	5,250	66.04
(Christian)	(1)						(1)					
Men (Christians)	1	14.28	24	16.67	600	10.82	2	20.00	30	16.48	1,500	18.87
(Christians, total)	(2)	(28.57)	(48)	(33.33)	(2,000)	(36.03)	(3)	(30.00)	(38)	(20.88)	(2,500)	(31.45)
Total	7	100.00	144	100.00	5,550	100.00	10	100.00	182	100.00	7,950	100.00

Table 3.
Residential Real Estate Transactions by Various Social Groups in Bāb al-Muṣallā, Third Sample (Rabīʻ al-Awwal 1, 1262-Rabīʻ al-Awwal 1, 1263/February 27, 1846-February 17, 1847)

	Buyers						Sellers					
Social group	*Contracts*	%	*Total shares*	%	*Cost (piasters)*	%	*Contracts*	%	*Total shares*	%	*Cost (piasters)*	%
Shaykhs	—	—	—	—	—	—	1	16.67	3	3.03	600	17.91
Ḥājjis	2	22.22	34	26.16	1,350	22.88	—	—	—	—	—	—
Ordinary people (no title)	5	55.56	48	36.92	2,450	41.53	2	33.33	36	36.36	1,450	43.28
Women	1	11.11	24	18.46	1,200	20.34	3	50.00	60	60.61	1,300	38.81
Men (Christians)	1	11.11	24	18.46	900	15.25	—	—	—	—	—	—
Total	9	100.00	130	100.00	5,900	100.00	6	100.00	99	100.00	3,350	100.00

Table 4.

Residential Real Estate Transactions by Various Social Groups in Bāb al-Muṣallā, Fourth Sample (Muḥarram 21, 1279-Muḥarram 10, 1280/July 19, 1862-June 27, 1863)

	Buyers						*Sellers*					
Social group	*Contracts*	%	*Total shares*	%	*Cost (piasters)*	%	*Contracts*	%	*Total shares*	%	*Cost (piasters)*	%
Shaykhs	2	9.09	33	7.78	4,250	3.67	2	9.09	48	10.81	14,570	12.91
Ḥājjis	4	18.18	80	18.87	24,512	22.05	1	4.55	8	1.80	2,000	1.77
Sharīfs	2	9.09	48	11.32	45,500	39.32	1	4.55	24	5.41	37,500	33.22
Military (*Aghas, Jorbajis*)	1	4.55	24	5.66	1,200	1.04	—	—	—	—	—	—
Ordinary people (no title)	4	18.18	78	18.40	6,750	5.83	7	31.81	150	33.78	21,700	19.23
Women	2	9.09	28	6.60	3,300	2.85	9	40.91	178	40.09	31,600	28.00
(Christian)							(1)	(4.55)				
Men (Christians)	7	31.82	133	31.37	29,300	25.24	2	9.09	36	8.11	5,500	4.87
(Christians, total)	—	—	—	—	—	—	(3)	(13.64)	(37)	(8.33)	(5,750)	(5.09)
Total	22	100.00	424	100.00	114,812	100.00	22	100.00	444	100.00	112,870	100.00

Table 5.

Residential Real Estate Transactions by Various Social Groups in Bāb al-Muṣallā, Fifth Sample (Dhu al-Hijjah 16, 1290-Dhu al-Hijjah 16, 1291/February 4, 1874-January 24, 1875)

	Buyers						*Sellers*					
Social group	*Contracts*	%	*Total shares*	%	*Cost* (piasters)*	%	*Contracts*	%	*Total shares*	%	*Cost (piasters)*	%
Shaykhs	2	12.50	25	10.41	2,400	5.90	2	16.67	20	14.81	4,770	28.01
Ḥājjis	7	43.75	94	39.18	18,031	44.33	—	—	—	—	—	—
Sharīfs	2	12.50	41	17.08	11,342	27.89	1	8.33	24	17.78	3,180	18.67
Ordinary people	—	—	—	—	—	—	4	33.33	22	16.30	3,308	19.43
Women	5	31.25	80	33.33	8,900	21.88	5	41.67	69	51.11	5,770	33.89
(Christian)	(1)											
(Christians, total)	(1)	(6.25)	(24)	(10.00)	(3,710)	(9.12)	—	—	—	—	—	—
Total	16	100.00	240	100.00	40,673	100.00	12	100.00	135	100.00	17,028	100.00

*In this sample, six purchase contracts and five sale contracts were paid in French gold pounds. One contract was paid in Turkish Majidi gold pounds; in addition, one purchase contract and one sale contract were paid in riyal fans (for coins at the time, see my book, *Essays on the Economic and Social History of Modern Syria* [in Arabic; Damascus, 1985], pp. 85-91). Because of discrepancies in the exchange rates of these currencies in the local, Ottoman, and international markets, I have used the exchange rates adopted by the Damascus Religious Court on Ṣafar 10, 1296 A.H./February 18, 1879 (Damascus Register no. 70, pp. 147-48) on the following basis: one French gold pound = 106 piasters; one Turkish Majidi gold pound = 122 piasters; one riyal fans = 20 piasters.

From these samples I selected real estate properties sold or puchased by individuals. Those properties which were sold or purchased by a group of partners belonging mostly to a single, big family were not counted because they were mainly inherited. Real estate transactions by individuals are more likely to show which social groups could afford to buy and which were compelled to sell for financial reasons.

In the first sample (1825-26), the equal number of purchasers and sellers reached a maximum of 40 contracts for each category, showing a stable real estate market, a tendency to avoid property concentration in a few hands, and a balance between individual and community properties. The number of individual contracts thereafter decreased, with a minimum in the 1834-35 and 1846-47 samples. The imposition of military conscription by the Egyptian rulers and the rebellion against them beginning in 1834-35 seem to have created an atmosphere of fear and instability unfavorable for investment.

On the other hand, military conscription limited rural migration to the city, where individuals could hardly escape the state's authority. Since 1844, the Ottoman army had been trying to subjugate the people of Damascus, but it was faced by the resistance of local military leaders, namely, those of the al-Mīdān area. This fact might explain the non-participation of the military in real estate transactions, in contrast to the period of the first sample (1825-26).

In the fourth sample (1862-63), individual buyers and sellers again increased in equal proportions; this was a period of quiet in the wake of the social and religious turmoil of 1860. According to al-Qasāṭlī, during the period 1861-63 business was excellent in Damascus; the products were good and a large amount of gold was owned by individuals.[35] In the fifth sample (1874-75), however, the proportion of buyers and sellers decreased again, partly because of the economic crisis resulting from a fall in silk prices and a drought. As a witness to these developments, al-Qasāṭlī relates that "the prices went higher and higher [in 1873] . . . Some poor people, in dire need, started eating herbs and plants. And there was, in 1875, a new epidemic of yellow fever that lasted two months; 9,200 people died, including 250 Christians.[36]

Since the participation of the military (*aghas* and *jorbajis*) in the real estate market was determined by the military situation and the attitude of the Ottoman state toward them, the five samples show them as the social group that participated the least in that market, with a total of 6 buyers and 3 sellers. The shaykhs came next, with a total of 5 buyers and 5 sellers. This small number might be explained by the fact that in Bāb al-Muṣallā few people had this title, either because there were few important religious centers or because the clergy of this neighborhood had no big money. It should also be noted that the shaykhs mentioned in the fifth sample were exclusively from the Maghrib. The third least participating group was the noble *sharīfs*, with a total of 9 buyers and 5 sellers. This small participation might be explained by the demographic structure of Bāb al-Muṣallā; the neighborhood was populated by people from the Maghrib, as well as by Turkmān, Bedouins, and migrants from rural areas, most of whom were not *sharīfs*. However, the fact that buyers were more numerous than sellers indicated a trend of stability among the noble *sharīfs* residing in the neighborhood.

The participation of the *ḥājjis*, that is, those Muslims who had performed the pilgrimage, in the real estate market was wider than that of the religious and military groups; they occupied second place after the women. Among the *ḥājjis*, there was a total of 29 buyers (the highest rate) and 14 sellers, which indicates a tendency to invest in real estate and to reside in Bāb al-Muṣallā. This tendency might be explained by a number of factors, namely, the location of Bāb al-Muṣallā on the way to Mecca and the fact that many residents of the neighborhood were originally from the Ḥawrān; they or their acquaintances in the country used to supply the Syrian pilgrim caravan and its guards with camels and food and often accompanied it. Moreover, many residents originally from the Maghrib had the title of Hājj.

The participation of the common people in the real estate market was equal to that of the *ḥājjis* (16 buyers and 20 sellers), but with some difference. Although the total of buyers and sellers was identical in both groups, buyers in the *ḥājjis* and the common people accounted for 618 and 448 shares respectively. In other words, common people were selling more than buying, most probably because of the troubled economic situation in Damascus at that time. This fact is evidenced by the low cost of real estate bought by common people compared with that bought by other groups.

Women were one of the most active groups in the real estate market, with a total of 18 buyers and 35 sellers. The proportion of sellers among women, 66 percent, is higher than for any other group; it shows that women invested in real estate more than in agricultural lands, which they could not exploit easily. This high participation was more than a mere liquidation of inherited assets; in the above samples, women appear as individual owners of purchased or sold estates, who enjoyed relative wealth and financial autonomy resulting from inheritance, work, dowry, alimony, or jewelry ownership. Most probably, women from rural origin had acquired those traits from the very nature of rural life.

The participation of Christian men and women is noteworthy; with a total of 16 buyers and 11 sellers, they ranked fourth, immediately following the women, *ḥājjis,* and common people, and showing a tendency to settle permanently in Bāb al-Muṣallā.

It is interesting to note, in these samples, the relation between the various social groups and the size of residential real estate transactions in terms of value and shares. The women remained first in purchasing and selling transactions (984 shares, or *qirāts*), followed by the *ḥājjis* (775 shares), the common people (575 shares), the Christians (339 shares), the *sharīfs* (272 shares), the military (164 shares), and the shaykhs (153 shares). This sequence in the size of residential real estate transactions is identical to the aforementioned sequence in purchase and sale contracts.

However, the sequence is different regarding the value of those transactions. The greatest amounts were paid by the *sharīfs,* with a total of 103,842 piasters and a price of about 382 piasters per share; these figures show a preference for distinctive residences as to quality and location. Second in order were the women, with a total value of 75,251 piasters and a price of 76.47 piasters per share, meaning that real estate properties owned by women were modest in quality, location, and size. The third were the *ḥājjis,* with a total value of 68,143 piasters and a price of 91.21 piasters per share. The fourth were the Christians, with a total value of 54,350 piasters and a price of 130.07 piasters per share; in terms of quality, location, and size, their real estate properties were superior to those owned by the women and the *ḥājjis.* The fifth group according to the value of their properties were the common people, with a total of 43,293 piasters. However, the price per share of their properties, which amounted to 75.29 piasters, ranks them sixth among the social groups. The total value of real estate owned by the shaykhs was 27,155 piasters, with a price of 150.16 piasters per share (the second best, following the *sharīf* group price). The least expensive were the properties of the military, with a total value of 9,000 piasters and a price of 54.11 piasters per share; these figures show a loss of status resulting from the reformation and modernization process initiated by the Ottoman state.

Economic Structure of Bāb al-Muṣallā

Economic activities in Bāb al-Muṣallā were focused on marketing and services. According to the registers of the Mīdān Religious Court, production activities were less important. In fact, the location of the neighborhood and the social structure of its population determined, to a great extent, the pattern of its economic activities.

The prime economic activity was the marketing of cereals, mainly in the numerous entrepôts (*bāykahs*) of Sulṭānī Street and those around the Muṣallā Mosque, which were flanked by large pieces of land. Other *baykahs*, on a smaller scale, were located in the alleys. The size of an entrepôt (*bāykah*) varied with the number of stone arches supporting its ceiling. The small *bāykah* consisted of four walls, a ceiling, and sanitary facilities; the middle-size *bāykah* had four walls, a ceiling supported by a stone arch, one door, and sanitary facilities. One large *bāykah* was owned by a lady, Raqīyah, daughter of Khāled Agha Qaṣṣāb Bāshī.[37] Another, located in front of al-Mazra'ah Alley, was for the sale of wheat; it had four walls and a ceiling supported by stone dividings, shop screens, and sanitary facilities.[38] Sometimes an upper level was built consisting of a *farankah*, with four walls, a ceiling, a door, and some windows; it was usually appended to an adjacent building, a residence, or another *bāykah* and was reached by a ladder.[39]

Although the *bāykah* could be used for selling many kinds of cereals, like the *bāykah* "for the sale of crops,"[40] some of them would specialize in a specific commodity, such as the above-mentioned *bāykah*, which specialized in wheat. Another is mentioned as specializing in straws; this one had four walls, a ceiling, a door, and sanitary facilities.[41] The owner of a *bāykah*, called a *bawāykī*, was known for buying up grains and selling them at exorbitant prices in out-of-season periods; as he became rich, he would lend to peasants and take a large portion of their crops. He would also cheat in measuring and weighing the crops.[42]

Some of the *bāykahs* were used not only for the marketing of cereals but also as hostels for peasants and their pack animals. One of them was a private *waqf* of the Sukkar family; it was located in front of al-Muṣallā Mosque and had hoes, two shops, a courtyard for tying up pack animals, certain rights, and sanitary facilities.[43] Of course, a *bāykah* of this size, with several buildings, was not covered by one ceiling, since it included an uncovered piece of land. We read, for instance, about "the rental of that piece of land without any building or plantation, located within the *bāykah*," in the private *waqf* of the Sukkar family, next to the house known as the "Sukkar family house" in Bāb al-Muṣallā.[44] It is interesting to note the dimensions of the rented piece of land in that *bāykah:* 37 cubits long and 30 cubits large; this unit is probably the Istambulic cubit,[45] equivalent to 68,5 centimeters.[46] Some of the *bāykahs* included an open place, like the Ṭuwayr *bāykah* in Sulṭānī Street close to the al-Qubbah al-Bayḍa and to the Ghawwaṣ.[47] Others included an open part and a covered part, like the *bāykah* in the Ḥabbālah Alley of Bāb al-Muṣallā, which "included a place partly open and partly covered, with four walls, a ceiling, a door and sanitary facilities."[48]

Among the other *bāykahs* whose owners and locations are mentioned in the records are the one belonging to Khalīl al-Taqī, called briefly the "Taqi *bāykah*," located in Sulṭānī Street,[49] and the *bāykahs* of Maḥmūd Agha Tello and Muṣṭafa Tello, both located on the east side of the street.[50] Two other *bāykahs* were located in the Arba'īn Alley and the Bādir Alley; another, the al-Zurayq *bāykah*, was west of the coffeehouse, in front of the Muṣallā Mosque.[51] It is clear, from the names of the owners, that the *bāykahs* were mostly owned by military *aghas* who monopolized the cereals trade in Bāb al-Muṣallā using their military influence. Moreover, some merchants became military men to protect their economic interests.

If the *bāykah* was originally used for the storage and marketing of cereals, other buildings, like the store (*al-makhzan*), the courtyard (*al-ḥawsh*), and the hostel (al-khān), were used for housing pack animals and, in some instances, their owners. The store is always described as a place for tying up pack animals; it consisted of four walls, a ceiling, a door, and sanitary facilities. In one instance, a store was taken from a house in the Arba'īn Alley before it was bequeathed as a *waqf* by its owner;[52] in another instance, a kitchen and a room were taken from a house bequeathed as a *waqf* in Sulṭānī Street and transformed into stores for tying up pack animals.[53] Other stores are mentioned, one in the Qubbah al-Ḥamra area, and two others in the Bādir Alley (the store of the Qara family and the store of the Muṣallā Mosque).[54] We can conclude from these data that the stores were of medium size and located in many areas.

As to the *ḥawsh*, it seems that changes were introduced in its use during the fifty-year period selected for this study. In contrast with the store, the *ḥawsh* was not taken from a house; it was mostly an independent piece of real estate. However, stores and *ḥawshes* were contiguous to residential buildings. A *ḥawsh* could be a part of a *bāykah;* it consisted basically of "an open place, four walls, a door, and sanitary facilities,"[55] and it was used to house pack animals in general. During the period under study, many *ḥawshes* were mentioned in the records as being located in the Mukhallalātī, Wasṭānī, al-Qubbah al-Ḥamrā, and Mujtahid Alleys. The *ḥawsh* was named after its owner (individual or family), like the Abdul Ḥaq Ḥawsh, the al-Kaḥil Ḥawsh, the Banī Mujtahid Ḥawsh, and the Banī Sukkar Ḥawsh.[56] Although the *ḥawsh* was originally used for housing pack animals, as mentioned earlier, it started to be used for residential purposes once a number of rooms were built in it. This change of pattern became more frequent after the 1860 events, when some Christians fled to al-Mīdān and Bāb al-Muṣallā from Mount Lebanon and even from the inner city of Damascus seeking refuge and security; in fact, the Mīdān and Bāb al-Muṣallā areas had no trouble during that period. In a lawsuit concerning the *waqf* of the Sukkar family and filed at the Mīdān Court on January 17, 1863, a *ḥawsh* located in the Sukkar family's *waqf* in the Baqqāra Alley was described as "comprising three square rooms for Christian residents."[57] The al-Kaḥil Ḥawsh in the al-Qubbah al-Ḥamra Alley comprised an open space, two square rooms, a kitchen, a toilet, and sanitary facilities, and was owned by Muslims; the identity of the residents, however, is not mentioned.[58]

In contrast with the numerous *bāykahs*, stores, and *ḥawshes*, there were few *khāns* located in Bāb al-Muṣallā; they were more related to trade activities for cereals, textiles, and condiments, as was the case for many *khāns* inside Damascus. The records mention the Abū Khalil Daqqāq's *khān* in Sulṭānī Street contiguous to the Uẓon Coffeehouse, the Abū Jawf *khān* close to the Ibn al-Taqi's *bāykah* in Sulṭānī Street, and another *khān* owned by Faris Agha Nūri close to the Muṣṭafa Agha Tello *bāykah* on the east side of Sulṭānī Street. Two other *khāns* are mentioned: the Fakhūra Khān in the Jūwwāni Alley[59] and the Banī Mujtahid khān.[60] The most frequently mentioned is the Dāwūd Dūmāni khān located in the Tayāmina Alley and known also as the Blacksmith khān; it is described as a place "for housing pack animals, consisting of an open space with an elevated pool, two *bāykahs*, three rooms, and a stone ladder leading to a rooftop, with three rooms and sanitary facilities."[61]

Another vital place for the rural people was the wood storehouse (*al-ḥāṣil*). The records mention, in 1825, the *ḥāṣil* of Shaykh 'Umar Efendi al-Mujtahid in Sulṭānī Street. Fifty years later (in 1874), his son, Shaykh Muḥammad Sa'īd Efendi al-Mujtahid, sold to another member of the family 13 2/3 shares of "the whole *ḥāṣil* used for the sale of wood, in addition to the oven (*ītūn*) within it," at a price of 50,000 piasters.[62] It is noteworthy that the Mujtahid family consecutively owned this wood storehouse for such a long time and that an exorbitant price (equal to that of several medium-size houses) was paid to purchase less than two-thirds of the storehouse; it shows that the wood trade was very lucrative for the Mujtahid family. The influence of this family and its religious status explain why an alley in Bāb al-Muṣallā was named the Mujtahid Alley.[63] It is confirmed, in the *Dictionary of Syrian Crafts*,[64] that the wood trade was very lucrative. The Mujtahid family also owned many private *waqfs*.

It is also noteworthy that the Mujtahid wood storehouse included a limekiln that used a variety of limestones; according to al-Qāsimi, it is not unusual for a *ḥawāṣli* (wood storehouse owner) to build a limekiln in his storehouse. Another limekiln was owned in Bādir Alley by Hajj

Anis Agha Sukkar, a big grain merchant and owner of a private *waqf.* On April 13, 1863, this limekiln was purchased by Ilyās Ibn Ibrāhim al-Ṣarjī for a price of 4,500 piasters; it was described, when sold, as comprising "a pit, a limekiln, a straw stack, an open space, and sanitary facilities."[65]

Among the service centers located in various parts of Bāb al-Muṣallā, there were three bakeries: one in Wasṭānī Alley, another in Tayāmina Alley, and the third in Bādir Alley. Only one public bath is mentioned, the Sanqar Bath on the west side of Sulṭānī Street; perhaps the residents were also using other public baths in Sūwayqah and Lower Mīdān. Three coffeehouses are also mentioned: one facing the Two Feast Muṣallā (Muṣallā al-'Idayn) on the west side (perhaps the Uẓon Coffeehouse), another named the Mujtahid Coffeehouse on the east side of Sulṭānī Street, and a third known as the Wasṭānī Coffeehouse (perhaps in Tayāmina Alley), described as consisting of four walls, a number of rounded stone benches, a stove for coffee cooking, an outside resting area, a ceiling, a door, and sanitary facilities.[66] The records also mention a mill, the Widows' Mill, "consisting of four walls, a ceiling, a door, a millstone, and some stores belonging, in part, to the Ḥaramayn *waqf.*"[67]

There were also, in the alleys of Bāb al-Muṣallā, various shops for manufacturing textiles, like the *alāja*, a striped fabric made of silk (weft) and cotton (warp), with a high price due to the prevalence of silk. A shop of this kind is mentioned as located in the Mukhallalātī Alley and as consisting of six looms; in 1826, its Christian owners sold it to a Muslim *agha.* Another was in Tayāmina Alley; it was purchased, in 1859, by Khawājā Jiryis Ibn Khawājā Yusuf al-'Absī and Khawājā Abdullah Ibn Khawājā Mikhā'il Barṣa (in equal shares) from Hajj Muṣṭafa Khalīl al-Zurayk; it consisted of four looms, with pleats, shelves, and sanitary facilities.[68] In Jūwwānī Alley, a single individual bought a textile shop (for *'abāyā* fabric) and the whole building in which it was located; the shop consisted of four walls and a ceiling, with windows and one door, and five looms with their equipment.[69] We know from the first examples that the textile workshops were distributed in the various alleys and mostly owned by one person, a fact which points to an individualistic pattern of business. When there was more than one owner, usually inheritance was involved. The textile business was not monopolized by any religious group; the ownership of the workshops was transferred among local residents from many denominations.

The last example of purchasing a shop and the building in which it was located suggests that the purchasing contract included neither the shop's equipment, namely, the *'abāyā* fabric looms and related tools, known as *gedik*, nor the right to use the shop's looms, known as *khulū* (key money). It was possible to purchase the shop's equipment and/or its key money without purchasing the shop itself or the building.[70] When the shop's land was a *waqf* that could not be sold, it was possible to sell the building and the shop, as well as the equipment and/or the shop's key money. Usually the contract specified clearly what was actually purchased. For example, when the contract specified that the whole shop had been purchased, it meant both the land and the building without the equipment and the right to use it, unless otherwise specified.[71]

The existence of a number of textile shops, including their equipment and key money, and the number of transactions effected in short periods show the difficulties faced by the Syrian textile industry (the *alāja* industry, in particular) during the nineteenth century because of competition by similar European products in terms of price, quality, and imitation of local models.[72] The domination of foreign capital is shown by the fact that most of Bāb al-Muṣallā real estate properties included in the fifth sample (1874-75), were sold in French gold pounds, because of the depreciation of the local currency (the piaster) and the lack of confidence in it.[73]

Most of the specialized shops in Bāb al-Muṣallā were grouped on the east and west sides of Sulṭānī Street. There were shops for making saddles or door frames, and others for tinsmithing, weaving, rifle repairing, and so forth. It is interesting to note that a great number of shops were endowed as private or public *waqfs* and dedicated to al-Muṣallā Mosque or al-Ḥaramayn.

It is possible, by reviewing some craft-related surnames of Bāb al-Muṣallā's residents, to gain a clear idea of the economic activities of the neighborhood, namely, the manufacturing of some products needed by rurals, the marketing of cereals, and the provision of various services. The following surnames were related to grains and cereals: al-Jammāl (the camel driver), al-Khānāti (the *khān* owner), al-Qabbānī (the weighing man), al-Mugharbil (the sifter), Abū al-Burghol (the Burghol merchant), al-Ṭaḥḥan (the miller), and al-Khawlī (the expert in farming and production; the plantation supervisor). Other surnames were related to products and services needed by rurals and local residents: al-Julaylātī (the maker of covers for pack animals), al-Baradi'ī (the saddle maker), al-Biṭār (the farrier), al-Zarābilī (the *zarboul* maker; a *zarboul* is a thick shoe for peasants), al-Ṣarmayātī (the shoemaker), and al-Basṭāṭī (the peddler). Other craftsmen provided services to both rurals and local residents, like al-'Akkām (the camel head driver, especially in the pilgrimage caravan), al-Mashā'ilī (the torchbearer accompanying the pilgrims), al-Sha'āl (the lamplighter), al-Bawāridī (the rifle repairman), al-Bunduqjī (the rifle maker), al-Masālkhi (the slaughterer), al-Qaṣṣāb Bashī (the chief butcher), and al-Dabbāgh (the tanner). Other surnames were related to the textile industry, like al-Ḥarirātī (the silkman), al-Ṣabbāgh (the dyer), al-Mulqī (an assistant to the weaver), al-Alajātī (the *alāja* manufacturer), and al-Farrā (the furrier). We also find other surnames, like al-Naḥḥās (the coppersmith), al-Mubayyiḍ (the whitener of copper cutlery), al-Ḥajjār (the stone-cutter), al-Daqqāq (a mason building walls with compressed clay), al-Dahhān (the painter), al-Qazzaz (the glassmaker), al-Qaḍamānī (the nut and bean merchant), al-Muḥammiṣ (the roaster), al-Nashawātī (the starch merchant), al-Laḥḥām (the butcher), al-Khabbāz (the baker), and al-Zabbāl (the garbage collector).[74]

When we consider these craft-related surnames and the names of the various alleys in which they lived, we find that no alley was restricted to residents from a single craft or a group of related crafts. In other words, there was no segregation of the alleys according to their residents' crafts; rather, each alley was inhabited by a mixture of people of all trades with various incomes. Thus the residents of a specific alley, although having different socioeconomic status, were living together in an environment of social integration and tolerance.

On another level, the real estate market played an active role in the economic life of Bāb al-Muṣallā. The amounts of money invested in the sector were huge in comparison with the prices in the Damascus area of agricultural land, commodities, and animals, as mentioned in the registers of the religious courts, in chronicles, and in reports by foreign consuls and other similar documents. The five selected samples show that the same persons purchased a number of residential properties and later sold some of them at different periods. It is noteworthy that women played a significant role in the purchase of real estate properties, in part or in total, because such investments were considered secure. Table 6 shows, in each sample, the amounts invested in real estate, the average price of a share, and the fluctuations resulting from the economic situation in general.

We note, in the second sample, a decrease in the average price of a share during the Egyptian rule; later, during the third sample period, we note an increase by about one-third, probably due to a depreciation of the piaster and to the adverse effects of European merchandise competition. During the fourth sample period (1862-63), the average price reached a maximum because of a fall in the piaster exchange rate to gold currencies, which were dominating the local exchange market;[75] an increase in mason wages and in prices of building materials;[76] and a rise in demand on real estate properties in Bāb al-Muṣallā, especially by Christians in the wake of the 1860 incidents. Again, during the fifth

Table 6.
Sale and Purchase Contracts of Real Estate Properties in Bāb al-Muṣallā, 1825-75

Sample	*Number of contracts*	*Total shares*	*Total costs*	*Average price of a share*
1825-26	50	936	43,618	46.60
1834-35	13	254	11,350	44.69
1846-47	11	178	10,335	58.06
1862-63	24	490	124,912	254.40
1874-75	17	283	55,442	195.91
Total	115	2,141	245,657	599.66

sample period, the average price decreased as a result of bad harvest, high cereal prices, and adverse general economic conditions, according to a contemporary chronicler, al-Qasāṭli (see *al-Rawḍah al-ghannā*).[77] An analysis of the contracts on which table 6 is based shows that, during the five sample periods, about 50 percent of the transactions were concentrated in three alleys of Bāb al-Muṣallā (see table 7). We note from table 7 that the al-Qubbah al-Ḥamrā area—including the Turkmān, Shār, and ʿAzzām Alleys and some buildings in Sulṭānī Street—had the highest proportion of sale contracts (estimated at 19.13 percent). In comparison with the Wasṭānī and Tayāmina Alleys—respectively second and third in the number of contracts—the al-Qubbah al-Ḥamrā Alley had the lowest costs, the highest being those of Tayāmina Alley (in spite of the low number of contracts). Of course, this difference is due to a difference in prices, the impact of which will be dealt with in the following section, which deals with the integration of various social groups.

In its various forms, the *waqf* played an important role in the economic life of Bāb al-Muṣallā. A great number of commercial, agricultural, and residential real estate properties—*bāykahs*, shops, gardens, pieces of land, houses—were endowed as public *waqfs* to the Bāb al-Muṣallā

Table 7.
Real Estate Transactions in Main Areas of Concentration in Bāb al-Muṣallā, 1825-75

Alley	*Number of contracts*	*% of total*	*Number of shares*	*% of total*	*Costs (in piasters)*	*% of total*
al-Qubbah al-Ḥamrā	22	19.13	416	19.42	23,031	9.37
Wasṭānī	19	16.52	337	15.73	29,610	12.05
Tayāmina	16	13.91	265	12.37	43,478	17.70
Total	57	49.56	1,018	47.52	96,119	39.12

Mosque or to the Ḥaramayn or as private "family" *waqfs*, especially to the advantage of some great families like the Sukkar or the Mujtahid family. It is difficult to determine, in the samples, the ratios of private to public *waqfs* and then follow the chronological variations of both types. In the history of Syria, the Ottomans of the sixteenth century were known for their great charitable achievements, such as the mosques built by some famous governors (*wālis*) and to which a high proportion of public *waqfs* were endowed. In the eighteenth century, however, this trend was reversed; to avert their confiscation by the state, a great number of governors and rich people started endowing their properties to private *waqfs*. It is equally difficult to know in Bāb al-Muṣallā the type of *waqf* to which many real estate properties (many houses, in particular) belonged, because the registers of the Mīdān Religious Court do not specify the type or the beneficiary. The registers also mention the endowment to a public *waqf* of a proportion of the rental of an endowed piece of land on which a real estate property was built. But, in spite of these uncertainties, it is possible to know, in each sample, the overall ratio of endowed to nonendowed real estate properties by examining the various kinds of (a) totally or partly sold properties; (b) rented properties; (c) properties submitted for consideration by the court in any kind of litigation; and (d) properties contiguous, from all sides, to the above-mentioned.

The totals of owned and (privately and publicly) endowed real estate properties were 586 and 62, respectively, the ratios of the latter and the former to the total being 9.57 and 90.43 percent, respectively. But it is not possible to assess the significance of these ratios without a comparative study of other neighborhoods of Damascus during the same period. Nevertheless, the high proportion of owned real estate shows a trend of property acquisition and settlement in the neighborhood, despite the fact that a great number of families were newcomers,

Table 8.
Ratio of Owned to Endowed Real Estate in Bāb al-Muṣallā, 1825-75

	Residential		*Commercial*		*Agricultural*	
Sample	*Owned*	*Endowed*	*Owned*	*Endowed*	*Owned*	*Endowed*
1825-26	182	5	13	5	2	—
1834-35	76	—	6	—	2	1
1846-47	40	3	13	9	—	1
1862-63	97	7	27	16	2	4
1874-75	101	8	20	2	5	1
Total	496	23	79	32	11	7

Table 9.
Number of Public and Private Waqfs in Bāb al-Muṣallā

Type of real estate	*Public waqfs*		*Private waqfs*	
Residential	12		11	
Commercial	13		18	
Agricultural	4		3	
Total	29	(47.54%)	32	(52.46%)

immigration from other regions was continuous, and the newcomers were very different from each other, probably people with low incomes. Moreover, the low number of public *waqfs* in Bāb al-Muṣallā can be explained by the scarcity of religious buildings in the neighborhood and, except for the Muṣallā Mosque, by their insignificance in comparison with similar buildings inside Damascus and in some places outside the city.

It is noteworthy that the Ottomans did not build, in the Bāb al-Muṣallā neighborhood, any mosque like those of Darwīshīyah and Sinānīyah or even like that of Murādīyah in the immediate vicinity of Bāb al-Muṣallā. Similarly, they did not erect in it any important building of public or private use. Therefore, there was no need for them to endow any kind of *waqf* to Bāb al-Muṣallā.

The 62 real estate properties endowed as *waqfs* in Bāb al-Muṣallā were not predominantly public *waqfs.* Most of them were private *waqfs* used by some notable families like the Sukkar and Mujtahid, in addition to some *waqfs* endowed to the Two Holy Places (Mecca and Medina). Table 9 shows the proportion of each type of *waqf.*

In terms of their beneficiaries, the 29 public *waqfs* could be classified in three categories, as in table 10.

Table 10.
Beneficiaries of Public Waqfs in Bāb al-Muṣallā

Type of real estate	*al-Muṣallā Mosque*	*al-Ḥaramayn*	*Unspecified*
Residential	4	2	6
Commercial	5	3	5
Agricultural	3	–	1
Total	12	5	12

In the "unspecified" category, not only the beneficiaries, but also their residence or location (inside or outside the neighborhood), are unknown. Some *waqf* ground rents are not included in table 10, like the ground rent of residential buildings whose land was a *waqf*, its structure a property, and its ground rent an endowment to a specific charitable organization. For instance, the house in the Jūwwāni Alley had a yearly ground rent of five *miṣrīyah* (one-eighth of one piaster) endowed to the *waqf* of the Shāmīyah Burrānīyah School in Damascus;[78] another house, in the same alley, had a yearly ground rent of twenty *miṣrīyah* endowed to the same school.[79] Another example is a house in the Wasṭānī Alley whose ground rent of fifteen *miṣrīyah* was also endowed to the same school,[80] known as one of the Shafi'ī schools. No other endowment of a ground rent is mentioned in the registers. Moreover, there is no evidence of the Muslim rite which was predominant in Bāb al-Muṣallā during the period under study; we know that the many residents from the Maghrib observed the Maliki rite.

According to Shaykh 'Abd al-Qādir Badrān (died in 1346 A.H./1927-28), known for his knowledge of *waqf* affairs, no *waqf* was endowed to the Muṣallā Mosque;[81] he probably had in mind the time it was built, in 1209 (606 A.H.). The existence, during the period under study, of *waqfs* endowed to this mosque shows that they were acquired by stages; or Shaykh Badrān may not have found, at the time of his writing, any *waqf* belonging to the mosque. It is interesting to note that the records of the Mīdān Religious Court mention, on the fourth day of February 1874 (16 Dhū al-Hijjah 1290 A.H.), a house on Sulṭānī Street as "formerly from the *waqf* of the Muṣallā Mosque and presently the residence of Shaykh al-Najjar";[82] it might be, therefore, that the mosque lost it through substitution or appropriation.[83] Because of the misuse of the *waqfs* at that time, the Ottoman authorities straightened up the *waqf* affairs in Damascus during the period of administrative reorganization. It is mentioned, in 1862, that the director of the Damascus *waqf* had attested to the sale of the equipment and key money of a *waqf* shop located in Bāb al-Muṣallā.[84]

In 1834, Muḥammad al-Baghdādī al-Qādrī was the administrator of the Muṣallā Mosque Waqf, and Ibrāhīm al-Qabbānī was the trustee. This *waqf* seems to have generated, at that time, an extra income which allowed the purchase of a *bāykah* and a garden in the Muṣallā Alley (Bādir Alley).[85] It was mentioned, about twenty-five years later, that Muḥammad Agha Ibn 'Ibrahim Agha al-Qabbāni was, by a decree from the sultan, the administrator of the Muṣallā Mosque Waqf.[86]

The *waqfs* endowed to the Two Holy Places were under the responsibility of Muḥammad Amin Efendi Aḥmad Efendī al-Islambūlī, general trustee of these *waqfs*. In 1864, Ḥusayn Agha Ibn 'Ali Agha al-Qarahiṣār was his representative in Bāb al-Muṣallā; one year later, another representative is mentioned: Maḥmūd Agha Ibn Aḥmad Jalabī Shaykh al-Arḍ.[87]

From an economic viewpoint, the most well-known private *waqfs* were those of the Sukkar and Mujtahid families; they were fundamental to the wealth of both families. The Sukkar were from Turkmān, of military origin; they emerged from the Janissary and their grandfather was Amir Ḥasan Agha al-Turkmānī, one of the famous Janissaries of Damascus during the first quarter of the seventeenth century.[88] Members of the Sukkar family kept using the military titles of *agha* and *jorbaji* even when they became grain merchants; in addition to the *agha* title, some of them were called "dean of merchants." During the period under study, the members of the Sukkar family had to supervise and speak for four big private *waqfs:* the *waqf* of their forefather Amir Ḥasan Agha al-Turkmānī, the *waqf* of their grandfather Muḥammad Agha Shubaṣi, the *waqf* of their grandfather Ibrāhim al-Bitār, and the *waqf* of their grandmother Ṣaliḥa Kadin Bint Ḥusayn Basha al-Arnā'ūt.[89] These *waqfs* consisted of *bāykahs*, coffeeshops, lands, shops, and houses.

The Mujtahid family was also noted for the exploitation of big private *waqfs;* like the Sukkar family, they took advantage of their military influence, although they were known as a family of science and jurisprudence. Shaykh Muḥammad Jorbaji al-Mujtahid was the superintendent of the *waqf* endowed by his great grandfather Muṣṭafa al-Ḥūrānī.[90] Because of the competition in economics and politics between the Sukkar and the Mujtahid families and because of their conflicting interests in renting real estate properties and in their roles as authorized representatives in lawsuits between individuals from different families, the registers of the Mīdān Religious Court are full of lawsuits between both parties.[91] Other families also took advantage of private *waqfs* on a limited scale, like the Kharraṭ and the Farrā families as superintendents of the *waqf* endowed by their grandfather Qara Aṣlān, and the Barūdi family as superintendents of the *waqf* endowed by their grandfather Sulaymān al-Khawwām.

Private *waqfs* were rented for a long period of time by their own beneficiaries or by other individuals; the rental was modest and a portion of it was deducted for repair costs. The leasing of a *waqf* for a long period of time with a fixed rental was a blessing for the tenant because of the additional profit resulting from currency depreciation, especially during the nineteenth century. In some instances, the *waqf's* superintendent increased the rental, even before the end of the leasing period.

Nevertheless, the *waqf's* tenant, being usually from one of the beneficiary families, received most of the *waqf's* earnings and used them to consolidate his economic and political influence inside and outside Bāb al-Muṣallā to the detriment of other beneficiaries from his relatives.

Socioethnic Integration in Bāb al-Muṣallā

Because of its location and the services it provided, Bāb al-Muṣallā was inhabited by various social groups. One of them was the famous Janissaries of Turkmānī and Kurdish origins, who gradually became a local community engaged in commercial activities, namely, the grain trade. Another group was the Maghribīs, who figured as soldiers. Most of these were members of the Zawāwa tribe from the Kabyle Mountains in Algeria, and some were from Tunis and Tripoli; they grew in number during the nineteenth century after the occupation of Algeria by France. al-Mīdān and, in particular, Bāb al-Muṣallā also received a great number of Christians from the Ḥawrān and other neighboring regions who took advantage of religious tolerance in Syria under the Egyptian rule; as a consequence, the Melkite Patriarch Maximos II Maẓlūm built, in 1834-36, two churches in the Mīdān Quarter: one in Bāb al-Muṣallā and the other in Qurashi Alley. In addition, Ibrāhim Pasha allowed him, in 1833, to build a cathedral in the Zaytūn Quarter in Damascus. Because of the increasing number of Orthodox Christians coming to Mīdān from the Ḥawrān and Rāshayyā, especially after the 1860 events, a church was also built for them in Qurashi Alley in late 1862.[92]

Given the wide variety of social groups that had successively inhabited Bāb al-Muṣallā and that were different in their origins, activities, socioeconomic levels, and immigration motives, the question is: How did they live together and how cohesively were they integrated?

In fact, the coexistence of these groups and their social integration are obvious from many viewpoints: the meshing of their residences, the absorption by the neighborhood of a great number of immigrants, and the continuation of this peaceful coexistence in spite of the turmoil and crises which shook Damascus and the region. Through the five samples of our study, the registers of the Mīdān Religious Court provide us with precise and documented information about the variety of those groups and the extent of their integration as it appears from the contiguity of their properties.

Table 11 includes information about the identity of buyers and sellers of various real estate properties and the identity of owners of properties

Table 11.
Identity of Buyers and Sellers of Various Real Estate Properties and of their Neighbors in Bāb al-Muṣallā, 1825-75

Identity	*Sellers*	*Buyers*	*Neighbors*	*Total*	*Percentage*
		First sample (1825-26)			
Maghribīs	8	2	3	13	4.41
Kurds and Turkmān	3	—	1	4	1.36
Egyptians	—	1	1	2	0.68
Military	7	5	4	16	5.42
Geographic Syrians	4	7	—	11	3.73
Christians	12	14	16	42	14.23
Unspecified (local)	55	43	109	207	70.17
Total	89	72	134	295	100.00
		Second sample (1834-35)			
Maghribīs	2	3	—	5	4.67
Kurds and Turkmān	1	—	1	2	1.87
Egyptians	—	—	—	—	—
Military	3	2	3	8	7.48
Geographic Syrians	2	1	—	3	2.80
Christians	2	8	2	12	11.22
Unspecified (local)	20	18	39	77	71.96
Total	30	32	45	107	100.00
		Third sample (1846-47)			
Maghribīs	—	—	—	—	—
Kurds and Turkmān	6	—	—	6	8.00
Egyptians	—	—	—	—	—
Military	—	—	2	2	2.67
Geographic Syrians	1	3	—	4	5.33
Christians	6	1	3	10	13.33
Unspecified (local)	15	14	24	53	70.67
Total	28	18	29	75	100.00
		Fourth sample (1862-63)			
Maghribīs	2	4	3	9	6.25
Kurds and Turkmān	—	—	—	—	—
Egyptians	—	1	3	4	2.78
Military	4	1	4	9	6.25
Geographic Syrians	—	1	—	1	0.69
Christians	3	17	9	29	20.14
Unspecified (local)	34	15	43	92	63.89
Total	43	39	62	144	100.00

Identity	*Sellers*	*Buyers*	*Neighbors*	*Total*	*Percentage*
		Fifth sample (1874-75)			
Maghribīs	1	6	2	9	4.15
Kurds and Turkmān	—	—	—	—	—
Egyptians	1	—	—	1	0.46
Military	—	2	4	6	2.77
Geographic Syrians	—	—	—	—	—
Christians	12	8	9	29	13.36
Unspecified (local)	70	30	72	172	79.26
Total	84	46	87	217	100.00

contiguous to the sellers and mentioned in the registers as part of the description of a transacted property. Despite the discrepancy in the number of real estate properties reviewed in the five samples, the ratios of social groups in each sample give a clear picture of the real estate market and the identity of buyers and sellers. In the five samples, the total number of sellers (274) exceeded the total number of buyers (207), which shows that ownership tended to concentrate in fewer hands. Four groups were constantly present in the real estate market: the Maghribīs, the Kurds and the Turkmān, the military, and the Christians; although Muḥammad ʻAlī Pasha ruled Syria for nine years, the presence of Egyptians did not last on a large scale after the retreat of the Egyptian army, especially in the Bāb al-Muṣallā neighborhood. Of course, people from other regions of Syria were also residing in Bāb al-Muṣallā, as in other neighborhoods of Damascus.

The Maghribīs were constantly residing in Bāb al-Muṣallā and were active in its real estate market. Their proportion in table 11 is about 5 percent, showing an uninterrupted flow of immigrants into Damascus. We know that a great number of them were residing in the Maghāriba Quarter south of Bāb al-Muṣallā in the ʻAmara neighborhood, the stronghold of Prince ʻAbd al-Qādir and his followers, as well as in other areas of Mīdān. In the five samples, buyers from this group reach a total of 15 and the sellers a total of 13; in fact, they were more active in the real estate market than the Kurds and the Turkmān, who did not increase in the same manner by receiving a constant flow of fellow immigrants. It is interesting to note that, in both the 1862-63 and 1874-75 samples, a number of Maghribī sellers and buyers of real estate property, especially in the al-Qubbah al-Ḥamrā area, had al-Zawāwī for a surname, as in the case of ʻAli Ibn Saʻid al-Maghribī al-Zawāwī.[93] Because of their wealth, the military (*aghas* and *jorbajis*) were more active in the real estate market than the Maghribīs; their share of the market was about 6 percent.

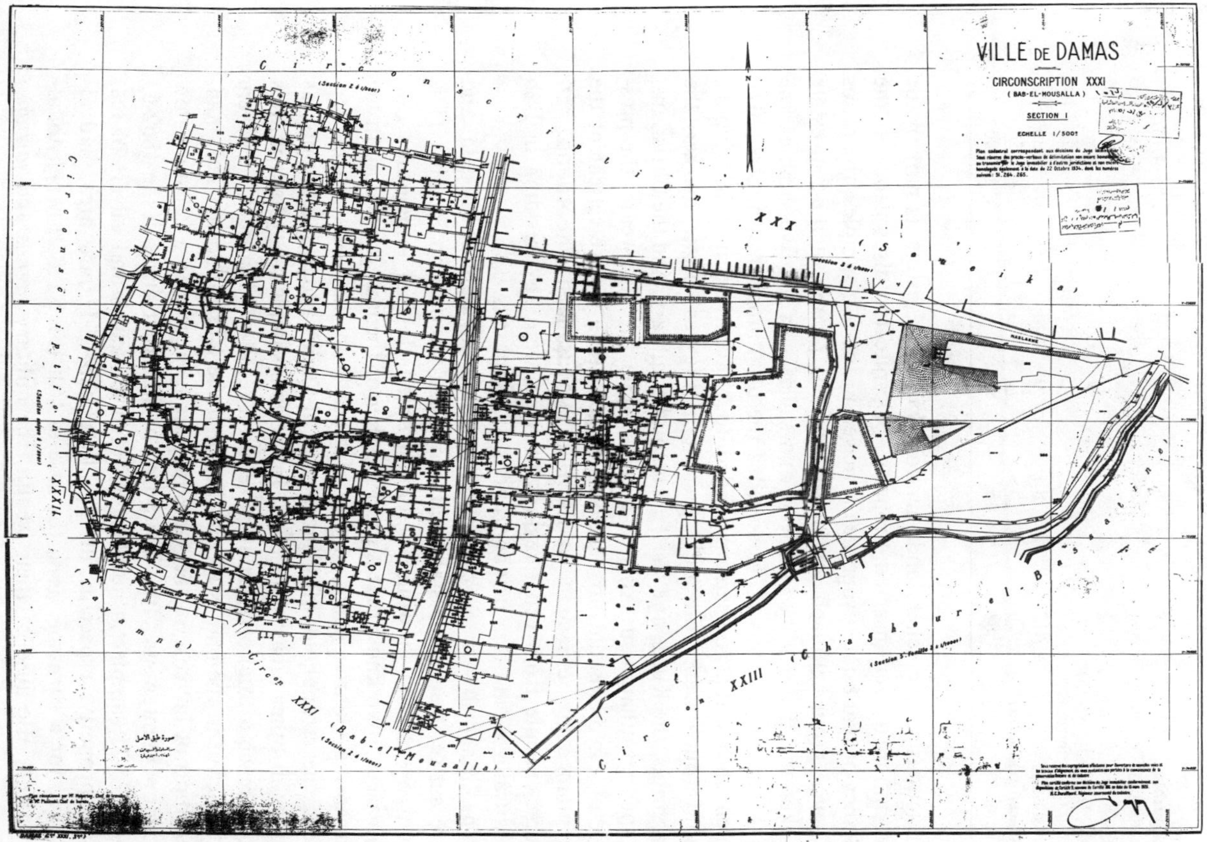

Figure 1. Damascus in the Middle of the Nineteenth Century (from J. Sauvaget, "Esquisse d'une histoire de la ville de Damas," REI, IV [1934]).

The second group in order of participation is the Christians, with an average share of 14.50 percent of the market, immediately following the share of the local majority of Muslims (about 71 percent). In fact, Christians coming from the Ḥawrān, the Wādī al-Tīm region, and the other southern regions reached al-Mīdān first; a great number settled in the area and some of them moved later to Damascus. The density of the Christian population was high in many alleys of al-Mīdān outside the Bāb al-Muṣallā neighborhood, especially in Qurashi Alley and in the alleys of Upper Mīdān.[94]

In the samples, we note that among the Christians, the buyers (48) were more numerous than the sellers (35). The increase in the number of Christian buyers is quite obvious in the 1862-63 sample. This increase was partly due to the fact that the Christians of al-Mīdān did not suffer, in general, from the social and confessional troubles which occurred in Damascus and Mount Lebanon in 1860. This atmosphere encouraged many Christians from outside the neighborhood to buy real estate properties in Bāb al-Muṣallā, as is shown by the 1862-63 sample, where we find, among the Christians, 17 buyers versus 3 sellers. Despite the fact that the average price of a real estate share in Bāb al-Muṣallā had reached during the 1862-63 period a peak of 254.40 piasters (compared with the average price in the other samples), there was a great demand for real estate. This demand could be explained by a number of factors: (a) the prosperity enjoyed by Damascus during that period;[95] (b) the payment by the Ottoman state of compensations for "property lost by theft and fire" to the Christian victims of the 1860 events;[96] (c) the fact that a number of Christians chose to return to Damascus after seeking refuge in Lebanon; and (d) an improvement of the treatment of Christians by the Ottoman state.[97]

The Christian presence was not restricted to a specific alley in Bāb al-Muṣallā. Although they lived in a number of alleys, the Christians generally concentrated in a specific alley because of the close relationships of immigrants from a given region. Located at the entrance of Bāb al-Muṣallā, Tayāmina Alley immediately attracted Christians coming from the south. The number of Christians in Bāb al-Muṣallā and especially in Tayāmina Alley later increased to such an extent that a French scholar wrote in 1931 about "a Christian quarter" in Bāb al-Muṣallā,[98] although the registers of the Mīdān Religious Court do not specifically mention a Christian quarter or alley in Bāb al-Muṣallā. They do mention, however, a Christian alley in Mīdān outside the Bāb al-Muṣallā neighborhood, in the context of recording a real estate sale on March 29, 1863 (Shawwāl 8, 1279 A.H.). But the seller and the buyers were Muslims,[99] a fact which indicates that the alley's name does not correspond to the identity of its whole population; it means, however, that a great number of Christians were living in it, possibly in a previous period.

Thus, there was no narrow religious spirit in Bāb al-Muṣallā during the period of this study. People from all denominations lived together, as is shown by their interlaced real estate properties mentioned in the registers as boundaries to other, transacted properties. For instance, Yusuf Shāhīn, a Christian, bought from 'Abbās Jaffāl half of the house located in the Wasṭānī Alley; to the south, the house was bordered by the street (with the door), to the east by the home of Ḥajj Khalifah al-Mugharbi, to the north by that of Hajj Ḍāhir, and to the west by that of Murād al-Darkazalli.[100] We also find some cases of joint ownership, and possibly of joint residence, between Muslims and Christians. For instance, Ilyās al-Qārūṭ, a Christian, bought from Muḥammad Ibn Ṣāliḥ Ibn Ḥassan al-'Asalī and his sister 'Ayshah all the *murabba'* (square room) which was inside the house of the sellers located in the Muṣli Alley in Lower Mīdān; to the south, the house was bordered by the home of Khalīl al-Rabbāṭ, to the east by the street (with the door), to the north by the home of the buyers, and to the west by that of the heirs of Abdullah Shāmīyah.[101]

Similarly, we find the same pattern of integration among people from different geographic origins. For instance, the Maghribīs lived in more than one alley in Bāb al-Muṣallā; they had no alley of their own. Turkmān Alley, was also integrated in the al-Qubbah al-Ḥamrā area. The alley of the Ḥawārinah is mentioned only once in the first sample; since it does not appear in other samples, we may conclude that it was integrated into another area.

We also find the same integration between various social and economic groups, as is shown by the size of homes and their range of prices in the same alley. Actually, there were no alleys for the rich and others for the poor. The fact that two alleys were named after the Sukkar and al-Mujtahid families is no evidence that they were restricted to members of those families; it also means that not all members of those families were rich. Moreover, depending on the location of the alleys and the professions of their inhabitants, prices of real estate were higher in some alleys than in others.

It is possible to note in table 12 the integration between various social and economic groups in the same alley by classifying, according to their price level, the real estate properties sold in full or in half (multiplied by two) in some of the main alleys known for their high frequency of real estate transactions.

Table 12.
Residential Real Estate Properties Sold in Bāb al-Muṣallā in Full or in Half, 1825-75, by Sample, Alley, and Price Level (piasters)

Alley	*Less than 500*	*501-1,000*	*1,001-2,000*	*2,001-3,000*	*3,001-5,000*	*More than 5,000*	*Total*
			First sample (1825-26)				
al-Baqqāra		2					2
al-Tayāmina	2	1	1				4
al-Jūwwāni			1	2			3
al-Sulṭāni		2	1				3
al-Qubbah al-Ḥamrā	3	2	2				7
al-Mukhallalātī	1	3	1				5
al-Wasṭānī	1		4	1	1		7
Total	7	10	10	3	1	–	31
			Second sample (1834-35)				
al-Baqqāra	1	1	1				3
al-Qubbah al-Ḥamrā	2	2					4
al-Wasṭānī	1	2	1				4
Total	4	5	2				11
			Third sample (1846-47)				
al-Jūwwāni	1						1
al-Sulṭāni		1					1
al-Qubbah al-Ḥamrā	1	1					2
Total	2	2					4
			Fourth sample (1862-63)				
al-Baqqāra			1			1	2
al-Tayāmina			1		1	3	5
al-Jūwwāni			1				1
al-Qubbah al-Ḥamrā			2	2	1		5
al-Wasṭānī			1			1	2
Total			6	2	2	5	15
			Fifth sample (1874-75)				
al-Baqqāra					3		3
al-Tayāmina					3		3
al-Sulṭāni					1		1
al-Qubbah al-Ḥamrā				1			1
Total				1	7		8

We note that, in the first three samples (1825-47), 42 out of 46 properties (91.30 percent) fall within the three first price categories, that is, up to 2,000 piasters. Within this distribution, 13 properties fall in the low price category, 17 in the higher category, and 12 in the third category. These figures show that price levels were balanced and consistent and that there were no gaps between low and high prices, probably because of closely similar social and economic standings among the inhabitants of those alleys. They also show that the purchasing power of the currency did not face major shocks, a fact which is consistent with the previous observation concerning the closeness of the average prices of a share in residential real estate of the first three samples.

In contrast, we note that, in the third and fourth samples, 17 out of 23 properties (73.91 percent) fall in the price categories above 2,000 piasters, and the other 6 fall within a category immediately preceding the others. This fact was not due to the scarcity of moderately priced houses and an increase in highly priced houses, but rather to an inflation caused by a fall in the exchange rate of the silver piaster to the gold currency (Ottoman and European), namely to the French pound, in which the cost of houses started to be paid, as is mentioned in the registers of the Religious Courts. We already noted that, in the fourth sample, the average price of a share of real estate was higher by 450 percent than in the third sample; then, in the fifth sample, it decreased by about 23 percent from the average price in the fourth sample. This decrease could be also explained by the local economic difficulties encountered during 1860-75 as a consequence of the 1860 events and of the instability of the domestic economy and its subservience to European capitalism. At that time, a group of local merchants and capitalists from all denominations took advantage of the situation and expressed their new standard of living by building luxury homes in Damascus.[102]

Despite the high prices of real estate properties in the fourth and fifth samples, they show some harmony; we find no gaps between low and high prices. As in the gradual difference of prices in the first three samples, this pattern shows a similarity in real estate prices and therefore in the socioeconomic status of the owners. Indeed, there was no big difference between the poor and the rich living in the same alley.

We also note, in the context of social integration, that women of Bāb al-Muṣallā were, in some aspects of public life—namely, the real estate market—as active as men and more active than their peers in Damascus. This participation is probably due to the rural origin of a great part of the Bāb al-Muṣallā population, since women usually played an active role in rural areas. It is significant that some women of Bāb al-Muṣallā bought real estate properties in their entirety; the purchase of a portion in one property or more was most likely the result of inheritance or a settlement (of rights) with relatives. Entire real estate properties bought and sold by women included residential and commercial properties within the neighborhood, as well as the tools and key money of shops. And properties fully owned by women were known by these women's names, as is mentioned in some cases when a property is delineated in the registers. For instance, we read, "Bordered, to the South, by the home of Raḥma Bint 'Idrīs and, to the West, by a portion, owned by Fāṭima Bint Abū al-Ḥassan al-Ḥawwārī."

It is interesting to note that most women who bought or sold entire real estate properties were not of local origin, as is shown by their names: 'Atiqa Bint Ḥusayn al-Fallāḥ, who bought the entire shop close to al-Muṣallā Mosque; Fāṭimah Bint Aḥmad Agha al-Turk, who bought with her own money the tools and key money of a shop in Sulṭānī Street; Zaynab Bint 'Umar al-Naḥawī al-Maghrībī, who bought for herself an entire house in Mukhallalātī Alley; and 'Abdah Bint Muḥammad al-Ṭarābulsī, who bought an entire house in al-Qubbah al-Ḥamrā.[103] These examples bear witness to the active role of women in the real estate market of Bāb al-Muṣallā; beside lending, real estate was, for them, the most secure investment.

Concerning their real estate transactions, women used to appear in the Mīdān Religious Court without attorney. Moreover, they worked, in some cases, not only as guardians of minor children but also as authorized representatives of men. This role of women in Bāb al-Muṣallā reflects a deep-rooted rural heritage. In the country, women played an independent role; they relied upon themselves in working, living, and defending their rights, whereas city women were more or less in seclusion and did not rely upon themselves to exercise their rights.

The social and economic structure of Bāb al-Muṣallā during the period under study would have more relevance if compared to the structure of other neighborhoods inside and outside Damascus. Such studies would help explain the social and economical background of the various population groups and would also help us understand their political and religious attitudes and their cultural orientation.

Notes

1. See the commentary of al-Shaykh Aḥmad Dahmān in his edition of *A'lām al-warā bi man wulliya na'n 'an Dimashq al-shām al-kubra* by Muḥammad Ibn Tulūn (Damascus: Ministry of Culture, 1964), pp. 6-7 and 51-52.
2. J. Sauvaget, "Esquisse d'une histoire de la ville de Damas," *Revue des études*

islamiques, 4 (1934): 460-69; R. Thoumin, "Deux quartiers de Damas: Le quartier Chrétien de Bab Musalla et le quartier Kurde," *Bulletin d'études orientales*, 1 (1931): 99-135.

3. Na'mān al-Qasāṭli, *al-Rawḍah al-ghannā' fī Dimashq al-fayḥā'* (Beirut: Reprint of the 1876 edition, Dār al-Rā'id al-'Arabi), p. 107.
4. al-Shaykh 'Abd al-Qādir Badrān, *Munādamat al-aṭlāl wa musāmarat al-khayāl* (Damascus: al-Maktab al-Islāmī, 1379 A.H./1960), p. 389.
5. al-Qasāṭli, *al-Rawḍah*, p. 111.
6. See "The Province Council. Damascus Register," 1200-1261 A.H./1844-45 A.D., pp. 355-58.
7. See for example, Muḥammad Ibn Ṭūlūn, *Mufākahat al-khullān fī hawādith al-zāman*, ed. by Muḥammad Muṣṭafa (Cairo: al-Mu'assassah al-'Ammah lil-Ta'līf wa-al-Tarjamah wa-al-Nashr, 1962-64), vol. 1, pp. 191-277, 250-52, 282. See also Ibn Tūlūn, *A'lām al-warā*, pp. 143-44.
8. See the author's book, *The Province of Damascus, 1723-1783* (Beirut: Khayat, 1966), pp. 161-69.
9. See, for example, the following works: André Raymond, *Grandes villes arabes a l'époque ottomane* (Paris: Sinbad, 1985); *The Great Arab Cities in the 16th-18th Centuries* (New York: New York University Press, 1984); Antoine Abdel Nour, *Introduction a l'histoire urbaine de la Syrie ottomane* (*XVIe-XVIIIe siècle*) (Beirut: Lebanese University Publications, 1982); D. Chevallier, ed., *L'Espace social de la ville arabe* (Paris: Maisonneuve et Larose, 1979); A. Bouhdiba and D. Chevallier, eds., *La Ville Arabe dans l'Islam* (Tunis: University of Tunis, CNRS Publication, 1982).
10. Thoumin, "Deux quartiers de Damas," pp. 101-2.
11. Mīdān Religious Court, Register No. 547, p. 172.
12. See Register No. 392, p. 16.
13. See Register No. 547, p. 272; Register No. 653, p. 50; Register No. 654, p. 94.
14. See Register No. 654, p. 54.
15. See Register No. 653, p. 54; Register No. 654, p. 97.
16. The garden is defined as including lemon, sweet lemon, citron, bitter orange, apricot, and peach trees, in addition to jasmine and other flowers (Register No. 333, p. 86).
17. See Register No. 333, p. 86.
18. See Register No. 333, p. 86.
19. See Register No. 501, p. 75.
20. See Register No. 501, p. 120.
21. See Register No. 653, p. 54; Register No. 654, p. 57.
22. About these alleyways, see Register No. 333, p. 92; Register No. 392, p. 247; Register no. 547, pp. 276, 278, 295.
23. See Register No. 547, p. 220.
24. See Register No. 547, pp. 229, 250.
25. See Register No. 547, p. 276.
26. See Register no. 307, p. 165.
27. See Register No. 654, p. 145.
28. See Register No. 654, p. 145.

29. See Register No. 307, p. 94.
30. See Register No. 307, p. 97.
31. See Register No. 392, p. 247.
32. See Register No. 392, p. 247.
33. See Register No. 307, p. 332.
34. See Register No. 333, p. 330.
35. al-Qasāṭli, *al-Rawḍah*, p. 93.
36. Ibid.
37. See Register No. 307, p. 80.
38. See Register No. 392, p. 251.
39. See, for example, Register No. 653, p. 112; Register No. 654, p. 165.
40. See, for example, Register No. 547, p. 196; Register No. 654, p. 208.
41. See Register No. 501, p. 28.
42. For more details, see Muḥammad Sa'id al-Qāsimi, *Qāmūs al-Ṣinā'āt*, (Dictionary of Syrian Crafts), vol. ed. by Ẓāfir al-Qāsimi (Paris-The Hague: Mouton, 1960), 1:55.
43. See, for example, Register No. 392, p. 329; Register No. 501, p. 11; Register No. 547, p. 171.
44. See Register No. 485, p. 78; Register No. 547, p. 173.
45. See Register No. 653, p. 6.
46. See my essay, "Gaza, Urban, Social and Economic Study" (in Arabic), published in my book, *Essays on the Economic and Social History of Modern Syria* (in Arabic; Damascus, 1985), p. 79.
47. See Register No. 307, p. 276.
48. See Register No. 654, p. 195.
49. See Register No. 307, p. 233.
50. See Register No. 653, p. 96; Register No. 654, p. 208.
51. See Register No. 481, p. 166; Register no. 547, p. 196.
52. See Register No. 333, p. 316.
53. See Register No. 510, p. 65.
54. See Register No. 307, p. 161; Register No. 547, pp. 1, 89.
55. See Register No. 392, p. 256.
56. See Register No. 307, p. 198; Register No. 333, pp. 349, 400; Register No. 653, p. 158.
57. See Register No. 547, pp. 154, 182.
58. See Register No. 333, p. 349.
59. At an unspecified date, a pottery was replaced by a house in Arba'īn Alley (Register No. 333, p. 411).
60. About these *khāns*, see Register No. 392, p. 312; Register No. 547, p. 264; Register No. 654, p. 208.
61. See Register No. 654, p. 110.
62. See Register No. 654, p. 94; Register No. 653, p. 50.
63. See, for example, 'Abd al-Razzāq al-Bitār, *Hilyat al-bashar fi tārīkh al-Qarn al-tlālith 'Ashar*, ed. by Muḥammad Bahjat al-Biṭār (Damascus: al-Majma' al-'Ilmi al-'Arabi, 1961-1963), vol. 2, p. 1131.
64. Ibid., vol. 1, p. 116.

65. See Damascus Register No. 547, pp. 89, 258.
66. See Damascus Register No. 653, p. 80; see also Register No. 481, p. 166; Register No. 547, pp. 171, 196, 232; Register No. 654, p. 94.
67. See Register No. 307, p. 82.
68. See Register No. 501, p. 101.
69. See Register No. 501, p. 155.
70. See, for example, Register No. 501, p. 118.
71. See, for example, Register No. 307, p. 16.
72. For details, see my essay, "The Damascene Economy facing the European Economy in the Nineteenth Century" (in Arabic), in *The Review of Historic Studies* (Damascus, in Arabic), Issues No. 17 and 18 (1984), pp. 115-159; published again in my book, *Essays on the Economic and Social History of Modern Syria* (in Arabic), pp. 241-85.
73. See, for example, Register No. 653, pp. 52, 54, 56, 96, 119, 120, 151, 158; Register No. 654, pp. 17, 54, 81, 97, 111, 115, 149, 220.
74. *The Dictionary of Syrian Crafts* (in Arabic) was used to explain some professions.
75. See my "The Damascene Economy," in *Essays* pp. 255-57.
76. al-Qasāṭli, *al-Rawḍah*, p. 92.
77. Ibid., p. 93.
78. See Register No. 307, p. 97.
79. See Register No. 397, p. 301.
80. See Register no. 307, pp. 255, 257; Register No. 333, p. 373.
81. See his book, *Munādamat al-aṭlāl wa musāmarat al-khayāl*, p. 389.
82. See Register No. 653, p. 54.
83. Concerning the appropriation of public *waqfs* by influential people, see Badrān, *Munādamat*, p. 53.
84. See Register No. 397, p. 301.
85. See Register No. 333, p. 86.
86. See Register No. 501, p. 65.
87. See Register No. 392, pp. 160, 355.
88. See Muḥammad Khalīl al-Murādī, *Silk al-Durar fī a'yān al-qarn al-thānī 'ashar*, (Cairo: Būlāq, 1301 A.H., 1883 A.D.), vol. 2, p. 62.
89. Concerning the exploitation of these *waqfs* by the Sukkar family, see Register No. 307, pp. 141, 161; Register No. 392, p. 529; Register No. 501, p. 264; Register no. 547, pp. 71, 75, 154, 196, 213.
90. See Register No. 307, p. 68; Register No. 547, pp. 45, 252.
91. See Register No. 547, pp. 45, 71, 213.
92. See al-Qasāṭli, *al-Rawḍah*, pp. 102-3; see also Thoumin, "Deux quartiers de Damas," pp. 113-15.
93. See Register No. 547, pp. 259, 267; Register No. 653, pp. 142, 158.
94. As examples of the purchasing of houses by Christians in the Qurashi, Muski, and 'Askari Alleys, see Register No. 485, pp. 24, 266.
95. al-Qasāṭli, *al-Rawḍah*, p. 93.
96. Ibid., p. 92.
97. Improvements in the treatment of Christians by the Ottoman state during

the Tanzimat period are reflected in the registers of Damascus Religious Courts. The Register No. 501 (1275-76 A.H.) of the Mīdān Religious Court refers to the Christian as the *ibn* of Mr. X. instead of the *walad*, which was constantly used in the past (see pp. 13, 14, and 101); and the word *ibn* is consistently used in the following registers. Instead of *Naṣrānī* or *Dhummī* or *'Isawī*, the registers start to use the term *Khristianī*, as in Register No. 547 (1279-80 A.H./1862-64) of the Mīdān Religious Court (see pp. 208, 224, and 309). At that time, the title *Khawāja*, associated with Christians, started to be used in the registers; the word, of Persian origin, means the merchant or the chief or the master; in Turkish, it becomes *Khoja* (Khojah), meaning the master. Later, the Christians were referred to as citizens of the Ottoman state (see the Mīdān Court Register No. 653 of 1290-91 A.H.; 1873-76), as in the following example: al-Khawāja Ilyās Ibn al-Khawāja Yūsuf al-Qārūt, citizen of the Ottoman state (*min ra'ayā al-dawlah al-'uthmāniyah*) as established by the Greek Catholic Patriarchate to which Ilyās belonged (see Register No. 653, pp. 38, 96, and 117). The Ottoman state had issued a decree (transmitted to the judge of Ghazza by the *wāli* of Jerusalem) ordering an inquiry into the identity of real estate buyers to ascertain their Ottoman citizenship. As regards Christians, the decree said, their identity could be established through their religious chiefs (see my essay on Gaza, p. 41); the purpose was to limit the purchasing of real estate by foreigners.

98. See Thoumin, "Deux Quartiers de Damas."
99. See Register No. 547, p. 241.
100. See Register No. 307, p. 165.
101. See Register No. 653, p. 38.
102. See al-Qasāṭli, *al-Rawḍah*, pp. 96-97. In the five samples of our study, the highest price of a house in Bāb al-Muṣallā reached 37,500 piasters; it was paid by al-Shaykh Muḥammad Sa'id Efendi al-Mujtahid, who, as an authorized representative of al-Sayyid Muḥammad Ṣāliḥ Qaṣṣāb, bought it from al-Sayyīd 'Abdallah Habbāb, on Dhū al-Hijjah 25, 1279 A.H./July 13, 1862 (see Register No. 547, p. 295). Three days later, the second highest price of 11,100 piasters was paid for a house located in Baqqāra Alley (see Register No. 547, p. 299).
103. See, for example, Register No. 307, pp. 52, 257, 314; Register No. 333, p. 369; Register No. 392, pp. 348, 355; Register No. 501, p. 44; Register No. 547, p. 254.

Imperial Germany: A View From Damascus

SAMIR M. SEIKALY

For early Arab thinkers engaged in the difficult task of mental rediscovery and renewal, the two capital cities of France and England served as two poles of positive intellectual attraction. Whether they traveled physically or, as it were, mentally, it was to Paris and London that they gravitated, drawn by the outer splendor of civilization or by the mighty minds active in scientific institutes and schools of higher learning. This fact is generally known and has been the object of comment and observation. Less known is the fact that some Arab intellectuals occasionally extended their vision beyond the confines of the inner Anglo-French zone and tried to establish for themselves, and for their readers, a reasoned understanding of the essence and operation of other European societies. The purpose of this study is to bring to light one instance of this type of activity: to analyze Muḥammad Kurd'Alī's comprehension of Imperial Germany's unique cultural ethos as well as his appraisal of its particular political evolution and rise to world prominence.

I

Even for those inhabitants of Ottoman Syria whose historic memory was short and whose geographic horizons did not as a rule progress beyond the limits of their own locality, Imperial Germany, in the first decade of the twentieth century, was a recognized—but somewhat distant—political and cultural entity.[1] Muḥammad Kurd'Alī was probably little known to most of his compatriots. But for a handful of educated Arabs and, we now know, for a few consular agents and European observers, he was more than an improbable composite name.

Muḥammad Kurd'Alī was not, in 1876, born to fortune. His father, Abdul-Razzāq, was at first an ordinary tailor. But driven by the need to provide for an expanding family, which in the male line alone numbered half a dozen, and attracted by the possibilities inherent in an expanding economy, Abdul-Razzāq left his craft and joined the merchant ranks of the city of Damascus. The risk taken by the father was great, but the reward, fortunately, was greater. After a somewhat hesitant start, Abdul-Razzāq eventually succeeded in firmly establishing himself as a retail trader operating from premises which he owned in that city. Following an increasingly prevailing pattern, Abdul-Razzāq used part of his newly acquired wealth to purchase a sizeable plot of the finest agricultural land in the fertile valley of al-Ghūṭa. The tailor become merchant was by now a gentleman farmer.

This remarkable parental act of economic transformation was imitated on an intellectual plane by Muḥammad Kurd'Alī himself. As his candid memoirs testify, Kurd'Alī's formal education, which terminated at the secondary level, was of the most ordinary type. In fact, the only outcome of upper-level study at a modern *rushdīyah* school appears to have been some facility in the comprehension and use of the Turkish language. The educational foundations for his subsequent intellectual prominence were laid, necessarily, elsewhere. Even as he attended secondary school, Kurd'Alī was encouraged by his father to begin the private study of the French language. But his real mastery of it, as well as his wide exposure to French thought, occurred when for a period of two years he attended the renowned Lazarist school at Damascus. How he gained command of the Arabic language, as well as his profound knowledge of its varied cultural manifestations, took a somewhat different form, but it revealed equal initiative and determination. In affording his son the opportunity to study French, Abdul-Razzāq was motivated by purely material considerations; knowledge of a European language was an asset in the business world and the world of government. It is probable that he may not have associated the study of Arabic with future material benefits; nevertheless, he made it possible for his young son to receive supplementary instruction in the Arabic language and a few other traditional Islamic subjects. But the critical development in Kurd'Alī's educational and intellectual formation occurred when he established for himself what can be most appropriately described as an inverted *ḥalaqah* (literary circle). Reversing the normal *ḥalaqah* pattern, he singly, and in a personal capacity, became the disciple of the foremost Muslim scholars of Damascus: Salīm al-Bukhāri, Muḥammad al-Mubārak, and Ṭāhir al-Jazā'irī.[2] As a result of their sustained and careful guidance, he was directed to the intellectual legacy of the Arabs and Islam, to the books on "language, literature, eloquence, sociology, history, jurisprudence, interpretation, and philosophy." Of that distinguished company, it was al-Jazā'irī who instilled in him an enduring love and respect for his

Arab heritage and a burning desire to promote educational and social reform, as well as the ability to express in lucid prose the imperative need for Arab regeneration.[3]

Muḥammad Kurd'Alī's literary career began somewhat inauspiciously. Upon the termination of his formal secondary education in 1897, and for a period of three years, he edited an insignificant weekly called *al-Shām*. His first journalistic experience was, in many respects, demoralizing, but, to adopt his own phraseology, "out of evil there emerged, unintentionally, some good." In the first place, he became adept at the art of journalistic ambiguity and dissimulation, necessary at the time if a comprehensive, gratuitous, and consistently ignorant censorship was to be evaded. But of far greater consequence was the fact that in editing what was in effect a simple bulletin, he found the time to write an essay on the Wahhabi movement, which was accepted for publication in the prestigious *al-Muqtaṭaf*. The year 1900, therefore, marked the genesis of Kurd'Alī as a journalist. Birth in his case, however, was followed by precocious maturity. For in less than six years, in addition to a stream of articles which he continued to contribute to *al-Muqtaṭaf*, Kurd'Alī—having taken up temporary residence in Cairo in 1905—edited two Egyptian dailies, first the little-known *al-Ẓāhir* and then the popular and influential *al-Mu'ayyad*. His greatest achievement, however, was to begin to issue in Cairo in 1906 his own periodical bearing the name of *al-Muqtabas*. In 1909, as a result of the temporary press freedom which the fall of 'Abd al-Hamid II allowed, Kurd'Alī moved his journal to Damascus and soon after crowned his journalistic career by establishing that city's first modern Arabic daily. Perhaps not very imaginatively, he called it, too, *al-Muqtabas*.[4]

In spite of the disadvantages that at times resulted from confounding one with the other, the periodical and the newspaper were together to emerge and maintain their position until the outbreak of World War I as the most vigorous and influential publications in the capital of the *wilāyah* of Syria. The importance of the two publications is locally attested by the wide welcome they received. It is also attested by the fact that their frequent disruption by administrative decree invariably elicited public disapproval and always evoked, in the Arabic press, open expression of support for Kurd'Alī whenever he was hauled to court to be judged, or misjudged, for his opinions.[5] Another, independent, proof is supplied by the testimony of informed foreign observers. The French consular agent in Damascus, Ottavi, never tired of reminding his superiors of the sway which Kurd'Alī and his publications exercised over Syrian public opinion. Indeed, in an elaborate attempt to exclude all negative reference to French foreign policy in the two *al-Muqtabas*,

Ottavi openly suggested that the silence of Kurd'Alī be bought. Ottavi thereby not only revealed the formative impact of the sister publications upon Syrian public opinion; he also exposed typical colonial wisdom as to the most effective method of dealing with independently minded native intellectuals.[6]

About the same time as Ottavi was recommending the merits of corruption, a German familiar with the region and its press was recording a less cynical estimate of Kurd'Alī and his journalistic reputation. Following a visit to Syria, which resulted in an encounter with Kurd'Alī himself, the German orientalist Martin Hartmann judged *al-Muqtabas* as qualitatively superior to similar Arab publications and noted that on that account—as well as their proprietor's courageous defense of Arab interests—they enjoyed wide circulation and considerable influence at the popular level and among the Arab elite.[7]

As the two foremost Arab publications in Damascus in their time and now as indispensable documents reflecting the evolution of modern Arabic thought and politics, the daily *al-Muqtabas* and the journal *al-Muqtabas* constitute the source from which will be derived Muḥammad Kurd'Alī's analysis, comprehension, and appraisal of the Imperial German experience as it developed before the war which ultimately destroyed it.

II

At first, that is, before his views echoed and were largely determined by the German-Turkish military alliance, Kurd'Alī regarded Imperial Germany as an integral but somewhat adolescent part of a more comprehensive whole to which—in his Arabic usage—he assigned the label *al-Gharb* (the West). To the East, *al-Gharb* ended where the borders of Russia and Turkey began, but to the West it overstepped the Atlantic to include within its boundaries the new but vigorous United States of America. In the writings of Kurd'Alī, *al-Gharb* figured as a complex, involved, and constantly evolving concept; but basically, and most fundamentally, it signified a cultural entity. In *al-Gharb* reason was emancipated and permanently in constructive motion. Overturning Marxian analysis—to which, incidentally, no direct reference seems to have been made in the two *al-Muqtabas*—Kurd'Alī insisted that it was reason, to begin with, that engendered, and institutions of learning that subsequently upheld, the superiority which in *al-Gharb* was evident in every sphere of human endeavor. Thus the inordinate political and military might of the West was the natural outcome and concrete expression of its material prosperity. But the generation of prodigious wealth was made possible, in the first place, by the tremendous advances in science, itself the product and embodiment of reason that was liberated, energetic, and bold.[8] Upon the pages of the two *al-Muqtabas*, France and its capital, Paris, frequently typified the essence and ascendency of *al-Gharb*. But for Kurd'Alī *al-Gharb* always comprehended Imperial Germany, and Berlin could as well represent Western potential, progress, and power.[9]

Although both Paris and Berlin could and did, equally and just as effectively, symbolize the external and visible aspects of Western civilization, the constituent parts of *Umam al-ḥaḍārah* (civilized nations) were not on that account identical or interchangeable units. Each unit, Kurd'Alī maintained, possessed its own specificity, its particular momentum and unique ethos. Thus, whereas Britain and France, as political subdivisions of *al-Gharb*, were the outcome of an organic and protracted evolution, Imperial Germany emerged as a result of a deliberate act of political transformation which completely and conclusively reversed the historic condition of German discord and dismemberment. Again, whereas the spirit and genius of France was embodied in her laws and legal systems, and that of Britain in her liberal political philosophy and representative institutions, Imperial Germany, Kurd'Alī affirmed, displayed her essence and uniqueness in her enduring educational traditions and in the multiplicity and sublimity of her intellectual creations. Paraphrasing what he claimed was a German aphorism, he noted that Britain exercised sovereignty over the sea, and France over the land, but Imperial Germany's special sphere lay among heavenly spheres, themselves the abode of reason (*Manzil al-'aql*).[10] The ultimate confirmation, as Kurd'Alī saw it, of the ascendency of reason in Imperial Germany derived from the organization of German society itself. In contrast with neighboring societies, in which individuals habitually overstepped their limits by succumbing to their inclinations, German society required its citizens to occupy the positions assigned to them by their natural dispositions (*fiṭrah*) and native intelligence. In this manner reason had created, and continued to uphold, a just and harmonious social order.[11]

Reflecting upon and attempting to understand the full implications of Imperial Germany's political evolution, Kurd'Alī observed that reason and the national idea were in that process intertwined. Indeed, it was reason, and by extension learning, which in the most adverse circumstances had allowed for the endurance of the German national idea. For at a time of military feebleness and complete political disarray, German intellectuals, in the privacy of their universities and institutions of higher learning, patiently forged and carefully nurtured the opposite notion of German unity and might. The result of their dedication and labor was to convince their students of the viability of the project of German unification and to demonstrate to the public at large its possibility and absolute necessity. But although the idea of German unity germinated in the university, it remained essentially an intellectual desire. Its transformation from the realm of the ideal and the intangible to the world of concrete reality occurred when it migrated from the university to the military barracks and ultimately to the battlefield. On the pages of *al-Muqtabas* the men of learning who had preserved the notion of German unity remain anonymous, but not its political architect. Bismarck was the first German statesman to concede the inadequacy of nationalist rhetoric and the insufficiency of intellectual invocations of German unity—and therein, according to Kurd'Alī, lay his realism. Bismarck was the first German statesman to realize that the time for the achievement of German consolidation had dawned, and it was he who had set out to determine its timing and the alternative means to bring it into being—and therein, according to Kurd'Alī, lay his genius. Because of Bismarck's premeditated policies, the birth of German unity came about in the "fire" of battle and by means of the sword (*al-nār wa-al-battār*). And yet for Kurd'Alī, although Bismarck's use of force was necessary, it was only a temporary measure. Once unity was achieved, force was relinquished and Germany reverted to its preoccupation with reason and the cultivation of the mind.[12]

The paramountcy of thought in Imperial Germany and the primacy of reason in the West did not mean that the *Umam al-ḥaḍārah* always conducted themselves rationally or behaved in a consistently civilized manner. For in one specific instance, in the exercise of imperialism, *al-Gharb*, as Kurd'Alī put it, oscillated in the direction of virtual insanity (*Junūn al-isti'mar*).

Imperialism, that is, the act whereby the West militarily overwhelmed the rest of the world and subjected it to its own political control, was, for Kurd'Alī, mindless because it was essentially superfluous. In the first place, in the order of world cultures, that of the West was the most dynamic and, in fact, in complete ascendency. Every culture, he wrote, possessed its own inner core which it ought to preserve; nevertheless, all traditional cultures, he admitted, had yielded to Western culture and in the process were being transformed by it. In a situation in which the West, on the cultural plane, was already reconstructing the world in its own image, imperialism, for Kurd'Alī, was both unnecessary and, because of the political friction that it generated, frequently harmful.[13]

In the second place, imperialism was especially futile because its particular form of military and political control was not a precondition for Western economic expansion. For just as the West enjoyed cultural preponderance, so too it commanded economic hegemony. In fact, because the West was the financial center of the world and its industrial pacesetter, it was inevitable that the remaining parts of the globe should be drawn into the orbit of its economy as providers of industrial raw materials and as consumers of its manufactured products. But, for Kurd'Alī, it was not inevitable that imperialism should intrude upon this unequal but reciprocal mode of economic exchange. Indeed, by its voluntary intervention, imperialism revealed its characteristic insanity and proved its own worst enemy. In embarking upon wasteful military conquests, imperialism merely dissipated the wealth which the West, to begin with, meant to enhance and which was, by the nature of the emerging economic world order, already at its disposal.[14]

In this respect and in contrast with England and France, Imperial Germany was not, as Kurd'Alī noted, fully demented. For whereas the two great European powers senselessly expanded their influence by military acts of annexation, Imperial Germany augmented and exercised its influence peaceably, by means, that is, of commercial exchange and by the diffusion into all parts of the globe of its scientific knowledge and industrial skills. In addition to its preference for a policy of pacific expansion, Imperial Germany, Kurd'Alī maintained, intentionally imposed constraints upon its colonial ambitions. England and France, he observed, cast themselves headlong into all manner of imperialist ventures (and misadventures) and in the process endangered the might that they meant to magnify. By contrast, because Imperial Germany prized its power, it deliberately increased its influence circumspectly and at a slow pace. In this manner, he argued, Prussia had at first gradually extended its sway over all the other German states and principalities. At present, that is, following unification, and in similar fashion, Imperial Germany was progressively extending its authority over adjacent territories and sharing the benefits of its advanced civilization among its less civilized European neighbors to the south and east.[15]

In Syria at the beginning of the twentieth century, the imperialist issue was not, for Kurd'Alī, conclusively settled. Before World War I and throughout its duration, he remained faithful to his conviction that Syria could avoid European annexation only if it maintained its historic links with the Ottoman Empire. Yet he fully realized that imperialist schemes and machinations were well advanced in his native land. The outposts, as it were, of European—that is French, British, and Russian—imperialism were foreign schools and foreign economic interests.

Although France, Britain, and Russia publicly claimed that their institutions of learning were exercises in charity and served to spread progressive and much-needed education, and although the three powers presented their economic involvements as acts of mutual benefit to themselves and—principally—to the Ottoman Empire, Kurd'Alī nevertheless regarded their actions in annexing parts of the Ottoman Empire as in fact falsifying all their claims and betraying their intention to eventually dismember the Ottoman Empire and partition its Arab provinces.

The case of Imperial Germany was somewhat less plain and therefore more difficult to encompass. In a lengthy article entitled "Us and Europe" in his journal, Kurd'Alī observed that the first formal encounter between Imperial Germany and its Ottoman counterpart at the Congress of Berlin was cordial and conciliatory. Bismarck, in 1878, could not fully restrain Russia, Britain, and France in their territorial claims, nor could he completely frustrate the Balkan nationalist drive for secession, but he did restrain the nation of which he was the representative. Bismarck's exercise in self-denial laid the basis for a policy which, in its fully developed form, amounted to placing the ailing Ottoman Empire under the permanent care and virtual protection of the mighty German Empire.[16]

In the same article, and almost in the same breath, the owner of *al-Muqtabas* expressed a number of reservations about the effectiveness of German support and its apparent altruism. German protection, he argued, was never fully effective, nor was it altogether altruistic and without reward. The limitation of German protection, he maintained, manifested itself on two successive occasions: in 1908, when it allowed Austria to annex Bosnia and Herzegovina, and in 1911, when it did not oppose the Italian conquest of Tripoli. In both instances, Kurd'Alī bitterly remarked, the new revolutionary Ottoman rulers of the Empire awaited a miracle that never transpired; they anticipated, in vain, the forceful intervention of the emperor who, at the tomb of Saladin in Damascus, had once proclaimed himself the protector of the Ottoman Empire and of the Muslims of the world.[17]

By contrast, the policy of defending the principle—but not necessarily the reality—of Ottoman independence and the integrity of the empire was not without rewards for Imperial Germany. On the political plane, German diplomatic ascendency in Istanbul, as exemplified by Baron Marshall, was unquestioned and practically unassailable. On the military plane, Germany's achievement was no less remarkable. As early as 1883 a German military mission had been invited to help in rebuilding the Turkish armed forces. Over the years military transactions had multiplied, with German officers serving as military instructors in the Ottoman capital, while Turkish military personnel acquired the art of modern warfare in the war academies of the German Empire. In 1913, the primacy of the German military presence was conclusively underlined by the dispatch of Liman von Sanders's mission to train and reorganize a demoralized Turkish army.[18] But for Kurd'Alī, the most substantial advantage which Imperial Germany derived from its rapprochement with the Ottoman Empire occurred at the material level. By military means, he observed, Germany had conquered Alsace-Lorraine. The Ottoman Empire, by contrast, had succumbed to Imperial Germany's economic drive. In that process, in the act of establishing commercial enterprises everywhere in the Ottoman Empire, in opening banks and in acquiring concessions, Imperial Germany, in the first decade of the twentieth century, was at the point of outstripping every other European power.[19] The mark of Germany's economic hegemony was the acquisition for itself of the choicest and most lucrative concession of all: the construction of a railway connecting Berlin to Baghdad. An editorial in the daily *al-Muqtabas* made the telling point (which has recently been rediscovered and reiterated by a number of historians) that over the Baghdad railway Imperial Germany was not, in fact, provoking the other major imperialist powers to the point of war. Rather, it was acting in concord with them or at least could secure their consent for the project at a price which, in the end, the Ottoman Empire paid. The proof of European accord was supplied by the cordial encounter of the kaiser and the czar in Potsdam, and by the fact that the concession provided Britain and France with the golden opportunity to define less ambiguously their respective spheres of influence in the Ottoman Empire. Thus, according to the same article, by determining with some precision their respective spheres of influence at the periphery—that is, in the Ottoman Empire—the European powers seemed to eliminate the threat of war at home.[20]

In the specific case of Syria, Imperial Germany, without the overt cultivation of any minority, followed in the path of other European powers that had preceded it to the area. By means of Catholic as well as Protestant German missionaries, it was developing a comprehensive system of elementary and secondary schools, constructing hospitals and erecting places of worship. By means of these institutions, Imperial Germany was transporting to the East the scientific attainments of the West; but at the same time, just like other parallel European institutions, these institutions were meant to serve German interests and enhance German prestige.[21]

In a leader in his daily *al-Muqtabas*, Kurd'Alī attempted a comparative analysis between the French and German varieties of imperialism. In the preceding pages of this survey, the general differences between the two have already been indicated. It remains here to note that for Kurd'Alī, when imperialism entailed human contact and exchange, the French variety was more tolerable, even more pleasing.[22] Although he conceded that the Germans, as far as learning Arabic was concerned, were exceptionally able linguists, he nevertheless found the Germans whom he personally encountered in their colonies in Palestine at once uncommunicative and somewhat supercilious.[23] In fact, in the specific context of Palestine, he found German colonies more attractive than the Germans who labored in them. For the colonies were models of modern efficient agriculture that he hoped would, by their example, revive and improve Arab agriculture in that part of Syria. As is well known, Jewish colonies were being established at the same time in Palestine. Of the two types, the German represented, for Kurd'Alī, the lesser danger. Unlike their Jewish counterparts, German colonies were, for the people working in them, an end in themselves, agricultural experiments without political associations. They were not, as in the case of the colonies established by Zionist agencies, the initial building blocks for a political edifice which, when complete, would result in the expulsion of the native population and would entail the creation in the southern part of Syria of an alien state.[24]

With the outbreak of World War I and the formation of the German-Turkish alliance, Kurd'Alī was denied the opportunity of independent reflection upon the general phenomenon of imperialism and its manifestations in his native land. In fact, he was practically denied the luxury of writing altogether. The daily *al-Muqtabas* ceased to appear, and the life of the periodical, with the exception of a few numbers which appeared in 1916, gradually came to an end. In these last issues of the periodical, Imperial Germany was present, not as a European power to be evaluated, but as an ally to be praised. Harking back to a prewar theme, Kurd'Alī called upon the youth of the Ottoman Empire to learn the German language in order to have direct access to the benefits of German civilization as contained in its arts, its sciences, and its economics. As the Western world that he knew and loved destroyed itself in a bloody war, Kurd'Alī called upon his readers to contemplate, in 1916, the miracle of Imperial Germany. The war had tested it, but its response was magnificent; indeed, in 1916, the entire world watched with awe and amazement the spectacle of Imperial Germany mobilizing her learning, economy, and society to fight a war in which she had already revealed her genius.[25]

The element of propaganda in all this is, of course, obvious. But the need to magnify the exploits of the Ottoman Empire's ally did not entirely eliminate the critical faculty of the owner of *al-Muqtabas*, nor did it deprive him of the spirit of dissent. The final article in which Imperial Germany figured carried the title "Jirmāniyā al-kubrā," or greater Germany. In it Kurd'Alī expressed the view that the creation of Mitteleuropa was both possible and—given Germany's military conquests in the opening stages of the war—even inevitable. But although he did not challenge the concept of a "greater Germany," he expressed doubts as to its territorial limits. Specifically, he did not wish for it to include Istanbul and the regions beyond it to the east. For this act of incorporation would deprive the Ottoman Empire of its essence: its language and culture, its customs and particular outlook on life. This is why, in closing the pages of *al-Muqtabas*, Kurd'Alī reminded his readers that the scope of German-Turkish relations ought not exceed the limits of a military and political alliance.[26]

But to leave the subject at this point would result in some distortion. For, in the final analysis, Imperial Germany's importance for Kurd'Alī derived from the fact that it fulfilled for him the function of a significant political as well as cultural symbol. Because of its disunity and weakness, the Ottoman Empire, he believed, could derive inspiration by contemplating, comprehending, and emulating the example of German unity. Imperial Germany symbolized what the Ottoman Empire could and ought to become.[27] And yet on the same political level and somewhat paradoxically, Imperial Germany, by its decentralized form of government and by the freedom that it allowed for its constituent units, actually showed what the Ottoman Empire should avoid, namely, excessive centralization. For Kurd'Alī genuinely believed that the attempt to reverse, at a late date, the historic loose pattern of relations between the center of the empire and its provinces would end by destroying the Ottoman Empire altogether.[28]

As an Arab intellectual who recognized the need to borrow from the West in order to begin the long and complex process of reform and regeneration, Kurd'Alī was confronted by the classic dilemma of what to retain from inherited traditions and what to adopt from imported innovations. How he resolved this problem in detail is beyond the scope of this analysis. Suffice it to note that he taught that Imperial Germany, at the beginning of the twentieth century, testified to the possibility of a resolution. Imperial Germany, Kurd'Alī maintained, did not renounce its past, nor was it entirely wedded to the new. It amalgamated selectively what was enduring in both. Therein lay for the Arabs of the Ottoman Empire the seeds for a solution to a dilemma which could be momentarily ignored but which would not go away on its own.[29]

Notes

1. The allusion here is to the German emperor's visit to Syria in 1898. By 1906 that episode, on the popular level, had been forgotten. In his two publications, Kurd'Alī did not single out that visit for special attention.
2. Based on a recently discovered manuscript, a book by Kurd'Alī, *al-Mu'āsirūn* (Damascus: Majma' al-Lughah al-'Arabīyah, 1980), contains biographical sketches of al-Mubārak and al-Jazā'irī and their pioneering work in education.
3. The best account of Kurd'Alī's youth and educational formation is provided in his autobiographical fragment contained in *Kitāb Khiṭaṭ al-Shām* (Beirut: Dār al-'Ilm lil-Malāyin, 1961) 6:333-347, and his extensive memoirs, *al-Mudhakkirāt* (Damascus: al-Tarraqi Press, 1948). Portions of his three-volume memoirs have been translated into English by K. Totah as *Memoirs of Muḥammad Kurd 'Alī: A Selection* (Washington, D.C.: American Council of Learned Societies, 1954).
4. The periodical *al-Muqtabas* first appeared in Cairo. In 1909, three years after its first appearance, Kurd'Alī moved it to Damascus, where it continued to appear until 1914. All the numbers have been bound into eight volumes. Numbers 7-12 of volume 8 actually appeared in 1916 following a two-year interruption due to the outbreak of hostilities in 1914. The first publication of the daily *al-Muqtabas* in Damascus actually occurred in December 1908. Despite frequent closure by the authorities, *al-Muqtabas* remained the leading Arabic paper in Damascus until 1914. For a history of Syrian journalism, see Sh. al-Rifā'i, *Tārīkh al-Ṣihāfah al-Sūrīyah* (Cairo: Dār al-Ma'ārif, 1969), and J. Ilyās, *Taṭawwūr al-Ṣiḥāfah al-Sūrīyah fī mi'at 'ām* (Beirut: Dār al-Niḍāl, 1982).
5. The preoccupation of the Arab press with, as it were, the journalistic destiny of Kurd'Alī is best exemplified by *al-Nibrās*. Owned and edited by Muṣṭafa al-Ghalāyini, the periodical frequently defended Kurd'Alī against charges brought against him by the authorities. See *al-Nibrās* 1 (1909), no. 7, pp. 261-63 and no. 8, pp. 300-304.
6. Volume 20 of Adel Ismail's *Documents diplomatiques et consulaires relatifs a l'histoire du Liban* (Beirut: Editions des Oeuvres Politiques et Histoiriques, 1979) reproduces several dispatches by Ottavi to his superiors at the Quai d'Orsay commenting upon the influence of the two *al-Muqtabas* and recording his conversations with Muḥammad Kurd'Alī himself.
7. Hartmann's evaluation of the two *al-Muqtabas*, their influence and principal role in molding Syrian public opinion, is found in *Reisbriefe aus Syrien*. In this paper I have drawn on an abridged translation contained in W. Kawtharānī's *Bilād al-Shām: al-sukkān, al-iqtiṣād wa-al-siyāsah al-Faransīyah fī maṭla' al-qarn al-'ishrīn* (Beirut: Ma'had al-Inmā', 1980).
8. For a systematic and detailed analysis of the evolution of the concept *al-Gharb* (the West) in the thought of Kurd'Alī, see my "Damascene Intellectual Life in the Opening Years of the 20th Century: Muḥammad Kurd'Alī and *al-Muqtabas*," in M. Buheiry, ed., *Intellectual Life in the Arab East, 1890-1939* (Beirut: American University of Beirut, 1981).

9. Prior to 1914 Kurd'Alī paid two extended visits to Europe, which did not include Imperial Germany. His impressions of Europe and what he regarded as the uniform character of its civilization were first published in *al-Muqtabas* 4 (1909), 5 (1910), and 8 (1914). In 1923 these same articles were subsequently published in book form under the title *Gharā'ib al-Gharb*, 2 vols. (Cairo: al-Maktabah al-Ahlīyah, 1923).
10. These themes are developed in some detail in Kurd'Alī's "Almānyā wa kullīyātuha," *al-Muqtabas* 6 (1911), no. 3, pp. 137-40.
11. See his leader entitled "Kayfa nastaqīm" in the daily *al-Muqtabas*, December 18, 1908.
12. See "Almānya wa kullīyātuha."
13. For the ascendency of Western civilization, see the references in note 9 above. In addition, see his important published lecture entitled "Ḥayātuna wa-al-ḥayāt al-awrūbbīyah," *al-Muqtabas* 8 (1914), no. 7, pp. 494-509.
14. His views about imperialism are scattered in numerous articles in his periodical. Most important of all is "Junūn al-isti'mār," *al-Muqtabas* 7 (1912), no. 1, pp. 60-65.
15. How German imperialism differed from other forms of European imperialism is found in "al-Almānīyah wa-al-Faransīyah," *al-Muqtabas* 8 (1914), no. 10, pp. 725-32.
16. "Naḥnu wa Awrūbbā," *al-Muqtabas* 7 (1912), no. 10, pp. 728-47.
17. The reference to the German emperor, his visit to Saladin's tomb, and his offer to become the protector of the Muslims is to be found in an article entitled "Awrūbbā fī Sūrīyah," *al-Muqtabas* 7 (1912), no. 3, pp. 160-68.
18. About German military involvement in the Ottoman Empire, see "Ḥawl al-bi'thah al-'askarīyah," the daily *al-Muqtabas*, December 22, 1913.
19. An account of German activities in Syria is found in "Awrūbbā fī Sūrīyah" and "Naḥnu wa Awrūbbā."
20. This perceptive analysis is found in "al-'Uthmānīyah wa Almānya," the daily *al-Muqtabas*, October 29, 1913.
21. The pitfalls of foreign activities—not excluding the German—for the Ottoman Empire are explicitly discussed in "'Alā'iquna al-dawlīyah," the daily *al-Muqtabas*, August 10, 1910. In that article Kurd'Alī regrets the fact that neutrality in politics (*ḥiyād*) is not possible for the Ottoman Empire.
22. For this comparative exercise, see "al-Isti'mārān al-Faransi wa-al-Almāni," the daily *al-Muqtabas*, October 12, 1913.
23. Kurd'Alī frequently praised ordinary Germans and German Orientalists for their knowledge of Arabic. Martin Hartmann was, for him, an example of a fair and knowledgeable Orientalist, although he disputed his generalizations about the incompatibility of Islam and progress. Kurd'Alī, incidentally, had learned about Hartmann's views by reading a French periodical. See "al-Islām wa-al-madanīyah," *al-Muqtabas* 4 (1909), no. 12, pp. 742-48.
24. For his views about German and Zionist agricultural colonies, see "Fī arḍ al-Jalīl," *al-Muqtabas* 4 (1911), no. 2, pp. 117-32.
25. See "al-Almānīyah wa-al-Faransīyah."
26. See "Jirmāniyā al-kubrā," *al-Muqtabas* 8 (1914), no. 10, pp. 732-38, as

well as "al-Ḥarb al-'āmmah," *al-Muqtabas* 8 (1914), no. 7, pp. 482-92.

27. About German unity and the need to emulate it, see the series of articles entitled "al-Waḥdah al-Jirmānīyah: numudhaj lil-waḥadah al-'Uthmānīyah," the daily *al-Muqtabas*, July 17, 18, 19, 1910.
28. Concerning the decentralized form of government in the German Empire and its suitability to serve as a model, see "al-Lamarkazīyah al-Almānīyah," the daily *al-Muqtabas*, August 12, 1913.
29. In relation to this dilemma and Imperial Germany's efforts at its resolution, see "al-Qadīm wa-al-ḥadīth," *al-Muqtabas* 4 (1909), no. 1, pp. 30-34.

The Egyptian Press Under Nasser and al-Sadat

A free press is the voice of the people;
a muzzled press is the mouthpiece
of the rulers.
—Muṣṭafa Amin

FAUZI M. NAJJAR

Egypt's modern political history is closely associated, if not identified, with the evolution of its press. The publication of *al-Waqā'i' al-Miṣrīyah* on December 3, 1828, marked the beginning of a contentious relationship between the ruler and the public. Newspapers published during the first half of the nineteenth century were not much more than official circulars and were little concerned with social problems. It was not until the coming of Khedive Ismā'īl that popular, nongovernmental newspapers began to appear. Despite censorship by the Khedive and, later, by the British authorities, the Egyptian press played a prominent and formative role in awakening national consciousness, laying down the ideological foundations of liberal thought, calling for national unity on a secular rather than on a religious basis, championing freedom of thought and expression, the rule of law, and women's emancipation, and bolstering opposition to the Khedive's arbitrary power and to the British occupation of Egypt.[1]

Prior to the 1952 revolution, Egypt was a constitutional monarchy alternating between libertarianism and authoritarianism. The press and the media system in general reflected the philosophy of the political order, and thus experienced varying degrees of freedom and repression. Having been in the forefront of the national struggle for independence, Egyptian journalists looked to the new revolutionary regime for a greater degree of self-determination and autonomy. Contrary to their expectations, and in total disregard of the revolution's principles, the relatively libertarian press system that had existed under the monarchy was replaced by a highly authoritarian one, as the following pages will try to show.

The Egyptian Press and the Revolution

Most Egyptian papers had welcomed the 1952 revolution as the dawn of a new era. The euphoria of the early days of the military takeover gave the press a measure of freedom it had never known before. But the honeymoon was short-lived once the new military rulers of Egypt sought to press the newspapers into the service of the revolution. Despite their claims that they would operate within the existing constitutional structure, the free officers proceeded to dismantle it. Having forced King Faruk to abdicate, they gradually began to destroy the nation's other political and constitutional institutions. On January 16, 1953, political parties were dissolved, their assets confiscated, and their newspapers suspended. Forty-two newspapers and magazines were ordered to cease publication on the flimsy grounds that they had appeared irregularly for a period of six months between October 1953 and March 1954.[2]

On September 16, 1952, the Revolutionary Command Council launched its own magazine, *al-Taḥrīr*, under the editorship of Aḥmad Ḥamrūsh, a leftist free officer, soon to be replaced because he had tilted in a communist direction. In April 1954, *al-Taḥrīr* became a weekly with Anwar al-Sadat as its managing editor. It ceased publication in 1959. In the meantime, the Revolutionary Command Council established its own political organization, the Liberation Rally, to mobilize public support behind the revolution. On December 7, 1953, the new political organization began publishing its own newspaper, *al-Jumhūrīyah.* At first, eminent writers like Tawfiq al-Ḥakim, Lūwis 'Awaḍ, Ṭahā Ḥusayn, and Najīb Maḥfūẓ wrote editorials and articles on a variety of subjects for the new publication, indirectly conferring legitimacy on the military regime.

Egyptian journalists, like all intellectuals in Egypt at the time, had expected the officers to return to their barracks after having cleansed the system of the sources of corruption. But a crisis of confidence unfolded when they realized that the new rulers had no intention of giving up power. Censorship was imposed, lifted, and reimposed in the name of "national security" and the prevention of sedition. Charged with inciting the public against the Armed Forces Movement, certain publications were suspended. Jamāl 'Abd al-Nāṣir (Nasser), who had emerged as the undisputed leader of the revolution, declared that freedom of the press meant freedom for the country's enemies.

The Case of al-Miṣrī

In no other case did the junta reveal its true intentions toward the press as it did in the case of *al-Miṣrī*, the Wafdist newspaper published by the Abū al-Fatḥ brothers. The fact that *al-Miṣrī* had supported the revolution wholeheartedly, and that Nasser had cultivated the friendship and confidence of its chief editor, Aḥmad Abū al-Fatḥ, did not deter the Revolutionary Council from closing the paper and confiscating its assets. The story of *al-Miṣrī*, which ceased publication on May 4, 1954, is widely known; only some of its salient features need be highlighted here.

By March 1954, the rivalry between Colonel Nasser and General Muḥammad Najīb, titular head of state, had reached the crisis stage, causing a rift within the Revolutionary Command Council itself. Najīb and Khālid Muḥyi al-Dīn favored a return to constitutionalism, whereas the rest of the members opted for an authoritarian regime. The press, *al-Miṣrī* in particular, upheld the cause of democracy, constitutionalism, and parliamentary life. In a series of bold and defiant editorials, Abū al-Fatḥ bemoaned the fact that the country was still without a constitution, that martial law was in effect, that detention camps were open, and that press censorship was imposed. He hailed democracy as the only guarantee of social peace, a healthy economy, and the rule of law. Moreover, *al-Miṣrī* printed a series of articles by Dr. Tawfīq al-Shāwī, professor of criminal law at Alexandria University who had been detained and released, describing the torture and the humiliations awaiting those who might enter Egyptian prisons.

Having failed to win *al-Miṣrī* to its side, Egypt's military regime on April 25, 1954, brought charges against Maḥmūd and Ḥusayn Abū al-Fatḥ (Aḥmad had already left the country) before the Revolutionary Tribunal. They were accused of having "inspired" antiregime press propaganda, of having established relations with foreign (Arab) governments opposed to the revolution, and of having engaged in nepotism. In addition, Ḥusayn was accused of having sought by illegal means to conclude an arms deal with the War Ministry. The verdict of the three-day military trial was a ten-year prison term and a fine of 1,358,438 Egyptian pounds for Maḥmūd, and a fifteen-year suspended prison term for Ḥusayn. Subsequently, Minister of the Interior Zakariyya Muḥyi al-Dīn ordered the closing down of *al-Miṣrī*, and the government took over custody of the Abū al-Fatḥ Publishing Company.[3]

The suppression of *al-Miṣrī* was condemned by press institutions, newsmen, and intellectuals all over the world as an assault on press freedom. It was no longer a matter of conjecture that it was another step toward consolidating the grip of the military on the reins of government. Guidance Minister Major Salah Salem, at a press conference on the second anniversary of the revolution, had said: "We have too many enemies, and we had to supress the most powerful one. *al-Miṣrī* was not only a newspaper; it was a political adversary."[4] The *al-Miṣrī* case was therefore meant as an example and a warning to those who opposed the military regime. Those who advocated the restoration of the constitutional system suffered similar consequences. Well-known journalists, like Fikrī Abāẓah, Iḥsān 'Abd al-Qaddūs, Aḥmad Bahā' al-Dīn, and Abū al-Khayr Najīb, were either arrested or dismissed from their work. Abū al-Khayr Najīb, chief editor of *al-Jumhūr al-Miṣrī*, was accused of contacting foreign agents and of violating the professional code of ethics. He was sentenced to fifteen years at hard labor and stripped of his citizenship.[5] Fikrī Abāẓah, elder statesman of Egyptian journalism and several times president of the Press Syndicate, was placed under house arrest after being dismissed from his work as board chairman of Dār al-Hilāl and chief editor of *al-Muṣawwar*, for expressing views contrary to government policy. He was reinstated on April 13, 1962, six months after he had published an apology on the front page of *al-Ahrām* of September 25, 1961. By silencing liberal journalists and suppressing dissident newspapers, the free officers had foreclosed the establishment of a free democratic government.

From Censorship to Ownership

The "March 1954 crisis" ended with Nasser assuming formal as well as actual power. The next phase was to witness the institutionalization of this power. Political parties had been dissolved and their newspapers suppressed. The Muslim Brothers Association was disbanded and its leaders jailed. So were those regarded as "enemies of the regime." Martial law, emergency regulations, and press censorship were retained. The Liberation Rally remained the only legal single political organization. There were short periods of relaxation of control, but they were designed to identify and trap the opposition.[6]

In January 1956, an interim constitution drawn up by the government was adopted, ending a three-year transition period. Instead of the traditional parliamentary system of government, the new constitution introduced a presidential system giving the president supreme powers in legislation, administration, and even adjudication. Freedom of the press was guaranteed in the new document, but it was qualified by the phrases "in the interest of the people," and "within the limits of the law."[7] On June 19, marital law and press censorship were lifted, in preparation for the first presidential election. Nasser was the only candidate; he was elected by a staggering majority.

Ignoring the constitutional guarantees of a free press, Nasser's government moved to extend its control over the newspapers and other instruments of mass culture. A decree was issued stipulating that any publication must be approved by the Censorship Department before it could be printed.[8] Moreover, new journals, like *Ṣabāh al-Khayr*, *al-Sha'b*, and *al-Masā'*, were licensed as proregime publications, and military officers became newspaper editors. In the meantime, President Nasser had expressed his preference for a press linked to the National Union—a reorganized version of the Liberation Rally. Consequently, an agreement to that effect was reached between the general secretary of the Union, Anwar al-Sadat, and the newspaper editors whereby the latter would constitute a committee on the press within the political organization, and the party would be represented by a special committee within each press establishment. In sanctioning the arrangement, Nasser called on the press to present the government program to the public, and on the National Union to play a positive role in guiding the press.[9] With this structural integration of the press into the government-controlled mass party, the next logical step would be formal nationalization.

The 1960 Press Reorganization Law

International as well as domestic developments in the late 1950s convinced President Nasser of the need for a statist-socialist system. The 1956 Suez War and the subsequent union with Syria, as well as the breakup of the United Arab Republic, pushed him toward "the society of sufficiency and justice." Greater socialization of the Egyptian economy would require greater control by the state over the means of information and guidance. Hence, the 1960 Press Reorganization Law.

May 24, 1960, was a watershed in the history of the Egyptian press. On that day, the president of the republic issued an executive order (Law 156) "reorganizing" the press. It was an act of nationalization except in name. Henceforth, the press would be the property of the people as represented by the National Union, Egypt's only legal political organization. Under the new law, dispossessed publishers were to be compensated, and any Egyptian wishing to work in journalism had to be licensed by the government party.

The four major publishing firms taken over by the government were Dār al-Ahrām, Dār Akhbār al-Yawm, Dār Rūz al-Yūsuf, and Dār al-Hilāl. The fifth publishing firm, Dār al-Taḥrir, had been established by the new regime, as already mentioned. The oldest and most respected of the nationalized firms was al-Ahrām, founded in 1875 by Gabriel Tackla and owned by his son, Bishara Tackla. A special committee was established to appraise the assets of the nationalized firms. Accordingly, the owners would be compensated in government bonds yielding 3 percent interest over a twenty-year period.[10] Dār al-Ahrām and Dār al-Hilāl were combined into one "institution," as the publishing firms were now called.

Why the Reorganization?

According to most observers, there was no emergency reason for the government action, which took everyone by surprise—including the publishers. The papers and magazines affected had been "cooperating" with the authorities, and in the case of al-Ahrām, its chief editor, Muḥammad Ḥasanayn Haykal, was Nasser's close adviser and friend. An oft-stated reason was the president's "annoyance at publishers for giving more space to sensational accounts of crime, divorce, and sex incidents than to the government's social and land reform."[11] The government's explanatory note stated that the publications were being taken from "capitalist owners and placed in the hands of the people to insure press freedom." Public ownership of the means of social and political guidance, the note continued, is inevitable in a democratic, socialist, cooperative society. Rather, it is the logical outcome of the founding of the National Union to direct the "positive national action" toward the construction of a society based on the principle of the people's sovereignty. Since one of the six principles of the revolution is "the ending of the monopoly and domination of private capital over the government," President Nasser asserted, "it follows that private capital should not exercise any control over the means of guidance."[12]

At his briefing of directors and chief editors of newspapers, the president criticized the "caricatures of naked women" and the gossip stories about "which woman runs after which man" that filled the pages of newspapers. He stressed that such accounts did not reflect the real character of Egyptian society. "The real picture of our country lies in the Nile Delta," he said, where people work hard to earn a living. He then asked: "Does a woman who leaves her husband and runs away with another man represent the society in which we live? Not in the least! Is our country reflected in what you call high-life society? Definitely not!"[13] Nasser made it clear that he wanted the press to address Egypt's social and economic problems and to mobilize public opinion behind his development program. Beyond criticizing government officials for failing to discharge their duties, and beyond reporting social contradictions requiring immediate attention, the press need not go. "Journalism is more of a calling than a commodity!" he asserted. Its function is to inculcate the socialist, democratic, cooperative ideology, but not to indulge in any political criticism.

Another reason for the takeover, President Nasser told the Egyptian editors, was that foreign embassies had been competing to control Egyptian newspapers through advertising. One advertisement that embarrassed the Egyptians was inserted by East Germany during a visit by Dr. Ludwig Erhard, West German minister of the economy. When Mr. Erhard left, the West Germans retaliated with counter-advertisements. At the same time, the Soviet Union and its allies, including Communist China, had spent $500,000 on advertising in the Cairo press in 1959. The Western nations had also inserted advertisements costing thousands of dollars.[14]

The nationalization of the press could not have been a complete surprise. For sometime prior to May 1960, Egyptian journalists, probably at government instructions, more than hinted that the press was called upon to play a positive role in national guidance. In *al-Ahrām*, chief editor Haykal accused the privately owned press of "levity" and of having been a "personal press," lacking faith in specific social goals. Fatḥī Ghānem and Iḥsān 'Abd al-Qaddūs, both writing in *Rūz al-Yūsuf*, argued in favor of the press assuming a role in national guidance. Even 'Alī Amīn, co-founder and co-owner of Dār Akhbār al-Yawm, attacked the lack of discipline (*infilāt*) of certain writers, who thought that freedom meant they could trample down the sacred values and higher ideals of society.[15] Although Nasser called on the journalists to "correct and not to flatter," the most they could come up with was to submissively ask for instructions as to how to implement the law.[16]

Was it Nationalization?

Whether the new law of the press meant "reorganization" or "nationalization" has been a subject of discussion and controversy to this day. The Egyptian government denied that the transfer of ownership from private individuals to the National Union constituted nationalization, a contention confirmed by the Council of State. The argument in the high court ruling was that newspapers were not public institutions, and that Law 156 simply transferred their ownership to the National Union. Regarding the legal status of the union, the Council of State ruled that it was not a public body, but a popular organization formed by the citizens to achieve the goals for which the revolution had been launched. In short, the National Union's ownership of the press was "a private ownership." Press institutions were operated by private companies, which were legal persons like any other joint-stock company. In its management of the press, the union would be governed by public law, and the press would be subject to the procedures of the civil code.[17]

Despite claims that the law of the press "guaranteed its independence of the administrative government machinery," a number of regulations and arrangements insured government control of Egypt's newspapers. First, the president of the republic was the president of the National Union—a government-established political organization—and cabinet ministers filled its leadership ranks. Second, the government appointed and dismissed editors and board members of the press establishments, and, third, the chief censor was a government-appointed official. Consequently, Egyptian newspapers dutifully echoed the regime's pronouncements and policies. For example, all newspapers endorsed Nasser's socialist legislation, his nonalignment policy, and his capricious squabbles with Arab and non-Arab leaders.

Reactions to the Press Reorganization Law

Within Egypt, the press welcomed the law as an act of "returning the press to the people." *al-Jumhūrīyah* proclaimed the following: "Public ownership of the means of guidance is a primary national necessity and a fundamental popular right; it renders the press less susceptible to deviations, and safeguards its true freedom."[18] The president of the Cairo Press Syndicate, Salah Salem, former member of the Revolutionary Command Council, expressed gratitude to President Nasser for transferring the ownership of the press to the people. "You have confirmed the true meaning of press freedom," he said in his telegram.[19]

Outside Egypt, the reaction was condemnatory. An editorial entitled "The Other Throne" in the Beirut daily *al-Nahār* said, "Yesterday, Egypt's other throne—the throne of her majesty the press—collapsed." It used to be said, the paper went on, "that two things would endure in Egypt, the Nile and the press. Yesterday, almost eight years after the July 23rd Revolution, only one remains." The rest of the editorial is worth quoting in full:

> In reality the decree . . . comes as though it were a mere formality, and an official sanction of a *fait accompli.* For a people denied political and parliamentary freedom, and the freedom to form political parties and organize trade unions,

freedom of the press becomes a kind of heresy. This is so even if the press had been "truly free." But the Egyptian press is no longer free—its loss of freedom is a logical outcome of the abrogation of all freedoms. Nationalization of the means of production was bound to lead to the nationalization of the means of information.[20]

The *al-Nahār* indictment was echoed elsewhere. At its Thirteenth Congress, held in New York on May 24, 1960, the International Federation of newspaper publishers denounced the takeover as an "intolerable and truly unbearable violation of freedom of the press." In a cable to President Nasser, the Overseas Press Club of America termed the government measure a "travesty of justice . . . Such action, of course, is the very opposite of press freedom. It is press tyranny, because as in the press of the Communist world, the press may print only what the government wants it to print so that the government can be beyond any criticism."[21]

Interestingly enough, the press in the Arab world, an area not noted for a free press, reacted with similar denunciations. Sudan's *al-Ra'ī al-'āmm* expressed "surprise" and "grief" over Nasser's decision to nationalize the press. "In view of Egypt's leadership role in the Arab-African world, the decision is so much more distressing and disappointing," the paper stated.[22] At the same time, the Jordanian magazine *Ḥawla al-'Ālam* accused the Egyptian president of concealing an inclination to oppression, and of a deep-rooted preference for terroristic methods.[23]

Impact of the Nationalization on the Egyptian Press

In the early years of the revolutionary period, the Egyptian press had suffered from government regulation and intervention. Newspapers like the outspoken *al-Miṣrī* were silenced and their owners dispossessed. However, journalists could still express their views on a variety of subjects, including calling upon the military to go back to their barracks. But the 1960 law transformed the Egyptian press into a "mobilization press" directed by the rulers to mobilize public support and to legitimize the regime. It is a characteristic of authoritarian and single-party systems, particularly in developing nations seeking fast economic and social development. One important feature of the "mobilization press" is that it "does not criticize the basic policies of the national government . . . [It] never criticizes the personalities heading the national government . . . It follows that there is no significant diversity on important political issues among newspapers."[24] In short, the reorganization turned the Egyptian press into a government agency exercising the only freedom available to it—the freedom to justify, support, and flatter.

With the establishment of the Arab Socialist Union (ASU) and the drafting of the National Charter in 1962, more precise ideological principles were set for the press to follow. The charter provided, in Nasser's words, "a single ideological line" (*khattan mabdā'iyan wāḥidan*) from which no one would be allowed to deviate. Various opinions could be expressed, and even encouraged, "but we will decide . . . whether such opinions are right or wrong," the president stated at a meeting of the ASU's parliamentary body. To illustrate his point, he gave Aḥmad Sa'id as an example: this garrulous radio broadcaster had, during the month of Ramaḍān, expressed certain views with which Nasser did not agree and to which he had made no objection, "but if he had said he was opposed to socialism," Nasser said, "I would have said No!"[25]

In Defense of a Guided Press

There were those writers and journalists who, either out of conviction or sycophancy, argued in defense of a "committed" or "guided" press. They wondered whether a developing society like Egypt could afford the luxury of a free press. "In a socialist society," wrote Aḥmad Ḥamrūsh, a former free officer and a Marxist writer, "the press can no longer remain . . . the foster child of a capitalist system. Rather, it must be a progressive press addressing a different kind of person—the socialist person—who builds his life and future by exertion and hard work . . . and who thinks in a different way from that of the person living in a capitalist society."[26] Ḥamrūsh, like many others, argued that the press, like the universities and other institutions of culture, must be placed in the service of society.[27] With such premises, the question becomes not whether the press is free or controlled, but whether it is rightly or wrongly guided!

Supporters of the new socialist ideology did not see, or did not want to see, any conflict between a "committed" and a "free" press. Ironically, four months before his arrest and imprisonment in 1965, Dār Akhbār al-Yawm's Amin had hailed Nasser's stance on the role of the newspapers in a socialist system as a commitment to a free press![28] With much less embarrassment, *al-Ahrām*'s Haykal asserted that "the most distinctive feature of the Egyptian revolutionary regime is . . . that it has not imposed any restrictions on the freedom of thought and expression."[29] To substantiate his contention, Haykal mentioned how in 1966 Tawfiq al-Hakim's play *Bank al-qalaq* (Bank of Anxiety), critical though it was of the Nasser regime, was published. However, he overlooked the fact that the play was written in such a manner that whatever criticism it implied would elude all but the most sophisticated readers.

The Press and the 1967 War

The 1967 war demonstrated the extent to which the Egyptian press had become a government mouthpiece. Before and during the early days of the fighting, newspapers played a decisive role in convincing the people of an impending victory while the Egyptian armed forces were suffering a shattering defeat. After Nasser confronted the Egyptian public with the truth, it was realized that more than slogans was necessary to restore faith in the regime and to chart a new course for the future. Either to provide an outlet for pent-up emotions and frustrations or to express a genuine concern for reform, the president lifted press censorship and called for "self-criticism" and "change." Seizing the opportunity, journalists and writers expressed themselves freely on subjects hitherto considered sacrosanct: the causes of the disaster, the nature of the political system, and the need for freedom and democracy.

Leading the campaign for a free press and a participatory democracy, Haykal published a series of editorials in *al-Ahrām* focusing on the "internal front." The first step toward victory, he argued, is to strengthen the internal front, not only by rebuilding the armed forces and increasing production, but also by liberalizing the political system and mobilizing public support through truth, freedom, and democracy. Encouraged by Nasser's speech to the fifth session of the National Assembly, Haykal attributed the weakness of the internal front to the "centers of power," as the rival factions within the Arab Socialist Union were known, and to the arbitrary conduct of certain government agencies, the intelligence agency in particular. He saw the remedy in the "institutionalization of the revolution" (*Taqnīn al-thawrah*) through a permanent constitution and the transfer of power from individuals to institutions.[30]

In response to a wave of criticism from all quarters, President Nasser proposed in early 1968 a new program of action stressing freedom of thought and expression, a more democratic Arab Socialist Union, and a free press. However, this March 30th program promised more than the regime was willing to deliver. The Arab Socialist Union elections returned the same "centers of power" to their leadership positions, and the freedom enjoyed by the press, thanks to the 1967 defeat, proved to be short-lived. Journalists who had "gone too far" found themselves subjected to the same police action of prewar days. For example, Dr. Jamāl al-'Uṭayfi, an eminent lawyer and writer, was detained for eight days for an article in *al-Ahrām* of May 8, 1969, in which he took the minister of justice to task for ignoring the very judicial procedures he was appointed to observe and safeguard. He was later released after a number of prominent writers appealed to President Nasser personally, and after Muḥammad Haykal threatened to resign from *al-Ahrām*.[31]

The Press as Scapegoat

In the wake of the 1967 defeat, the Arab Socialist Union's General Congress considered in its September 1968 conference the reorganization of the party and the press. One of the resolutions called for "the study of the state of the press, and for its reorganization on the basis of the principles of the people's ownership of the instruments of guidance, and the goals of a socialist society."[32] The press and the political organization received a large share of the blame for the "setback" for having failed to "deepen public awareness." "The press," wrote Maḥmūd Amīn al-'Ālim, leftist writer and Dār Akhbār al-Yawm board chairman, "did not as much get involved in the radical social transformation as it tried to reconcile itself to it, and may, at times, have by devious and skillful means tried to block its drive." In fact, he went on to assert, "while certain newspapers overtly championed the revolution, they have covertly served as strongholds of counterrevolution, and as agencies of espionage and sabotage."[33] Neither the National Union nor the Arab Socialist Union had, in al-'Ālim's opinion, been able to advance the socialist phase of the revolution. He charged that the press had been transferred from private to public ownership only in financial terms, not in political ideological, or organizational terms. He said that the press had been run according to the principles of private enterprise, that is, for pure monetary gain, and often at the expense of its political mission. In conclusion, al-'Ālim called for a reorganization of the press to make it a more effective tool in the hands of a reorganized political organization for a more positive reconstruction of society.[34]

In a more forceful manner, Dr. Mukhtār al-Tihāmī, professor of journalism at Cairo University and one of the early advocates of public ownership of the press, urged its mobilization for socialist reconstruction in the service of the masses. He wrote that the socialist theory of information rested on two fundamental principles: first, public ownership of the press, and second, firm linkage of the media to the socialist society and the needs of the masses. He accused the press of having failed to fulfill the functions specified for it in the charter. To turn it into a more effective instrument in the service of society, al-Tihāmī proposed the following: (1) a more thorough control of the press by the Arab Socialist Union, (2) complete party control over editorial policy, (3) financing of press institutions from other sources than advertising, and (4) training of journalists for the role they are expected to play in a socialist society.[35] Champions of a free press were by this time silenced.

Ill health, the humiliation of defeat and of the Israeli occupation of Sinai, and the deterioration of inter-Arab relations had sapped Nasser's physical and mental energy. He looked like an aged lion in a cage, as his aides, cognizant of his imminent death, intensified their vying for office. Under these circumstances, press freedom was of no immediate concern. Newspapers continued toeing the government line in dull uniformity. Under Nasser's protection, only Haykal of *al-Ahrām* had the temerity to challenge the "clergy" of the ASU. But even the great Haykal was more apologetic for the regime than critical of it. In a socialist society, freedom of the press, it was reasoned, was a luxury no developing society could afford. By the time President Nasser died in September 1970, the uniformity in press coverage had reached a cynical level, prompting the Syrian poet Nizār Qabbāni to compare Egyptian newspapers to the "death notices" posted on city walls.

The Press Under the Sadat Regime

In volume 1 of his four-volume *Shakhṣiyat Miṣr* (Egypt's Distinctive Character), Dr. Jamāl al-Dīn Ḥamdān writes:

> In Egypt the ruler is regarded as a god until he falls. He is above criticism until he departs. He is the history and geography [of Egypt] until he is replaced by someone else. He always fancies Egypt as his private property, his hamlet or his larger village. He is the state and the fatherland. Loyalty to the fatherland is synonymous to loyalty to his regime, and to him personally . . . He regards any criticism of Egypt as criticism of him personally and, hence, an unforgivable treason.[36]

Although this description fits all of Egypt's rulers, from the pharaohs to Nasser, it is most apt in the case of President Anwar al-Sadat, who assumed office following the former's death. Contrary to all appearances and pretenses, al-Sadat surpassed his predecessor in tightening control over the press. His attitude toward the press—indeed, toward all public institutions—stemmed from a self-perception that he knew better than the Egyptians what was good for them. He regarded himself as the head of the Egyptian family (*rabb or kabīr al-'ā'ilah*) and the Egyptians as his children (*'awlādī*). Two American political scientists have aptly described al-Sadat's regime and his style of government as "the return to traditional patrimonialism."[37]

Despite his promise to restore to the press its lost freedom, the new president not only availed himself of the already institutionalized mechanisms of control, but he also proceeded to refine them through legal and constitutional enactments, as will soon be described. al-Sadat's standard rationalization was that "freedom without responsibility becomes lawlessness or undiscipline (*tasayyub*)." As he promulgated a constitution to introduce the form if not the substance of democracy, he continued to propagate his patrimonial philosophy of government. Unfortunately for al-Sadat and for Egypt, this political schizophrenia led, ultimately, to his assassination. But that is another story.

The Press in the State of Institutions

After getting rid of his opponents in what he called a "corrective revolution," President al-Sadat advanced the idea of a "state of institutions" to replace the rule of one man and to guard against the emergence of new "centers of power." The Arab Socialist Union—the stronghold of these centers—was the only existing political organization, but by the time its General Congress concluded its proceedings in July 1971, al-Sadat's supporters had occupied the key positions in its hierarchy. The "institutionalization" of the state went hand in hand with the consolidation of al-Sadat's grip on the reins of government. Although the constitution guaranteed freedom of the press, the president, as head of the ASU, could still control what the newspapers published by appointing editors and newsmen. Invoking the state of war with Israel, al-Sadat declined to lift censorship. However, in response to an appeal from the Press Syndicate, and as a gesture of goodwill, he issued an executive order restoring twenty-nine journalists and writers to their jobs, from which they had been transferred under the Nasser regime.[38]

Neither this gesture of goodwill nor the president's promises of liberalization assured the Egyptian public of the future. Exhausted by two decades of the Nasser regime and humiliated by the 1967 defeat, Egyptians agitated for more freedom and for the liberation of Sinai from Israeli occupation. Student organizations reemerged, pressuring the government to fulfill its promises. Wall newspapers reappeared on the campuses of Egypt's major universities. Egyptian journalists and writers were more outspoken in their interviews with foreign correspondents and in their reporting to foreign newspapers. This was more than al-Sadat could take. In a speech to the People's Assembly on January 31, 1973, he accused this "misguided gang" (*zumra ḍāllah*) of feeding foreign correspondents with false news about Egypt and of inciting the public against national unity. A few days earlier, it was reported that four journalists, writers, and other intellectuals and professionals were dismissed from the ASU, in what was believed to be the beginning of a major purge. Having lost their membership in the union, the disenfranchised were expelled from their jobs by order of the Disciplinary Committee of the People's Assembly.[39]

More disturbing to President al-Sadat were the students' demonstrations and riots. The post-Six Day War period witnessed the reappearance of the Student Movement as a force to be reckoned with. Frustrated over the continued Israeli occupation of Sinai, and perturbed by state control of the "instruments of information" and by the absence of genuine democracy in Egypt, university students revolted in anger. They set up "committees for the defense of democracy," and in their wall posters described the state as one of "repression, a police state" and decried "the cessation of political life in Egypt," which limited political activity to "cheering on special occasions."[40] The great shock occurred when the Press Syndicate, in one of its general assembly meetings, admitted not only the existence of certain "negative phenomena that have inhibited the press from fulfilling its role," but also that some journalists had described the al-Sadat regime as a reign of repression and terror. To add insult to injury, a statement, said to have been prepared by no less a person than the playwright Tawfiq al-Hakim and signed by a number of intellectuals, was published simultaneously in Cairo and Beirut, describing Egypt's future as "gloomy" (*ka'īb*), and warning that the country was heading for disaster. At the same time, *al-Jumhūrīyah* and al-Ahrām came out in support of the students (accused by the government of being Marxists), calling for complete freedom of the press.[41]

However, al-Sadat made it clear that he would not tolerate any criticism, especially when he was preparing for war against Israel. The least he would expect was a quiet, if not cooperative, domestic front. Having subdued the journalists, he now could grant them clemency. On the occasion of the third anniversary of Nasser's death, al-Sadat announced his decision to restore the journalists to their jobs and to drop all charges against the rioting students. Having decided to launch the October 1973 war and to "move the peace effort forward," a divided domestic front was the last thing Egypt's president wanted. Moreover, a message from the expelled journalists affirming their loyalty to the "fighting leader" and promising to stand "as a single line behind you in the great battle for the liberation of our land" could not but have had a disarming effect on the father of the Egyptian family. However self-serving al-Sadat's step may have been, it was acclaimed by the

Press Syndicate as a "just and revolutionary decision," and welcomed by *al-Jumhūrīyah* as a "great decision by a great man."[42]

Toward the Institutionalization of Press Control

With the Egyptian armed forces gaining ground in the early days of the war, al-Sadat's popularity soared. Not only did he enjoy complete support from the press, but journalists volunteered to serve on the battlefront. Overnight, he found himself a hero in Egypt and in the whole Arab world. His decisiveness, courage, and qualified victory earned the president unprecedented adulation from people and newsmen alike. Despite a few skeptical commentaries on the real accomplishments of the battle, the aftermath of the 1973 war ushered in a honeymoon between the regime and the press. In January 1974, Muṣṭafa Amīn was freed and restored to the world of journalism after having spent nine years in jail on charges of passing state secrets to U.S. intelligence. His brother, 'Alī Amīn, was brought back from exile to become chief editor of *al-Ahrām*, replacing the celebrated Muḥammad Haykal, who had been dismissed after seventeen years of service. Enjoying such genial popularity, the next logical step for the president to take was to lift press censorship, except for military matters, effective February 9, 1974. In return, he entrusted chief editors with responsibility to supervise what was published. Subsequently, the Egyptian press enjoyed a wide measure of freedom lasting for almost two years.[43]

Two considerations may have been behind President al-Sadat's lifting of press censorship. First, he may have had a desire to create the right atmosphere for his *'infitāḥ*, an open-door economic policy which he was about to unveil in the October Paper of April 1974, a blueprint for postwar economic recovery and prosperity. Second, he may have planned to unleash the press against the regime of his predecessor. Whether a de-Nasserization process had been intended or not, opponents of the revolutionary regime took advantage of the opportunity to mount a wild campaign against the "totalitarian character" and the "abuses" of the Nasserist system of government. The attacks and revelations went beyond any contemplated limits, forcing the president to order a halt and to assume part of the blame for all the blunders that had been committed.[44]

Whatever his real motives in lifting press censorship may have been, al-Sadat was acclaimed by journalists and writers as a champion of freedom. As they hailed his decision, they also reflected on the conditions under which the Egyptian press had to function. In his column "Fikrah," 'Alī Amīn reminded the president that freedom "is a right the people have earned by their sufferings," and he warned that it was their responsibility to safeguard it and never to surrender it, because "freedom is like honor; a minor scratch on it would develop into a festering sore."[45] In an opinion editorial, Najīb Maḥfūz, Egypt's great novelist and writer, had some poignant observations to make on freedom and press censorship. "The crushing weight of censorship," he wrote in *al-Ahrām*, "has created a grim atmosphere verging on suffocation. It also has bestowed sanctity on the state, its institutions, and its men. So much so, that resort to rationalization, hypocrisy, and surrender to fate has become rampant. Consequently, Egyptian society has been afflicted with schizophrenia and negativism, and characterized by alienation and irrationality." Strongly supporting freedom of expression, Maḥfūz stressed that "in the realm of thought and debate there is no sanctity except for free opinion . . . there is no rule except that of reason . . . and there is no certainty except that of the scientific method, which opens before man the way to enlightenment and progress. Only the weak, the deviant, and those bent on fanaticism and oppression," he concluded, "detest free opinion, whereas it is esteemed by the strong who have an unshakable confidence in themselves and their people."[46]

The lifting of censorship generated a debate among writers and journalists over whether press freedom should be unconditional or subordinated to social and political considerations. 'Ali Amīn and Muḥammad Sayyid Aḥmad traded arguments on this issue, with Amīn supporting complete freedom and Sayyīd Aḥmad, a Marxist, questioning unconditional press freedom. Freedom is meaningful only if it is freedom for society as a whole; in other words, a free press should be committed to championing the aspirations of the masses, Sayyid Aḥmad maintained.[47] For completely different reasons, President al-Sadat himself began to wonder about an unrestrained press. In a meeting with newsmen in late August 1974, he affirmed his commitment to press freedom because "it is an intrinsic part of the state of institutions," but he also did not expect the press to use its freedom to distract people from the real challenges that confronted them by focusing on the negative aspects (*al-salbiyāt*) of Egyptian life and policy.[48]

A controversy between *al-Ahrām*'s famous cartoonist Ṣalāḥ Jāheen and the minister of justice (also the Socialist prosecutor-general) put the regime's commitment to press freedom to the test. It started with a cartoon by Jāheen chiding the minister for having concluded in an official investigation that nobody in particular could be blamed for the poor quality of Cairo's drinking water. The cartoon depicted the minister, Muṣṭafa Abū Zayd Fahmī, announcing that the culprit was the same unknown persons responsible for the burning down of the

Cairo Opera House three years earlier and for other major fires laid to negligence. In a letter printed in *al-Ahrām*, the minister charged that he had been defamed, and later brought suit against Jāheen. Journalists, lawyers, and members of the People's Assembly came to Jāheen's support, and under this relentless pressure, Fahmī finally dropped his libel suit. The case was hailed as a triumph of press freedom under al-Sadat, although some high government officials were getting increasingly nervous about press probings into their affairs.[49]

In mid-December, the president formed a committee of four people (the People's Assembly speaker, the prime minister, the minister of the interior, and the first secretary of the ASU's Central Committee) to draft a press reorganization plan. No representative of the press was included. Two weeks later, al-Sadat announced that the press would be turned into a fourth branch of government (fourth estate), and that a supreme council for the press would be formed. Ownership would be 51 percent for the ASU, and 49 percent for editors and workers of press institutions.[50] These proposals betrayed al-Sadat's impatience with the way journalists were exercising their newly acquired freedom, as it also betrayed his resolve to bring the press under his control without appearing too authoritarian: in other words, to institutionalize the press as part of the regime.[51]

The Supreme Council for the Press

In late 1974 and early 1975, President al-Sadat found himself in a dilemma. He had initiated a policy of economic and political *'infitāḥ*, committed himself to building a "state of institutions," and lifted press censorship. Yet he not only did not receive the kind of enthusiastic support he had expected, but instead was confronted with criticism and opposition. How could he silence his critics while maintaining a democratic and liberal facade? As far as the press was concerned, al-Sadat had come up with the idea of self-censorship, but how to institutionalize it? The answer was a press council that would draw up a press honor code and supervise its implementation.

The idea was not new; it had been suggested by the Press Syndicate as early as 1964. Under the 1960 Press Law, the syndicate had no power over its own affairs. The president of the republic, in his capacity as head of the Arab Socialist Union formed and dissolved editorial boards, and expelled or transferred journalists at will. Moreover, the syndicate had to put up with interference and conflicting instructions from ministers and the ASU's "centers of power." It was in the hope of recapturing its independence and of clarifying its relations with the government and the union that the Press Syndicate proposed a charter (*dustūr*) for the press and the establishment of a Supreme Council for the Press. The idea of such a council in Egypt was indeed an innovation, although England had had one for many years—admittedly for different purposes. However, it took ten years of discussions before a press council was established by al-Sadat on March 11, 1975.[52]

It was in the constitutional debates of 1971 that the question of a Supreme Council for the Press (SCP) was formally raised. Proposals for its organization and powers were drafted by the Constitutional Committee after hearings were held on the subject. However, it was clear that the proposals were designed to conform to President al-Sadat's directives that the Supreme Council for the Press would be responsible for the "political and ideological direction (*tawjīh*)" of the press, and would have the power to punish journalists who deviate from the ethical code.[53] In a subsequent meeting with newsmen on December 2, 1977, al-Sadat revealed his true intention by suggesting that the minister of information prepare a coherent information plan for the press to follow, and that Arab Socialist Union's secretary for culture, thought, and information be the head of the Supreme Council for the Press, and help draft its code of honor. Despite the input by the Press Syndicate, the whole issue subsided. While the president kept newsmen occupied with their own problems, he continued to ponder what his next step would be.[54]

For the next four years, press reorganization, which by now had become a euphemism for press manipulation and control, relinquished its priority in the president's mind to the October War, the Disengagement Agreements, and the transformation of the Arab Socialist Union into a multiparty system. It was therefore to everyone's surprise that al-Sadat, in his capacity as head of the Arab Socialist Union, issued on March 11, 1975, a decree setting up the first SCP under the chairmanship of first secretary of the Arab Socialist Union.

After defining the press in the Arab Republic of Egypt as "an independent national institution" entrusted with "promoting the goals and values of society" (Article 1), the decree outlined the powers and functions of the SCP. In summary form, the SCP "shall draw up the press honor code . . . coordinate the activities and relations among press institutions . . . look into violations of the honor code . . . and license newspapers and journalists" (Article 3). More important was the composition of the Supreme Council for the Press, and how the members were to be chosen. According to Article 5:

The SCP shall be organized under the chairmanship of the First Secretary of the Central Committee of the ASU, and shall consist of the following members: (1) Minister of Information, (2) ASU's Secretary of Propaganda and Socialist Thought, (3) Deputy Speaker of the People's Assembly, (4) President of the Press Syndicate, (5) a Court of Appeal judge, (6) three members chosen from among board chairmen and chief editors of press institutions, (7) three public figures, (8) Dean of the Faculty of Communication Arts of Cairo University, (9) two Council members of the Press Syndicate, (10) three journalists with no less than fifteen years of service, to be nominated by the Press Syndicate Council, (11) the chairman of the federation of printers and publishers. Appointments are subject to the approval of the President of the ASU (President al-Sadat).[55]

Although the decree did little more than to sanction a fait accompli, it nonetheless generated a controversy regarding its constitutionality. Writing in *Akhbār al-Yawm* of May 24, 1975, the distinguished attorney Muṣṭafa Mar'i questioned the president's authority to regulate the press without submitting the matter to the People's Assembly. He argued that al-Sadat, in his capacity as head of the Arab Socialist Union, could only regulate the nationalized press. Yet the decree granted the SCP sweeping powers to regulate and control the profession of journalism as a whole. In Mar'i's judgment, the decree violated the freedom of the press provision of the constitution by designating the press as a state institution and by conferring on the SCP the monopoly power (*'iḥtikār*) to license newspapers and journalists.[56]

A debate over the constitutionality of the president's action ensued between Mar'ī and Khālid Ḥassūnah, senior judge of the court of appeal. Ḥassūnah, an appointed member of the Supreme Council of the Press, chided Mar'i for failing to consider all of the legal and constitutional aspects of the matter, pointing out that the decree was in line with the Press Reorganization Law (156) of 1960 and the Press Syndicate Law (76) of 1970. He mentioned specifically the last paragraph of Article 2 of the latter law, which states, "The syndicate shall exercise its activities within the framework of the Arab Socialist Union." The law also specifies that no one could work as a journalist without being a registered member of the Press Syndicate—a step that required the approval of the Arab Socialist Union. Ḥassūnah concluded that these two laws authorized the ASU to regulate the press as a whole, and not only the nationalized newspapers. Moreover, he pointed out that Article 114 of the same law defines *ṣuḥuf* as "all newspapers, magazines, and all other publications appearing periodically under the same title."

While Mar'ī invoked Article 45 of the constitution, which guarantees press freedom, Ḥassūnah insisted that it should be interpreted in light of Article 5, which confers on the president the authority to issue such a decree and to regulate the press as he sees fit.[57] Noted for a distinguished career in the defense of freedom, Mar'i dismissed Ḥassūnah's arguments as self-serving. In an article in *al-Akhbār* of May 30, 1975, he pointed out that the law authorized the ASU to supervise (*yushrif*) but not to hold a monopoly over the press. He also questioned whether Law 76 (1970) would allow the Arab Socialist Union to supervise the Press Syndicate, let alone the whole journalistic profession. In conclusion, Mar'i laid all the emphasis on Article 45 of the constitution, and found nothing in Article 5 that would abrogate it.[58]

This is one of many examples of how President al-Sadat, with the complicity of loyalist lawyers and legislators, manipulated the law to tighten his control over the instruments of information in Egypt. As head of the ASU, he could appoint and dismiss SCP members at will, restrict the activities of dissidents, or punish those who did not display the required enthusiasm for his policies. Journalists were not unaware of such legal artifices, but there was little they could do beyond resigning, a course of action not totally exempt from risk. Hardly four months after the establishment of the Supreme Council for the Press, one of its prominent members, 'Abd al-Raḥmān al-Sharqāwi, then board chairman of Dār Rūz al-Yūsuf, tendered his resignation, charging that the council did not provide the necessary protection for the freedom of expression in a controversy that developed between Dār Akhbār al-Yawm (*'Ākhir Sā'ah*) and Dār Rūz al-Yūsuf. Although al-Sharqāwi was later persuaded to withdraw his resignation, the incident highlighted the tension between al-Sadat and those who sought to defend press freedom.[59]

The government did not seem to mind the wrangle; it tried to exploit it as a proof of the existence of free speech. With most Supreme Council for the Press members being loyalists (the chairman was Dr. Rif'at al-Maḥjūb, first secretary of ASU's Central Committee), al-Sadat was not even disturbed. He had already insured that dissident journalists were excluded.[60] And in order to suggest a course of action to the other members, he called the SCP for an "orientation" program on May 16, 1975, five days before the newly appointed council held its first meeting. In his statement, he asserted that "free speech had been abused in a manner harmful to Egypt's interests." Referring to the country's conditions in the post-Six Day War period, the president complained that "we were torn to pieces, but instead of some of these journalists trying to heal wounds, or relieve the pains, they rendered them worse in a way that was immature and irrational." To make it clear that he regarded free speech as subordinate to other considerations, he echoed one of his recurring refrains: "If freedom of speech is sacred, Egypt is more sacred."

Accordingly, for the press to play its proper role in his regime, "it will have to be transformed into a state institution legitimized in constitutional documents." As a first step in that direction, the president suggested that the council draw up a press honor code, keeping in mind that "everything in this world, including freedom, is subject to constraints (*ḍawābiṭ*)—and freedom of expression is no exception." After expressing his disappointment—even exasperation—in some journalists, he insinuated that he expected the Supreme Council for the Press to act as his watchdog, keeping members of the press in line.[61]

Since constitutional changes establishing the press as a state institution were many years into the future, how would the Supreme Council for the Press supervise (*yushrif*) a national institution that did not yet exist constitutionally? The question may be superfluous since the president had envisaged for it only a temporary and limited role. Let the journalists be occupied with (a) drawing up a press honor code, substituting self-censorship for the official censorship that had been lifted, (b) establishing new pay scales, and (c) allocating the dividends accruing to them from their 49 percent ownership of press institutions. By retaining in his own hands the most effective means of controlling the press—the power to appoint and dismiss the chief editors—al-Sadat left no doubt as to who would dictate what the newspapers could and could not report.

Anwar al-Sadat had often followed the policy of the carrot and the stick, preferring the first but never hesitating to use the second if he thought opposition to, or criticism of, his policies went beyond certain limits. As he contemplated the best methods to institutionalize the press as a part of the state system, he thought that the Press Council would monitor journalists and prosecute violators of the press honor code, that is, the official line. At the same time, through the council's licensing power, the state had complete control over the selection of journalists and the granting of franchises to newspapers.[62]

The Press as a Branch of Government

In the spring of 1976, President al-Sadat decided that the limited freedom the Egyptian press had enjoyed had served its purpose—the demythologizing of Nasser. Journalists and writers had been delirious in exposing the evils of the totalitarian (*shumūlī*) system that dominated Egypt for eighteen years. The virulence of the attack, even against Nasser and his family, was so embarrassing that al-Sadat had to call it off, as mentioned above. However, not one to shun an opportunity to remind the press of its limits, he used the occasion to illustrate how it had abused its freedom by defaming the dead leader. "This is shameful," he averred hypocritically, "and contrary to the ethical values and traditions of our society."[63]

It is doubtful whether this was the only reason behind al-Sadat's decision to restore censorship. Circumspect as the press tried to be, there were yet a number of journalists, especially those writing for foreign publications, who sought to discredit al-Sadat's open-door economic policy and his close friendship with the United States. Moreover, the president was about to embark on some radical changes in his policies, and he saw no reason why they should be jeopardized for the sake of press freedom. Domestically, he considered abolishing the ASU and legalizing a multiparty system, if for no other reason than as a goodwill gesture to the United States and the Western world. In foreign policy, al-Sadat was contemplating a dramatic step toward a peaceful settlement with Israel. It was largely for these latter reasons that he wanted to silence his critics. In a speech before the People's Assembly on March 14, 1976, he bitterly attacked the press, and soon after, reinstituted censorship and ordered a major reshuffle of newspaper editors. It was, in the words of an eminent Egyptian journalist, a move to "inspire terror" and not that "transient courage" that marked the previous two years of qualified press freedom.[64]

The second half of 1976 found Anwar al-Sadat experimenting with the *manābir*, the ideological platforms of organizations within the framework of the Arab Socialist Union. Three platforms, representing the right, center, and left, competed in the parliamentary election of late October and early November of the same year. With his center party (the Arab Socialist Union) in complete control of the People's Assembly (82 percent of the seats), the president, in a historic statement before the newly elected body on November 11, announced the transformation of the three platforms into political parties. He projected at the same time that his decision would entail revision of the basic laws of the ASU, freedom of political parties from ASU control, and freedom for each party to manage its own affairs within the limits of the law.

In general, Egyptians welcomed the new measures as positive steps toward genuine democracy. Although the center party dominated the assembly, opposition parties and independents were represented. Even the leftist al-Tajammu' of Khālid Muḥyi al-Din managed to win three seats. Feeling confident, al-Sadat decided to comply with the International Monetary Fund's insistence that the public deficit be reduced by lifting subsidies on such necessities as flour, rice, sugar, macaroni, and so forth. Rioting broke out on January 18 and 19, 1977, with thousands of Egyptians rampaging through the streets of Egypt's major cities, burning cars, looting shops, and attacking all symbols of wealth and affluence. Shaken by the events, the president immediately rescinded the price increases and called in the army to restore order.[65]

While the leftist opposition proclaimed the "bread riots" a "popular uprising" against al-Sadat's economic liberalism (*'infitāḥ*), the embattled president called them "an uprising of thieves" and a "counterrevolution." He blamed "communists" for instigating them, and ordered the arrest of all suspects, including a number of students who had participated in a series of demonstrations against his policies. However, having established order, al-Sadat proceeded to defuse public anger by holding a series of meetings with university professors, labor unions, and students. As he embarked on his public relations campaign, the nationalized press continued its relentless attack on "subversive elements" and "misguided youth."

In his dialogue with the students, President al-Sadat heard more than he had bargained for. Rejecting the president's charge that the students had engaged in sabotage, Sha'ban Ḥāfiẓ al-Shāfi'i, president of the Federation of Egyptian Students, blamed the government's "economic measures" for what had happened. Pointing to the growing economic disparities between the "new class of parasites" and the masses of Egyptians, the student leader pleaded with the president not to place any new burdens upon the "toiling masses." He also called for *al-infitāḥ* geared to production and not to consumption. In response to Sadat's criticism of the students' "wall newspapers," Shāfi'i asserted that neither the government-controlled newspapers nor the rest of the media reflected the real sufferings of the people. Instead, they practiced sensational and misleading journalism by falsifying facts, distorting history, and flattering government officials.[66]

From Democratic Pretensions to Authoritarianism

The January events were a turning point in the political thinking of the Egyptian president. Besides being disruptive of public order and the economy, the riots were a personal embarrassment and an affront to al-Sadat's "glorified sense of self." Instead of relaxing controls and introducing the "genuine democracy" he had often promised, he went on to curtail whatever political freedom of expression had existed. With a People's Assembly "stacked" with his supporters, al-Sadat enacted a number of laws giving his government absolute power over all aspects of life in Egypt. Two weeks after the riots, he issued an executive order relating to the "protection of national unity and security." Law 2 (1977) banned all secret organizations hostile to the social order and imposed severe penalties on those engaged in sabotage or in inciting the public against the state, its laws, regulations, and property.[67]

Soon after, another presidential order authorized the Niyābah 'Āmmah (*Parquet*) to prosecute all crimes laid down in Law 2 before state security tribunals.[68] More restrictive of political freedoms was the Law of Political Parties of July 1977. Subject to the discretion of the state, political parties would be legalized and allowed to publish their own newspapers.[69] This legislation proved to be the most powerful weapon in the hands of public authorities to check and control political activities in Egypt.

Having armed himself with statutory powers against any possible opposition, Egypt's president embarked on his most dramatic action—the trip to Jerusalem. The impact of this impulsive and perplexing journey on inter-Arab politics and the Palestinian-Israeli conflict remains a subject of controversy to this day. Our immediate concern, however, is with the role the Egyptian press played in this whole episode. Coverage of the president's visit to Israel by the nationalized press gave the impression that Egyptians were solidly behind their leader. This was not the case. Reading only the government-controlled newspapers, one would never have known that opposition parties, especially al-Tajammu', special groups, private individuals, and students, demonstrated in the streets and distributed leaflets and flyers denouncing "this act of national humiliation." Also ignored by the official press were reports of arrests in Cairo, Alexandria, Sharqīyah Province, and the Canal Zone. The news of the resignation of Egyptian Foreign Minister Ismā'il Fahmi and his deputy Muḥammad Riyāḍ, protesting al-Sadat's purely personal and peremptory decision, was reluctantly published, without ever mentioning the reasons for their resignation, not to mention printing the texts of their letters of resignation, which were made available to foreign reporters. Only *al-Aḥrār*, organ of the Liberal Socialist Party, published Fahmi's picture with the text of his letter of resignation.[70]

al-Sadat's peace mission to Israel in November 1977, followed by the Camp David Accords in September 1978 and the signing of the Egyptian-Israeli peace treaty in March 1979, catapulted him to the center of the world stage. He won the Nobel Peace Prize and was called a "man of peace" and a "great statesman." *Time* magazine chose him as the 1977 "Man of the Year," and news producers created a living legend of the son of the Nile. Is it any wonder that all this public idolization went to his head, making him more sensitive to, and intolerant of, criticism? With little or no pretense, the "new pharaoh," as he was later called, turned against his critics with a vengeance, restricting their activities and curtailing their freedom of expression.

The first to suffer the initial blow of the president's anger was the leftist al-Tajammu' party and its organ, *al-Ahāli.* On August 2, 1978, the *niyābah* of state security ordered the confiscation of the Wednesday issue of *al-Ahāli*, charging it with publishing false reports and biased editorials offensive to Arab-Islamic sensitivities. The paper allegedly defended the role of the Soviet Union and Cuba in fighting the insurgents in the Ogaden and Eritrea. The South Cairo Court of First Instance upheld the *niyābah*'s action with the reasoning that "to defend these two states at a time when they are supporting Ethiopia in liquidating the Arab Somali rebels and the Muslims of Eritrea is offensive to Arab-Islamic feelings." Moreover, the court ruled that *al-Ahāli*'s editorials kindled public passions and threatened public peace by inciting class hatred and sedition in violation of the penal code. The government ordered the closing of *al-Ahālī* indefinitely.[71] With voices of dissent deprived of their most influential platform, al-Sadat could pride himself on the "unanimous" support of the Egyptian people as portrayed by his official press.[72]

Opposition to al-Sadat's authoritarian regime and to his flamboyant style of government was growing, especially among Muslim fundamentalists, who bitterly resented his Jerusalem visit, and among workers and peasants, who suffered most from the effects of his economic policies. Fully aware of the importance of keeping control of public opinion, he began to take steps to integrate the Egyptian press into the state apparatus. In early 1979, the president appointed a Committee on the Institutionalization of the Press, entrusting it with the task of drafting proposals regarding the fourth estate. Although a good number of journalists were included on the committee, the chairmanship went to Manṣūr Ḥasan, minister of state for presidential affairs and minister of culture and information. Under his "guidance" the committee could only draw up what the government wanted.

There were expressions of anxiety, for many feared that the press would turn into a government agency and that commitment (*'iltizām*) to the constitutionally established social norms would turn into forcible acceptance (*'ilzām*) of faits accomplis. One intriguing argument advanced in support of institutionalization was that it would help remove from the people's minds the ideological ambiguities that accumulated after eighteen years of totalitarian rule. Institutionalization would also reinforce the democratic experiment initiated by al-Sadat in his corrective revolution of May 15, 1971. Another equally intriguing argument was that Egypt could not afford (politically, not economically) to have privately owned papers become "political shops (*dakākīn siyāsīyah*) as is the case in Lebanon, and in some European countries."[73]

Over a period of sixty days, the Committee on the Institutionalization of the Press held a series of hearings at which interested organizations and individuals were given the chance to present their views, although government thinking on the subject had already been leaked. The case for a free press was, however, presented by the Press Syndicate, which stressed press freedom as an "essential ingredient of freedom in general, a fundamental expression of democracy," and "an inalienable public right."[74]

Likewise, the Lawyers Syndicate warned in a memorandum against turning the press into a "fourth power" owned and controlled by the proposed Consultative Assembly in the name of the people. In addition to depriving the press of its independence and freedom, the government scheme would also rob it of its character as a free occupation and would transform journalists into state employees.

Moreover, investing the Supreme Council for the Press with power to purge nonconformist journalists by refusing them membership in the syndicate constituted a violation of Article 23, paragraph 4, of the Universal Declaration of Human Rights, according to the lawyers' statement. Furthermore, the appointment of the SCP members by presidential decree, as proposed by the government, would be incompatible with the proposed constitutional amendments legalizing a multiparty system, with each party having the right to publish its own paper.[75]

Ignoring public opinion, the Sadat government went ahead with its proposals for the constitutional amendments legitimizing, among other things, the press as a "fourth power" of the state. It only took the People's Assembly three days to approve them, and on May 22, 1980, the Egyptian people endorsed them in a referendum. The added articles concerning the press, Articles 206-211, define it as "an independent power of the people," fulfilling its role in accordance with the constitution and the law. Articles 207 and 209 affirm the independence and freedom of the press "in the service of society," and establish "public control" over press institutions. Article 211 gives the SCP responsibility to strengthen press freedom and independence, preserve the fundamental constituents of society, and help safeguard national unity and social peace.[76]

A constitutionally mandated law pertaining to the "Power of the Press" (Law 148) was enacted by the People's Assembly and promulgated by the president of the republic on July 14, 1980.[77] The new law regulates the relations of the Egyptian press with the state. It defines the press as "an independent public power" discharging its mission "in the service of society" (Article 1). Press freedom is guaranteed provided it contributes to the creation of the "free climate [necessary] for the development of society," and for the enlightenment of the people (Article 2).

Carefully worded are the provisions delineating the rights and responsibilities of journalists. In whatever they report or publish, journalists "shall be bound (*yaltazim*) by the basic constituents of society stipulated in the constitution."[78] Freedom to publish newspapers is guaranteed only for political parties and legal persons "within the limits of the law" and subject to the approval of the SCP, which is basically a government agency (Articles 13 and 18).

What proved to be the more radical innovation was the provision that "national newspapers" "are the private property of the state, with the Consultative Assembly exercising the rights of ownership." Accordingly, the speaker of the assembly presides over the meetings of the Supreme Council for the Press, whose members are appointed by a presidential decree (Articles 22-28, 36, 48). In the judgment of most observers inside and outside Egypt, Law 148 ended whatever semblance of freedom the Egyptian press had. Coming on top of a number of statutes limiting all freedoms of public expression, the law betrayed most eloquently the fraudulence of al-Sadat's much-vaunted "state of institutions."

Careful analysis of the constitutional and statutory changes reveals the subtlety with which the al-Sadat regime coopted the press and made it almost impossible for anyone to criticize the government with impunity. The ambiguous and elastic language of the law made it susceptible to any interpretation the ruler chose. Who, for instance, is to define the moral and social constituents of society? How is the press to safeguard national unity and social peace? How can the press be "free and independent" and at the same time be "bound" by all sorts of restrictions?

To most Egyptians, the idea of the press being a fourth power was bewildering. Even those who supported the Sadat regime had serious misgivings about the new status the press had acquired. It is a "legal illusion," wrote Muḥammad 'Asfūr, an eminent Egyptian professor of law.[79] The distinguished journalist Muṣṭafa Amin referred to the constitutional amendments as "the massacre of the press." "To call the press the fourth power," he wrote, "is no guarantee of its freedom, just as to place the sign "Egyptian University" on the gate of the Limān Ṭurrah prison does not turn it into one . . . Newspapers cannot be free so long as they are owned by the government . . . Neither are journalists free so long as they are appointed and dismissed by executive decrees."[80] Jalāl al-Din al-Ḥamāmṣi, dean of Egyptian journalists, went further to charge that the Consultative Assembly was a mere facade, a mask, behind which the head of state personally controlled the newspapers.[81] Many members of the press were stunned, but there was nothing they could do. Those who could not tolerate al-Sadat's high-handedness left the country to write for Arab publications. The "expatriate journalists" had to await the death of the president to be able to return to their homeland.

Conclusion

Before the July 1952 revolution, Egyptians used to refer to the press as "Her Majesty" (*ṣāḥibat al-jalālah*) in deference to its independence and to its being above parties. Even the term *fourth estate* in its political, not legal or constitutional, sense was adopted from Western usage in recognition of the power of the press. The notion of the press as a branch of government was alien to Egyptians, as it was to most others. Rather, the press was regarded as a force to oversee and restrain the conduct of government by exposing its corrupt practices and failures, and by disseminating the right kind of information.

In the postrevolutionary period, the Egyptian press experienced troubles and setbacks verging on adversity, as we have seen. Despite differences in style, both Nasser and al-Sadat tended to regard the press, indeed all mass media, as an appurtenance to their regimes, the function of which was to mobilize public support for their policies. This tendency to regard the media as a handmaiden to the state has prevailed in most developing nations. Rulers tend to regard themselves or their mass political organizations as the sole representatives of the public interest. They know better than the people what is good for them. Such an attitude—more conspicuous in al-Sadat's case—could only lead to intolerance of any criticism or opposition.

Whereas Nasser was more subtle and less concerned with legal and constitutional forms than al-Sadat was, the latter was no less authoritarian. More than Nasser ever did, al-Sadat made ample use of the news conference to communicate his wishes and his displeasure to the press. However, whenever his wishes were not heeded, he was just as ruthless as Nasser in punishing the dissidents.

The temptation to compare the conditions of the Egyptian press of the pre- and postrevolutionary periods is compelling. Under the monarchy, the press was, to a large extent, independent and free. No public figure, from the king down, had been spared the newsmen's gibes and mischievous jokes. It is true that some of them were punished and their newspapers suspended, but there was much greater tolerance on the part of political leaders and government authorities toward their critics than Nasser and al-Sadat would ever have been inclined to show. If a free press is at the core of a democratic system, the Nasser and al-Sadat regimes fell far short of their pretensions.

Notes

1. Farūq Abū Zayd, *al-Ṣiḥāfah wa qaḍāyā al-fikr fī Miṣr* (Cairo: Kitāb al-Idhā'ah wa-al-Telefiziyan, 1974); Ghalī Shukrī, *al-Thawrah al-mudāddah fī Miṣr* (Beirut: Dār al-Ṭali'ah, 1978), p. 375; Rūz al-Yūsuf, 2679 (October 15, 1979), p. 8.
2. *al-Waqā'i' al-Miṣrīyah*, June 7, 1954.
3. Aḥmad Abū al-Fatḥ, *L'Affaire Nasser* (Paris: Plon, 1962), pp. 152-73; 'Abd al-Latif al-Baghdadi, *Memoirs*, I (Cairo: al-Maktab al-Miṣrī, 1977), p. 170. Maḥmud Abū al-Fatḥ, "The *al-Miṣri* Case" (a memorandum submitted to the United Nations in November 1954); Layla 'Abd al-Majīd, *Ḥurīyyat al-Ṣihāfah fi Miṣr* (Cairo: al-'Arabī, 1983), pp. 19-20; "Blood and Tears in the Story of the Egyptian Press," a mimeographed sheet, dated June 18, 1971, in the Archives of *al-Ahrām*. On May 25, 1985, the High Administrative Court in Cairo ruled that there was no evidence that *al-Miṣrī*'s license had actually been withdrawn. Despite this ruling, *al-Miṣrī* may not be able to publish without fulfilling requirements stipulated by the Press Law of 1980.
4. Maḥmūd Abū al-Fatḥ, "The *al-Miṣrī* Case," p. 33.
5. *Rūz al-Yūsuf*, 2678 (October 8, 1979); Muṣṭafa Amin, *Ṣāḥibat al-Jalālah fi' al-Zinzānah*, 2nd ed. (Alexandria: al-Maktab al-Miṣrī al-Ḥadīth, 1974), pp. 196-202; 'Abd al-Majīd, *Hurīyyat*, p. 27.
6. Cf. Ṣabrī Abū al-Majd, "The Story of the Most Important Referendum by the Egyptian Press," *al-Muṣawwar*, July 4, 1975, pp. 10-13.
7. Article 45 of the 1956 constitution.
8. *al-Waqā'i' al-Miṣrīyah* 92 (h) (November 18, 1956).
9. 'Abd al-Majīd, *Hurīyyat*, p. 54.
10. *al-Ahrām*, May 24, 1960. Article 5 of Law 156 was later amended by executive order to provide an overall compensation of a nominal value of 15,000 Egyptian pounds in the form of bonds at 4 percent interest, and for a period of fifteen years. *al-Jarīdah al-rasmīyah*, 301, December 31, 1963.
11. *New York Times*, May 25, 1960.
12. *al-Ahrām*, May 25, 1960. All translations from the Arabic in this study are rendered by the author.
13. *Times* (London), May 31, 1960; *al-Ahrām*, May 30, 1960.
14. *New York Times* and *al-Nahār*, May 31, 1960.
15. 'Abd al-Majid, *Hurīyyat*, pp. 64-66.
16. Jalāl al-Din al-Ḥamāmṣi, *Aswār ḥawla al-ḥiwār* (Cairo: al-Maktab al-Miṣrī, 1984), p. 173.
17. *al-Ahrām*, December, 26, 1961, and April 16, 1962; *al-Jumhūrīyah*, April 16, 1962.
18. *al-Jumhūrīyah*, May 25, 1960.

19. *New York Times*, May 26, 1960. See also A. A. al-Maghribi, *Khabāyā al-Ṣiḥāfah* (Cairo: al-Maghrabī, 1975), pp. 70-74.
20. *al-Nahār*, May 25, 1960. All translations are by the author.
21. Reuter and AP Wire Reports in *al-Ahrām* Archives.
22. *al-Ra'i al-'Āmm*, May 27, 1960.
23. *Ḥawla al-'Ālam*, June 10, 1960. It is to be remembered that Egyptian-Jordanian relations at the time were at their lowest ebb.
24. William A. Rugh, *The Arab Press* (Syracuse: Syracuse University Press, 1979), pp. 31-35.
25. See *al-Ahrām*, February 26 and March 12-13, 1965.
26. *al-Jumhūrīyah*, August 5, 1963.
27. Cf. F. M. Najjar, "State and University in Egypt during the Period of Socialist Transformation," *The Review of Politics* No. 1, (January 1976): pp. 57-87.
28. *al-Ahrām*, March 13, 1965.
29. Ibid., August 11, 1967. See also Ibrāhim Nawwār's views on a "committed press" in *al-Muḥarrir*, September 28, 1966.
30. *al-Ahrām*, July 28, November 17, and December 1, 1967.
31. 'Abd al-Majid, *Hurīyyat*, pp. 106-7.
32. *al-Ṭali'ah*, vol. 4, no. 12 (December 1968), pp. 51-57.
33. *al-Akhbār*, December 28, 1968.
34. Ibid.
35. "Freedom of the Press and the March 30th Program," *al-Jumhūrīyah*, April 26, 1968; cf. *The Charter* (Egyptian Information Department, English version), p. 46.
36. Quoted in *al-Sha'b* 239 (July 3, 1984).
37. James A. Bill and Carl Leiden, *Politics in the Middle East* (Boston: Little, Brown and Co., 1979), pp. 228-35. At one of al-Sadat's public appearances, an Egyptian wit raised a poster with the words "Welcome Papa Sadat."
38. Executive Order No. 580. *al-Jarīdah al-rasmīyah* 20b (May 20, 1972); *al-Ahrām*, March 26, 1972.
39. *al-Akhbār*, January 19, 1973; *New York Times*, February 4, 1973; *al-Muṣawwar*, March 9, 1973. President al-Sadat had offered to lift official censorship on condition that the press itself would exercise self-censorship by drawing up a viable press honor code and scrupulously observing it. Two attempts to convene the Press Syndicate's General Assembly to approve a code of honor draft failed for lack of a quorum. See *al-Ṣayyād*, August 3, 1972, pp. 58-59.
40. *al-Nahār Supplement*, January 30, 1972.
41. Mūsa Ṣabrī, *Wathā'iq Ḥarb Uktūbar* (Alexandria: al-Maktab al-Miṣrī al-Ḥadīth, 1974), pp. 280-94.
42. *al-Ahrām*, June 28, 1973; *al-Ahrām* and *Al-Jumhūrīyah*, September 29-30, 1973, *al-Jumhūrīyah*, October 2, 1973.
43. *al-Ahrām*, February 8, 1974.
44. Typical of the writings of this period are a number of works by Ibrāhim 'Abduh, Muḥammad 'Abd al-Raḥīm 'Anbar, Ibrāhim Si'dah, and Muḥammad 'Abd al-Salām.

45. *al-Ahrām*, February 11, 1974.
46. Ibid., February 22, 1974.
47. Ibid., March 10-25, 1974.
48. Ibid., August 29, 1974.
49. *New York Times*, November 13, 1974; *al-Ḥamāmṣī*, *Aswār*, pp. 170-71.
50. *al-Ahrām*, February 3, 1975.
51. One such journalist was Muḥammad Haykal, former chief editor of *al-Ahrām*. Haykal, who had been dismissed from his job by al-Sadat, wrote a series of articles for the Arab press underscoring the risks involved in the Sinai Disengagement Agreements. This did not please the president, who imposed strict censorship on Arab papers coming into Egypt, and, according to Damascus Radio, confiscated all of those issues that carried portions of Haykal's editorials or other criticisms of the Disengagement Agreements. Opposition within Egypt was voiced by students at Cairo and 'Ayn Shamsh universities, who denounced the agreement as *'ittifāqīyat al-naksah* (setback agreement), and condemned the alliance between Egypt and the United States and the abject surrender to the Zionist enemy (Press file in *al-Ahrām* Archives).
52. *al-Ahrām*, November 8, 1964; Muṣṭafa Bahjat Badawī, *Min Mudhakkirāt Ra'īs al-Taḥrīr* (Cairo: Dār al-sha'b, 1976), p. 312.
53. *al-Jumhūrīyah*, July 15, 1971.
54. *al-Ahrām*, December 3, 1971, and January 1, 3, 1972.
55. *al-Maghrībī*, *Khabāyā al-ṣiḥāfah*, pp. 86-88; *al-Ahrām*, March 12, 1975.
56. Reprinted in Muṣṭafa Mar'ī, *al-Ṣiḥāfah bayna al-sulṭah wa-al-sulṭān* (Cairo: 'Ālam al-Kutub, 1980), pp. 96-100.
57. Ibid., pp. 101-3. Article 5 of the constitution states: "The ASU confirms the authority of the alliance of the working forces of the people through political action which its organizations exercise among the people and in various organs assuming responsibilities of national action." The Arab Republic of Egypt, Ministry of Information, *The Permanent Constitution of the Arab Republic of Egypt*, Cairo, 1971.
58. Mar'i, *al-Ṣihāfah*, pp. 104-6.
59. *al-Ahrām*, September 8, 1975, October 2, 1975.
60. Three leftist journalists, Ḥusayn 'Abd al-Rāziq, Salamah Abū Zayd, and 'Adil Ḥusayn, who were nominated by the Press Syndicate, were refused appointment to the council. *al-Ahrām*, May 12, 27, 1975.
61. *al-Ahrām*, May 27, 1975.
62. Badawi, *Min Mudhakkirat*, pp. 314-15.
63. Quoted in *al-Ahrām*, June 27, 1977.
64. al-Ḥamāmṣi, *Aswār*, p. 49.
65. Ḥusayn 'Abd al-Rāziq's *Miṣr fī 18 wa-19 Yanāyir* (2d ed., Beirut: Dār al-Kalimah, 1981) contains the best record of those events.
66. Text of the dialogue in Ḥamāmṣī, *Aswār* pp. 227-91.
67. *al-Jarīdah al-rasmīyah*, no. 5 (b) (February 3, 1977).
68. Presidential Order no. 92, *al-Jarīdah al-rasmīyah*, (February 17, 1977).
69. *al-Jarīdah al-rasmīyah*, no. 27 (July 7, 1977).

70. *al-Waṭan* (Kuwaiti newspaper), November 21, 1977; Ṣalāh Qabaḍayā, *Ṣaḥafī ḍiḍ al-ḥukūmah* (Cairo: Kitāb al-Ḥayāt, 1980), p. 75.
71. *al-Ahrām*, August 3, 1978. *al-Ahālī* did not resume publication until May 19, 1982, seven months after al-Sadat's assassination.
72. *al-Waṭan*, November 21, 1978, reported an Egyptian journalist who had the courage to ask at a meeting of the Press Syndicate: "Is there no single voice of dissent in the whole of Egypt . . . If there is—and we know there are many—why does not our press, which claims to be free, publish one single opinion of dissent?"
73. *al-Ahrām*, December 3, 1979.
74. *Mustaqbal al-Siḥāfah fī Miṣr* (Cairo: Dār al-Muwqif al-'Arabī, 1980), pp. 230-34.
75. Ibid., pp. 245-48.
76. *al-Jarīdah al-rasmīyah*, no. 26 (June 26, 1980).
77. Ibid., no. 28 (b) (July 14, 1980).
78. See pt. 2, chap. 1, of the 1971 Egyptian Constitution.
79. *Mustaqbal*, pp. 140-41.
80. Ibid., pp. 279-80.
81. Ibid., pp. 225-26.

Index

Abābīl, 78
Abāẓah, Fikrī, 329
Abbas I, 145
Abbasids, 71, 213
'Abd al-Ḥamīd II, 46
'Abd al-Nāṣir, Jamāl, *See* Nasser, Gamal Abdel
'Abd al-Qaddūs, Iḥsān, 329
'Abd al-Qādir (al-Amīr), 77, 301
'Abd al-Rāziq, 'Alī (Abdul Raziq), 165n.18, 189, 218, 223, 229n.64
'Abd al-Rāziq, Mustafa, 209, 211
'Abduh, Muḥammad, 45, 210-211, 214, 219, 225
'Abdullah, Amir (Later King), 248, 250
Abī-Rāshid, Ḥanna, 265n.9
Absolute, The, 75
Abū al-Fatḥ Brothers, 328
Abū Barzah, *See* Ibn Barza
Abu-Izzeddine, Najla, 32n.5
Abū Ḥanīfah, 84, 194
Abū Kāmil, *See* Ibn Aslām, Shujā'
Abū Nūwās, 185-186
Abū Tammām, 185-186, 195, 198-199
Abū 'Ubaydah, 197, 273
Abū Zayd, 197
Abyssinian Invasion, 76
Acculturation, 176, 178
Adonis ('Alī Aḥmad Sa'īd): 183-204; on Arab heritage, 188; criticism of, 193; methodology, 190; on modernity, 186; view of history, 192; view of Islam, 203
Aflaq, Michel, 22
al-Afghānī, Jamāl al-Dīn, 172, 218
al-Ahālī (Newspaper), 351
Ahl al-ḥall wa-al-'aqd, 49, 216, 218
al-Ahrām (Newspaper), 331, 340
al-Ahrām, Dār, 330-331
Akhbār al-Yawm, Dār, 330, 337, 346
Algebra, 98
al-'Ālim, Maḥmūd Amīn, 337
Almohades, 91
Almoravid Dynasty, 91
Althusser, Louis, 165n.15
American University of Beirut, 3
Amīn, Aḥmad, 210-218; and Muslim-Copts relations, 212; on religion and science, 217; and Shari'ah, 216; and Western Civilization, 212-213
Amīn, 'Alī, 335, 341-342
Amīn, Muṣṭafa, 341, 353
Amīn, Qāsim, 209
'Ammūrīyah, 198-199
'Amr Clan, 247
'Anbar School, 259
Apollo Group, 186
'Aql, 184
al-'Aqqād, 'Abbās Maḥmūd, 163, 218; on democracy, 222; on evolution, 226; on existentialism, 226; on freedom, 220; on Islam, 223; on reason, 223-225; on religion, 222
Arab, 147; civilization, 8, 10, 31, 54; empire, 144; identity, 21; intellectuals, 53, 163, 189, 311; mentality, 186, 190, 203; nation, 10, 23, 31; nationalism, 20-22; society, 7-9, 22, 26, 31, 56, 58; thought, 7, 30-31; *see also* under culture
Arab Socialist Union, 335-336, 339, 344, 346, 348
Arabia, 232
Arabian Peninsula, 235, 237
Arabic Language, 149
Arabism, 56
Arabs, 167, 202, 215, 233; attitude towards past, 6; compared to Europeans, 147
Archemides, 105, 111n.22
Aristotle, 86n.2, 112, 123
Armed Forces Movement, 327
al-Arna'ūṭ, Ṣāliḥah, 298